Our Country

The North's Civil War
Andrew L. Slap, series editor

Our Country

Northern Evangelicals and the Union during the Civil War Era

Grant R. Brodrecht

FORDHAM UNIVERSITY PRESS
NEW YORK 2018

Fordham University Press also publishes its books in a variety of electronic formats. Some content that appears in print may not be available in electronic books.

Visit us online at www.fordhampress.com.

Library of Congress Cataloging-in-Publication Data available online at https://catalog.loc.gov.

Printed in the United States of America

20 19 18   5 4 3 2 1

First edition

Contents

Author's Note

The bibliography for this book can be found on the web at https://fordham.bepress.com/history/13/. It is also available in the e-book versions of this title.

Introduction: "Long Live the Glorious Union"

Nobler, freer, and more glorious,
Shall the future Union be:
O'er the despot's rod victorious,
All the lands its strength shall see.
North and South in one dominion,
One in freedom evermore,
O'er one land on loving pinion
Shall the lordly eagle soar:
Northern lake and Southern harbor,
Cotton-field and prairie wide,
Seaside slope and greenwood arbor,
All shall boast the Union's pride.

—Dwight Williams, "The Union as It Shall Be," quoted in Jesse T. Peck, *The Great Republic, from the Discovery of America to the Centennial, July 4, 1876*

On March 4, 1865, the day that Abraham Lincoln delivered his second inaugural address and looked ahead publicly to the Union's restoration, George Peck envisioned the end of the Civil War by putting the finishing touches on a collection of his sermons to be published under the title *Our Country: Its Trial and Its Triumph, a Series of Discourses Suggested by the Varying Events of the War for the Union*. The Methodist Peck—an antebellum circuit rider and holiness teacher, a wartime pastor in Scranton, Pennsylvania, and the eventual maternal grandfather of Stephen Crane—intended to present signed copies to Lincoln, Secretary of State William Seward, and Secretary of War Edwin Stanton.[1] Although the politically moderate Peck had long opposed slavery, he, along with many other northern evangelicals, was not an abolitionist. During the Civil War he had come to support emancipation, but, as it was for Lincoln, the conflict remained first and foremost about preserving the Union.[2] Peck's devotion to the Union flowed in part from a lineage of which he was proudly aware. His father descended from New Haven colony's Puritan founders; his paternal grandfather likely died in the Revolution; three of Peck's paternal uncles fought in the war, with two being captured by the British; and Peck's maternal grandfather died at Valley Forge. To George Peck, the Union was "our country."[3]

His thoughts following South Carolina's attack on Fort Sumter four years earlier exemplify a reflexive love and sense of responsibility for America that persisted among northern evangelical Protestants throughout the Civil War and Reconstruction. "This glorious land is ours," he announced. "Let it never be divided." Let an American citizen travel to other countries "and have his passport demanded" at every turn. "Then let him return home and travel from Maine to New Orleans, up the father of waters to St. Paul, then let him cross the plains to California, then visit Oregon and . . . the Rocky Mountains, and then let him return to his home in the east." Surely an American would "recollect that he has traveled for thousands of miles, and has not crossed the boundaries of his own country and has not once been asked for his passport; what must be his admiration of the real sublimity of this great Republic?" Would a loyal American ever want to see his country "cut up into petty independencies?" Instead, "Let that tongue be palsied," Peck concluded, "that does not shout in the highest key, 'Long live the glorious Union!'" That Union, Peck proclaimed, had been "bequeathed to us primarily by God, and secondarily by our fathers." That Union was, then, "Christian America."[4]

Peck was not alone in this view. Even if all northern evangelical Protestants could not individually boast of a comparable lineage and despite the fact that some gave extraordinary attention to the issue of slavery in particular, a great many presumed responsibility for the fate of the Union as a specifically Christian country. It was that which southerners threatened to destroy. Northern evangelicals' "proprietary" regard for Christian America, considered within the context of crises surrounding the Union from the Civil War to the 1880s, is the focus of this book.[5] Stated succinctly, the thesis is that throughout the Civil War and Reconstruction many northern white evangelicals subordinated particular concern for the four million African American slaves—and then ex-slaves—to a larger vision for the Union's persistence and continued flourishing as a specifically Christian nation.

Evangelicalism and Christian America, North and South

With origins in seventeenth-century transatlantic pietism and the eighteenth-century Great Awakening, evangelicalism connotes a fervent, multidenominational expression of Protestant Christianity that became centrally important in

American culture during the nineteenth century. Richard Carwardine, while contending that Civil War–era evangelicalism was "the most powerful of all the era's subcultures," estimates that nearly 40 percent of the American population was sympathetically under its sway; Mark Noll goes so far as to say that "the country's ethos was predominantly evangelical," while including the Civil War era as part of what he refers to as "the era of 'Christian America.'"[6] Evangelicals resided primarily within denominations of British origin and were predominantly at home among Congregationalists, Presbyterians, Methodists, and Baptists, although they also could be found among low-church Episcopalians, African Americans, various Protestant sects, and even European confessional communities such as Lutherans and the German and Dutch Reformed. Characterized negatively, many evangelicals were self-consciously not Roman Catholics, and this particular disposition constituted a crucial aspect of their identity. Positively, evangelicals shared several distinctive characteristics: First, they regarded the Bible, when read in a seemingly straightforward, commonsense manner, as fundamentally authoritative regarding salvation, religious practice, and morality; second, they insisted on the necessity of an individual conversion experience or spiritual transformation linked to the salvific work of Christ on the cross as revealed in the Bible; and finally, evangelicals stressed the resultant necessity of an energetic Christian life, which included strenuous, self-disciplined personal piety and holiness, in addition to the importance of ostensibly Christlike action in the form of evangelism and often sociopolitical reform.[7] Although denominational differences over various aspects of faith, practice, and ecclesiology were important—which sometimes found the more creedal or liturgical-minded Protestants residing ambivalently on the margins of evangelicalism, particularly regarding revivalism and the role of subjective experience in conversion and sanctification—this summary definition encompasses most Civil War–era Trinitarian Protestants.[8]

Because of the importance of personal piety and godly behavior, evangelicalism may appear excessively individualistic, but evangelicals almost universally insisted that transformed individuals must actively work to bring about a Christian society.[9] Following in the wake of the American Revolution, which provided great religious, political, and geographical space for action, this social impulse most visibly manifested itself through various voluntary benevolence and reform efforts during the Second Great Awakening.[10] Questions about how slavery fit within the expanding Christian republic and what, if anything, ought to be done regarding the institution or its westward expansion would ultimately lead to war, but the desire to Christianize America remained a central and continuous feature of nineteenth-century evangelicalism, and this included southern evangelicals, many of whom consequently strove to remain committed to the Union during the sectional crisis of the 1850s. As one historian notes, antebellum southern evangelicals, no less than northern evangelicals, "insisted that the United States had been founded as a Christian nation" and that evangelicalism "was vital to [its] preservation."[11] Furthermore, evangelicals nationwide assumed that America existed in some sort of Old Testament–like covenantal relationship with God, and for many that assumption was bound up with millennial desires to establish an exemplary American republic that would serve as God's providential means of establishing the heavenly kingdom on earth. Irrespective of millennial beliefs, however, the covenantal mind-set meant that evangelicals habitually assumed that America was morally responsible before God, with divine blessings and curses linked to collective behavior.[12] Evangelicals' individualistic faith, held in common by northerners and southerners, thus was tempered by a concern for the nation.

Even though evangelicalism pervaded both sections, by the 1850s sectional differences were becoming manifest. North and South were "emerging as separate peoples," in Eugene Genovese's words, even if "they looked like a single people to foreign visitors and to many among themselves."[13] Divergent sectional self-understandings, each rooted in distinct socioeconomic systems and associated cultures, in conjunction with differing views of the nature of the federal Union and the Constitution that governed it, were infused with and received support from white evangelical Protestantism. Perhaps Europe's wars of religion had crossed the Atlantic after all, for what constituted a properly Christian and American Union was at the heart of the sectional crisis that became the Civil War. As Saint Augustine made known in the fifth century, Christians in search of an eternal city are always temporally located somewhere, shaping and being shaped by their specific time and place; the "city of God" is thus never completely separate from the "city of man," and by 1861, evangelicals North and South were entangled with their respective section's vision for the way things ought to be in Christian America.[14]

Even as the South produced cotton for world markets within a modernizing, liberal capitalist system and relied on northern banking, shipping, and customers to make immense profits, white southerners generally retained a traditional understanding of society, which they increasingly and defensively regarded as superior to that of the North. In the idealized southern understanding, individuals existed interdependently within a hierarchical, organic, and honor-based community of mutual obligations, while an enslaved African American labor force formed society's base. Although southern evangelical leaders often related uneasily to the classical, honor-based culture of southern gentlemen, and although they at times expressed ambivalence, if not guilt, about the actual practice of slavery, from the 1830s onward they never seriously challenged the southern social order or its "peculiar institution." In fact, arguments that both the Bible and the Constitution countenanced slavery were readily made, and through the 1850s white southern evangelicals vigorously championed what they believed to be a God-ordained way of life—including its racial assumptions—in the face of northern criticisms.[15]

Those criticisms flowed in part from a different social understanding taking shape in the North by midcentury, an understanding that many of its advocates, including evangelicals, increasingly insisted represented the American way of life and which should thus eventually infuse the entire Union. Northern evangelicals were, as Daniel Walker Howe contends, "champions" of a modernizing way of life centered on the free individual's attainment of "a new personal identity as both follower of Christ *and* rational, autonomous individual." Such twice-born, self-making individuals were also co-laborers seeking to achieve a thoroughgoing, morally disciplined, and rationally ordered Christian society, with such an aim comporting well with the Republican Party's free-labor ideology that gloried in individual freedom, equality of economic opportunity, social mobility, and progress. Despite overlap with many southerners concerning the importance of the evangelical new birth and freedom in Christ, and although northerners in the Whig-Federalist tradition maintained affinity for a national organic understanding of society, the southern individual's importance, identity, and exercise of liberty were more thoroughly embedded within a traditional, premodern social structure than in the North. Northern and southern evangelicals thus had diverging visions for the way things ought to be in the Union, and the linchpin had become race based slavery.[16]

Evangelicals in the South and the North had been debating the biblical rightness or wrongness of slavery and the matter of Christian slaveholding since the 1830s. Although most northern evangelicals were not immediatist abolitionists, they were increasingly convinced that slavery was incompatible with the spirit of the New Testament and, therefore, the Christian American republic. To southern evangelicals, a plain, commonsense reading of both the Old and New Testaments clearly permitted the institution of slavery, though they believed that the actual practice of it sometimes fell short of biblical ideals and needed reforming. In southern eyes, however, criticism of slavery per se threatened the Bible's authority, and this was compounded when northern evangelicals appeared to have found common cause with heterodox abolitionists. When southerners looked north, they saw a biblically deficient, atomistic Yankee society of striving and often secularizing individuals, a society filled with heretical William Lloyd Garrisons and eventually fanatical John Browns. The debates over slavery led to the Union's two largest Protestant denominations, Methodists and Baptists, splitting along sectional lines in 1844 and 1845, respectively, and the Presbyterians, next in size, being disrupted in part by arguments over slavery in 1837. By 1850, to both northerners and southerners, slavery had come to "symbolize all that was right or wrong" about the South. Americans' common evangelicalism had not been sufficient to hold the denominations together, and it would not hold the Union together for long once the nation began debating the extension of slavery into western territories during the Mexican War.[17]

Continuing criticism of the slave-based southern way of life during the 1850s, combined with Republican efforts to restrict slavery and elect a president committed to such, precipitated an array of emotions and attitudes among white southerners, eventuating in the secession of eleven states and their attempt to forge a separate Christian American nation. Perceived northern aggression left them feeling surrounded, alienated, dishonored, insulted, and outraged. Those who had come to perceive of themselves, in Drew Gilpin Faust's words, as "the most godly of Americans," found themselves having been impugned at every turn throughout the 1840s and 1850s, and it was gallingly unjust to them that, as equal members of the Union, they might be denied the right to transplant their way of life into the common federal territories. Having created a slave-based society, "[white southerners] could claim with some justice," Edward Ayers says, "that they were doing . . . nothing that the Bible and the Constitution did not at least tacitly sanction." Their status in the Union "seemed to change virtually overnight."[18] Following Lincoln's election in November 1860 and the subsequent succession of southern state secessions, southern evangelical leaders from the major denominations would provide widespread, vocal support for disunion and the creation of a presumably superior slave-based, Christian nation.[19]

The clash of Christian cultures had come to a head. Many northerners had come to perceive a southern slave-power conspiracy seeking to use the federal government to nationalize slavery, while many southerners feared shameful Yankee enslavement by a northern-controlled federal government that sought to nationalize its understanding of freedom.[20] In that context, white southern evangelicals, no less than their northern counterparts, thought of America as that which had been providentially created by God through the agency and blood of the Revolutionary founders; it was the South's Union too—until it no longer appeared so. To southern evangelicals, northern religion was irreparably diseased, and northerners had long ago departed from the original federal compact's permission and protection of slavery; separation, as an act of self-preservation and faithfulness to both God and the spirit of the American founders, was the only available option.[21] In order to separate, southerners went through the process of deratifying the Constitution, state by state, and in so doing left little doubt that slavery was, as Alexander Stephens infamously put it, the "cornerstone" of the new Confederacy.[22] In that process, they powerfully linked their cause to America's revolutionary beginnings. "Liberty," as William Cooper explains, "had always meant control of one's own affairs and institutions, of one's destiny," and "that destiny was inextricably caught up with black slavery." In the spirit of 1776, white southerners were unwilling to suffer under what they perceived as tyrannical, dishonorable rule from afar.[23] By April 1861, many southern evangelicals had thrown their weight behind states' rights, compact theory, and the right of revolution, and in their support for the new Confederacy they retained their traditional covenantal understanding of Christian America. But Christian America had moved south, and southern evangelicals were assured that God would bless their obedient efforts to create a godly, slave-based republic.[24]

Of course, northern evangelicals retained their own covenantal understanding of Christian America, and it would inform their outlook and actions throughout the Civil War and Reconstruction. As indicated above with George Peck, preserving the Union—not dissolving it—was an act of faithfulness to God and the Founding Fathers. Foremost in northern evangelicals' minds was the ingrained assumption that God had been at work since the seventeenth-century colonial settlements, providentially creating and sustaining a whole, Christian American people until himself. It was as though southerners were selfishly and shortsightedly forgetting that glorious heritage and choosing to remember America's past differently. The glory of the Lord had not departed the North for the South—northern evangelicals, like their southern brethren, surely felt a great obligation to faithfully remember God's historical activity, but on the entire Union's behalf. And yes, this included remembering their redemption from British tyranny during the Revolutionary War, but faithful remembering necessitated preserving that Union, which had been purchased with both northern and southern blood. Following the shedding of much more northern and southern blood during the Civil War, faithful remembering would mean infusing the restored Union with the spirit of affective sectional unity and evangelical morality. In short, northern evangelicals were convinced that the Union as Christian America was a sacred trust that must be preserved.

Northern Evangelicalism, the Civil War, and Reconstruction

Northern evangelicals from all denominations held some such view during the war and beyond, although it was perhaps most pronounced among Methodists, Presbyterians, and Congregationalists. It was among those three denominations that I began exploring the northern evangelical quest for a Christian America during the Civil War era. Richard Carwardine's *Evangelicals and Politics in Antebellum America* initially inspired the project; I too sympathized with the conclusions of "ethnocultural" or the "new" political history, which brought attention to the importance of religion in relation to national politics, in addition to sharing his method of taking evangelicals' public and private words to be indicative of "real" fears and aspirations.[25] I have approached my own sources similarly, while of course recognizing the embeddedness of those fears and aspirations within their sociopolitical context. I began by looking at three ostensibly representative figures: the Methodist Peck, Philadelphia's Old School Presbyterian Henry Boardman, and New York City's Congregationalist George Cheever. Boardman, like Peck, was moderate to conservative concerning slavery-related issues.[26] Cheever, however, was an uncompromising radical and likely the most prominent evangelical abolitionist of the era.[27] Though he disagreed with the others over how to tackle slavery and related issues, and in that regard he serves as a foil throughout the book, all three exemplified northern evangelicals' proprietary disposition toward the American republic.[28]

I subsequently cast the net as widely as possible to include sources from the major Protestant denominations. The book thus rests on a selection of sermons, denominational newspapers and journals, autobiographies, archival personal papers of several individuals, and the published and unpublished papers of Abraham Lincoln, Andrew Johnson, and Ulysses S. Grant. I read all of these sources with my eyes specifically open to expressions of evangelicals' sense of responsibility for America, while keyed to issues of national and presidential politics, and the book is organized accordingly. Although such a traditional method is not the only way to organize American history, it remains useful, and—perhaps it goes without saying—presidents do matter.[29] Arguably, Civil War–era presidents mattered greatly, and for many northern evangelicals specifically who resided in the White House symbolized much about the Christian republic's covenantal standing before God. In addition, with a mind-set familiar with both the Old Testament and classical history, northern evangelicals assumed, in agreement with other Americans, that individuals were the most significant shapers of history under God's providence.[30] Sermons, print media, and private letters related to national politics, then, provide a glimpse of northern evangelical preoccupations, fears, and hopes regarding the country. As Martin Marty has said, the intersection of the presidency and religion reveals "the deepest definitions of a people, the highest points they reach, [and] the most idolatrous depths in which they wallow."[31] During the Civil War era, northern evangelicals reflected and helped shape mainstream Republican/Union party political culture during the Lincoln, Johnson, and Grant presidencies. In Johnson's case, evangelicals, like many other northerners, eventually viewed him as a traitorous, Jacksonian Democrat at heart. When it came to Lincoln and Grant, most northern evangelicals saw fit leaders and saviors of the Union that was their Christian country.

One final and important note regarding the book's research and method is in order, particularly as they relate to the thesis and its potential significance. I specifically read the sources with the discourse surrounding Union in mind, and given the book's contention—that many northern white evangelical Protestants subsumed issues associated with African Americans under their larger vision for the Union's persistence and continued flourishing as a Christian nation—two interrelated historiographical implications emerge. First, not only does the book complement, if not expand, our understanding of why white northerners zealously fought from 1861 to 1865, but second, it assists in making more comprehensible Reconstruction's arguable failure to secure for the ex-slaves political, civic, and socioeconomic equality within the American republic.[32] However, northern evangelicalism has been insufficiently related to that failure within the predominant historical narrative.[33] Given evangelicals' central place in nineteenth-century American culture, it stands to reason that a fuller understanding of the Civil War era ought to take into account more centrally their thoughts, sentiments, and expectations.[34] As the abolitionist evangelical George Cheever believed, northern evangelical devotion to the Union hindered abolitionist dreams for a racially equitable America. Such an interpretation should give us pause, then, as we strive to better understand African American freedom and equality during the Civil War and its aftermath.

To be sure, scholars have demonstrated overwhelming northern evangelical support for the war effort, though they have not focused on the Union per se. Unsurprisingly, most scholarship focuses on slavery and related issues—and perhaps focuses disproportionately on abolitionists—usually within the context of nationalistic beliefs in providence, America's covenantal relationship to God, and millennial zeal flowing out of the Second Great Awakening. On this view, evangelicals blended patriotism with their belief in God's providential activity, such that God, in bringing about the culmination of world history, guaranteed the success of northern arms in order to provide an exemplary, slave-free republic for all the world to see. James Moorhead's *American Apocalypse* has been seminal in that regard. Furthermore, some have argued that the war transformed many evangelicals into abolitionists, suggesting in turn that evangelicals entered Reconstruction eager to include African Americans as fully equal partners in a restored Union. This is the view of Harry Stout in *Upon the Altar of the Nation*, and his interpretation meshes well with Edward J. Blum's *Reforging the White Republic*. On Blum's telling, the Civil War hopefully fractured the widespread antebellum notion of a great white Protestant republic that had been in the making, only to find northerners during the 1870s repudiating a war-produced commitment to abolitionist ideals and then willingly reconciling with white southerners in order to reforge that white Protestant republic by century's end. In other words, evangelicals tragically participated with other northerners to slam shut the window of opportunity that they themselves had helped to pry open during the war.[35]

Although I agree on a number of particulars and although I have benefited immensely from the large body of scholarship on Civil War–era northern evangelicalism, there are still a few points of divergence. First, a paradigmatic focus on millennialism potentially obscures the reality of evangelicals' elementary understanding of their nation as the Union. This is not to deny that millennial beliefs were powerfully present, especially in relation to antebellum reform movements and ideas about America's republicanizing mission to the world, or to deny that during the war evangelicals often understood the Union in such terms. But it is to say that Union is the larger category. Just as with scholarly debates about Puritanism, the desire to produce or preserve a biblical commonwealth (in this case a godly Union) may be distinguished from a belief in the exemplary mission of that society or a belief that history is about to culminate within one's own time and place.[36] Irrespective of millennial beliefs, then, evangelicals could be like other northerners, at least insofar as they were deeply concerned about the type of country they were creating for themselves and preserving for their children and grandchildren. At bottom, it was the Union that was in a life-and-death struggle, whether one had infused it with millennial import or not. Turning to slavery and issues of racial justice, I do not want to leave the impression that they were not on evangelicals' minds—abolitionist or otherwise—for they certainly were; however, as with millennialism, we should comprehend slavery-related matters within evangelicals' continuous concern for the Union. Although it is true that the bulk of northern evangelicals opposed slavery on some level by 1861, most had not been abolitionists.[37] Consequently, even if the Civil War softened the already "soft racism" that Alexander Saxton has ascribed of antebellum Whig-Republicans, which included many evangelicals, it is implausible to view the Civil War as dramatically transforming northern evangelicals into racial justice advocates.[38] It is more plausible to view the majority as leaving the war in terms of a continuous devotion to the Union, even as that devotion now included emancipation.

Thus even though slavery and emancipation are at the fore of scholarly understanding of the Civil War era's meaning and importance, I am not convinced that this was necessarily the case for the majority of northern evangelicals at the time—just as it was not for northerners in general.[39] That the Union was the primary lens through which many northerners, evangelical or otherwise, viewed the war and slavery-related issues should not be terribly surprising. Relying on data from 1860, which reveals that 98.8 percent of the northern populace was white, Gary Gallagher contends in his *Union War* that "most [white northerners] thought in terms of a white republic because, in almost every way that mattered in their quotidian lives, they inhabited one." The vast majority "could go about their lives without encountering many, if any, African Americans." Additionally, most African Americans were concentrated in the North's largest urban areas, which meant that most parts of the North were "even more blindingly white." Combining that demographic reality, then, with the deep civic-religious affection for the Union that animated so many antebellum white northerners suggests that most focused primarily on the fate of the Union during the Civil War era; they considered the fate of African Americans when radicals and events forced them to do so. In the case of northern evangelicals in particular, they did so as part of their larger concern for the Union's continued existence and flourishing as a Christian nation.[40]

With that overarching preoccupation in place, many evangelicals entered Reconstruction expecting to see the emergence of a speedily restored and culturally homogeneous Union, a Union strengthened by God through the defeat of secession and the removal of slavery as secession's cause. The expectation was that such a Union would be one in which evangelical Protestant moral and political assumptions would be even more culturally dominant than they had been during the antebellum period. And yet obstacles to a secure and thriving Union on northern evangelical terms threateningly appeared along the way to that imagined Union, coming in the form of Lincoln's assassination, Andrew Johnson's defiant leadership, white southerners' recalcitrance, and the presence of various so-called problem groups such as the ex-slaves, Roman Catholics, and Native Americans. With many northern evangelicals already at home in the Lincoln-led

Whig-Republican political tradition, victory in war cemented their allegiance to the Union-saving Republican Party and ensured the continuance of their jealous concern for the Union as "our country" through Reconstruction and beyond.[41]

Twenty years after George Peck published *Our Country*, the Congregationalist minister Josiah Strong published his better known and notorious work of the same title. When it appeared in 1885, evangelicals were long accustomed to meeting the sorts of "perils" that Strong saw threatening the country's survival, Christianization, and status as the world's greatest republic. His work flowed from a mind-set habituated to perceiving threats to "our country." It was a mind-set that ironically had helped ensure the end of slavery in defense of the Union while predisposing many northerners to look past, if not forget, the ex-slaves following the war.[42]

Evangelical Unionism as Ethnocultural Nationalism

In choosing to refract northern evangelicals' proprietary vision for America through the prism of Union, I have attempted to give some old sources a new read, and as part of further introducing the book, it is necessary to unpack the Union's meaning further. "No idea said more to Americans or they to it, than did the guises of Union between 1776 and 1861," the historian Paul Nagel stated in 1964. Tracing the transition from an early understanding of Union as a pragmatic experiment in federative polity among the colonies-become-states to a subsequent view of Union as a material and geographic fact delivered by the market and various antebellum technological developments, such as railroads, canals, the telegraph, and the press, his book was the first sustained look at the concept of Union. By the eve of civil war, eighteenth-century fraternal or familial feelings had combined with mid-nineteenth-century commercial self-interest and ideas of inevitable American progress, the advancement of democratic liberty, and providential national mission to produce a near-idolatrous attachment to the Union.[43] Thus George Peck's evocative praise of the Union in 1861 was not uncommon, even as his understanding of it came adorned in evangelicals' Christian American garb.

The Union was an all-encompassing civic-religious symbol and national entity. As *Harper's Monthly* optimistically proclaimed following the 1854 Kansas-Nebraska Act, the providential Union wondrously combined North and South into an organic whole, with the "Puritan on the one side [and] the Cavalier, the Huguenot, and the Scotch-Irish on the other."[44] With "Union" and "nation" functioning as coincident terms in common American usage, this love affair with the

Union may be viewed as the American version of romantic nationalism that was contemporaneously exercising its spell over Germans and Italians.[45] Although many southerners, particularly those in the Upper South, remained devoted to the Union until the very end, and perhaps even in romantic terms of affective oneness, there were many other southerners who nevertheless regarded it in terms of confederation and compact—understandably so by 1861, since they certainly perceived themselves as a "beleaguered" minority for whom such a view made good practical and existential sense.[46] In seceding and forming the Confederacy, southerners took any romantic sense of organic national oneness that had been directed toward the Union and transferred it to their new southern nation. "War and the ensuing reconstruction," William Freehling has concluded, "[then] forged a consuming southern nationalism around this prewar kernel of nationalism."[47] Northerners, for their part, carried their devotion to the entire Union's oneness into the war and beyond, while presuming that their way of life was the American way. It was to a vision of a familial, organic Union, materially united more strongly than ever, that the Whig-Republican Abraham Lincoln referred in his 1858 "House Divided" address. That Union signified Lincoln's free-labor, self-improving vision of America as "the last best, hope of earth" and whose perpetuity he would defend at a cost of at least 600,000 American lives.[48] For northerners, then, the concept of Union concerned more than simply the issue of federal-state relations and a utilitarian compact that allowed for loose cohesion among its members. Instead, as object of affection and imagination, it referred to one whole people and encapsulated all that was seemingly good in America—republican liberty, equality of opportunity, free labor, material prosperity, progress, hope, and glorious world prominence.

The Philadelphia Presbyterian Henry Boardman, likening the Union to the Israelites' "ark of the covenant," revealed how affection for the Union imperceptibly rooted itself in the northern evangelical consciousness. The Union, he said following the Compromise of 1850, "was the repository of our most precious national mementoes, the symbol of the Divine presence with us, and the pledge of his future protection," and such a sentiment could not "be ascribed to any specific training."[49] Perhaps it is helpful to consider Boardman's thought in terms of what the philosopher Charles Taylor has termed, in a very different context, a "social imaginary"—something which helps people make sense of or give meaning to social life in a taken-for-granted fashion. Taylor says, "I am talking about the way ordinary people 'imagine' their social surroundings, and this is often not expressed in theoretical terms, it is carried in images, stories, legends, etc." In other words, "The social imaginary is that common understanding which makes possible common practices, and a widely shared sense of legitimacy."[50] As Boardman reflected on the Union and its meaning, he seems to have been giving expression to something like Taylor's social imaginary. "We have inherited [devotion to the Union] from the mothers who bore us" and "inhaled it in the air," Boardman said. It has emerged "from the scenes of our firesides, from our daily employments, from our journeys, from our sanctuaries, from our national anniversaries, from all our experiences and all our associations." As the nineteenth century proceeded, for Boardman and many Americans, love for the Union had "become a part of our being. And this it is which, under God, has made the Union so strong; it is because its roots are struck down into our hearts, and so interlaced with the very framework of our moral being, that they seem to belong to our personal identity."[51] Reflecting on the war's beginning, Washington Gladden, the future Social Gospel advocate, simply described the task of preserving the Union as "our religion."[52]

Despite the Union's centrality to mid-nineteenth-century Americans, attention to its importance has been slight since Nagel's book appeared during the Civil War's centennial. Perhaps now, following the Civil War's sesquicentennial, the Union will once again become more central to our understanding of the era. After Nagel, a good place to begin is with Rogan Kersh's *Dreams of a More Perfect Union*, which reveals continuous preoccupation with the Union into the 1890s. Suggesting that Union has taken a back seat to republicanism and liberalism, he argues for the importance of Unionism's emphasis on affective bonds as distinct from civic virtue or self-interested striving.[53] A subsequent treatment that focuses specifically on the Civil War comes from Gary Gallagher. Recognizing that Americans at both the academic and popular levels have diminished if not effaced the centrality of the Union to those who fought in the war and supported the northern war effort, Gallagher's *Union War* represents a much-needed summons to reconsider our understanding of the Civil War North. He suggests that contemporary Americans have difficulty grasping the Union's historical importance because of our interest in freedom and the simple fact that freedom is much easier for most to comprehend as a noble aim of the Civil War (and Reconstruction). "The concept of the Union," he says in an earlier book examining the Civil War in film and art, "is much more nebulous." Although Gallagher, like Kersh, does not focus on evangelical devotion to the Union, he rightly says, "Recapturing how the concept of Union resonated and reverberated throughout the loyal states in the Civil War era is critical to grasping northern motivation. No single word in our contemporary political vocabulary shoulders so much historical, political and ideological meaning; none can stir deep emotional currents so easily."[54]

Our Country, then, explores northern evangelical Protestantism within the context of that pervasive devotion to the Union. Some evangelicals appear as typical adherents and promoters of it, while some abolitionist evangelicals were never able to entirely transcend it in their struggle for racial justice. To northern evangelicals the word "Union" certainly referred to the American territory—consisting of all the existing states and those to be added—and it often included the Constitution and federal government. Most important, however, the term connoted a country formed by the providential hand of God, in addition to the idea that it should remain whole and filled throughout with evangelical Protestantism. As a result, although their country was a federal union of states with a representative central government overseeing a vast and growing territory, many northern evangelicals envisioned the Union, above all, as a homogeneous national community consisting of one whole, historically formed Christian people.[55]

In addition to being unwilling to let the South go and presuming that the northern way of life was the American way of life, this meant that, strictly speaking, they were thinking of the Union as a Christian *nation*. One scholar has helpfully defined a nation as "a territorial relation of collective self-consciousness of actual and imagined duration," characterized as "spatially expansive" and "temporally deep," and such a definition meshes well with evangelicals' understanding of the Union. Members of a nation as such perceived themselves as "being related not only to those in the present who share in those territorial traditions, but also those in the past who performed activities in that territory. . . . Thus, the territory and its past are recognized as being one's own, as belonging to oneself and to those who are territorially related to oneself."[56] Of course, just what constituted the "territorial traditions" and who was being more faithful to them was at the center of the sectional dispute. Many northern evangelicals, as we shall see, energetically desired to see realized a homogeneous and specifically Protestant culture for the entire Union, a quest that brings to mind George Fredrickson's contention that nineteenth-century northerners had a "'psycho-social' wish" for homogeneity. That desire thus found northern evangelicals engaged in a fair bit of wishful imagining about the Union's oneness.[57]

The intersection of Union with nationalism is germane at two particular points. First, some scholars have emphasized weak or nascent nationalist ideas before 1861 and then focused on the transformative power of the Civil War as the means of producing a stronger national consciousness and a more powerful and even militarized central government. In other words, the Civil War transformed a loose union of states into the modern, globally powerful American nation-state.[58] Although I do not challenge the view that the war precipitated extensive thought about the United States becoming a nation, transformed and modernized the economy, and laid the groundwork for significant changes in the power and reach of the central government, evangelicals (like many other loyal northerners) went to war, entered Reconstruction, and advanced their understanding of America in terms of the prevailing discourse centered on Union. Furthermore, an emphasis on allegedly weak antebellum nationalism overlooks the fact that scores of evangelicals were continuously interested in questions concerning the extent to which they were a whole Christian people, and in that sense a nation, before, during, and after the Civil War. To these northerners, Union carried significant connotations that we miss if it is too readily swallowed up by notions of the emergent modern nation-state. It was not as though Union talk and associated concerns began only in the war and then ceased afterward, and this seems to have been particularly true of many evangelicals, who, like many other northerners, continuously used the terms "country," "nation," and "Union" synonymously.[59]

Thus northern evangelicals refused to see their country rent in 1861 and would continue to insist on national oneness after 1865. For even as many evangelicals realized that cultural differences between the sections were bitterly real, and though they perceived southerners' defense of slavery as the root cause of secession, they still insisted that God intended oneness for the American Union. The New School Presbyterian George Duffield Sr. asked following the Compromise of 1850, "Who can be ignorant that by the good providence of God, the national Union of these confederated States, bound together under the same constitution, forms the elements, the life and soul, of that civil, political and social prosperity, distinguishing us as *a people*?"[60] Accordingly, when it came to defending the Union after Fort Sumter, moderate and conservative white evangelicals shared George Peck's jealous and proud regard for the country. "The union of these states is a real union," the Old School Presbyterian Charles Hodge asserted during the first year of the war. "It is not a mere association, such as binds together nations of different races, languages, and political institutions. . . . The union of this country therefore, is determined by the homogeneity of its people, by its history, and by its physical character."[61] Or, as Yale's Congregationalist *New Englander* put it, "The people of these United States are one in their historical antecedents and associations. . . . Hence, secession does violence to history, to nature, and to our organic life."[62] In continuity with their antebellum vision for their Christian nation, many evangelicals would continue to insist on the reality of a whole and homogeneous American people throughout the war and Reconstruction, despite recognizable cultural differences between North and South and the perceived disruptive presence of various ethnic and religious groups. In that sense, as the historian David Waldstreicher has argued regarding nationalist celebratory activities during the early republic, evangelical ideas, sentiments, and practices regarding the nation were simultaneously unifying and divisive. That is, northern evangelicals continued to desire the reality of a unified and homogeneous American people, and this desire necessarily had the potential to divide and exclude precisely because it sought unity primarily on northern evangelical terms.[63]

Consequently—and here we come to the second significant point of intersection between Union and nationalism—rather than viewing northern evangelical devotion to the Union primarily in terms of civic nationalism, this book importantly reveals that at least some evangelicals retained significant elements of ethnocultural nationalism.[64] In brief, civic nationalism means that membership in the American nation (or Union) would be theoretically in keeping with what we now regard as the egalitarian spirit of the Declaration of Independence and thus open to all on the basis of citizenship under the national government.[65] Civic nationalism would include a common commitment to a set of shared ideals such as the rule of law, ordered liberty, equality of opportunity, republican aversion to inherited class distinctions and privileges, tolerance of ethnocultural differences, representative and participatory institutions as the locus of democratic conflict, majority rule circumscribed by the protection of certain basic rights available to all, and so forth. Or, as David Hollinger puts it, "Nationality . . . is based on the principle of consent and is ostensibly open to persons of a variety of ethno-[cultural] affiliations." Civic nationalism is, then, a theoretically inclusive vision that looks primarily to a "common future" based on certain agreed-upon democratic and republican ideas.[66] As the story goes, and it does make for a good narrative, northerners' inclusive civic nationalism triumphed over a southern and more exclusive form of ethnocultural or romantic nationalism rooted in such factors as a common language, religion, and culture, and perhaps, in James McPherson's words, "a belief in the common genetic or biological descent of the group."[67] Thus, as McPherson puts it in *Battle Cry of Freedom*, "Union victory in the war destroyed the southern vision of America and ensured that the northern vision would become the American vision." On this view, Abraham Lincoln and many public-minded northerners came to perceive the Union in civic nationalist terms.[68]

However, while Lincoln's flexible thought and leadership compelled many evangelicals seemingly to share the ideals and speak the language of civic nationalism, many willingly subordinated concern for the fate of African Americans to their vision of national Christian oneness and were often skeptical of them and other perceived outsider groups in terms of fitness for citizenship in their Christian nation. That is, northern evangelicals' nationalism exhibited something like what one historian has attributed to Theodore Roosevelt's turn-of-the-century nationalism, namely a "divided" or "contradictory" form; it would be a mistake, therefore, to view northern evangelicals as having rid themselves entirely of ethnocultural or romantic nationalist elements in the wake of the Civil War.[69] In fact, the antebellum problem of the cultural one and the many became even more pressing after the war. Not only did evangelicals often share ambivalent, racialized perceptions with other northerners when thinking about the presence of non–Anglo-American groups in their country, they continued to insist that their own religious and moral assumptions should be the foundation for the Union's common culture—hallmarks of ethnocultural nationalism. Perceiving themselves as the nation's rightful proprietors, largely within the Federalist-Whig-Republican tradition, evangelicals had long been about the task of producing a unified Christian American people. In other words, evangelical devotion to the Union contained and retained "ascriptive elements" from the antebellum period through Reconstruction. Northern evangelicals imagined the Union on their own terms and were preoccupied with sustaining it as a whole Christian people permeated by a homogeneous Christian culture.[70] Thus, although they could give voice to a free-labor American dream of material and moral transformation, seemingly open to all, including the ex-slaves in particular, northern evangelicals nevertheless often insisted on more than a shared commitment to civic ideals as the basis for inclusion in their country. Victory in the Civil War solidified their vision for the nation, with potentially significant implications for the course of Reconstruction and beyond.

1 "The Uprising of a Great People"

A Providential Union

> Is such a government to die? Is its life and light to go out in blood? Forbid it, O my God!
>
> —Henry A. Boardman, The War (2), April 28, 1861

Following the Civil War, former Confederate Vice President Alexander Stephens likened Abraham Lincoln to Caesar, the "destroyer of the liberties of Rome!" Lincoln's nationalist construction of the Constitution and his use of executive power to prosecute the war and end slavery suggested the comparison. Writing to Americans who likely knew the Bible better than they knew classical history, Stephens also compared Lincoln to Hazael, an obscure oppressor of ancient Israel. Either way—classically or biblically—Lincoln embodied tyranny, and Stephens contended that Lincoln's "irrational" devotion to the Union drove him to consolidate federal power at the expense of the states, to make emancipation a war aim, and to violate the civil liberties of thousands of political opponents during the war. "The Union with him, in sentiment," Stephens said of his former congressional colleague, "rose to the sublimity of a religious mysticism."[1] Regardless of the overall merit of Stephens's interpretation—Mark Neely, for instance, has referred to it as "the constitutional moralizing of sore losers"—Stephens was not wrong to emphasize Lincoln's religious-like devotion to the Union as crucial for understanding what transpired between 1861 and 1865.[2] That devotion was particularly attuned to northern evangelical hearts and minds, and because his public words seemingly reflected their own understanding of the Union, Lincoln received their support throughout the war.

Even in early 1861, prior to his inauguration, evangelical resonances were apparent in Lincoln's speeches. "We are," he said to an Indiana gathering on his way to Washington in February 1861, "bound together, I trust[,] in christianity [*sic*], civilization and patriotism, and are attached to our country and our whole country. While some of us may differ in political opinions, still we are all united in one feeling for the Union." What "the salvation of this Union" needs, he said to another Indiana audience, is "but one single thing—the hearts of a people like yours." Alluding to Christ's remark to Saint Peter in Matthew 16:18, Lincoln continued, "When the people rise in masses in behalf of the Union and the liberties of their country, truly may it be said, 'The gates of hell shall not prevail against them.'" Given the importance of heartfelt, pious feeling and commitment to evangelicals, similar romantic utterances delivered during the war would only draw them closer to Lincoln while he acted to save the Union.[3]

Although they, like Lincoln, did make actual arguments on behalf of a perpetual Union, their arguments often came infused with civic-religious sentiment and appeal. Henry Boardman provided emblematic expression of that just prior to South Carolina's December 1860 secession. "The love of Union is too strong," he said, "to be suppressed when danger threatens. . . . When [the Union] is imperiled, our fears and anxieties can no more be repressed, than could those of the Hebrews when the ark of the covenant was in jeopardy." With words that echoed beyond the war, he insisted, "We are one people, Our government is one. We are one in our achievements and traditions; one in our rights and interests. . . . The Union is too sacred a trust to be sacrificed except upon the most imperative grounds." Though not insensitive to southerners' feelings of injustice and dishonor within that Union, Boardman did not believe that the controversy surrounding slavery's expansion, the return of fugitive slaves, and ultimately the election of a Republican president warranted secession.[4] In contrast to growing southern defensiveness and regional self-consciousness during the 1850s, which southern evangelicals substantially reflected and to which they contributed, northern evangelicals were increasingly animated by a vision of the whole Union persisting as a distinctly Protestant republic.

Consequently, support for Lincoln flowed from that vision. Prior to Fort Sumter, he had enjoined northerners, "It is your business to rise up and preserve the Union and liberty," and evangelicals would do their part. Although many wanted peace to the last, once the shooting began they threw their support behind him and his efforts to save the Union.[5] Cincinnati's Methodist pastor Granville Moody, who would become personally acquainted with Lincoln and Andrew Johnson, embodied that spirit by volunteering to lead the 74th Ohio Regiment; he was wounded three times during the war and breveted to Brigadier General in 1865 for his gallantry at the 1862–63 Battle of Stones River. His colleague William P. Strickland recalled that Moody believed that crushing the rebellion was "the most sacred duty of every liberty-loving American citizen."[6] Many northern evangelicals understood liberty in Whiggish-Republican terms, thus the Union was that exceptional place wherein striving individuals were politically, economically, and religiously free to make the most of life under God; this was Lincoln's meritocratic, free-labor America intermingled with evangelical Protestantism.

By 1861 the contrast between northern and southern understandings of liberty within the Union had become stark. Henry Ward Beecher, perhaps the nineteenth century's most famous evangelical, made the sacred, free republic the centerpiece of his sermon two days after Fort Sumter. "God, through our fathers," he said, "committed to us certain [republican] institutions, and we will maintain them to the end of our lives, and to the end of time." It was "those institutions," Lincoln had earlier said, "which have made us free, intelligent and happy—the most free, the most intelligent and the happiest people on the globe."[7] And thus, before it was anything else to northern evangelicals, the Civil War was a crisis of the Union's existence brought on by southerners in defense of a slave-based way of life that increasingly appeared to be incompatible with the highest ideals of the Protestant republic. Stunned by the attack on Fort Sumter, Boardman perceived it as treachery "laid open." The South actually sought "to destroy the Union."[8]

To grasp the depth of northern evangelicals' devotion to that Union, and then in turn their support for Lincoln, their habituated, often unselfconscious covenantal approach to the republic must be kept in view. This was an integral aspect of their quest for a Christian America, and northern victory would ensure its influence through Reconstruction and beyond. Of course, southern evangelicals were devoted to the Confederate cause and struggled for its existence within a similar framework, though defeat would require them to comprehend and remember the war much differently than victory would enable northerners to do.[9] Appropriated from the Old Testament and inflected by American experience since the seventeenth century, the covenantal disposition came in the form of a syllogism. The major premise maintained that God providentially dealt with all nations or peoples just as he dealt with individuals. Analogous to a father chastising a son, this meant that God would bless or curse in order to bring about increased faithfulness. Judgment in the form of national extinction was also possible, however, and when coupled with republican insecurity, such a potential often left northern evangelicals with a foreboding sense of the Union's fragility—particularly during a civil war. The crucial minor premise, though adhered to somewhat nervously in relation to the reality of older European nations, posited that Americans constituted an actual people. The necessary conclusion held that God was dealing particularly with them from 1861 to 1865, and this implied that they must respond with requisite gratitude, humility, and repentance in order to ensure the Union's survival. Furthermore, few northern evangelicals questioned whether a faithful response included a vigorous defense of the Union, for it was God's Union, and to do other than defend it militarily was a sure sign of ingratitude.

Whether held by radicals, moderates, or conservatives, the force of this syllogistic disposition transcended denominational lines and helped ensure that scores of northern evangelicals would intensely resist national disintegration. As a group of northern Baptists declared in May 1861, just prior to Tennessee becoming the final state to join the Confederacy, "We are threatened to be rent as a people." That Union "bought at Bunker Hill, Valley Forge, and Yorktown, was not, without our consent, sold" when seceded states formed a confederacy. "We dispute the legality of the bargain," they resolved, "and in the strength of the Lord God of our fathers still hope to contest, through this generation, if need be, the feasibility of the transfer."[10] Most northern evangelicals would contest the transfer.

Sharing Lincoln's "mystical Unionism," his public words often reflected the essence of their providential understanding of the Union and its obligation to God. Lincoln was someone far different than a tyrannical Caesar or Hazael; with the exception of some radical abolitionists, most notably George Cheever, a great number aligned themselves with the president in his defense of the Union. In accordance with their covenantal understanding, he was to them a heaven-sent defender and savior.

The Supremacy of Providence

In his second inaugural address, Lincoln looked back at the origin of the war with what are now well-known words. "Both parties deprecated war," he said, "but one of them would *make* war rather than let the nation survive; and the other would *accept* war rather than let it perish. And the war came." The last sentence perhaps reveals his sense of the war having providentially overtaken the nation. One historian has suggested that Lincoln became "obsessive" in his struggle "to fathom the part that Providence [played] in the war," and one of Lincoln's evangelical contemporaries approvingly observed what some historians have stressed of late: "Nobody can understand [Lincoln] who does not regard [his] solemn sense of being an agent of God in a great work as the back-ground of his whole policy."[11]

And Lincoln provided ample evidence for the plausibility of such a view. As president-elect, he publicly referred to himself as "a mere instrument, an accidental instrument" who might "serve but for a limited time"; on another occasion prior to his first inauguration, while expressing anxiety "that this Union, the Constitution, and the liberties of the people shall be perpetuated," he said, "I shall be most happy indeed if I shall be an humble instrument in the hands of the Almighty, and of this, his almost chosen people." At some point during the war Lincoln privately meditated on the probability that both sides in the war were unwittingly serving as God's "human instrumentalities" to accomplish "His purpose." In April 1864, Lincoln remarked to the Kentucky newspaperman Albert G. Hodges regarding the emergence of his emancipation policy: "I claim not to have controlled events, but confess plainly that events have controlled me. Now, at the end of three years struggle the nation's condition is not what either party, or any man devised, or expected. God alone can claim it."[12]

Perhaps above all, Lincoln's widely reprinted remarks given in February 1861, on the occasion of his leaving Springfield for Washington, set the tone for evangelicals' support over the next four years. What occurred on that occasion appears to have been a very evangelical moment. With great emotion and tears, Lincoln struggled to speak of the task before him, suggesting that it was a burden heavier than that "which devolved upon any other man since the days of Washington." Without the "the aid of Divine Providence," Lincoln offered, Washington would have failed, and "I feel that I cannot succeed without the same Divine aid which sustained him." According to *New York Herald* reporter Henry Villard, Lincoln's exhortation to the audience to pray "elicited choked exclamations of 'We will do it; we will do it.'" The presidency had come upon Lincoln just as a civil war was about to come upon the nation, and together Lincoln and the nation would struggle to understand the providential meaning of it all.[13]

To George Peck, the war had "thrust itself upon our attention." He had expected that the Union would survive the secession crisis, and this was rooted in historical experience. He remembered the Missouri Compromise and had participated in the political wrangling and compromising that had taken place over the next forty years. He had been a delegate at every Methodist General Conference since 1824, and during the 1840s and 1850s he was intimately involved in Methodist debates over slavery. In those debates the moderate Peck strove to mediate between two uncompromising "ultraist" positions on slavery, and as editor of the denomination's official newspaper he hoped to maintain peace by restricting discussion of the slavery issue following the Compromise of 1850. Peck was consistently concerned for the persistence of the Union and the unity of the Methodist Church. Like many in the Whig-Republican political tradition, he tended to regard himself as essentially apolitical and therefore reserved his harshest criticism for those whom he perceived to be elevating the interests of party or section over the good of the whole. In describing the ideal

American character, he alluded to the iconic Whig statesman Daniel Webster in saying that "no limited, local, sectional, partisan feeling should enter into the composition of his political character, or the formation of his political creed. [His] maxim should be: Our country, our whole country, one and inseparable." Despite decades-long anxiety over the fate of the Union, it had survived previous threats through compromise. It is understandable, then, that the war's beginning was "startling."[14] Perhaps the sense of shock is lost on us, however, because the story of the Civil War and its meaning, as Ed Ayers has stressed, have become satisfactorily "self-evident"; or, although it may be true that the Civil War "never goes away," to borrow James McPherson's memorable phrase, perhaps that never going away is akin to background noise.[15]

Being overly familiar and maybe even satisfied with the story and its meaning to us, we take little notice of the existential impact of the war's actual arrival on the people who could not know with clarity what the future held—even for those believers in a God who controlled all mundane events. Eliza Gilmore, the evangelical mother of the future head of the Freedmen's Bureau, Oliver Otis Howard, remarked that she could not entertain the possibility of a permanently divided country and thus looked for the providential coming of another great Whig statesman, a second Henry Clay, to stave off war and restore the Union.[16] When the war did begin, a writer in Princeton's staid *Biblical Repertory and Princeton Review* recalled the feeling as "impossible to describe—there is nothing like it in history." The sounds from Fort Sumter could be heard "through the telegraphic wire, with strange thrills, by every man and woman and child. The nation awoke, as in a moment, to the conviction that . . . its very existence [was] in peril." The war's coming meant the possibility of disunion, that which so many northerners dreaded and many doubted would occur.[17] Whereas abolitionists like Frederick Douglass prophetically saw the beginning of slavery's demise during the secession winter and said, "Let the conflict come, and God speed the right," others disbelieved and dreaded God's permission of war.[18] Eliza Gilmore said she "never expected to live to see such a state of affairs as this, [and] I think it calls upon every Christian to seek to know the most sure spiritual manner the Sovereign God can be approach'd and to supplicate his divine assistance in our Country's behalf."[19]

Most important, the war's coming startled so many northern evangelicals because—unlike southern evangelicals—a sundered Union had become incomprehensible to their self-understanding as American Christians. Perhaps attempting to reassure southerners, the conservative Charles Hodge succinctly expressed the prevailing sentiment when he said in early 1861, "It is not a question simply of the extension or non-extension of slavery, of the triumph of one system of labour, or form of social life over another." No, "it is the question, whether we are to continue to exist as a nation, or become a congeries of independent nations."[20] The politically moderate Congregationalist pastor Wheelock Craig, reflecting a few weeks after Sumter, marveled at the "mysterious inspiration" that "instantaneously roused the unanimous heart of the North. . . . My heart bleeds to think that it has come to this. But since it has come, and in a way so purely providential . . . I cannot help most strongly hoping for Northern success and victory."[21] Southern evangelicals, for their part, marveled at the Confederate unity that seemed to be emerging after Fort Sumter, viewing the fort's surrender as a sign of divine approval that would induce hesitant Upper South slave states to throw in their lot with the already seceded states. And three days later, Lincoln's call for 75,000 volunteers to put down the rebellion served to further compel holdouts to join the Confederacy, while it left northerners even more amazed at the spirit of unity pervading their section of the country.[22] "Sentiment" for the Union, Syracuse's New School Presbyterian Sherman B. Canfield recalled, was "kindled into a flame as by a breath from the God of our fathers," and that sentiment became "words and deeds when the intelligence was flashed throughout the land that the secessionists had opened their war against the Union . . . trampling on the time-honored symbol of our national sovereignty." The response to secession was nothing less than "the Uprising of a Great People" urged on by providence. Northern evangelicals of various stripes rehearsed a historical narrative that interpreted America as a whole, predominantly Protestant, people who had existed since the Puritans in a special relationship with the God of the universe. When the war came, they scrambled to discern the unthinkable, understanding its coming and associated events in the only way they could—by refracting it all through this well-entrenched historical lens.[23]

Northern evangelicals, as centrally as any other Americans, took for granted God's providential supremacy, whether this pertained to an individual's pilgrimage through life, changes in the weather, or events on the battlefield. Theirs was a protean assumption that would survive the war and remain important through Reconstruction.[24] Although some might acknowledge, as one Philadelphia Baptist did, "that it is a delicate, and indeed a presumptuous task to infer the special designs of God, from the peculiarity of human affairs," most did not shy away from attempting to do so in some manner. Mundane events were always signs, even if one's vision was "limited" or "easily biased by partisan sympathies."[25] The abolitionist pastor of New York City's Congregational Church of the Puritans, George Barrell Cheever—although a frustrated, angry critic of Lincoln, as well as of Lincoln's evangelical supporters—exemplified the evangelical view of providence. Throughout his life he drew great personal comfort from an exalted understanding of God's sovereignty, while nevertheless acting quite vigorously in the world. "Step by step God carries us on," Cheever remarked while struggling to keep the abolitionist newspaper *Principia* financially afloat in 1863, "and we know not whether the next step is to be on firm ground, or in a quagmire; but really it is no matter, if God only holds us by the hand and we hold on fast to him." Cheever piously assumed and insisted on the priority of God's special providence in all things—individually and nationally.[26] For northerners, whether God was a Unionist, abolitionist, or something in between was another matter. "It is God who knows full well how," one Brooklyn Presbyterian said, "at certain conjunctures, military victory is the defeat of the moral [slavery] question, and how, in those junctures, moral victory demands military defeat. . . . He it is who can bring into existence, and harmonize, all action, military, moral, civil, ecclesiastical, domestic and foreign . . . to secure the high design of His providence." Above all, Henry Boardman insisted, the plain tenor of scripture seemed clear: There were no accidents in God's world, regardless of the difficulty involved in comprehending the "inscrutable" swirl of events surrounding the success or failure of the Union army or its relationship to the issue of slavery.[27]

Like most northerners on the home front, evangelicals anxiously sought to make sense of the war by means of personal letters and various forms of secular and religious media that brought news from the battlefield. Boardman was disconcerted that evangelicals engrossed by the war were neglecting basic Christian practices such as scripture reading, prayer, Sabbath observance, and church attendance. "We are," he observed in October 1862, a month after Antietam, "breathing an intoxicating atmosphere—an atmosphere which excites and distracts the mind." Thus he struggled to remind his flock, and likely himself, that "the soul cannot live on newspapers." Of course, it was unsurprising "that there should be a general craving for news. . . . There are too many husbands and fathers, sons and brothers, in this deadly strife, for the fact to be otherwise." The Methodist abolitionist Gilbert Haven remarked similarly during Grant's 1864 Overland Campaign, though with less concern, that "telegrams, not texts, are our spiritual food. The battle, not the Bible, draws our attention. The lives of myriads, nay, the life of the nation hangs on the dreadful die."[28]

With war news foremost in mind, northern evangelicals instinctively cast events in terms of God's interposing hand. For instance, the Baptist pastor Joseph Gilmore, frustrated by two-plus years of failure in the eastern theater, perceived no great Union generals—even after extolling Ulysses S. Grant's western victories at Vicksburg and Chattanooga. Gilmore, son of New Hampshire's Whig-Republican governor and best known for his wartime hymn "He Leadeth Me," suggested that God was directly leading Union forces in order to prevent northerners from idolatrously worshipping "the vessel" of divine grace. Is there any Union general, Gilmore rhetorically asked, who "has even the ghost of a chance to fill the Presidential chair? God is taking all the glory to himself." As with Old Testament Israel, "The Lord of Hosts" was leading the Union, "and in his name do we set up our banners." After Grant's celebrated promotion in March 1864, the African Methodist Episcopal Church's *Christian Recorder* voiced the same sentiment. Glory belonged only "to Him that loved us, that died for us, that is now at the right hand of God the Father for us." In actuality, most had little problem focusing on the divinely chosen vehicle. One Washington, D.C., lover of the Union, while providing the obligatory qualification that God was the ultimate source of any success, nevertheless sought to reward God's earthly instruments. Excited by Lincoln's September 1864 Thanksgiving proclamation—and the victories at Mobile and Atlanta that lay behind it—he sent one hundred dollars to Secretary of War Edwin Stanton with the instruction that Grant give it to those "who will unfurl the Stars and Stripes" in Richmond.[29]

In practice, then, most assumed that God and northerners were somehow working in tandem to accomplish his purposes. This was evident when Luther Peck wrote to his father George in late July 1864, "I have strong hope in Grant and Providence," or when the Methodist layman Loring Grant jubilantly wrote George Peck in anticipation of northern voters serving as God's instrument to reelect Lincoln in 1864. Both Luther Peck and Loring Grant revealed an implicit aspect of the doctrine of providence, namely that God ordinarily used particular means or secondary causes in governing the world. In fact, George Peck's brother Jesse, a future Methodist bishop and Syracuse University founder, would write a lengthy narrative centered on God's "unimpaired sovereignty" and use of means in directing American history. Even for these Methodists, who vehemently argued against Calvinists on behalf of some form of human agency in personal salvation, it was inconceivable that Grant or Lincoln ever really moved independently of God.[30] For northern evangelicals God was actively sovereign over the course of the war, whether mediately or immediately.

A truly contingent world was inconceivable, and it was difficult for evangelicals in either section to sympathize with one who might think differently. Only the foolishly proud or intellectually deficient person would think that God was not providentially present in the war; of course, sectional allegiance or prior understanding of the war's meaning clearly influenced how one discerned the workings and meaning of that providence. Howard Crosby, the great-grandson of a Declaration of Independence signer, a renowned New Testament scholar, the pastor of New York City's Fourth Avenue Presbyterian Church, and one who would go on to become president of the American Philological Association and chancellor of New York University, announced with great confidence that it was a person of limited vision who could not move beyond the instrumental relationship between tactics, for instance, and the outcome of a particular battle to see the ultimate hand of God.[31] Citing both Union victories and defeats, Buffalo's Henry Smith rhetorically asked midway through the war, as a means of shoring up confidence, "My friends, can any sane man imagine the possibility of [God's] absence from Sumter, and Manassas, and Ball's Bluff, and the swamps of the Chickahominy; from Fort Jackson and Fort Henry; from Fort Donaldson [Donelson] and Shiloh; from Vicksburgh [Vicksburg] and Port Hudson; from Antietam and Gettysburg?"[32] With the same aim in mind, that of acknowledging providence, a southern evangelical easily could have uttered the same words, since the list also contained Confederate victories and defeats. And southerners could be just as confident as northerners that victory signified God's favor.[33] The A.M.E.'s *Christian Recorder*, with a very different understanding of the war's potential providential meaning in mind, marveled in early 1864 that "we are in the midst of a revolution whose issue is beyond the ken of mortal[s]," being "borne on by a resistless power . . . like ships on the ocean's breast, God only knowing whither."[34] Above all, as Henry Boardman stressed, though God used secondary causes to accomplish his purposes, "those causes [were] controlled by the great First Cause."[35]

Undoubtedly, actually to live by such a doctrine required patient faith in God, which likely proved difficult for Boardman and others. "Every practicable mode and means of protection [should] be employed" to save the Union, he urged his parishioners, and they should "plan and work as if everything depended upon ourselves." However, the trick was to "*feel* that our efforts are *nothing without God*. Commit all to Him [and] His sovereignty." In the context of civil war, Boardman knew that the temptation to impatience and bitterness was strong. "War," he bluntly said, "lets loose the worst passions of human nature," but he hoped that trust in God's providence could rein in such passions, especially as he anticipated the war's end. Boardman believed his stance to be the most logical and optimistic starting point, for to disbelieve in providence was "dismal atheism." Relative to other Protestants, those in the Reformed (or Calvinist) tradition, like Boardman, most consistently stressed the doctrine of God's sovereign control. Nevertheless, he rightly assumed that his views would be acceptable to "Christian men of all sects and all political parties" who sought to preserve the Union. He remarked to a multidenominational audience late in 1864, "Your theology recognizes a Providence . . . which comprehends all creatures and all events. You believe that whatever is, is by his appointment or by his permission; that, while he cannot ordain moral evil, he can permit it; and that what he permits, is just as essential a part of his plan as what he ordains." Alternately, as he had put it a few years earlier, "Nothing exists but by his ordination. Nothing happens but as he bids or permits it to happen. . . . It must be so. An infinite and perfect God must exercise an absolute and universal dominion." God either prescribed or permitted all earthly events according to an inscrutable, all-encompassing will, and Boardman championed the idea as well as anyone.[36]

Boardman did, however, represent the moderate to conservative portion of the Republican spectrum regarding society and the priority of Union over emancipation as a war aim—a good distance from a George Cheever or a Frederick Douglass.[37] Illustrative of Boardman's social thought is a sermon on Romans 9:20 that upheld the sovereignty of God as the one "great fact" of life. The King James text reads: "Nay but, O man, who art thou that repliest against God? Shall the thing formed say to him that formed it, Why hast thou made me thus?" Boardman admitted that as he looked at society and its problems, especially in a city like Philadelphia, "this whole scheme of things in the midst of which we are placed, is a mystery." Even in the most prosperous communities, "the symbols of our ruin and misery are all around us, and we cannot escape from them." One did not have to look hard to see that "the masses are groaning under the curse . . . of labor, and struggling with the trials of poverty," and it would be easy "to find fault with the economy under which we are placed." Nevertheless, "the man who spends his life in quarreling with what he calls his 'fate,' or less ambiguously, in reproaching Providence for not making him other than what he is, or placing him in different circumstances, is but augmenting his burdens every day and dispersing the gloom around his path." From his position as pastor of well-to-do businessmen and those like the prominent jurist Horace Binney, Boardman's public theology was perhaps understandable. Regardless, for Boardman it was incumbent on all believers, and really all Americans, to recognize and submit to God and God's sovereign governance of the American Union.[38] During the Civil War that meant supporting Lincoln and the appropriate military and political means against both southerners and those northern Democrats opposing Lincoln. Both groups were choosing to be on the wrong side of providential history, even while many of them professed just as strong a belief in providence as Boardman did.[39]

A Covenantal President

In seeking to preserve the Union, President Lincoln publicly recognized God's providence in proclaiming or recommending nine days of fasting, prayer, or thanksgiving during the war.[40] His Confederate counterpart Jefferson Davis directed southerners similarly, calling for ten national days of fasting, humiliation, or thanksgiving. He said more than Lincoln likely ever would have, however, when he exclaimed to a gathering in Georgia in fall 1864, "I believe that a just God looks upon our cause as holy, and that of our enemies as iniquitous." Alluding to the Old Testament, he said that God "in His good Providence will assist us, and never desert the right."[41] Although cynicism, in addition to complaints that the proclamations unduly mixed the sacred and the secular, could be heard in both sections—perhaps less so in the more thoroughly evangelical South—their issuance by both presidents underscores the central importance of evangelicalism to Civil War–era Americans. Each side desired to see realized its respective vision for a properly Christian American republic, and one historian has referred to Lincoln's use of the religious days in particular as "a national charge of adrenaline" that, in effect, licensed ministers "to wave the Union-Republican flag from the pulpit."[42] Lincoln's first proclamation, issued a few weeks after the stunning defeat at First Bull Run, urged clergymen to lead the nation before the one true God. The president proclaimed:

> It is fit and becoming in all people, at all times to acknowledge and revere the Supreme Government of God; to bow in humble submission to his chastisements; to confess and deplore their sins and transgressions in the full conviction that the fear of the Lord is the beginning of wisdom; and to pray, with all fervency and contrition, for the pardon of their past offenses, and for a blessing upon their present and prospective action.[43]

Lincoln fulfilled the role of national covenantal leader to a tee and gained northern evangelical affection in the process.

Although Lincoln's deference to God's providence might appear formulaic, it should be remembered that Lincoln regularly sat under the preaching of the Old School Presbyterian pastor Phineas D. Gurley at Washington's New York Avenue Presbyterian Church. Similar to Boardman's sermons, Gurley's sermons expressed the essence of Old School Presbyterian evangelicalism. Characterized by great pathos and reverence for God as the transcendent sovereign of the universe, Gurley's preaching pressed hearers in a very evangelical way to be confronted by that God and to make one's peace with the divine through Christ by being "born again." Speaking at the funeral of Lincoln's son Willie, Gurley brought the all-controlling will of God to the fore: "All those events which in any wise affect our condition and happiness are in his hands, and at his disposal." Seeking to instruct and console the Lincolns, Gurley continued, "Disease and death are his messengers; they go forth at his bidding and their fearful work is limited or extended according to the good pleasure of his will."[44] In short, Gurley urged faithful submission to God's superintendence of temporal life as the foundational truth for living. This was a kind of faith, in other words, that comprehended all earthly events—such as the death of a son or a civil war—in terms of God's transcendent greatness and goodness.[45]

Although Gurley's influence plausibly helps explain Lincoln's unceasing desire to make sense of the war under God, Lincoln also said that he preferred Gurley's preaching to that of other preachers because it was largely apolitical. In fact, because Gurley "confined himself so strictly to the simple preaching of the Cross," as the pastor of New York's Fifth Avenue Presbyterian Church put it, some accused Gurley of disloyalty to the Union cause, even while the president attended Gurley's church.[46] Extant sermons do suggest that Gurley stuck to matters of Christian faith and practice in his regular preaching, and he did present himself as disinclined to speak to political matters. "When therefore," he said, "I speak of our national affairs, either in the pulpit or out of it, I speak, not as a political partisan, but as a believer in the Triune God . . . and as an humble interpreter of his word and providence." Perhaps conscious of criticism, Gurley dropped his guard slightly on August 6, 1863, in response to Lincoln's July call for a day of Thanksgiving following the July victories at Gettysburg and Vicksburg. While exhorting his hearers—including Lincoln—to ultimately rest and trust in the sovereignty of God, Gurley pleaded that he was "honestly devoted to the preservation of the Union." Remarkably, he portrayed the Union's salvation as of a piece with the most important event in Christian history (and thus, for Christians, the history of the world): "He, who made the crucifixion of Jesus by wicked hands the most glorious event in the annals of the universe, can turn the dark night of our national adversity into a morning of gladness and a day of splendor such as neither this nor any other nation has ever seen before."[47]

Lincoln's Democratic opponents did not fail to see the easy fit between the president and clergymen such as Gurley. During the campaign of 1864 they cast a cynical glance at the proclamations, and it is noteworthy that four of them occurred during the election year. Democrats ridiculed Lincoln and supportive evangelicals:

> Let pious preachers who profess their enemies to love,
> Proclaim aloud that war is right, and sanctioned from above;
> That "Peace on earth, good will to man," has filled the world with strife,
> And God will love and bless the man that takes another's life.
> Then sound the tocsin—havoc cry—let slip the dogs of war;
> Let brother against brother fight, each other's name abhor;
> Let them beat out each other's brains, destruction deal around,
> Then proclaim a thanksgiving, and sacred peals resound.[48]

Although some clergymen professed to understand the criticism, it seems clear that most supported Lincoln's public deference to God. For example, prior to commending Lincoln's August 1863 proclamation as "a noble Christian document," Henry Smith allowed that it might be the work of "shrewd politicians." However, he quickly reassured his audience that because rulers in a republic are "fellow citizens" who would "reap in private life the harvest which they have sown in their public capacity," they would not risk facing their neighbors' retribution back home. Most likely, Smith did not really question Lincoln's sincerity, and thus he was similar to others who so strongly believed in the virtue and crucial significance of publicly recognizing God. The Pittsburgh Presbyterian John W. Bain, recollecting Lincoln's request for prayer and his stated need for divine guidance when he left Springfield in 1861, categorically rejected the possibility that Lincoln's words were "merely a political bid for Christian favor," while across the state, near Philadelphia, Norristown's Episcopal rector John Woart believed that most Christians throughout the Union responded to Lincoln's calls with "gratification."[49]

Undoubtedly, Lincoln's perceived sympathies with evangelicals engendered a great deal of affectionate support in return. One of the most celebrated instances came in response to his May 1864 thanksgiving recommendation. The Methodist General Conference appointed a group, which included George Peck and Granville Moody, to meet Lincoln and convey their "sympathy with him . . . , and [pledge] our prayers 'for the preservation of our country undivided, for the triumph of our cause, and for a permanent peace, gained by the sacrifice of no moral principle, but founded on the word of God, and securing righteousness, liberty, and equal rights to all.'" Lincoln responded warmly: "It may fairly be said that the Methodist Episcopal Church, not less devoted than the best, is, by its greater number, the most important of all. . . . God bless the Methodist Church—

bless all the churches! And blessed be God, Who in this, our great trial, giveth us the churches." It was particularly significant that Lincoln, "the very impersonation of a care-worn, weary man," in the words of Peck, "read the last sentence with a reverence which seemed to indicate deep religious feeling."[50] To emphasize Lincoln's deep religious feeling is unsurprising, coming from an evangelical, but what is perhaps more notable is that doing so overcame or obscured the fact that Lincoln's language about God was usually broadly theistic at best. To fill the president's words with Trinitarian (and evangelical) Christian substance and import was a short, easy, and unreflective step.[51]

In addition to their construal of Lincoln's words, many evangelicals nationwide assumed that the renowned Methodist Bishop Matthew Simpson had the ear of Lincoln and others in the administration.[52] John Lanahan, an Alexandria, Virginia, Methodist pastor and Simpson confidant, contended that "Mr. Lincoln held [Simpson] in the highest esteem, and attached much importance to his counsel. . . . The same is true of [Secretary of War] Stanton; he not only manifested great respect, but even love; he was invariably present to hear the bishop preach." Lanahan further stated that "Bishop Simpson's arrival in Washington was always the occasion of interest and courtesies from the chief men of the government and of Congress. . . . During my residence of some fifteen years in Washington I have known of very few who received more attention and manifestations of respect from leading men. . . . Mr. Lincoln and Mr. Stanton took him to their bosoms."[53] Many northern evangelicals eagerly latched on to such anecdotes and perceptions of Lincoln's openness to evangelical religion, with one pastor admitting after Lincoln's death that "we wished him [to be] good."[54] A certain satisfaction and comfort could be derived from the perception that the president was one of them; that is, to have someone with such authority apparently sharing their religion functioned to reassure evangelicals during a time when many aspects of their religious outlook, including providence, were beginning to be seriously challenged. Furthermore, possessing direct access to presidential power potentially symbolized and authenticated their presumptive status as the nation's rightful proprietors. Finally, there is also little doubt that many, particularly Methodists, viewed Simpson's relationship with Lincoln as a means to government appointments, either as a vehicle for furthering the evangelical agenda or mere office-seeking.[55]

Above all, it is likely that many desired Lincoln to be sufficiently religious for existential and theological reasons related to their overarching concern for the continuance of the Union as Christian America. As indicated above, evangelicals reflexively assumed that divinely sent blessings and curses correlated with the degree to which the nation lived up to its obligations to God. Consequently, Jesse Peck, Henry Boardman, and many others repeatedly maintained that a minimal obligation of any nation, let alone one like America with its sacred history, was to publicly acknowledge God as the world's true sovereign. A nation that failed to do at least that was flirting with disaster. Because nations, unlike individuals, "cannot be punished in the world to come," the possibility of temporal punishment threatened with great urgency. God could only dispense justice to nations within the flow of history, and clearly war was among the most striking means God might use to express his displeasure and get a nation's repentant attention. A final judgment in the form of national extinction was always a potentiality, and thus it was imperative to properly respond to God's prodding.[56] This is precisely what northern evangelicals saw Lincoln doing with his proclamations. A Baptist from Cleveland remarked in late 1864, "It is hopeful to see a nation while breasting the full stress of a gigantic civil war, pause, in the midst of its vast activities, to remember . . . its obligations to God, to ponder upon His dealings with it."[57]

Until Lincoln's October 1863 plea for a national thanksgiving, individual states rather than the president, issued summons to celebrate the November holiday, and this was not lost on some northern evangelicals.[58] New Jersey Presbyterian Joseph Symmes extolled the fact that "the highest officer in the land" had finally made the holiday national, thus marking an "epoch" in the nation's history. To recognize God as such was a needed correction from the dangerously secularizing trajectory he perceived America to have been traveling along since the late eighteenth century. "Hitherto," Symmes contended, "our public documents were too generally such as heathen or infidels could approve. There has been a marked advance in this respect."[59] The radical *Independent* agreed that "it is a happy augury that the day appointed for Thanksgiving is the same in all the loyal states. The festival of the Puritans becomes the festival of the nation." Accordingly, the paper published a specially prepared hymn, "Give Thanks All Ye People," which, evidently Lincoln had seen and "approved." At long last Thanksgiving was becoming a national holiday, initiated by the highest civil official in the land, Symmes said, "the legally appointed, and therefore divinely constituted head of the nation." New York's Samuel Bell could not resist drawing a parallel between Lincoln's nationalization of Thanksgiving and the ancient Hebrew Feast of Tabernacles.[60]

Ancient Israel

Most evangelicals in both sections had for some time looked to the Old Testament narrative of God's covenantal dealings with ancient Israel as particularly instructive for understanding how God deals with all nations in general and America in particular. Southern evangelicals retained the analogy following secession and regarded themselves during the war as being in bondage to a Pharaoh-led Egypt that would not let the Confederate Israel go.[61] Of course, northern evangelicals continued to think in terms of the entire Union—though beset by rebellion—as analogous to ancient Israel. At war's end Edward Norris Kirk, the well-known antebellum reformer and long-time pastor of Boston's Mt. Vernon Congregational Church, instructed northerners: "To know God in his providence we must become familiar with his treatment of the Jews. The Old Testament must enter into our education. He made his providence more marked and distinct with them than with any other people."[62]

In maintaining the comparison, however, northern evangelicals perpetuated a nagging ambiguity. First, they did not always explicitly claim that the United States was the "New Israel." That is, on one level they regarded historical Israel as the uniquely chosen people of God, such that the Christian church became the primary fulfillment of Israel as the nonnational people of God dispersed among the world's nations. On another level, however, and not necessarily at odds with the idea of the Christian church as the New Israel, northern evangelicals simply assumed the applicability of comparing Old Testament Israel to the United States. The words of Micah, for example, "belong to the American people now just as much as to the Hebrew people," stated the evangelical Episcopalian Frederic Dan Huntington. Henry Boardman confidently proclaimed, "The points of resemblance . . . have been too often dwelt upon to require any special elucidation. We have been accustomed to illustrate our bondage and our deliverance, the formation of the Union and its extraordinary growth and prosperity, by corresponding facts in the annals of the chosen people." Indeed, the parallel with Israel was too ingrained in the American Protestant tradition, while American history itself seemed to provide powerful confirmatory evidence of God's miraculous dealings with them as a people. Northern evangelicals continually recited American history as providential history, thereby reinforcing their determination to preserve the Union. "Like [Israel] we have felt that we were in the peculiar care of the Supreme Being. . . . And it must be conceded, that He has blessed us as He has blessed no other nation within the last seventy years—nor, indeed, since the Christian era," Boardman said.[63]

Moreover, as Boardman suggested a decade earlier, the inability to perceive this redemptive history was seemingly on par with sinful unbelief. "No man who believes that there is a Providence can take even a brief retrospect of our history . . . without discovering innumerable evidences of his benignant agency," he said.

The person who cannot "see a Divine hand directing and controlling the whole course of our affairs, from the landing of the colonists at Jamestown and Plymouth until the present hour, would hardly have seen the pillar of cloud and of fire had he been with the Hebrews in the wilderness." It was clear to Boardman and others: "This Union is not the work of man. It is THE WORK OF GOD."[64]

For northern evangelicals, similar recitations of American history as providential history would encompass victory and extend through Reconstruction and beyond, often with the preservation of the Union as the high point of the story. These narratives served as both cause and effect of a mind-set that would not allow northern evangelicals to easily forget what they believed God had done for them throughout their nation's history, but particularly during the years 1861 through 1865. "God is on the throne, our fathers' God and our God," Lincoln's pastor Phineas Gurley said during the war. "He has ever been manifestly and marvelously the Guardian-God of the Republic." Therefore, "we must not be faithless, but believing." This imperative was at the core of Old Testament–style covenantal theology, obligating northern evangelicals to jealously guard their national story and pass it on to their children—just as God repeatedly instructed ancient Israelites to do regarding events such as the Exodus and entrance into the promised land. George Peck did his part by placing America's "rich heritage" at the end of a divine narrative that included New Testament Christianity and the Protestant Reformation. God was making a Christian and republican people unto himself. Only in America, Peck stressed, were people free from the twin despotisms of monarchy and Roman Catholic "popery." Political and religious liberty were two sides of the same coin in such a narrative, and some version of this story was nearly axiomatic for most Civil War–era northern evangelicals. The Confederate quest for independence obviously threatened the whole enterprise; not striving to preserve the Union was therefore monumental betrayal.[65]

Northern evangelicals simply assumed that all Americans, including southerners before they seceded and then after the war, had a responsibility to protect such a historic, divine Union. Therefore, despite charges that he "preached politics," those such as Peck felt great pressure to discuss "questions of patriotic duty" and "national questions in the pulpit where [he] saw fitting opportunity." In essence, evangelicals devoted to the Union viewed themselves as playing the part of providential mouthpieces no less than southern evangelicals felt compelled to defend their godly, slave-based republic in the making. For example, Peck said he had no other choice than to denounce "the crime of the South" and explain "what [he] held to be the duty of the Christian citizen." In the spirit of Old Testament Israel, Peck believed all clergy were obligated to serve as the Union's "watchmen."

Both state and church would rue the day that clergymen became "dumb dogs" and refused to "sound the note of alarm" in the face of obvious danger. The seceded states, in their "madness, had plunged the nation into the horrors of fratricidal war." This was unthinkable to northern evangelicals who had internalized some form of the Christian America narrative over the course of the nineteenth century. "The only alternative left us," Peck said as he recalled the war's beginning, "was either to resist with all our strength, or be torn in pieces." He admitted, "I saw no way to escape national destruction but by the most vigorous and determined resistance."[66] As a threat to the Union's very existence, the war—and ultimately victory—hardened this tradition of looking to Old Testament Israel as the paradigm for American society and history. This hardening, however, ensured that the line between the Christian church, as the people of God, and the exceptional American nation, as the people of God, would remain fuzzy well into the future.

Some compounded the ambiguity by conflating God's dealings with Israel and his dealings with other Ancient Near Eastern nations. On the one hand, for example, Byron Sunderland, an Old School Presbyterian in Washington, D.C., in 1863 appeared as a Jonah prophesying to a nation steeped in wickedness. While comparing America to Nineveh, the capital of pagan Assyria, he wondered aloud whether there was a "sufficient number" of faithful and repentant Americans—clearly this meant a remnant of faithful evangelicals—for God to "interpose" and spare the nation. If not, he feared that the Union's permanent "dissolution" was near. On the other hand, Sunderland came to the pulpit as a Hebrew prophet, essentially charging the nation as the collective people of God with having broken its covenant through various personal sins. Here he continued in the American jeremiadic tradition of confronting the nation with a "shopworn" list of its sins for which, he assumed, it knew in its heart of hearts it was guilty of committing. On this point, northern and southern evangelicals sounded identical to one another, each responding to the vicissitudes of war with jeremiadic sermons and tying the fate of their respective cause to individual morality. "Vast numbers" of Americans, Sunderland representatively said, have rejected "the Gospel of Jesus Christ," which amounted "to a national sin of the deepest dye." Given the prominent place of Protestantism in American history and culture, he assumed that Americans as a whole should have known better. Consequently, in his view, God's potential judgment in the form of disunion should have been unsurprising.[67]

Joseph S. Grimes similarly conflated Nineveh and Israel in early August 1864, when northern morale reached its lowest point in the war. First, Grimes cast Lincoln's July call for a day of prayer and fasting as exactly parallel to "the Ninevitish

King" responding to Jonah's warning of impending destruction. However, without missing a beat, Grimes then quoted 2 Chronicles 7:14, where God referred to Israel as "my people," and applied such words to America. It did not matter to Grimes that not everyone shared his understanding of the nation's covenant obligations before God; it really did not matter what other nonevangelicals thought, for the gravity of the times called for appropriate action, and this meant first and foremost a humble acknowledgment of the nation's sin before God. In a scene replayed in both the North and the South at various moments throughout the war, he indicated that the providential state of the war had reached a crisis point. It was not a time to be giving heed to the cavils of the "infidel" interlopers in their midst, nor a time for political dialogue or compromise. How appropriate that the executive of the nation was calling all Americans to act as the people of God that so many presumed the nation to be.[68]

For those northern evangelicals who did put great stock in Lincoln's public words, and it appears that plenty did, they were clearly aware of others who attached little or no significance to the president's calls. For example, Grimes knew that "unreasonable men" might mock and sneer at "God's servants" for emphasizing Lincoln's proclamations of fast and thanksgiving days. But that only exacerbated the danger.[69] Bernard H. Nadal, a Methodist who lived in Washington, D.C., renowned as a "strong believer in the Union" and a purported friend of Lincoln's, reacted angrily to the perceived lack of seriousness. He lamented that the president did not somehow use his executive authority "to stop the scenes of amusement, the 'fast-day theatricals and picnics,' which fill the newspapers with their advertisements, and which turn the President's fast-day into bitter mockery, or into a broad farce."[70] Similarly, Frederic Huntington expressed shock at what he saw in Boston in April 1864, with Grant's Overland Campaign set to begin and more death to follow. How could it be, he asked, that so many "should stand on this verge of awful destinies, trifling, grasping, dancing and making merry, as if it were all a masquerade of pleasure-seekers to vanish in a night?" He worried that the president's proclamations might be of little avail if not joined by corresponding action by citizens. Thus he concluded that the humble reverence, "which the nation's God designs by his discipline, and demands in his Word, [is] not generally produced." Although Lincoln had directed them, "We are not repentant. We are not sobered. We are not on our knees. We are not a people bringing forth fruits meet for repentance."[71]

Such comments exemplify a key aspect of the covenantal mind-set, which left evangelicals in both sections susceptible to rapid mood swings in relation to news from the battlefield or changing political developments. While Confederates struggled to secure their existence as a people, northerners sensed that the Union's continued existence hung in the balance through much of the war. This unsettled, anxious state of being describes both abolitionists and nonabolitionists in the North, and Cheever illustrates the point well. He regularly alternated between despair and hope, pessimism and optimism. In one context, for example, he was greatly encouraged by an opportunity to speak prophetically to the Senate regarding "the State of the country, and God's demands upon the government and people." In another context, when the war was going badly, he retreated to the sovereignty of God to find a silver lining in military downturns. "We must thank God and take courage," he wrote to his wife in June 1863, "even if we cannot take Vicksburg, which seems to be not very probable. . . . Disasters are still good for us, [perhaps] our government will be compelled to change its ways, and strike at slavery in full earnest." Still again, not one month later, Cheever rejoiced to his sister Elizabeth Washburn at "the news of our victories [at Gettysburg and Vicksburg] by the mercy of God. . . . It is an interposition in our behalf, that, if our government know how to avail themselves of it, and to follow it up, morally as well as martially, will save the country." In supporting the northern war effort, Cheever envisioned the emergence of a Union that provided a just home for African Americans, but when that sort of Union was nowhere in sight, he became disgruntled and disillusioned. Thus he was filled with despair once again in 1864, just as Grant's Virginia campaign began: "We have as much reason to tremble for our country as Eli had to tremble for the Ark of God." As David Blight has said of Frederick Douglass's struggles to maintain belief and hope in providence, "A reformer's cause is always to some extent at the mercy of events."[72]

For Cheever, this meant that even while he maintained a sense of his own peculiar, prophetic responsibility to help bring about the Union's proper form of Christianization, he also viewed himself as part of a faithful, though beleaguered, minority to whom few listened. That sense of alienated distance from other Americans was continuous with abolitionists' antebellum experience, and to some extent it paralleled antebellum and postbellum southerners' experience of estrangement as well. Cheever was displeased throughout the war with Lincoln for his Union-first approach and his perceived slow and incomplete emancipation measures during 1861 and 1862, for failing to use ex-slaves as soldiers during that time, and then, after the government eventually allowed for the use of African American troops in the summer of 1862, for inequities regarding officer commissions, bounties, and regular pay. Accordingly, Cheever interpreted the New York City Draft Riots in July 1863 as coming from the hand of God against Lincoln's Unionism. "The country is reaping the fearful consequences of the President's indecision and failure at once to organize colored troops," he wrote to his sister on July 15. That very day, Lincoln issued his first "Proclamation of Thanksgiving," to be observed on August 6. Having fled to Saratoga Springs because of the riots, Cheever lamented to his sister on August 5, "So long as we war against the blacks and refuse to give them their rights, so long will God war against us, and in the end will take our rights from us, unless we repent." And then he excoriated the president: "Instead of confessing our guilt and announcing it in sackcloth and ashes, tomorrow we are invited to a day of thanksgiving for our victories, with not one intimation of humiliation before God, or confession of great sin, or intention of justice."[73]

Though Cheever's abolitionism set him apart from the bulk of northern white evangelicals, and clearly from southern evangelicals, his providential and covenantal outlook did not. Like so many, he hung on nearly every event, constantly scrutinizing and reinterpreting the course of the war in order to comprehend the ways of God. With the benefit of hindsight this worldview was nearly irrefutable to its adherents. Any sort of human or natural evil could be providentially explained as the result of national disobedience or sin. Perhaps one could never be sure if and when there was sufficient holiness and obedience in the land to keep judgment at bay, but one could usually be certain when the level of holiness was insufficient. The war itself provided evidence of that; one did not have to look far to discern the terrible hand of God summoning his people. Regardless of the interpretive difficulties involved, evangelicals nevertheless assumed that they possessed an ability to perceive God's workings in the world, an ability that unbelievers necessarily lacked. Consequently, in the case of northern evangelicals, they viewed themselves as ultimately responsible for the continued life of the Union, regardless of what others thought. It was clear to them that God was dealing with the nation just as he had with Ancient Israel (or Nineveh). Precisely what a proper response to God entailed, beyond increased personal holiness, is what divided Cheever-like abolitionists from other northern evangelicals—and southern evangelicals for that matter.

Heaven-Sent Defender and Savior

Cheever aside, most northern evangelicals heard President Lincoln speaking as one of them, and perhaps never more so than in his March 1863 national fast-day proclamation. At the urging of James Harlan, a Methodist senator from Iowa, the Senate requested that Lincoln proclaim a national day of prayer and repentance. In response, the president issued a prototypical covenantal proclamation. Coming after three and a half months of winter inactivity, and with Burnside's disaster at Fredericksburg—where Union forces suffered nearly 13,000 casualties to the Confederacy's 5,300—fresh in mind, Lincoln came forth as a covenant leader to remind northerners of their obligations before God. First, he said, "It is the duty of nations as well as of men, to own their dependence upon the overruling power of God" and then "to confess their sins and transgressions, in humble sorrow." They could do so, he reassured northerners, in the "hope that genuine repentance will lead to mercy and pardon." Above all, he implored them "to recognize the sublime truth, announced in the Holy Scriptures and proven by all history, that those nations only are blessed whose God is the Lord." Predicated on the assumption that "nations like individuals are subjected to punishments and chastisements in this world," Lincoln implied that "the awful calamity of civil war . . . may be but a punishment, inflicted upon us, for our presumptuous sins, to the needful end of our national reformation as a whole People." Continuing the jeremiad, Lincoln proclaimed, "We have forgotten the gracious hand which preserved us in peace, and multiplied and enriched and strengthened us; and we have vainly imagined, in the deceitfulness of our hearts, that all these blessings were produced by some superior wisdom and virtue of our own." According to the covenantal logic, the conclusion easily followed: "It behooves us then, to humble ourselves before the offended Power, to confess our national sins, and to pray for clemency and forgiveness."[74]

Most northern evangelicals were not like Cheever, for they wanted to see and hear good omens where they could be found, and Lincoln had provided just that with such proclamations. Thomas Nelson Haskell's response to this particular call provides an excellent example of evangelicals filling Lincoln's words with hopeful meaning. "Our republic," Haskell said, "is falling down, convulsed before the Prince of Peace, and through the President's proclamation, and every penitential prayer, is crying, 'Lord, if thou wilt, thou canst make me clean!'" The mere fact of Lincoln's "fully recognizing our national dependence upon God" was as important for preserving the Union as anything else he might do as the executive of the country. Lincoln, quite simply, was properly acting the part of a Christian nation's leader. The Lutheran John K. Plitt agreed, contending that "the most hopeful posture of the Nation may be that of the bowed suppliant crying to Heaven for mercy." When long-awaited military success came in late summer 1864, Lincoln knew to remind northerners that it was incumbent upon them to recognize whence their deliverance had come. In response, evangelicals regarded Lincoln as most fittingly occupying the executive seat of the government. As the Brooklyn Congregationalist Joseph P. Thompson put it in September 1864, "Well does the President . . . call upon us as a Christian people to make devout acknowledgment of 'the signal success that Divine Providence has vouchsafed the operations of the United States fleet and army.'" By calling for "devout acknowledgment to the Supreme Being in whose hands are the destinies of nations," Lincoln had tapped into the very heart of the northern evangelical worldview, and he was able to do so without mentioning Christ.[75] Like Lincoln, evangelicals possessed something akin to a mystical attachment to the Union, and in their case it was rooted in a well-entrenched understanding of the Union as a Christian republic for which they were particularly responsible. Undoubtedly, the good will generated by the nine proclamations that Lincoln delivered during the first three years of the war helped him during the campaign and election of 1864.

2 1864

Annus Mirabilis

> A scene of grandeur never before witnessed in any age or in any country, has just been displayed on the foreground of our national history. . . . Never, before the Great Reformation, was there such an event in political history.
>
> —Nathaniel West, *Victory and Gratitude*

On January 1, 1865, Boston's Methodist abolitionist Gilbert Haven proclaimed 1864 as America's "wonderful year." Alluding to Dryden's poetic commemoration of 1666 as Britain's *Annus Mirabilis*, the pastor announced, "Much more will the year 1864 stand forth in our annals as wonderful." The effusion stemmed from Lincoln's reelection, which, when coupled with an improving military situation, seemed to guarantee the Union's preservation; furthermore, having long railed against Americans' caste-like treatment of blacks, Haven rejoiced with millennial ardor at the prospect of a racially just Union emerging from the war. For the optimistic Haven, as for Frederick Douglass, Union and emancipation were not mutually exclusive—the two aims always went hand in hand. Proud of his lineage that extended back through the Revolution to Puritan New England, Haven had served as chaplain of the 8th Massachusetts early in the war and envisioned a Christian America especially characterized by racial justice and harmony. That vision distinguished him from centrists such as George Peck—and from Lincoln—who consistently comprehended slavery's demise within a more basic commitment to the Union. Perhaps this was never more apparent than in 1864.[1]

The war's evolving aim certainly reflected white evangelicals' widespread misgivings regarding slavery—it was a moral blot on the republic and the cause of the war—but during 1864 many downplayed slavery-related issues. Contrary, then, to the desires of those like Haven—or the angrier George Cheever—mainstream northern evangelicals viewed the election of 1864 fundamentally in terms of saving the Union. The abstraction that was "our country" overshadowed the abstraction that was the American "Negro." What Frederick Douglass observed about the Republican/National Union Party, in a letter to the evangelical editor Theodore Tilton, surely applied to many northern evangelicals at home in the party: "Slavery, though wounded, dying and despised, is still able to bind the tongues of our [R]epublican orators. . . . To all appearance we have been more ashamed of the Negro during this canvass than those of 56 and 60. . . . The Negro is the deformed child, which is put out of the room when company comes."[2] Given the widespread perception that Democrats sought a peace settlement granting southern independence, he realized that Republicans were not likely to make slavery and race central to the campaign.[3] Sensing that most Republicans feared "the charge of being the 'N----r' party," he resignedly supported Lincoln. For many evangelicals, devotion to the Union as Christian America, when coupled with northern racism and Democrats' insistent bifurcation of Union and emancipation as war aims, meant that the "deformed child" would be left outside. Like Lincoln, many refused to accept a situation that would find two nations emerging from what had heretofore been one. To that end, subordinating slavery-related issues to Union appeared necessary.[4]

If things were not quite as Haven imagined, 1864 still turned out to be a wonderful year to most. Lincoln's reelection did ensure the Union's survival, and Ulysses S. Grant had emerged as a hero. Although Grant's Virginia campaign faltered during the summer, precipitating much anxiety, that development heightened the election's importance. The year 1864 was nothing if not a scrape with national death; before and after the election, evangelicals cast the year as the dénouement of the war, if not the nation's entire history. The enhanced drama benefited Lincoln, for the more desperate things appeared, the more desperately evangelicals supported him. At first glance, this appears counterintuitive, since historians generally agree that late-summer military successes rallied the northern populace around Lincoln. While likely true regarding old Whigs, War Democrats, and some radicals, others became more supportive of Lincoln as their sense of crisis grew. Matters related to slavery would have to wait for war's end.[5]

High Hopes with Grant

Amherst College's Congregationalist clergyman-president William Stearns opened 1864 by thanking God that "we have still a country" and auspiciously announced, "The war will be brought to a righteous close. Liberty and law will be established, and we may hope for the time when the whole nation will become . . . 'One Huge Christian Personage.'" Liberty and Union meshed readily in this evangelical vision for America—with secession defeated and its cause, slavery, purged, a revitalized national Christian organism awaited. Union triumphs at Gettysburg and Vicksburg in July 1863, followed by November victories around Chattanooga, provided the basis for optimism.[6]

Lincoln boosted morale further on March 9, 1864, when he promoted Grant—the hero of Vicksburg and Chattanooga—to the newly revived rank of lieutenant-general and named him commander of all Union forces. On commissioning Grant, Lincoln said, "As the country herein trusts you, so, under God, it will sustain you." Grant knew how to respond publicly; anticipating the confrontation with Lee, he recognized "the full weight of the responsibilities now devolving upon me" and in turn acknowledged his limitations with an endearing and memorable humility. If those responsibilities are met, he said, "it will be due to those armies, and, above all, to the favor of that Providence which leads both nations and men." Right words indeed for an eager nation.[7] George Duffield Jr., a Presbyterian pastor in Galesburg, Illinois, who was a well-known hymn writer, the son of a famous New School Presbyterian pastor and reformer, and the great-grandson of a renowned colonial revivalist and chaplain of the Continental Congress, recalled the intensity and anticipation prior to Grant's Virginia campaign as being unequaled by any other moment in the war, so much so that many brought it to "the communion table itself!"[8] George Peck's brother, Jesse Peck, portrayed Grant's promotion as another glowing instance in the Christian republic's godly narrative and packed it with great covenantal significance. "Never did two men rise more grandly up to the highest responsibilities: God was, to their great minds, the sovereign and trust of the nation."[9] Evangelicals relished the fact that both the chief executive and the highest ranking military officer seemingly exemplified essential Protestant and American traits.

Amid the widespread northern excitement over Grant's promotion, evangelicals contributed to the lasting image of Grant as an unassuming republican, even Christian, savior of the Union. Though not quite the Cincinnatus-like figure George Washington had become, Grant was close. As the *Independent* reported, the westerner arrived in the capital without an entourage, "simply, unostentatiously, scarcely expected, and remained but for a day or two." He was "a cool man," duty-bound to finish off the Confederacy and uninterested in adulation or politics. Jesse Peck professed amazement at the "greatness" and "simplicity" of Grant's plan for Union forces to simultaneously strike Confederate forces on all fronts.[10] This classical republican image of a stoical, virtuous, and self-effacing Grant merged easily with biblical and evangelical imagery. Haven said Grant was "as little and unknown as David among his flocks" and "would have remained unknown but for that God saw his heart was simple, right, and true."

Furthermore, in Haven's hands, Grant became sufficiently antislavery, if not abolitionist.[11] Grant certainly was no George McClellan, the "young Napoleon" who sought "to conquer without God"; nor was he any of the other generals who had failed against Lee.[12]

However, there were some voices sounding a slightly different note on the eve of Grant's Virginia campaign. Erastus Wright, of Springfield, Illinois, self-described "old Friend and neighbor" of "Honest Abe," provides one memorable example. The sixty-five-year-old abolitionist sent Grant, America's "Joshua," a congratulatory, advice-filled letter. Claiming to express "the Mind, the Will, [and] Judgment of the Great God our Maker," Wright urged Grant to honor God in his new capacity by dealing justly with African American soldiers—which meant ensuring equitable pay, enlistment bounties, and officer appointments. Neglecting to do so would mean contending against God: "Old Pharaoh . . . tried it . . . and perished." Under Lincoln's leadership "this blind wicked Nation is on the same track and happy will it be if we escape," he prophesied. "Rob the nigger, hold a Fast to propitiate the favor of God! What a botch! . . . We are bleeding. We ought to bleed, it is just we should bleed and let me say Dear General Grant *we shall bleed* until we . . . are willing to do *Justice*. Measure the same justice to the black man as to the white." A Joshua or a Pharaoh to Christian America—the choice was Grant's.[13]

Despite abolitionist nemeses like Wright, the Union cause continued to subsume slavery-related issues, while confidence in Grant and Lincoln as Christian republican heroes rose. The Boston Congregationalist Andrew Stone, a pious Calvinist and moderate abolitionist, allowed that Lincoln had not moved fast enough regarding emancipation, but he still reassured his Park Street Church that under Lincoln's leadership the southern attempt "to dismember our broad country" was almost spent. Stone, who pastored the church from 1849 until 1866 and briefly served as chaplain for the 45th Massachusetts Infantry Regiment, stressed that his congregants must not lose sight of the war's larger significance with Grant's campaign about to begin: "We have two things to do as Christian patriots, to save the land and to save it for God. This land was for him; this nation founded for him."[14] Assuming the primacy of saving the Union, George Peck stressed the crucial importance of recognizing Grant's generalship and Lincoln's presidency as further evidence of America's divine narrative.[15]

Northern optimism soared following Grant's first encounter with Lee in early May. Initial indications suggested victory in Virginia's dense Wilderness west of Fredericksburg, near the old Chancellorsville battlefield. The *New York Tribune* reported, "We have reason to believe that a very few days now will settle the fate of the rebellion. It is staggering to its fall from the crippling blows of Grant, and cannot survive the summer." The *Christian Recorder* echoed that news, referring to Grant's initial actions "as a magnificent success."[16] On May 9 Lincoln responded with a Thanksgiving recommendation well suited to evangelical ears: "Enough is known of the Army operations within the last five days to claim our especial gratitude to God; while what remains undone demands our most sincere prayers to, and reliance upon, Him, without whom, all human effort is vain." He then recommended "that all patriots, at their homes, in their places of public worship, and wherever they may be, unite in common thanksgiving and prayer to Almighty God." It was this recommendation that inspired the Methodist delegation that included George Peck and Granville Moody to meet Lincoln in Washington. Afterward Peck observed that "the enthusiasm was contagious" in the city, and on seeing wounded Union soldiers from the Wilderness, he recollected, "I was almost ready to say, 'Would that I were young again, that I might join this band of heroes, and face the storm of war on the plains of Virginia.'" On the evening of May 9, Lincoln directed a serenading crowd's thoughts toward God in covenantal language. "While we are grateful," he said, "to all the brave men and officers for the events of the past few days, we should, above all, be very grateful to Almighty God, who gives us victory."[17]

The buoyancy soon subsided, however, as Grant did not achieve the anticipated victory. May 9 had also found Lee's men constructing the earthworks south of the Wilderness, near Spotsylvania Court House, which would become known as "the Bloody Angle." Three days later some of the most savage combat in recorded history occurred, with soldiers battling hand to hand amid cold rain, hail, and fog for twenty hours. Many of the 21,000 casualties lay atop one another in muddy, blood-filled pools. This occasioned Oliver Wendell Holmes Jr.'s well-known reflections on the apparent futility of the fighting, while from afar other northerners struggled to comprehend the hellish news.[18] "The piled dead lie before our vision," Gilbert Haven said to his congregation, "ghastly, torn, trampled, their eyes glazed, or 'staring in muddy impurity.' The wounded, sinking, fainting, groaning, bleeding, fill our souls with inexpressible anguish." Most striking, however, was the galling reminder that they were involved in a civil war; it simply should not be that "our sons and brothers have been wrestling in a death struggle with [southerners] who should [also] be our sons and brothers." Still, Haven could not resist portraying southerners as savages. "Our ears are filled with the hurrahs of our boys as they fly up the steep sides of rebel earthworks," he said in contrast to "the Indian yells of our foes, as they leap in mighty masses upon our serried columns." Perhaps comparing rebels to the stereotype of uncivilized Indians made it a bit easier to comprehend.[19]

Regarding perceptions of southerners, many evangelicals—like other northerners—equivocated. At one moment, a battle like Spotsylvania could bring about an emphasis upon nearly insurmountable differences between two peoples. At another moment, fervent desire for a restored Union found conciliation and American homogeneity at the fore. The latter impulse to oneness, with Christian themes intertwined, was clearly manifest in a December Thomas Nast cartoon in *Harper's Weekly*. Titled "The Union Christmas Dinner," Nast's print implicitly supported Lincoln's mild reconstruction policy and portrayed the president's familial understanding of the Union. Lincoln is shown welcoming Jefferson Davis and Robert E. Lee in from the winter cold. While they stand beneath the angelic proclamation announced at Christ's birth, "peace on earth, good will toward men," northern governors sit at the dinner table awaiting Confederates' return to the Union family. Corner insets portray warm northern conditions for reunion. In one inset "Victory" holds out "the olive branch to submission," while another shows Lee bowing and presenting his sword to "Unconditional Surrender" Grant. A third finds southern troops beckoned, "Lay down your arms and you will be welcome," while a fourth inset displays an elderly man embracing a younger man in tattered clothes, with the caption reading, "The return of the prodigal son." Absent from Nast's cartoon are references to slavery or African Americans, and yet by that time Lincoln was uncompromising when it came to emancipation as a condition for peaceful reunion. Lincoln, like many northern evangelicals, assumed that most southerners were heartfelt Unionists who had been duped by the "slave power"; in time, with secessionists removed and the region under the ameliorative influence of northern institutions, the South would come to resemble the free-labor North.[20]

Back in the summer, with the Union army slowed before Richmond, that hoped-for day appeared far distant. In July Grant commented, "If the rebellion is not perfectly and thoroughly crushed it will be the fault and through the weakness of the people [of the] North." Northern evangelicals, however, refused to be among those submitting to their country's disintegration.[21] Henry Darling, pastor of Albany's Fourth Presbyterian Church and future president of Hamilton College, likened the war to Absalom's treacherous rebellion against his father David, insisting that the North press on with "every element of its strength." To talk of trusting God was insufficient and sanctimonious, for it is ordinarily "through the instrumentality of second causes" that God works—in this case,

Union arms. To steel northern resolve, Darling drew a Manichean-like conclusion: "Our present struggle is either all wrong, and every man who gives it the slightest encouragement is to be condemned, or it is right, and we are all together bound at whatever cost, to carry it out to a triumphant conclusion." Darling's remarks carried not-so-subtle jabs at Lincoln's critics; failing to support the Union wholeheartedly made one complicit in the sin of lawless rebellion.[22] As 1864 wore on, Grant strove to carry out a promise made the day before the fighting at the Bloody Angle. Grant had said, "I propose to fight it out on this line if it takes all summer," and indeed, unlike previous Union generals, he did remain steadfast despite mounting losses. None were more shocking than those on June 3 at Cold Harbor, just outside Richmond, where Union troops likely suffered 7,000 casualties in less than a half-hour. Overall, through the first week of June, Grant's Army of the Potomac had suffered approximately 55,000 casualties out of the 118,000 troops that began the campaign. After Cold Harbor, and at the price of 10,000 more casualties, Grant moved south to Petersburg to begin what would become a nine-month siege. With the army stalled, criticism of Lincoln came in from both left and right in what was becoming a "long summer of discontent."[23]

Radicals and Democrats

In response to the staggering casualties, George Cheever's sister wrote to him, "You are undoubtedly watching the progress of our armies with the same intense interest that prevails everywhere. How fearful and terrible are the recent battles! . . . Oh, how terrible and awful is this fearful conflict in our nation." To Cheever, long displeased with Lincoln, slowed military progress confirmed that God's hand was raised against the Union, and Cheever likely experienced a mix of satisfaction and anger as a result, since he had not bought into the early optimism prior to the Wilderness and had forecast more defeats as a consequence of racial injustice. However, Lincoln's May 9 proclamation likely only made Cheever's blood boil; here was Lincoln presumptuously counseling northerners to render God thanksgiving rather than repentance, and it could not have been lost on Cheever that Lincoln's words likely engendered more affection.[24]

Nor could Cheever have asked for a better opportunity to express his indignation than the one he received from the wife of Iowa's Methodist Senator James Harlan. She invited Cheever to preach a "bold, manly" sermon before Congress in late May that would expose Congress's "cowardice" for not "freely" addressing "the many wrongs that are being perpetrated daily [against African Americans]." Though not his first time speaking before Congress, Cheever still jumped at the prospect of speaking prophetically within the nerve center of the world's foremost Christian nation; perhaps some might reconsider their support for Lincoln and thereby propitiate God's covenantal wrath. Angry over pay inequities between white and colored soldiers, Cheever thundered that congressmen should be grateful that God had kept Confederates from Washington. Lawmakers had insulted God and outraged "humanity by legislating against the whole Colored Race." Though unsparing toward Congress, Cheever saved his harshest criticism for Lincoln's use of emancipation as a Union-saving war measure, referring to "the enormous wickedness of any ruler refusing to fulfill . . . justice, or daring to apologize for the act of emancipation as if it were a crime, or to refuse it until compelled into it."[25]

Cheever was pleased with his address, but the political situation left him distressed. Often oscillating between despair and hope, a conversation with his friend Salmon Chase, Lincoln's nettlesome treasury secretary and the early presidential favorite of Cheever and many radicals, left him low. Resignedly, he wrote his wife, "I am great afraid that Mr. Lincoln is to be there another four years. . . . We shall see. God is the Judge. He putteth down one, and setteth up another." Unfortunately for Cheever, God did not stop Lincoln's progress. On June 8, following the horror at Cold Harbor, the newly christened National Union Party nominated Lincoln. Furthermore, Cheever's incessant criticism began to wear thin on family and friends, who supported the president for doing the best he could under trying circumstances. Lincoln's acceptance of Chase's resignation on June 30 left Cheever furious. Commenting in covenantal terms, he said, "Thus Mr. Lincoln is hurrying the country toward ruin." Always one to remind himself and others, however, Cheever hastened to add, "God is at the helm, and our trust must be in Him."[26]

Meanwhile, Cheever had sided with other prominent nonevangelical radicals, including Parker Pillsbury and Wendell Phillips, to support "The Pathfinder," John C. Frémont. To Cheever, Frémont was the only permissible option for an evangelical. On July 11, Cheever hosted a campaign event at his church and delivered a scathing speech against the president. The immediate context was Lincoln's pocket veto of the Wade-Davis Bill, a bill passed on July 2 directly challenging Lincoln's prerogative in reconstructing the Union. Enraged at Lincoln, Cheever also vented his spleen at fellow evangelicals, clearly believing that he and they collectively occupied the pivotal position in the republic. Back in 1860 they had abandoned their proprietary responsibility by choosing Lincoln and the Republican agenda of the nonextension of slavery, but 1864 offered another opportunity to do right. To Cheever it was indisputable that the temporal ruler "must be just," and he believed there was indisputable evidence that found Lincoln wanting; to wit, only when the Union cause appeared dire did he offer the Preliminary Emancipation Proclamation following Antietam, and only then as a Union-saving "bribe" for rebel states to return with their slaves. For Cheever the crux of the problem was, in fact Lincoln's pragmatic Unionism.[27] Referring to Lincoln's public letter of April 1864 to Albert Hodges, in addition to Lincoln's famous August 1862 reply to Horace Greeley, Cheever proclaimed, "Events control Lincoln, not conscience, nor justice, nor God." Cheever exasperatedly wondered, "Can a Christian man . . . vote for one who abjures moral considerations, and acts only from expediency and necessity?" Lincoln, like Pharaoh, "chose that . . . the country [be] destroyed with divine judgments, before he would 'let the people go.'" Cheever never overcame the fact that it was, as he put it later, "Mr. Lincoln's policy" of "Union first, and slavery left for after consideration." Lincoln was unfit to lead a Christian republic; why would more evangelicals not see this?[28]

Cheever found it impossible, then, to join others in lauding the Emancipation Proclamation. As New Hampshire Baptist Joseph Gilmore portrayed events, America's God had compelled Lincoln and the nation to "do unto others as we would have others do unto us." Northerners "little dreamed" of emancipation initially; rather, "we thought only of a constitution trampled in the dust, a solemn union causelessly broken, a flag insulted, a nation of freemen wronged." God, however, freed the president of "constitutional obligations" hindering him from touching slavery in "the sovereign States," and thus "the Emancipation Proclamation is not, as many expected, a dead letter. There are one million freedmen in our land to-day." In response to such interpretive efforts that integrated emancipation into the Union's divine narrative, Cheever pointed out that most northerners still did not include African Americans as fully equal Americans. In political, civic, and social terms, African Americans were generally second-class members throughout much of the North. Consequently, Cheever suggested an alternative historical narrative. Paraphrasing Psalm 106:15, a passage chastising ancient Israel for seeking its own way independently of God, Cheever informed his audience that God had given northerners their "desire"—Lincoln's first term based on Republicans' nonextension policy—but had "sent leanness"—in the form of consistent military defeat—as a result of continued racial injustice. Thus Cheever met defenders of Lincoln's gradualism with sarcasm and anger. To the "contented" majority, blind to God's ways, he said, "It is God's war for justice, not ours for [U]nion. . . . God's thunderbolts smite the country, and the land now is smoking with his wrath, because of the continued injustice to the black race. Yet you propose to build up your white empire still, on their exclusion from it, as a caste."[29]

Cheever was a prophet crying in the wilderness, since the president would continue to receive evangelical support.[30] On July 2, the day of the Wade-Davis Bill's passage, Congress adopted a Concurrent Resolution requesting that Lincoln "appoint a day for humiliation and prayer." It beseeched him to exhort northerners

> to confess and to repent of their manifold sins; to implore the compassion and forgiveness of the Almighty, that . . . the existing rebellion may be speedily suppressed, and the supremacy of the Constitution and laws of the United States may be established throughout all the States; to implore Him as the Supreme Ruler of the World, not to destroy us as a people.

Lincoln reissued the resolution and appointed August 4 "as a day of national humiliation and prayer." The call seemed especially timely, coming at a moment that Gilbert Haven described as "probably the gloomiest since the night of war closed us in." With Grant stalled before Petersburg following the July 30 Battle of the Crater, Jesse Hough of Williston, Vermont, revealed great faith in Lincoln, using the appointed day to chastise what he perceived as unbelief within the national covenant community. "If the army is in motion, the masses are hopeful," he observed, "even though it be marching towards some Bull Run, or Chancellorsville. If, on the other hand, [Grant] bides his time, as at Vicksburg, or meets with temporary disaster, as at Petersburg, the multitudes . . . are ready to despond." Rejecting the siren call to abandon Lincoln, he said, "God knows how to wait." And northerners should too, while trusting in Lincoln, Grant, and God. Hough keenly observed the mercurial evangelical spirit of 1864, and remarked, "The battles of the Wilderness were not over, before the air was filled with eager prophecies that Grant would enter Richmond before the 4th of July. It is August now, and they who shouted Hosanna but yesterday, are to-day in the slough of despond." Hough particularly indicted brethren like Cheever who continued to oppose the president. "The assault on Petersburg has failed; the Secretary of the Treasury has resigned. . . . The administration [must] be changed; and the gloomy seers discern naught in the national sky, but the blackness of darkness." Hough, hopeful that Grant would succeed at Petersburg just as he had at Vicksburg, advised those critical of Lincoln to quit "dwelling upon the mistakes" and being so quick to discount his "successes."[31]

Hough's supportive effort was especially crucial in the face of virulent Democratic hostility, since some Unionists were identifying critics like Cheever as aiding the opposition.[32] Lincoln had maintained a coalition of War Democrats and Republicans, but its collapse was realistically possible by mid-1864. While the line between extreme anti-Lincoln Democrats—the Copperheads—and the rest of the party was fuzzy, few would have objected to speaking of Lincoln as an unsophisticated, tyrannical "ass." Democrats of any stripe reminded northerners that Lincoln had suspended the writ of habeas corpus, countenanced the arrest of nearly fourteen thousand people, tried civilians in military courts, shut down opposition newspapers, initiated conscription, overseen the nation's first income tax, allowed for the creation of inflationary "greenbacks," and, worst of all, offered up Union soldiers "as a holocaust at the shrine of Abolitionism."[33] One Pennsylvania Democrat responded to Lincoln's August call for prayer and humiliation by proclaiming, "God's curse is upon the land. Does it become us to acknowledge the truth, and pray for forgiveness of God for any and every part we may have taken in upholding the sins and abominations of this wicked administration . . . to put on sack-cloth and retrace our steps [?] . . . Oh God, give us Peace!"[34] And many were ready to make peace. At the Democrats' August 30 convention in Chicago, their platform described the war as a "failure" and called for an immediate armistice. Although not all Democrats agreed with this notorious "peace plank," most shared the Copperheads' racism and avowed hatred for the tyrannical Lincoln.[35]

The following doggerel encapsulates the most spiteful Democratic opinion, mixing a view of the proper role of religion in the country with economic issues, opposition to conscription, criticism of increasing casualties, and an implicit appeal to Revolutionary-era patriotism—all wrapped in vicious racism:

> We are taxed on all goods by kind Providence given,
> We are taxed on the Bible that points us to Heaven,
> And when we ascend to the Heavenly goal,
> They would if they could, stick a stamp on our soul.
> And it's all for the nigger, Great God can it be.
> The home of the brave and the land of the free!
>
> But this is not all, not the money alone,
> Does the Rail-Splitter claim for to build up his throne,
> If you haven't three hundred [dollars] your body must tell,
> And if killed in one month, it's all very well.

And it's all for the nigger, Great God can it be.
The home of the brave and the land of the free!

Now boys will you tell me just what it has cost,
To elect Old Abe Lincoln and all his black host?
Just five hundred thousand our country's best blood
Have been slain, and their bodies lie under the sod.
And it's all for the nigger, Great God can it be.
The home of the brave and the land of the free![36]

War Democrats thus faced great pressure to distance themselves from Lincoln. It likely mattered little when those from the newly dubbed National Union party praised War Democrats for sticking by the president, or, as one evangelical put it, for having "nobly 'come out from among [the Copperheads],' and cleared their skirts of all complicity."[37] As the infamous Roman Catholic editor James McMaster said at the Chicago convention, "Show me a War Democrat to-day and I will show you a shoddy Abolitionist in disguise. . . . He is a Judas, and should be cast out as an enemy to humanity and to God."[38] McMaster was the flipside of Cheever. To zealots in either party, there was little room for nuance, prudence, or pragmatism, whether considering fellow party members or opponents. Some Democrats thus attempted to tar Lincoln with Cheever-like abolitionism, and then, by extension, War Democrats for supporting Lincoln's war effort. The irony, of course, is that Cheever despised Lincoln for his Unionism. Nonetheless, in Democratic propaganda, evangelical radicals like Cheever, who were "fomenting war fever" on behalf of "darkies," represented the true spirit of Lincoln's party.[39]

Unsurprisingly, then, War Democrats found themselves in a tight spot. Presenting themselves as patriotic, Union-loving Americans, they also stood with Copperheads seeking to capitalize on bad economic or military news. Attempting to escape the dilemma, the party nominated George McClellan, the Army of the Potomac's former commander who had fostered an image of himself as a dashing war hero with superior intellect and military acumen. Despite McClellan's participation in the arrest of Maryland state legislators in 1861, which assisted Lincoln's efforts to keep that state in the Union but angered Democrats, what mattered more to some was that McClellan subsequently opposed Lincoln's conduct of the war. During 1862, for instance, McClellan insubordinately criticized the president's decisions and refused to acknowledge directives; privately, McClellan pompously described Lincoln as "an idiot," "nothing more than a well-meaning baboon," and "the original gorilla." Although demonstrating strong organizational skills and impressive strategic thinking, McClellan had been hamstrung by cautious indecision, and during 1864 evangelicals did their part to disparage him. New York's Presbyterian minister Marvin Vincent, who would later become a well-known New Testament scholar, sarcastically commented, "Under [McClellan] organization was to be perfected. Under him the army was to be led to certain victory." Still others reminded the North of his ostensibly disgraceful tenure as commander of the Army of the Potomac, first during the Peninsula Campaign and then following Antietam. Fairly or unfairly, many simply regarded him as a Copperhead.[40]

Saving the Union

Lincoln could not expect to receive Copperhead backing, of course, or perhaps that of unforgiving radicals such as Cheever, and thus he needed substantial mainstream evangelical support. In 1864 many evangelicals would prove faithful to the president, and in the process they would explicitly subordinate slavery-related issues to the Union. Again, it helped that Lincoln and Congress chose resonant language for the August day of humiliation and prayer. Though such calls and the clerical responses might appear formulaic, asking God "not to destroy us as a people" nevertheless meshed seamlessly with a covenantal mind-set ever aware of threats to the Union. National destruction was always possible, never more than in 1864. Henry Darling praised the government's timeliness, and the Pennsylvania Presbyterian Joseph Grimes suggested that calling on God's mercy was "the nation's last hope beneath impending ruin." Most seemed to sense the danger by late August, with Lincoln himself expressing doubt that he would be reelected and convinced that a McClellan presidency meant permanent disunion.[41]

That potentiality was utterly unpalatable to evangelicals, whose national self-understanding promised victory and a strongly holistic Union. Rather than Cheever's forecast destruction, God's loving chastening was the more attractive interpretation and justification of God's ways to the American people.[42] To inspire steadfastness, Joseph Gilmore quoted Hebrews 12:6, "Whom the Lord loveth he chasteneth, and scourgeth every son whom he receiveth," and assured his audience that despite military defeats, "the eagles of the Republic have steadily pressed onward towards the goal which now rises clear and distinct before us. We have met with reverses. We should have expected them." Blending fear for the republic's survival with a positive vision of one, whole Christian American people, Gilmore also saw God at work fashioning a modern nation-state. Witnessing "a government," Gilmore said in support of Lincoln, "which can levy taxes, enforce conscriptions, put down insurrections and carry to a successful issue civil war" meant that an actual nation was emerging from what had heretofore been "a community of states." Oneness was overcoming both confederation and regional differences: "The people of the West and the East, the North and the South have come to better understand each other's character" through this exercise of centralized power. Referencing Saint Paul's First Letter to the Corinthians, he continued, "The people of the loyal States have learned that their interests are identical—that if 'one member suffer, all the members suffer with it.' . . . On God's anvil . . . we are fast being welded into one people." He forecast a splendidly restored Union, one that functioned like Saint Paul's vision of the church as the body of Christ; in fact, the civic-religious nation seemingly had replaced the church. "Yes," Gilmore said, "the day will come when loyalist and rebel will be mentioned only in history—Northerner and Southerner shall be merged in the more glorious name of American—when one united people, faithful to each other because true to God, shall fill each smiling valley and cluster on the towering slopes of every hill from the Atlantic to the Pacific."[43]

In praising the utility of a strengthened government in bringing about American oneness, Gilmore also alluded to traditional Democratic fears of consolidation and government overreach, fears that evangelical Unionists downplayed or dismissed as a disloyal threat to the Union's glorious future. Even if some concerns were justified, as Hartford's famous Congregationalist Horace Bushnell allowed, the "true soul of loyalty" will never "bear a look of sympathy or suffer a suspicion of connivance, with disorder and rebellion." There would be time following the war "to mend the abuses of the laws."[44] Regarding civil liberties, the prestigious Presbyterian pastor-scholar Howard Crosby bluntly asserted—in New York City no less, the center of northern Democracy and site of murderous draft riots the year before—that it does not follow that "I turn traitor and give aid and comfort to the rebellion" in the face of "arbitrary arrests made by the Government in its prosecution of this war." The government's actions were pragmatically justifiable as temporary, Union-saving means. Pulling fewer punches, Poughkeepsie's Edward Crosby asserted that squabbling over civil liberties was simply a "pretext for complaint and opposition [by] those . . . bitterly hostile to the party in power"; challenging Lincoln's admittedly "extra-constitutional measures" reflected desperate partisanship that threatened the continued "existence of our nationality." It was plain to Crosby that "fear of federal encroachment and government tyranny" was "either grossly exaggerated or wholly insincere and hypocritical."[45] In the tradition of antiparty partisanship, then, supporting Lincoln was an American, republican, and Christian duty, not merely a Republican one. God's permission of such a national trial aimed to create a stronger, more coherent Christian American people, and the Methodist Bernard Nadal therefore insisted that loyal northerners must resist the temptation "to falter" in the face of "high prices, high taxes, and profuse shedding of blood," regardless of Democratic criticisms. At bottom, the Democratic threat to the Union was of a piece with the Confederate one.[46]

In that respect, publicity surrounding the Chicago Democratic Convention and its peace platform went a long way toward solidifying evangelical support for Lincoln. Haven bemoaned the shameful disgrace of "thousands upon thousands of traitors, a generation of vipers, . . . assembled in one of our greatest cities." The *Independent* said, "The Chicago platform fell upon the country like an insult, rousing loyal men to indignation and opposition." Any reasonable person would see "the turpitude of the Chicago scheme for the overthrow of the Republic." According to Howard Crosby, Democrats presented a simple choice to northern voters in 1864: act as God's arm of vengeance and destroy the rebellion, or make peace with the South. If they chose the latter, by electing McClellan over Lincoln, they should also wait for God's wrath. The nationally known Pittsburgh Presbyterian Herrick Johnson's shrill remarks went further, suggesting that those who "think more of their party than of their country" were in concert with Satan. Johnson juxtaposed those complaining about taxes and inflation with a heroic Union soldier "who lay there with both legs [cut] off up close to his thighs, and yet who said with a smile, as his great loss was referred to, 'I believe my country demanded it, and my God demanded it.'" Partisan Democrats were ready to "betray our holy cause."[47]

Following Farragut's August capture of Mobile Bay, Sherman's early September capture of Atlanta, and Sheridan's victories in the Shenandoah Valley during September and October, Democrats would be hard-pressed to continue describing the war as a failure. The cumulative effect left some southerners deflated and many northerners invigorated. There is evidence that some southerners were reconsidering the rightness of their cause and God's favor on the Confederacy, particularly regarding slavery. Cheever, having correctly gauged a softening of radical opinion, agreed with such southerners insofar as he interpreted the turn of events as a bittersweet interposition of providence to save Lincoln.[48] Theodore Tilton's *Independent*, far from an unambiguous Lincoln backer, consequently portrayed the election as a question of "the life or death of the Republic" and thus supported the president.[49] Enjoying a play on Grant's words from earlier in the summer, Haven insisted that northerners must "fight it out on this line, if it takes the whole century." The Christian church, he said, having sustained Lincoln in prayer, must "march to the ballot-box, an army of Christ, with the banners of the Cross, and deposit, as she can, a million of votes . . . to secure the reelection of Abraham Lincoln."[50] Although not forgetting slavery-related issues, even abolitionists beat the Union-saving drum on behalf of Lincoln.

This was far easier to do for those less conflicted about the war's meaning in the first place. Toward that end, George Peck transparently compared Lincoln to ancient Israel's "President" Nehemiah, "a man of much prayer and great faith in God" who courageously and prudently led the Israelites out of their Babylonian captivity to rebuild Jerusalem's walls. Instead of receiving universal support, Nehemiah faced "a mongrel mass of people . . . accustomed to have their own way" and who disliked "the *puritan* rule of the new governor." Such "secessionists" and their "tools" were "the open enemies of *President* Nehemiah and his administration." Like Nehemiah, the godly, wise, and "puritan" Lincoln faced severe opposition from his own "mongrel mass of people"—treasonous southern leaders and northern Copperheads who would rend the Union. Ignoring "their national relations, and [turning] their back upon the old flag," such "wicked" and "cunning" men had been "waging every sort of war against good old Nehemiah, who is hard at work, day and night, at the broken walls of the glorious old union." Peck angrily denied the Democratic "taunt" that the war was a "nigger war brought on by a pack of fanatics" bent on abolition and racial equality; the war always was a war "for law and order, for constitutional liberty, for the defense and preservation of the nation's life." Endlessly portraying themselves as merely aiding their country, Peck and northern evangelicals were consummate antipartisan partisans in 1864.[51]

The most notable example of this came from the Methodist Bishop Matthew Simpson, who repeatedly delivered one particular address throughout the North. Perhaps as well known as Henry Ward Beecher, Simpson—who had practiced medicine briefly before becoming a minister, was outspokenly antislavery during the 1850s, and then, prior to becoming a bishop in 1852, was a professor at Allegheny College, president of Indiana's Asbury College (later DePauw University), and editor of the *Western Christian Advocate*—was the most sought-after speaker during the fall, evangelical or otherwise. Occasionally fetching over four hundred dollars per speech, Simpson claimed to "stand far above all party dialect," despite his evocative reference to a "rail-splitter" becoming president. Encouraged by letter writers insisting that he owed it to the country to deliver his "war speech," Simpson presented Lincoln as embodying America's finest attributes and hopes. In the context of a civil war and Democrats' threatening peace plank, a vote for

Lincoln became a vote for the Union's continued existence and republican possibilities. In the words of one late-nineteenth-century biographer, Simpson became "the evangelist of patriotism, . . . pleading the loyal cause with such power that where despair had reigned, he left hope and confidence in God."[52]

In claiming to transcend party, Simpson downplayed the importance of slavery. Emancipation was a by-product, he said, "but this war ought not be carried on for the purpose of destroying Slavery, or for any other purpose but for the simple purpose of restoring the authority of our Government. That is the only object for which the war should be waged." Foreshadowing evangelical racial ambivalence during Reconstruction, and perhaps reflecting Lincoln's continuing ambivalence, Simpson recommended colonization in either Africa or the American Southwest—the latter as a buffer with Mexico—as the best means of dealing with the freedmen at war's end. Simpson portrayed the Republican/National Union party as antislavery but nonabolitionist, while claiming that a vote for Lincoln was strictly a nonpartisan vote for the supremacy of the Union and all that it symbolized. The Union, whose life was hanging in the balance, was that which made a story like Lincoln's possible. For evangelicals, that Union was God's historic, providential creation.[53]

On no other issue did evangelicals' antiparty partisanship and their understanding of the sacred Union better merge than in discussion around its origin and nature. The states' rights position held that the sovereign states created the Union in 1787–88 when they ratified the Constitution, thus making the Union a divisible compact from which states might one day secede through a process of de-ratification; the nationalist position contended that the Union signified one, whole sovereign American people who predated the Constitution, such that it was indivisible and perpetual. Confederates and many northern Democrats held the former view; Lincoln and the Whig-Republican tradition, including many evangelicals, maintained some version of the latter. Americans had struggled theoretically and practically with this problem of federalism—of the one nation and the many states—since the writing of the Constitution, largely because the document was ambiguous about the matter. Consequently, as Harold Hyman observes, wrangling over the Union had "provided a generation with unprecedented expertness" in constitutional theory. From the ratification struggle to the secession crisis of 1860–61, "the conviction was general that no aristocracy existed with respect to the Constitution." In short, "the Constitution was everybody's business," regardless of how "distasteful" legal professionals might have found "the unending intrusion of common folk into constitutional questions." Among such common folk were evangelicals, and Hyman says no intruders were more "obnoxious" than the "'pulpit politicians' sermonizing over the Constitution."[54] During the war northern evangelicals joined the discussion as a means of buttressing confidence in the cause for which the war was being fought. Given that evangelicals had long regarded the Union as one, whole Christian people, they readily supported Lincoln's nationalist position.

George Peck's input in late 1863 is illustrative, and others made the case in 1864. Misleadingly contending that the Constitution was ratified by popular vote, Peck stressed that the appearance of "the doctrine that each separate state is a sovereignty in itself" came well after ratification, originating with Jefferson's Republican opposition to the Federalists. That opposition, he said, was born of an unrepublican and un-Christian "spirit of faction," which was itself rooted in "human selfishness." Although Peck's telling was not entirely accurate, both to the method of ratification and because many opposed ratification precisely because they feared a consolidating central government that threatened to swallow up the states, he and other evangelicals insisted that state sovereignty (and secession) was an American heresy.[55] Perhaps most important, Peck reached back in time, to the Puritans, to locate a preconstitutional American people—or "nation." Those first Americans were, then, the providentially planted people of God and the religious predecessors of nineteenth-century evangelicals. Such an assumption undergirded evangelicals' sense of proprietary responsibility to argue against those southerners and Democrats who threatened to bring the enterprise to an end. To evangelical Unionists, one whole Christian American people adopted the Articles of Confederation before the states even existed, and it was that sovereign whole people who subsequently came together "in order to form a more perfect Union."[56] This argument consequently promised to nullify the view that the Constitution created the Union as a divisible compact of sovereign states, and, to Peck, it implied the Union's perpetuity. "When the federal Constitution was adopted by a popular vote an obligation was entered into, by the whole people [and] necessarily made for all time. . . . The very idea of a nation supposes adhesiveness and permanence." For Peck and others, "the right of secession, once admitted," meant that "our nationality is gone forever." As an added touch, Peck referred to Daniel Webster's words, which so many Americans knew by heart, and urged, "May the whole people respond . . . 'Union and Liberty, now and forever, one and inseparable.'" Peck's identification with the great Whig defender of the Union, his belief in the Puritans as the originating source of one, whole American people, and his opposition to states' rights exemplified the conjunction of a traditional Federalist-Whig-Republican view with evangelicals' providential historical understanding.[57]

It was Lincoln's articulation of the Websterian narrative to which Peck was clearly alluding. Responding to secession in his first inaugural address, Lincoln had said, "Perpetuity is implied, if not expressed, in the fundamental law of all national governments. . . . No government proper, ever had a provision in its organic law for its own termination." Furthermore, history argued for the Union's perpetuity. Reaching back to the Articles of Association in 1774 and the Declaration of Independence of 1776, Lincoln found a Union of one whole American people preceding the Constitution; that Union subsequently delivered the Articles of Confederation, with its reference to a perpetual Union, and followed up with the Constitution and its aim of perfecting that perpetual Union. As Lincoln later put it in July 1861, southerners had "invented an ingenious sophism," a "rebellion thus sugar-coated," with their compact theory. He never could bring himself to refer to secession as secession, because he denied its legal possibility. "The states," he said, "have their *status* IN the Union, and they have no other *legal status*. . . . The Union and not themselves separately, procured their independence, and their liberty. . . . The Union is older than any of the states; and, in fact, it created them as States."[58]

Having drunk from the same Unionist well, clearly evangelicals were echoing Lincoln's Websterian argument, but they went further by packaging their understanding of the Union's preconstitutional origin in their understanding of the nation's divine history. Notably, Lincoln's pastor Phineas Gurley further revealed the mixture when he asserted that God's purpose in the war was to form "a more perfect union." To Gurley that meant Americans "shall become, in a fuller, loftier sense than ever before, that united and happy people, whose God is the Lord." Northern evangelicals had little choice but to insist on the preconstitutional existence of one perpetual American people, regardless of the exact historical origins.[59] In the opinion of New School Presbyterian Albert Barnes, if "the Union under the constitution was a mere confederacy," it was not an actual Union.[60] Following Lincoln's reelection, Horace Bushnell prominently insisted, "We had, in fact, the name [of United States] upon us, before we spoke it, and the constitution in us, before we saw it on paper—the Philadelphia Convention did scarcely more than draw out the constitution already framed by Almighty God, in the historic cast of our nation itself." And looking ahead to Union victory, he expectantly proclaimed, "We shall be no more a compact, or a confederation, or a composition made up by the temporary surrender of powers, but a nation—God's own nation, providentially planted."[61]

In the face of Democratic criticism regarding war aims, many evangelicals rehashed nationalist arguments in 1864, and in so doing supported Lincoln and downplayed emancipation. The pious Methodist lawyer of Trenton, New Jersey, James Rusling, who was also a Union officer and one who had served under and been recommended for promotion by McClellan, reasserted that the Founding Fathers had located sovereignty in the collective American people.[62] "It was 'We The People,' not 'we the states,'" who ordained and established the Union. That Union, he added, perhaps echoing Lincoln's Gettysburg Address, was "established by the whole people, for the people." Recounting the struggle between Hamiltonians and Jeffersonians, Rusling insisted that the debate was being settled in favor of the former—unless Democrats won the election. Therefore, Rusling offered a plug for the ex-lawyer Lincoln, casting the war as the culmination of "the great [legal] case of the nation *versus* the states." The states, as the "defendants," had concluded that the "plaintiff did not mean to prosecute." However, the plaintiff "was goaded to think better of his cause" and "found a proper attorney in a certain honest lawyer from Illinois." The trial was being decided "at the bar of History, before the great Judge of nations as well as men." Rusling also took pains to remind that the war was not an abolitionist war: "Our real struggle, as a nation, to the calm eye of history, rises higher than the question of slavery, and is rather an armed resolve of the national government to assert for itself, at last, authority and power."[63]

For many evangelicals Lincoln's reelection thus sounded the death knell on the "heresy of state sovereignties." The Union, understood as one Christian American people, was becoming a more secure reality. In fact, one of the reasons that Gilbert Haven proclaimed 1864 as America's wonderful year was because the question of the Union's nature was nearing resolution. "1864, it will be said by the future historian, settled the question of America's nationality. No longer will State-rights resolutions vex and frighten the people." Lincoln's reelection and continued prosecution of the war to victory would end the matter forever.[64]

Denouement

By the fall, most knew the election would determine the fate of both Union and slavery. The abolitionist Oliver Johnson sent a last-gasp letter hoping to persuade Cheever to vote for Lincoln: "If Lincoln is reelected," Johnson wrote, "slavery and the Rebellion will soon die—if McClellan . . . then slavery will be nationalized, our army disbanded, and the rebellion will prove a revolution. What a day for our nation! None greater before the judgment." Cheever believed that Lincoln's reelection would preserve the Union in the short run, but he prophesied in covenantal terms the Union's ultimate destruction; a Copperhead revolt, reminiscent of the 1863 draft riots, would destroy the "Northern government," and Cheever was not about to vote for Lincoln. Northerners had been selling their souls for a mess of Union pottage for three years, setting themselves "against God" by refusing to emancipate all slaves everywhere and by their injustice to African Americans. Northerners could now wait for "the utter and hopeless destruction . . . of what remains of our union" at the hands of God's instruments.[65]

Cheever was wrong, of course, and others filled Lincoln's victory with a different covenantal meaning. The Congregationalist Increase Tarbox thankfully noted the "religious solemnity" that marked the Union-saving election and asserted that those unable to construe it as part of God's redemptive narrative for America were like those who lacked "eyes to see" and "ears to hear" Christ's gospel. The target of his comment was not primarily abolitionists such as Cheever, however, but Democrats. And Tarbox was not alone in this. One Brooklyn Presbyterian mocked Democrats for their cold-hearted and unrepublican selfishness. Insisting that American history had always been Christian history, their complaints evoked no sympathy. With words calculated to marginalize and shame, he concluded, "Let the ignoble and unpatriotic, who now so sadly mourn that they have no country to love and none to save, yet willingly partake of her unexampled blessings, sneer at a sentiment which all history, nature and revelation alike have hallowed." Democrats had a country to love, but the onus was on them to conform to political and cultural reality; if they could not, he implied, they should leave, for they were resisting God's providence. More specifically, conformity meant assimilation into the evangelical-inflected Whig-Republican tradition, which was about to emerge victorious from the war.[66] Although many evangelicals anticipated a reborn Union characterized by unprecedented oneness, it is doubtful that the place of African Americans was foremost in their mind.

To Gilbert Haven they were, however, and with the Union's nature settled, the election of 1864 became to him a referendum on emancipation and a potent symbol of a glorious future.[67] Haven suggested that the outcome at least revealed that northerners supported a Union-saving effort that included the Emancipation Proclamation, even while he believed that they and Lincoln had to be coaxed by the hand of providence. Accepting the reality of slowly turning political and cultural wheels and even lauding Lincoln's wisdom, Haven was simply pleased that many loyal northerners had inched closer to his viewpoint. Accordingly, rather than criticize, he relished what Lincoln's victory seemed to further indicate. In addition to Union and emancipation, Lincoln's reelection signified to him "the triumph of the equal rights of all men, without distinction of color or origin." Haven was particularly enthused by Lincoln's elevation of abolitionist Salmon

Chase to Supreme Court Chief Justice, replacing Roger Taney, the despised author of the majority opinion in *Dred Scott*. An American racial millennium was coming into view, and this prospect, as much as anything else, made 1864 wonderful. Haven zealously anticipated Chase uprooting "with his judicial ax not slavery alone, but its worse roots, caste and prejudice, and all the undemocratic and unjust treatment of our fellow-citizens and fellow-men." Perhaps the glory of the moment had blinded Haven.[68]

Not George Cheever. Despite being wrong about Copperhead violence following Lincoln's reelection, his insistence that evangelicals' Unionism overshadowed their concern for the freedmen appears accurate. The war had never become the abolitionist war he desired it to be, even with emancipation. Cheever suspected that there were far too many like Sherman Canfield of Syracuse, New York, people who were antislavery precisely because slavery "is the only thing which ever seriously imperiled our National Unity." In fact, Canfield was most pleased that God was answering the question, "Shall we have one Country and be one People, or shall we have groups of States remaining together at their option?"[69] The San Francisco Presbyterian Charles Wadsworth's views exemplified Cheever's fear even more strikingly. To Wadsworth, who is best remembered, incidentally, for a relationship with the poet Emily Dickinson, Lincoln's victory most importantly signaled increasing affective oneness among those who shared a "common land of precious memories and glorious hopes." America, Wadsworth said, would cease to be a "conglomerate" of separate "peoples"; rather, "like the celebrated Corinthian brass, an amalgam of all metals," America would become that "composite" where "the best qualities of the iron Saxon, the volatile Frenchman, the grave Spaniard, the reflective German, the effervescing Italian, and the warm-hearted Irishman shall be harmoniously blended in one type of American manhood." Remarkably managing to include the Irish, Wadsworth's interpretation of the election's meaning left African Americans unmentioned.[70]

Henry Boardman, perhaps a more prominent figure than Wadsworth, did not neglect to discuss them in his postelection sermon. In truth, they were very much on his mind while anticipating the war's end. He forthrightly asked, "What is to be done with four millions of emancipated blacks?" Boardman knew slavery's end involved "all the delicate problems pertaining to the relations of the Federal and State organizations," and, because "the whole social structure" of the South was "pervaded" by the "colossal institution" of slavery, he had more questions than answers. How would the "inferior race" be provided for, controlled, and educated? Could slavery's destruction "be so guided and mollified as to be made a savor of life, and not of death?" Knowing that white southerners would not greet emancipation as northerners were in the process of doing, Boardman could only point his hearers to God. "Happily, there is one resource left us; it is the only one. 'The foolishness of God is wiser than men,'" Boardman said, quoting Saint Paul's First Letter to the Corinthians. God knows "what is best for the slave and for the master; for the South and for the North, and for both combined. If He has decreed that the system shall be annulled, He knows just how it should be done; and how the African should be cared for; . . . and the country healed of its wounds."[71]

The overwhelming difficulty arising from emancipation brought forth an even more troubling and significant problem for Boardman, namely that of restoring an affective Union. As he put it, "can these two peoples"—white northerners and white southerners—"ever again become one nation," or would something like the Habsburg Empire emerge, "a collection of provinces inhabited by distinct races, speaking different tongues, alien from one another in all their traditions, and having almost nothing in common but their allegiance to the same sovereign"? The latter was not a true union and would be a "burlesque upon the idea of a republic," where oneness of "sentiment and sympathy" must bind citizens together. The war, whose cause Boardman knew to be slavery, had alienated North and South "as much in feeling as in form." Hatred and a thirst for revenge must be replaced by "ancient concord." From a human perspective, the task was daunting; from the standpoint of faith, God could "fuse these discordant fragments into a homogeneous mass." Here Boardman's covenantal understanding of the Union and the presumed central importance of evangelical Christianity came to the fore. Though implicating evangelicals, North and South, in "bringing on the war, and protracting it," Boardman proscribed—in imitation of Christ—sedition, rebellion, and revenge. Not only would Christlike behavior "mitigate the horrors of this contest," it would also bring covenantal blessing from God upon the nation's rulers in the form of wisdom and courage. Evangelicals, then, "are doing more, whether for good or ill, to shape the destiny of the country than any other equal portion of our people." As Boardman looked ahead to Reconstruction, evangelicals' faithful presence in America was more important than "Cabinets and armies; for Cabinets and armies will properly fulfil their mission only as the Church fulfils hers."[72]

Wonderful year it might have been to Gilbert Haven and even to Henry Boardman, but the sorts of questions raised by Frederick Douglass remained. What was the status of African Americans in the soon-to-be restored Union? Had the election provided solid hope that they would be welcomed into the American body politic as fully equal citizens? Or did the election actually foreshadow their continuing relegation to second-class status? It is clear that issues associated with racial justice had taken a backseat to the Union's preservation during the 1864 campaign, with evangelicals contributing to that reality, and ultimately it is difficult to determine the degree to which the election was a referendum on emancipation. It is safe to say that a large number of nonabolitionist evangelicals were solidly behind Abraham Lincoln, not only because of deep affection for him personally, but because they regarded emancipation as helpful in preserving the Union, solidifying its status as a nation and not a confederation, and because they came to regard slavery as incompatible with a Christian republic. By 1864, then, the bulk of northern evangelicals had included emancipation as part of the ongoing narrative of Christian American history, which many of the extant postelection interpretations reveal.[73]

At bottom, however, in the face of terrible casualties and Democratic peace overtures during the summer of 1864, the fate and plight of African Americans was subordinate to the overarching concern of plenty of evangelicals to preserve their Christian country. The New School Presbyterian George Duffield Jr. provides a fine example of this, especially as he was one for whom emancipation and Union were intertwined. Nevertheless, he recalled that during the summer of 1864—a time he referred to as "the great Peace Panic"—the question of the nation's survival crowded out all other concerns. "Then indeed was the very hour and power of darkness," he said. Another evangelical observer recalled in very similar terms: "The year 1864 was a very *gulf*, into which the floods of death and desolation had emptied themselves. It was satan's hour, and the power of darkness. Copperheadism was rife and rampant. . . . Then came that election in November—the most memorable in our annals." To a great many evangelicals, the election was the denouement of the war's divine narrative and, had Lincoln lost, of the nation's entire history. A Lincoln defeat surely would have engendered serious soul-searching; victory, however, confirmed and hardened evangelicals' vision of the nation as a Christian country, along with the persistent presumption that they were the primary interpreters of its meaning, hope, and promise. As many northern evangelicals construed things, 1864 was thus a wonderful year, and victorious evangelicals looked ahead to the postwar period with visions of an organic Christian republic emerging. What to do with the "deformed child" in their midst was another question entirely.[74]

3 "The Harvest of Death Is Complete"

Imagined Unity

> "If thou rememberest that thy brother hath aught against thee . . . go and be reconciled to thy brother." It may cost a struggle to do this; for pride and passion would hold them back. But it would be a harder struggle not to do it.
>
> —Henry A. Boardman, *The Peace-Makers*

In January 1865, the future head of the Freedmen's Bureau, Oliver Otis Howard, hoped that in the providence of God "some wonderful thing will soon happen, so as to let us return to peace and prosperity."[1] Howard was not alone in anticipating the war's end, and undoubtedly for many northerners in general, peace simply meant an end to four years of killing and a return to some semblance of normalcy. But for many northern evangelicals in particular an end to hostilities also brought an obligation to more securely and homogeneously Christianize America. One Cincinnati Presbyterian remarked in April 1865, "The Christian sentiment of the country has grown to be the controlling element in the war" and "the soul of the nation's loyalty, the heart of its patriotism"; northern Christians had "sanctified the Union, by making it a symbol of all that is highest and holiest in the Christian aspirations of the nation," and Reconstruction, as a postscript to the war, would come "directly within the province of Christian truth and duty."[2] Public-minded northern evangelicals were ecstatic when the war ended and the Union was preserved, and, despite Lincoln's assassination and the anger that followed, they would look ahead to Reconstruction as a moment during which affective national Christian oneness would be more fully and strongly attained than ever before in American history.

This impulse to oneness came to the fore in an article in the January 1865 issue of Yale's *New Englander*. Although written by one with questionable evangelical credentials, former Union colonel William Grosvenor—a man expelled from Yale in the 1850s and court-martialed in 1864, on both occasions for alleged sexual improprieties—the essay's appearance in such a prominent evangelical journal suggests that it was indicative of evangelical reflection and sentiment. Grosvenor, having portrayed the election of 1864 as perhaps the nation's severest test within the war, which was itself "a test of all that makes a people great," utilized evangelical imagery in looking ahead to "the new-birth of the nation." Unprecedented unity would be the salient feature of the born-again republic. It was "a fiat of the Almighty" that within America's boundaries there should be "one nation and but one." A civil war, however, had revealed "that we had never been one people, and that a true nationality . . . had never existed." Instead, "heterogeneous populations, hostile systems, and irreconcilable ideas had only been placed in contact, and held to bare juxta-position by a constitutional compact." Continuing with a metaphor more mundane than evangelical rebirth, Grosvenor insisted that "no chemical union" had ever occurred. "For that the white-hot crucible of civil war" became necessary, and Reconstruction would complete the "process of amalgamation." A "permanent nationality" would leave behind the tenuous, constantly threatened confederated existence that had seemingly characterized the Union's entire history. Although he gave slight attention to evangelical Christianity and rooted his argument primarily in the classical republican tradition, Grosvenor nevertheless sounded a theme of national oneness that preoccupied northern evangelicals.[3]

In doing so, however, he criticized Lincoln's desire to quickly restore the Union, and in that respect perhaps distanced himself from evangelicals. Grosvenor warily believed that Lincoln's moderate-to-conservative stance toward the South represented widespread northern sentiment, and he specifically worried that the northern public might be inclined to hastily accept something like Lincoln's Ten Percent Plan. That plan, though requiring acceptance of emancipation and excluding some high-ranking civil and military officials from public life, was lenient toward ex-rebels and flowed from Lincoln's unwavering desire to restore the Union. It would permit ex-Confederate states to be governed by a nucleus of southern loyalists and be readmitted when 10 percent of a state's registered 1860 presidential voters took an oath of future loyalty.[4] Lincoln insisted until the end of his life that southern states never left the Union, referring to the controversy over the states' status as a "pernicious abstraction." The states, led by a minority of misguided, rebellious individuals, were merely "out of their proper practical relation to the Union; . . . the sole object of the government, civil and military, . . . is to again get them into that proper practical relation." Grosvenor suspected that many sympathized with Lincoln because of "the very depth of their horror of treason and secession, and their resolve to maintain the Union at all hazards."[5] Perhaps he was correct. Major Republican newspapers were supporting Lincoln's policy by April as the best means of achieving "a quick termination of the war and a restoration of a harmonious Union." Grosvenor insisted, however, that Lincoln's plan meant that a few loyal Unionists would be surrounded by many more disloyal and bitter ex-rebels. The states would "have to be propped up by bayonets," hardly making them "fit members of the federal family." It would be a nominal Union at best.[6]

Consequently, though the desire for a speedily restored Union likely was widespread, the means for achieving it produced disagreement. Grosvenor's impulse to unity pushed him toward congressional radicals such as Thaddeus Stevens and Charles Sumner—at least regarding the seceded states' status, for Grosvenor stressed that his thoughts about Reconstruction had "nothing to do with slavery or confiscation" of rebel property. Grosvenor fused Stevens's theory of conquered provinces with Sumner's idea of state suicide and reversion to territorial status, not because he sought to radically remake the South, but because he believed that federal oversight of the seceded states was necessary for the realization of a more affective, organic Union. This was an end that he shared with Lincoln, but Grosvenor's blueprint required more time, in order that "we may carefully discriminate between leaders, whose deep-dyed guilt [deserves] punishment . . . and the truly loyal men, to whom may be safely entrusted the privileges of citizenship." Northerners were willing to pardon and be "magnanimous," he said, "but they will not consent to see those whose rebellion has cost the nation all this treasure and blood, this agony and shame, return at once, without penance or probation, to the full enjoyment of privileges and blessings preserved only by loyal sacrifices and sufferings." With prudence, patience, and improved republican statesmanship, southern states could be properly reconstructed under loyal local leadership. He concluded, in language well suited to the *New Englander*'s audience, "Let us hope that [the God] who has brought hither this strangely composite people" would see to the emergence of a more homogeneous and stable postwar Union.[7]

Grosvenor had articulated a vision for the Union that evangelicals generally shared, with many seizing on the events of March and April 1865 to proclaim the emergent reality of that which they so eagerly desired—a national Christian organism characterized by affective oneness. That is not to say that evangelicals were not thinking about the necessity of receiving tangible signs of southern repentance, for they certainly were, particularly following Lincoln's assassination. Nevertheless, amid loud cries for vengeance and justice, alongside apprehension about Andrew Johnson's presidency, the impulse to true national oneness remained strong. Whether the nation was reborn or refined, plenty of northern evangelicals earnestly hoped that differences between North and South would be effaced in a gloriously restored and reconciled Union.[8]

Binding up the Nation's Wounds

When Abraham Lincoln delivered his second inaugural address on March 4, 1865, reunion and a slave-free American republic appeared as actual possibilities. Even while he did not venture to predict the war's actual end, the president could still plausibly announce that recent events provided "high hopes for the future." For he knew that a day earlier Lee had made overtures to Grant in hope of ending the siege of Petersburg and, in turn, the war, while Sherman's army, having already notoriously burned Columbia, South Carolina, continued to move north through secession's birthplace.[9] In addition, Lincoln knew that eighteen states had ratified Congress's proposed amendment to abolish slavery, to which Lincoln earlier had referred as "a King's cure for all the evils" associated with the war. No longer would the republic be divided or marred by the presence of slavery, and, in fact, Lincoln said further, "It winds the whole thing up."[10] Lincoln had refused to budge when it came to the possibility of a negotiated peace that would recognize Confederate independence or permit reunion with slavery remaining. He was getting what he desired, a restored Union and a constitutionally legal and permanent end to the republic's "peculiar institution." Finally, and also the day before the inaugural address, Congress had established the Bureau of Refugees, Freedmen, and Abandoned Lands—the Freedmen's Bureau—as the primary agency to oversee the postwar South.[11]

Lincoln was indeed looking ahead with high hopes when he delivered his second inaugural speech as a sermon on national reconciliation. There is a sense in which he had been waiting for the day since the war began—not because it officially began a second term, but because it marked the beginning of the Union's restoration to its proper condition. The Princeton theologian Charles Hodge approvingly commented that Lincoln's "ruling idea" in reconstructing the Union "was to disturb as little as possible existing relations, to inflict as few penalties as possible, and to restore all rights and privileges as fully and as rapidly as was consistent with public safety."[12] In March 1865 it was now a matter of waiting for Confederate surrender. Like George Peck, who said that "reconciliation upon the condition of submission is Christian," Lincoln still required Confederate submission, militarily and regarding emancipation, despite the warmth of his message. Even as Lincoln expressed magnanimity toward the South and humility regarding providence and the rectitude of the Union cause—"with malice toward none;

with charity for all; with firmness in the right, as God gives us to see the right"—he also urged, "Let us strive on to finish the work we are in." That "work" was to defeat the Confederacy. After victory, in other words, they could turn "to bind up the nation's wounds; to care for him who shall have borne the battle, and for his widow, and his orphan—to do all which may achieve and cherish a just, and a lasting peace."[13]

With deep roots stretching back through the Whigs to the Federalists, Lincoln and many evangelicals continued to envision America ideally as a family. North and South were supposed to be one; in large part, this was what the war had been fought over. The Philadelphia Baptist Reuben Jeffery interpreted Lincoln's familial vision of the Union as his presidency's most important providential meaning. The president recognized, Jeffery said, that American history to that point "was only a period of assimilation and development." The country's true telos was to become a national "organic entity." As a result, when Lincoln urged "'charity for all and malice towards none,' he at once turned towards his deluded and disappointed countrymen, not to triumph over their mortification, but to assure them of the sincerity of a brother's love."[14] Even Andrew Stone of Boston's Park Street Church, who had abolitionist sympathies and perceived the presence of too much "magnanimity," dreamily anticipated that day when the American flag once again flew over "a family of brothers." Arguably, it was because Lincoln similarly thought the two sections were supposed to be one that he could hint at northern culpability in slavery and urge, in Christ's words, "let us judge not that we be not judged." Accordingly, the New Hampshire Congregationalist and Dartmouth College trustee Pliny Day understood Lincoln's address as a conciliatory, Christian gesture to the South. Alluding to the prophet Micah, Day proclaimed that Lincoln "dared to recognize the hand of God in the rule of nations, and to exhort the people to do justly and love mercy." Lincoln's instruction to the nation "came from a mind imbued with the spirit of the gospel."[15] Of course, the president could speak as such because the American family was about to be reunited largely on his terms.

Evangelicals had been hearing Lincoln speaking their covenantal language for four years, and not surprisingly the inaugural address received approbation from some quarters precisely for its ostensible recognition of God's providential historical care for the Union. New Jersey's Old School Presbyterian William Blackburn, who in 1884 would become the first president of the University of North Dakota, discerned in Lincoln's words "a most remarkable proof of [the president's] faith in the God of our fathers," while finding further evidence that the president regarded himself "only as an agent in God's hand; a mere pilot under a great commander, a subordinate under the God of nations."[16] One Methodist interpreted the speech even more explicitly in covenantal terms, asserting that Lincoln had publicly acknowledged God on behalf of the American people and was charging them in the style of an Old Testament prophet with having generally forgotten God's historical activity on their behalf.[17] Alexander Bullock, longtime antislavery Whig-Republican and future governor of Massachusetts, praised the address for its "apprehension of the Divine Word" and because it revealed Lincoln's humble acknowledgment that "he could not foresee all that might happen" in striving "to keep step with the majestic marches of Providence."[18] The day following the inaugural address, Gilbert Haven voiced the thoughts of many when he referred to it as "the saddest, most solemn, most religious message ever delivered by an American President," and he subsequently referred to it as "the most truthful, humble, and Christian [word] that a ruler ever addressed to his people." Always out in front regarding matters of racial justice, Haven believed Lincoln's address was most noteworthy because it acknowledged the hand of a covenant-keeping God in bringing judgment upon the whole nation for slavery. He did forebodingly predict future judgment if the nation refused to rid itself of racial prejudice, but perhaps, once again, his millennial zeal overshadowed his fears. Underestimating the cultural and socioeconomic shock that defeat and emancipation would bring to the white South, even he thought emancipation would be a near-panacea—something akin to Lincoln's "King's cure"—thus paving the way for the Union's smooth reunification under America's covenantal God.[19]

Despite resonances between Lincoln and northern evangelicals regarding the Union, and despite Lincoln's lack of religious orthodoxy, it has perhaps become second nature among historians to accentuate the relative theological profundity and humility found in Lincoln's second inaugural address. At first glance, there is much to commend that approach, for plenty of evangelical interpretations do appear more celebratory, facile, and confident than Lincoln's.[20] Insofar as that is true, however, the difference may be partially explained by the different social functions of president and clergyman, especially considering the role of proprietary watchmen that America's evangelical clergymen had traditionally presumed. This meant that many clergymen were vocationally constrained to interpret the hand of God more often, more specifically, and more vocally than Lincoln. In doing so they sanctified the Union cause for the northern populace, which Lincoln seemed pleased to permit. Furthermore, while certainly recognizing Lincoln's humility and the fact that he increasingly and sincerely wrestled with the war's providential meaning, it remains true that he astutely knew that it was in the Union's best interest to measure his words, lest he alienate radicals, War Democrats, border-state and southern Unionists, or soon-to-be-defeated Confederates. Prudence had dictated that he leave the unmeasured words to others. What recedes from view, then, in addition to evangelical resonances, is Lincoln's undying vision for a restored, still-great Union within the context of factious domestic politics and a fast-approaching Reconstruction. Although Lincoln eloquently articulated hermeneutical humility about providence in his address, in addition to suggesting northern complicity in slavery, he retained hopeful belief in the ultimate success of the Union cause, as well as in the South's instrumental responsibility for starting the war. To be sure, it was a chastened Union shorn of slavery, but it still remained the last, best hope of earth and that for which so much blood had been spilled under his vigorous leadership. Though God likely never became to Lincoln the sort of personal redeemer championed by evangelicals, God did remain to Lincoln the Union's redeemer. In short, Lincoln, like his contemporary evangelical admirers, had not entirely transcended deep civic-religious affection for the Union. It is noteworthy that Lincoln's pastor, Phineas Gurley, commended the president precisely because his trust in God's sovereignty was bound up with his commitment to the Union. The second inaugural address makes much sense when viewed through the prism of Lincoln's civic-religious Unionism, certainly with emancipation added, and within the context of the Union's restoration that he already had attempted to commence.[21]

Consequently, though often more eloquent and nuanced, the substance of Lincoln's thought could still sound quite similar to that of those evangelicals who also had come to perceive the mysterious, awe-inspiring, and chastising hand of God in ending slavery. As George Peck said just prior to Lincoln's address, "The logic of events proved that the successful prosecution of the war for the Union would be the means of the emancipation of the multitudes . . . in slavery." Though secession was the "most malignant" of all evils, slavery was still "our great national sin, and our greatest disgrace."[22] By 1865, many had come to believe, in the words of one Old School Presbyterian, that "the Providence of God is plainly teaching that the institution of slavery in this country must be abolished." The "whole land" has "been made to mourn" because of slavery. Just after the inaugural address, Henry A. Boardman remarked, "And now [slavery's] removal has come. Not in a way which any one . . . could have anticipated. Not in the way which many amongst us believed would be the wisest and best way. . . . But the vast stream of Providence rolls on regardless of men's plans and opinions; and he who will not yield to the current, must be swept away by it." Regardless of how uniquely Lincoln perceived matters in suggesting that God's chastisement had come upon the entire nation for slavery, or whether at the president's behest or not, by 1865 there were many evangelicals, radical and conservative alike, who occupied ground next to Lincoln. As Boardman stressed, "[God's] controversy was no less with us than with our [southern] brethren." It appears that more than a few evangelicals believed like Lincoln that God had brought the entire country along, preserving the Union and ending slavery.[23]

Of course, those more inclined to an abolitionist position told a similar story, but it was a story about those who had to be moved—unwillingly or unwittingly—by the hand of providence. For instance, Gilbert Haven suggested that "our passion for the Union" was the means of northern victory, but more importantly he believed that devotion to the Union was the divinely chosen means to bring about emancipation. He reiterated a narrative common among radicals that portrayed Lincoln in particular as one who reluctantly accepted abolition and gradually came to see God's hand in events. As was the case following the election of 1864, some radicals were simply pleased that so many had eventually arrived at the same position and in turn marveled at the providence of God. The New Bedford abolitionist Alonzo Quint, who served as chaplain of the 2nd Massachusetts Infantry for nearly three years, appeared to relish the irony of destroyed northern commerce that had rested on compromise with slavery from the country's beginning. "The sin you agreed to," he said to his maritime and mercantile audience, "shall be your curse."[24]

Regardless of how long northerners in general and evangelicals in particular were interested in dwelling on their own culpability in the sin of slavery, or in questioning the degree to which they might or might not "see the right," plenty were ready, with Lincoln, "to bind up the nation's wounds." Perhaps it is here that evangelical self-assuredness appears in sharp relief. Several insisted that even if the North shared responsibility for the historical perpetuation of slavery, they had adequately responded to God's chastisement by eventually advocating emancipation and then integrating it into the narrative of God's ongoing process of fashioning a Christian republic unto himself. Both abolitionist and nonabolitionist evangelicals commented in such terms. As Boston's moderate abolitionist Andrew Stone put it, "Of this one sin we are wringing our skirts clear; and this avenging judgment [in the form of civil war], which converted us, is passing by." After George Peck stated that slavery had brought the wrath of God upon the entire nation, he revealingly asserted that the pending Thirteenth Amendment had "relieved the general government of all further responsibility in the matter"; the thorn in America's side had been removed. Nathan Rice, pastor of New York's Fifth Avenue Presbyterian Church, essentially agreed, saying, "Slavery, the bone of contention, the gigantic evil which has been the occasion of the war, has been swept away." Articulating a covenantal understanding of the nation as clearly as anyone, he assured his audience that the country could move on regarding the matter of slavery: "God never visits a people with judgments for sins after those sins have been abandoned." Sufficient punishment had occurred in the form of over one million dead and maimed soldiers. "Thank God that the iniquity is expiated; that the sin is forgiven," abolitionist Alonzo Quint proclaimed.[25] With both slavery and secession vanquished, the time to bind up the Christian nation's wounds was indeed at hand.

Victory and Peace

About a month after the inauguration, beginning on Saturday, April 1, the war came to a rapid and seemingly providential end. Near Five Forks, Virginia, just to the southwest of Petersburg, Union forces under Philip Sheridan crushed Confederate troops under George Pickett. The next day, Confederate president Jefferson Davis received news from Robert E. Lee that the capital would have to be abandoned. Davis received Lee's dispatch just as he was about to receive the Eucharist at St. Paul's Episcopal Church, a turn of events that Gilbert Haven cast as the ironic providence of God on display. Comparing Davis to Pharaoh seeking to preserve slavery, Haven brashly remarked, "Davis received his death-blow in the church of his idolatry, at the altars of a false god [slavery], whom he had set up in the place of the true God and our Savior Jesus Christ. . . . Fitting was the hour and spot of his destruction."[26]

Although many had been forecasting the end for months, evangelicals remained tethered to war news, watching the sacred Union's narrative unfold before their eyes. They made much of the Confederacy's sudden collapse at Five Forks. Among some, this provided further indication that God still reigned over the nation, and in turn, it inspired "hopes of a speedy and enduring peace."[27] Despite the fact that God sometimes seemed absent during the war, the events of early April stood as a bulwark against the temptation to disbelieve in America's God. The Rhode Island Congregationalist pastor James G. Vose, exemplifying pervasive nineteenth-century American republican insecurity vis-à-vis Europe, in addition to the evangelical penchant for real-time emending of the country's divine narrative, compared the battle to earlier European battles such as Leipzig, Austerlitz, and Waterloo. "Which of them," he asked, "was equal in value or results to this?" Five Forks essentially ended the war, and Vose announced, "No more division, nor talk of division; no more secession, or talk of secession, in Southern State or Northern State, in Eastern State or Western State, but one country till the end of time." Then he added, foreshadowing many northerners' expectations for Reconstruction, nothing less than the victorious Union spirit "shall infuse every part and portion of the South, and men shall wonder and be astonished that rebel leaders ever laid their sacrilegious hands upon the ark of our holy covenant."[28] In that respect, one Chicago Baptist admitted that his "joy was subdued by sadness." As he reflected on events following Richmond's fall, and considered that his country would be whole again, he said, "It is sad that there should have been a war such as has raged . . . ; sad to think how many precious lives the war has claimed . . . ; sad even to look southward and observe what a ruin rebellion has plucked down upon whole States."[29]

The joy would not be subdued for long. Two days later, on April 3, Lincoln walked through Richmond to the cheers of Union soldiers and ex-slaves. One northern evangelical recalled marveling at this "triumphal entry," declaring that it easily surpassed the glory and significance of Washington's entry into Trenton. Only Christ's entry into Jerusalem was superior.[30] On April 9, Palm Sunday, Lee surrendered his Army of Northern Virginia to Grant at Appomattox, effectively ending the war. Confederate troops under Joseph Johnston would surrender to William Sherman a few weeks later in North Carolina, and at the end of May in Texas, Kirby Smith would surrender the last significant group of rebels. America's covenant God had preserved the Union.

But his providential permission of Confederate defeat left scores of southerners stunned, mystified, and largely unrepentant. The Confederacy's covenant God had not allowed the exemplary slave-based republic to come into existence after all, though for a while some were convinced that he still would see to it. Because Confederates had been engaged in a "just and holy war," as one cavalryman remarked, God "in his own good time" would yet grant them their separate nation. Emma LeConte, a seventeen-year-old from Columbia, South Carolina, cried out in disbelief as the Confederacy crumbled: "They say *right* always triumphs, but what cause could have been more just than ours?" Once the Confederacy's defeat became official, great numbers of southerners simply refused to acknowledge that their quest had been wrong or that they were guilty, even if they had been militarily overpowered. With an outlook infused by the Psalms and drawing solace from the sufferings of Job and New Testament Christians, southern evangelical clergy labored to reassure the South that although God had inscrutably chastised the Confederate Israel, he was actually preparing them for a greater future. The seeds of the Lost Cause were in the ground, although hindsight suggests that many northerners underestimated the depth of white southerners' commitment to slavery and independence.[31]

Henry Boardman, for his part, certainly anticipated difficulties in restoring the Union, particularly because of slavery's centrality to the southern way of life, but even he might have inadequately discerned the extent to which southerners would be uninterested in reconciling with an alien, conquering Yankee nation. When Boardman came to his Philadelphia pulpit on April 9, he was obviously unaware of events unfolding in Virginia between Grant and Lee, but the war's end was in view and the South was on his mind. Instead of delivering a traditional Palm Sunday message commemorating Christ's triumphal, kingdom-inaugurating entry into Jerusalem, he explored the implications of Christ's kingdom for the soon-to-be restored American Union and what was required of northerners in particular. Boardman emphasized that Christ's kingdom, and by analogy the American nation, was supposed to be characterized by "peace between man and man." It was therefore incumbent upon northerners to regard defeated southerners in the spirit of Christ, who said, "Blessed are the peace-makers." Recalling the purpose and power of Christ's first-century gospel to overcome "hereditary enmity" between Jews and Gentiles, Boardman urged his audience to resist the spirit of revenge, for true Christians would strive "to overcome evil with good." Boardman reinforced his appeal to the Beatitudes by returning to the more common, and perhaps more powerful, analogy between the American Union and Ancient Israel. "Can there be a Christian here," he asked his audience, "who is willing that a tribe should die out of our Israel? God forbid." Just as when the tribe of Benjamin warred with fellow tribes, the temptation to vengeance was understandably strong. "Passion would have prompted it. But the natural affection, piety, and patriotism, forbade." Moreover, Boardman hoped that "an injured and suffering nation, in the flush of victory, while yet mourning their own dead, [would] come together to weep over the terrible but righteous retribution they had visited upon their brethren, and to plead with their covenant God to preserve the tribe [the South] from extinction." Having disavowed any interest in dictating policy to the president or Congress, he sorrowfully asked his congregation, "Is not the whole South a desolation? 'A voice of wailing is heard. . . .' Is not this enough? Can you still talk of vengeance?"[32]

Henry Boardman reflected widespread northern sentiment that the defeated South should be dealt with in a kindly manner as the surest means of reconciliation, specifically rooting the impulse to national oneness in his understanding of the demands of Christ's inaugurated kingdom. Significantly, however, Boardman was largely silent about the implications of that kingdom regarding the soon-to-be ex-slaves or how they might figure in the Union's restoration. Perhaps unsurprisingly, when he spoke of North and South he essentially meant a white North and a white South—and hence a white re-Union. Here, as in his reflections following Lincoln's reelection, he had not forgotten about African American slaves, for Boardman stressed that in the providence of God they had been freed, which he believed was monumentally significant. But he said little more at that point. Along with the ex-slaves, he waited "to see the result of this stupendous revolution."[33]

Regardless of what was to come for the freedmen, he was like many others looking ahead to a new, stronger Union emerging from the war. Washington Gladden, recollecting years later that there was widespread sorrow for the defeated South, approvingly quoted an early postwar sermon regarding defeated southerners: "If we could have saved their lives and their property and their pride and at the same time have saved the nation, I do not know who would not have chosen it. There is nothing like hatred or vengeance in the . . . North toward . . . the South. There has only been a stern determination that they should not rend the nation asunder." Northern kindness and patience, the minister insisted, would "establish new relations of friendship which shall be far closer and more enduring than the old ones were." To Samuel Babcock, rector of St. Paul's Episcopal Church in Dedham, Massachusetts, Union victory and slavery's end meant that "all the disturbed elements of the land" would be readjusted "so that all parts thereof, North and South, East and West, might be reconsolidated into an Union that could never again be severed." Similarly, Henry Ward Beecher described an exhilarating feeling of national oneness upon hearing the news of Appomattox: "How these tidings swept away the divisions among men!"[34]

Not surprisingly, Lee's surrender set off wild celebrations and produced scores of sermons and speeches throughout the North. For example, an estimated 100,000 people paraded in Chicago on April 10, and years later the Brooklyn Methodist William H. Boole remembered "at least 10,000 people" in New York City singing the "doxology, as if they were members of a World Convention of the best Christians." Gordon Hall, the pastor of Edwards Church in Northampton, Massachusetts, spoke in covenantal and civic-religious terms that the celebrations were a response to the mercy of "the God of our Fathers." God had preserved the republic, and thus Hall said, "Lord thou hast done great things for us, whereof we are glad." One Boston area pastor suggested that the joy during the week was "far greater" than Israel experienced following the Babylonian captivity. Albany's Warren Hathaway described the week's festivities not as "a Roman saturnalia, but a patriotic, Christian jubilee." Of course, it was Christian and not Roman. As one historian has observed about earlier national celebrations, the associated rhetoric of nationalist speakers and politicians aims "to create what they promote—the nation."[35]

In the case of northern evangelicals, it was the specifically Christian nation. Insisting so strongly and so often about national unity, which they would continue to do after the war, suggests that some knew that their hopes did not quite match the reality being proclaimed. Evangelical rhetoric may be viewed as an act of imagining and even insisting on the reality of a whole Christian American people, historically formed by and ultimately accountable to God. In seeking to create that which had not been fully realized, however, such rhetoric simultaneously divided and unified, excluded and included, repelled and invited. For example, Andrew Stone resented conservative Democrats—whose hands, he said, "would never take up a gun" or whose voices "prophesied defeat"—for audaciously celebrating in response to Appomattox. Yet Stone also envisioned "a great, free, united, happy land,—[rising] fresh from this baptism of blood." The cultural and political tension among northerners, which he knew was quite real, would nevertheless somehow vanish after the war. Paradoxically, Democrats were excluded from participating because of past behavior while being expected to conform and act within the nation in terms of unspoken or ill-defined expectations.[36] Perhaps the paradox would be resolved and oneness realized when Democrats simply kept their opinions to themselves and remained out of sight. This was not quite inclusive civic nationalism.

Wheelock Craig, pastor of Trinitarian Congregational Church in New Bedford, Massachusetts, also appreciated the formative role that the week's celebration could play in forging a harmonious postwar Union, but he did so in a far more welcoming and comprehensive manner. Although it is unlikely that Craig was a Democrat, Stone's criticisms would have found their mark in Craig, a pietistic and Christocentric Calvinist whose circumspection, liberal learning, and literary bent set him apart from many evangelicals. Craig's unswerving Unionism and associated criticism of emancipation as a war measure had made some in New Bedford, which had long been a destination for the Underground Railroad and thus traditionally hospitable to abolitionism and African Americans, suspicious of his fidelity. Smarting from such criticism, he insisted that his previous questioning of Lincoln's leadership was actually rooted in patriotic loyalty to the nation—rather than mere party—and he was therefore behaving in a more American manner than were his critics. Consequently, in the aftermath of Lee's surrender, Craig took the opportunity to chastise those who sought to proscribe Lincoln’s critics from celebrating. He said,

> There are some who appear to feel that they and their chosen associates have a monopoly of the joy . . . ; and when they meet persons not of their own clique, there is a look in their eye, or an utterance from their lips, which says, What! Are you glad too? What right have you to participate in such gladness?

Craig appreciated the irony that found those who had vocally longed for peace during the war being told that they should not now be celebrating the peace that had finally come. Continuing to defend himself and others, he said, “Some of the most joyful hearts to-day are those whom the Pharisees of loyalty and patriotism would shut out of their synagogue.” It would be far preferable to “let the men of every shade of opinion, in oblivion of the past, come freely forward upon the broad national platform, and join us. . . . All who occupy that platform hold out to every one accepting it the hand of welcome.”[37]

Critical of fellow northerners whom he regarded as acting primarily out of partisan interest rather than a republican and Christian concern for the good of the whole nation, Craig sought to widen the circle of loyalty to include all who were devoted to the Union. In doing so, he marveled at the “inscrutable allotments” of God’s providence that had conjoined radicals such as William Lloyd Garrison and Wendell Phillips with moderates such as Lincoln and William Seward and even conservative Democrats. “One cannot help feeling,” he said in words that echoed Lincoln’s second inaugural address, “that this whole tissue of events is a historic mystery, a providential riddle, whose only solution lies in the consideration which seems to have escaped us all, that certain schemes of man run in accordance with, and others stand in antagonism to the eternal purposes of God.” In the face of this, he concluded that Americans must humbly conform their thoughts and activities to God’s will and guidance. As part of such conformity, northerners should seize on the post-Appomattox euphoria and allow it to function as a “truce of God,” where “all private grudges and differences were forgiven and forgotten. It is no time now for acrimonious judgments and resentments. Let us make it the era of good feeling.”[38]

While striving to transcend partisan loyalties in the North, Craig joined with other northerners in hoping that sectional differences would melt away. This hope rested on a distinction many had made between secessionist leadership and the southern populace, a distinction Andrew Johnson maintained and which would later influence northern evangelicals’ initial approval of him. According to this thinking, most southerners before and during the war had been hounded and duped by the "slave power," that supposed ruling cabal of planters and politicians bent on secession in order to protect slavery. Thus Craig said, "Those who have violated the laws will be taken . . . as felons . . . . If their case calls for clemency, this prerogative is intrusted [*sic*] to the executive power." Regarding "those who have not violated the laws," he continued in reference to the mass of southerners, "Christ bids us, Love one another as brethren, and judge not that ye be not judged." Pliny Day, a Congregationalist, spoke similarly on April 13. "When the wicked leaders are disposed of according to their deserts," he advised, "we should be magnanimous." All others they should regard and treat "with tenderness and forbearance." Day urged every government and public official having anything to do with the South to "make up his mind to treat his southern friends with magnanimity." Although no northern official should hide from southerners "his abhorrence of treason, nor conceal from them the fact that their iniquities have made rivers of blood, and cost untold treasure," such public men must "remember that these same brethren and their children are members of our great household. They are to live and die in our political family, and are to be made an arm of strength to us." Distinguishing between southern leadership and ordinary southerners, then, potentially reduced the tension between the desire for justice and the impulse to unity and mercy. Those like Day and Craig ideally envisioned a healed Christian Union, whole and nonpartisan, wherein all sorts of divisions were erased. Craig said further, "Bowing in penitential sorrow before the throne of [God], let us forgive and love one another, and see to it that peace and good will prevail between the various parties, and classes, and households, which subdivide the people in church and state." Only those, he continued, "who will not abide by this good rule come under the ban of social outlawry, as a traitor against the common weal."[39]

Rooted in republicanism and their providential and covenantal understanding of the Union, the impulse to national unity was fully displayed on Good Friday, April 14. That day, at Fort Sumter in Charleston harbor, South Carolina, Major Robert Anderson raised a tattered American flag up the flagstaff. Exactly four years before, as commander of the fort's garrison, he had lowered that same flag upon surrendering. This commemorative event, taking place where the war began, symbolically marked its end. Organized by Secretary of War Stanton, it was an event infused with evangelical meaning. As part of the ceremony, a clergyman read four covenantal Psalms, all portraying the joy of God's people being redeemed and delivered. The selection of those particular Psalms made great sense: The God of all nations, in his covenant faithfulness, had saved "His anointed." Given that clear meaning and application to the American people, the reticent and pious Major Anderson believed a religious ceremony conducted solely by clergymen would have been more appropriate. Nevertheless, persuaded to speak, he said to the assembled crowd, "I thank God that I have lived to see this day, and to be here, to perform this duty to my country. My heart is filled with gratitude to that God who has so signally blessed us, who has given us blessings beyond measure. May all the world proclaim, 'Glory to God in the highest; on earth peace; goodwill toward men.'"[40]

Following Anderson's brief words a band played "The Star-Spangled Banner," and then Henry Ward Beecher, among the most popular and electrifying orators in America, delivered the main speech. Beecher recalled his feelings while watching Anderson and then looking upward prior to speaking. It was as if, he said, "the heavens had broken and poured down their influences on me, I could not have been so surcharged, and so borne away, as I was in that strange and surpassing moment. . . . I dissolved, and cried like a child, like a woman, or rather, like a *man*." Amid weeping, fainting, and praying, "men clasped each other in convulsions of emotion." The American flag, rising again with all its stars intact, he said, symbolized that "not one State shall be struck from this nation by treason. . . . Not a state is blotted out. Hail to the flag of our fathers and our flag! . . . And glory to God who, above all hosts and banners, hath ordained victory and shall ordain peace." Of course, it would be a peace in which the states existed as subordinate parts of the whole, and thus, as if Charleston's citizens were listening to him, Beecher proclaimed, "This is the flag of sovereignty. The nation, not the State, is sovereign!" Oh for those colonial and Revolutionary days, he reminisced, when South Carolinians knew neither section nor state, but only America. "There is scarcely a man born in the South who has lifted his hand against this banner, but had a father who would have died for it. Is memory dead? Is there no historic pride?" If that appeal were insufficient, both North and South, he reminded, "read the same Bible." This latter fact, Beecher thought—instead of giving northerners pause to consider and temper their own self-righteousness, as Lincoln had counseled—should have spurred southerners to repentance and conciliatory oneness as evangelical Americans. A divided or fragmented America was not God's intention for this Christian country. Surely many in the crowd at Fort Sumter saw in the flag hope of a re-United States, where differences among citizens and regions were subsumed rather than accentuated in a new and permanent Union. Undoubtedly some had feelings of communion based on their participation in a just-completed war that indeed had preserved that common history to which Beecher pointed.[41]

With 3,000 freedmen in the audience, it is also likely that others imagined the emergence of a new, racially and culturally inclusive America. Two days earlier Gilbert Haven dreamily imagined a soon-to-be-realized racial millennium, when God will have reunited all Americans "in one blessed brotherhood of blood and love." This would begin in the South, when "the daughters of these haughty Southerners, who have shrunk from [blacks] as leprous, shall yet gratefully accept the offers of the sons of their father's slaves. . . . Not ten years may pass ere such marriages will be frequent."[42] Perhaps, then, the events of April 14, 1865, symbolized a sort of civic-nationalist moment of possibility for abolitionists.

However, in all likelihood, April 14 was not necessarily that moment for most. Some evangelicals revealed that they were not as much interested in forging an inclusive and pluralistic society as they were in controlling the pluralism they saw increasing around them, and such anxiety would color their thought and activities throughout Reconstruction. For one thing, the sheer size of the republic, with its regional, cultural, and religious diversity, proved distressing. For example, the president of Indiana's Wabash College, Joseph Tuttle, was disconcerted by "the want of homogeneousness" at war's end. Such concern, along with the hope of sectional restoration, precipitated more pronouncements of unity from others. Pliny Day, contemplating the incorporation of new western states and the reincorporation of ex-Confederate states into the Union, remarked that we "should be like so many strands, twisted into a massive cable. . . . Let us replace among our Stars and Stripes, our national motto, '*E Pluribus Unum*.' Let us draw the cords of union strong around ourselves; then we shall be a tower of strength."[43]

As subsequent chapters will reveal, during Reconstruction and beyond evangelicals would continue to regard and proclaim the Union as a singular, uniform people being formed by God. This would involve both subjective and objective aspects; that is, strong feelings of communion were bound up with an ostensibly common history, language, culture, and religion. And so-called outsiders were expected to conform themselves to this vision for the Union. The antebellum problem of incorporating perceived outsiders thus remained. It would become only more pronounced as evangelical expectations of unity and uniformity rose alongside increasing religious and ethnic pluralism and an increasingly recalcitrant white South.

For the time being, a day such as April 14, 1865, was an opportunity to see a fuller realization of that national Christian organism, which evangelicals so earnestly longed for and had been interpreting the Civil War as producing. In that vein, the New Hampshire Episcopalian bishop Carlton Chase had earlier suggested to Lincoln that he declare Good Friday a national day of prayer and fasting because "that day would be agreeable to Christian people of all denominations."[44] In Philadelphia's First Baptist Church, George Dana Boardman eagerly fused the most important moment in Christian history—the death and resurrection of Christ—with the end of America's Civil War. It was a Good Friday indeed; the "God of our fathers," who had been at work in ancient Israel, subsequently within the history of the church, and finally in America, had brought the nation through civil war, preserving a people and destroying slavery. Boardman thought it quite fitting to be celebrating the Sumter flag-raising in church on the day that began the Easter celebration. For just as he believed Christ's substitutionary death symbolized the vindication of God's law, so did the re-raising of a trampled-upon flag symbolically vindicate God's "ordinance of earthly government." Above all else, a flag flying once again over Fort Sumter symbolized that "the American Republic is not a league but a nation; not a confederacy, but a people; not a congeries of States, but a Union. . . . The American Union is a vital, organic nationality, pervaded by a common life, which binds together in indissoluble union each and every member, thus making the whole absolutely ONE."[45]

Lincoln's Assassination

On Good Friday evening, John Wilkes Booth shattered the euphoric feelings of national oneness when he entered Lincoln's box overlooking the stage at Washington's Ford's Theatre and mortally shot the president. The fact that "God has permitted this great calamity is all we can say," Elizabeth Howard wrote her husband. "[Only] He can lift the dark cloud and show us the silver lining." Following directly on the heels of the glorious events at Fort Sumter, the assassination left people groping to describe the shock that came, in the words of another evangelical, as "a crash of thunder from an unclouded sky." According to John E. Todd, "Not even the intelligence of the first assault on the flag at Sumter has so stirred the depths of popular feeling." Similar to Elizabeth Howard, all he could say was that he knew God still lived. Lincoln was dead before northerners had even "recovered from the ecstasies of delight occasioned by the victories unprecedented in modern warfare, and which gave promise of speedy peace." Some people received the news of Lee's surrender and Lincoln's assassination in the same moment, and such simultaneity precipitated further speculation about God's mysterious hand upon their nation. George Peck simply recalled, "Sunday was a day of darkness. . . . Never before, not even when George Washington died, had this nation felt so bitter a sorrow." As Phineas Gurley declared during Lincoln's state funeral in Washington, northerners had located their "best hopes for the true and speedy pacification of the country, the restoration of the Union, and the return of harmony and love" in Lincoln.[46]

On April 19, the day of Lincoln's funeral, pastors and preachers throughout the country strove to convince their respective audiences to comprehend Lincoln's death just like they had God's dealings throughout the country's exceptional history.[47] The Baptist pastor William Hague urged his congregation to remember the biblical God and resist the temptation "to yield for a moment to doubt or fear or dark forebodings, like those who adore no God but chance or fate, or blind, inexorable law." He admitted that it "seems so mysteriously *ill-timed*" to ably harmonize "with a cheerful, hopeful view of those kind designs and wise forecastings of Divine Providence that insure our national welfare, and our progress in a bright national career of honor, glory, strength, freedom, and prosperity." Gurley also retreated to the mystery of God's sovereign will, just as he had done at Willie Lincoln's funeral. On this occasion, however, he directed his reassuring words to an entire country rather than to grieving parents: "[God] may chasten, but he will not destroy. He may purify us . . . in the furnace of trial, but he will not consume us." Gurley reminded his hearers that "[God] has chosen us, as he did his people of old, in the furnace of affliction; and he has said of us, as he said of them, this people I have formed for myself; they shall show forth my praise." The Unitarian Warren Cudworth sounded a similar theme, remarking that the God who brought the Puritans to America was somehow at work in the assassination. Alluding to Saint Paul's letter to the Philippians, Cudworth urged, "Let us rely upon Him, therefore; assured, that, having begun a good work among us, he will carry it on to a successful termination." The concurrence of Lincoln's death, Good Friday, and the Sumter flag-raising provided hopeful, if mysterious, evidence of God's sovereign hand. "Yes, it was meet that the martyrdom should occur on Good Friday," the Baptist Cephas Crane said. "It is no blasphemy against the Son of God and the Savior of men that we declare the fitness of the slaying of the Second Father of our Republic on the anniversary of the day on which he was slain. Jesus Christ died for the world; Abraham Lincoln died for his country." In one way or another, pastors and preachers sought to comfort their listeners by reminding them that such an event was of a piece with God's history in dealing with both ancient Israel and America.[48]

Clearly, however, not everybody attempted to calmly theologize and neatly fit the assassination into America's divine narrative in quite the same manner. Although it is likely that some white southerners genuinely mourned Lincoln's death, and some in occupied areas, fearing retribution, disingenuously made a public display of such, still others felt free to express their satisfaction at the assassination of the man whom they believed had tyrannized the South. In East Texas, for instance, Marshall's *Texas Republican* proclaimed, "It is certainly a matter of congratulation that Lincoln is dead because the world is happily rid of a monster that disgraced the form of humanity."[49] Even some northern radicals felt just as free to express themselves. For David Banks, of Stanwich, Connecticut, who was an acquaintance of George Cheever's, Lincoln's death did little to ameliorate his view of the man, and Banks could hardly restrain his anger in a remarkable letter to Cheever. In covenantal terms, Banks perceived it as fitting that God would remove Lincoln in response to the vain "shouting and huzzaing" following Lee's surrender. God rebuked the foolish northern masses for following and adoring the Unionist Lincoln. His death, Banks said, "is a signal rebuke to this wild and intoxicated nation." In response to a question from his wife about whether he was "sorry or glad that Lincoln was killed," Banks communicated to Cheever, "I replied that I rejoiced that God rules—if God wanted Lincoln in that position longer he would have kept him there, but that he was removed . . . was an evidence He did not want him there any longer." Perhaps, Banks sarcastically speculated, he might be arrested by the authorities "for not joining in the multitude in magnifying or praising our dead President; but he was not *my* president, for I did not vote for him [a second] time." Views like those of the abolitionist Banks infuriated the Dutch Reformed pastor William Gordon, who angrily called out those "feloniously clapping their hands over [Lincoln's] murder." Though likely directed at northern Democrats, many of whom might have been in his audience, he also might have had radicals and even southerners in mind when he rhetorically asked, "Are we not all brethren? Are we not all bound up in the same national interest!"[50]

George Cheever, in his sermon of April 21, could not be as open as Banks, though Cheever, like Banks, was no more pleased with Lincoln in death than in life. Nevertheless, he knew well enough to moderate his public comments. Referring to Lincoln as a "martyr" was about as far as he would go in positively eulogizing the president. However, Cheever representatively suggested that God intended the assassination to reveal the South's true character, which would finally induce the North to deal appropriately with southerners. Lincoln's death was, ironically, "the proper fruit of a Slaveholder's Rebellion" that the president had never seriously confronted. Lincoln "was too gentle, too lenient, to deal out justice," Cheever said. Such a view, expressed by other radicals, brought an angry reply from the moderate Presbyterian Albert Barnes. He quickly discounted those evangelicals keen on discerning God's displeasure with Lincoln's magnanimity. Throughout the war, he insisted, Lincoln had always managed to strike the right balance between conflicting ideas—between justice and mercy, or firmness and softness—and had consequently preserved the Union and ended slavery. It served no fruitful purpose to speculate further about the ways of providence.[51]

Although much less driven by the impulse to quick restoration than those like Barnes, Cheever did similarly distinguish between southern leadership and the southern masses in calling for punishment. For moderate and conservative evangelicals, as for northerners generally, culling the most notable leaders held great symbolic value, while seemingly paving the way for the desired reunion. The New School Presbyterian theologian Henry Boynton Smith said, "Our only safety is in expelling the leaders or executing them." Not insignificantly, with a few months having passed following the assassination, the influential Henry Ward Beecher would question whether the North should even go that far.[52] For radicals like Cheever, however, punishing the South was the foundation for making the South over in an even more radical image as the basis for a renewed and homogeneous Union. Those southerners who were behind slavery, secession, and civil war had to be purged. As Cheever emphasized, the true spirit of slavery had been plainly revealed in the assassination—"the slaveholding aristocracy must be annihilated." Nevertheless, he seemed to realize, even at this early stage, that the prospects for a thoroughgoing reconstruction were slim and that many in the North were anxious for restoration. "I fear," he said in standard covenantal terms, "we are laying foundations for a new controversy of God with us."[53]

Not surprisingly, angry calls for vengeance were heard in the immediate aftermath of the assassination. For example, as part of a list of notorious southern acts—Preston Brooks's caning of Charles Sumner, the sack of Lawrence, Kansas, the first shot at Fort Sumter, the slaughter of black Union troops at Fort Pillow, and the horrible treatment of Union prisoners at Andersonville Prison—the Long Island Methodist Charles Backman painted the South in the worst possible light. He repeated what had become an oft-told story, that Confederate troops "buried our fallen heroes faces downward at the battle of Bull Run [and subsequently] took their sacred skulls and used them for drinking cups." In light of such a story, he mocked those who would refer to southerners as "our erring brethren."[54] According to one Providence, Rhode Island, Congregationalist, northern designs to be magnanimous and merciful, to welcome southerners "back to the family circle," would have to wait. Edward S. Atwood seconded that opinion. He allowed that "[Lincoln] would have smoothed the way of return to amity and union; his hand would have sown the seeds of forgetfulness on the graves of the past; he would have tempered justice with mercy, and taught even vengeance to say amen." Now, however, justice must prevail over mercy, and thus, he added, "Let not the babble of *magnanimity* be heard in our streets."[55]

Frederick Douglass, who esteemed Lincoln more highly than many other radicals, resisted criticizing him but interpreted his death similarly. "Only the other day," he remarked two days after the assassination "it seemed as if this nation were in danger of losing a just appreciation of the awful crimes of this rebellion. We were manifesting almost as much gratitude to Gen. Lee for surrendering as to Gen. Grant for compelling him to surrender! Republics have short memories," he continued, and "I was afraid the American people were growing weak." Perhaps, he permitted, it was "in the inscrutable wisdom of Him who controls the destinies of Nations" that Lincoln had been murdered, but "let us not be in too much haste in the work of restoration. Let us not be in a hurry to clasp to our bosom that spirit which gave birth to Booth." Douglass hoped that a magnanimous North had been stopped in its tracks, and in calling for sweeping punishment of southerners, he hoped for the emergence of a racially inclusive republic.[56]

A New Era Dawning

Despite the anger and calls for vengeance or justice, voices calling for magnanimity and unity were still heard in the aftermath of Lincoln's assassination, and this increased as time passed. The abolitionist Jonathan Jenkins seemed to realize this in July, when he alarmingly noted the "disposition" among some in the North "to tame down the severity of justice, and to demand clemency and even full pardon for all classes of offenders against the justice and majesty of our government, whether traitors, armed rebels, or assassins." Among the less radical, Lincoln's death became an opportunity to relish and continue to proclaim national oneness, despite white southerners' lack of genuine interest in such. Henry Ward Beecher took solace in the "sublime sorrow that in a moment swept down lines and parties, and covered up animosities, and in an hour brought a divided people into unity of grief and indivisible fellowship of suffering." He concluded, "Men will receive a new impulse of patriotism for [Lincoln's] sake, and will guard with zeal the whole country which he loved so well." According to Buffalo's New School Presbyterian Joel Bingham, despite the assassination, one thing was certain: "It is settled whether the United States be a nation, [a] living and indivisible unity of life, or whether it be a loose and lifeless conglomeration of thirty-six supreme sovereignties." Furthermore, though acknowledging stories of atrocious southern behavior, Bingham presciently looked ahead to a day when patriotic Americans would make civic-religious journeys to Washington's

Mount Vernon, Virginia, and Lincoln's Springfield, Illinois. "The path of patriot pilgrims will henceforth branch alike northward and southward to the resting place equally of the Founder of American Liberty, and of the Destroyer of American Treason and Traitorous Slavery." The Methodist Seth Reed simply asserted that the assassination will be the occasion of "a holier, stronger bond of Union to this nation." The Philadelphia Baptist Reuben Jeffery saw God opening a "new era in American history" through the assassination. Future Americans would refer to April 14, 1865, as "the Good Friday of American Redemption," the day when "American nationality" emerged. A month or so removed from the event, when emotions had subsided a bit, Charles Hodge noted something similar. He looked back at the national funeral for Lincoln as a great moment of unity for the Union—around noon on April 19 "millions of people were [simultaneously] on their knees before God." This was a glorious portent in Hodge's view.[57]

The New Hampshire Congregationalist Henry Elijah Parker, who had been a chaplain of the 2nd New Hampshire volunteers and would later be a professor of Latin at Dartmouth for over twenty years, took one of the most optimistic and interesting views of all. With a restored Union coming into view, he suggested that "this fearful event will have a mighty and happy tendency to unite our people," for Lincoln's death would, in fact, ease southern animosity with surprising rapidity. "This act," he continued, "will utterly destroy what little remaining sympathy there was in any quarter for the failing cause of the confederacy." The animosities of southerners and northern Democrats had been centered in the person of Abraham Lincoln, and "those animosities, to a great extent, will be buried with him;—while even where, to any extent, they may partially or temporarily remain, his sad and wicked end will greatly soften and ameliorate them." The unity that appeared to be dawning at war's end, but which seemed utterly threatened by the assassination, was now even closer to realization. Parker, like others, could interpret the assassination within the larger stream of America's redemptive history, "exactly in the line of God's dealings with us ever since the commencement of our difficulties."[58]

On this view the assassination of Abraham Lincoln was no different than the opening attack on Fort Sumter or, for that matter, any other event in the nation's divine history. The God in whom Abraham Lincoln had seemingly trusted, as many evangelical religious leaders reminded their audiences, was still alive and caring for the nation. "The Lamb that was slain," Detroit's New School Presbyterian George Duffield Sr. said, still "rules in providence and guides the destiny of nations." America's God, "the God of our Fathers," he said, would bring them through the latest crisis. Glancing back at the end of the war eight months later,

John W. Adams thankfully announced, "The harvest of death is complete. God has stretched out his hand and has stayed the tide of blood. In his own way, and in his own good time, he has put an end to the rebellion." A new era was dawning, an era that would be marked by "a unity of interest, pride, and destiny."[59] That same God who carried the Union to victory would sustain Lincoln's successor, Andrew Johnson, in bringing about a reunited land.

4 From Moses to Joshua

> Of all the men that have occupied the presidential chair, not one . . . has displayed more wisdom in the solution of practical questions . . . than has President Johnson. . . . God appointed him almost without our knowledge or forethought, one so well fitted to take up the work. . . . Perplexing questions were to be settled. Difficult knots were to be untied. But he has taken up and untangled thread after thread of our national affairs; and with a firm purpose, a skillful hand, and a clear head, he has gone on weaving that garment which is yet to cover the body of these states in a common brotherhood.
>
> — Henry Ward Beecher, Sermon, November 2, 1865

Speaking on April 19, 1865, the day of Lincoln's state funeral in Washington, Jeremiah Rankin, the abolitionist pastor of Trinitarian Winthrop Church (Congregational) in Charlestown, Massachusetts, and the future president of Howard University, compared Lincoln to Moses, and Andrew Johnson to Joshua. Like Moses overlooking the Promised Land but prevented by death from going in with his people, God permitted Lincoln to catch only a glimpse of the "whole nation" about to be reunited. And, as with Moses's successor Joshua, God would permit Johnson to lead America into its promised land of a restored Union that now included liberty for all.[1] Other evangelicals echoed Rankin's expectation regarding Johnson, and some explicitly encouraged him to follow in Lincoln's steps as a willing vehicle of providence to speedily restore the Union. With Congress in recess until December, Johnson had a relatively free hand to direct Reconstruction and produce sectional reconciliation.

For the last half century or so, historians generally have understood Johnson's actions during this period as crucial for the course of Reconstruction and the subsequent history of African American civil rights. In retrospect, with the defeated South arguably "pliable," or at least awaiting clear terms of settlement, this immediate postwar period may be viewed as a propitious opportunity to have guaranteed the ex-slaves equal membership in the nation. But Johnson never articulated unambiguous, mandatory terms, and, furthermore, Johnson's approach to the South was predicated on white southern leaders' cooperation and the widespread northern assumption, shared by plenty of evangelicals, that generosity and leniency would engender white southern agreement in forging a new, slave-free Union. In looking to indigenous southern leadership, Johnson was largely following Lincoln, but this approach meant that the ball was also largely in the white South's court. And white southerners, in possession of power and prerogative, would prove to be little interested in much more than being reintegrated politically into the Union. Johnson, instead of insisting on Army-enforced conditions that minimally would have permitted the ex-slaves to obtain or retain confiscated or abandoned southern land, granted suffrage for black males, and stringently proscribed ex-Confederate officials from public life, instead returned much of the land to the original owners, hardly considered black suffrage, and pardoned thousands of ex-Confederate leaders following professions of loyalty.[2] As events unfolded in 1865, Johnson "emboldened" many white southerners in an unyielding and defiant desire to manage their own affairs. This meant that the ex-slaves would remain "outside the bounds of citizenship," and by December 1865, with the Thirteenth Amendment's ratification pending and southern states ready to send representatives back to Congress, Johnson was eager to pronounce the Union restored.[3]

During 1865, as will be seen, northern evangelicals were among those supporting and encouraging Johnson, thereby sharing in and reflecting a widespread "trust-Johnson" sentiment. Evidence suggests that he received broad northern evangelical support into early 1866, with many sharing his leniency toward the white South while looking for him to bring about sectional reconciliation. As a result, the immediate postwar period does not appear to have been a predominantly inclusive, civic-nationalist moment receiving widespread encouragement from evangelicals. Though they would be troubled by news of white southern defiance and racial violence, in addition to Johnson's role in such developments, plenty of northern evangelicals nevertheless supported him through 1865 as part of their desire to see a fuller realization of affective national oneness.[4]

Encouraging Johnson

Following Lincoln's death, Johnson's public words were consonant with evangelical expectations of the president of their Christian republic. Expressing deep sadness and humility, Johnson deferred to God's sovereignty immediately on taking office; Benjamin French, a Washington bureaucrat and Lincoln holdover, commended Johnson's remarks as "worthy of a statesman and a Christian," informing him that they would have great public effect.[5] Shortly thereafter Johnson spoke of the American people as specifically Christian and recognized "an inscrutable Providence" that had made him president. This was a more sober man than the one who had delivered a drunken inaugural harangue before the Senate in March.[6] Any hints of piety or deference to providence reassured wary evangelicals, with the response of Hartford Baptist Cephas Crane revealing much about their assumptions and aspirations. Crane, who had met Lincoln alongside George Peck and Granville Moody in 1864, admitted he had "lost faith" in Johnson following his "maudlin" inaugural speech; subsequent remarks, however, convinced Crane that "there has been wrought a marvelous change in the man." Although such comments are indicative of evangelical belief in the importance of dramatic personal transformation, Crane's affection for America also convinced him that Johnson had significantly changed: "For, friends, I know that God will save this nation. Our whole history, and especially the history of the last four years, would be nothing else than an excrescence upon the trunk of time, if we should not reach a higher national perfection and prosperity." Boston's popular Congregationalist Edward Norris Kirk simply remarked, "He has repented: this is all we ask of him."[7]

Many evangelicals resultantly pledged prayer and support for Johnson. Wheelock Craig observed that "Providence" seemingly surrounded him "with the panoply of a wonderfully unanimous cordiality and approval," and in a flush of Christian patriotism he said, "We are with you; count us on your side. . . . Keep the ship of state headed as President Lincoln had headed her, . . . and all that we can do, we will do, to assist you in sailing her." On April 19, New York Methodists informed Johnson of how "pleased" they were with his public words, while suggesting that perhaps some had judged him prematurely. Although John Bain, pastor of United Presbyterian Church in Canonsburg, Pennsylvania, pleaded that Johnson needed prayer following his "unhappy conduct" at the inauguration, Bain still suggested that some had been too "hasty and harsh," condemning "him as if he was a confessed inebriate, a confirmed sot." If he was a "drunkard," Bain retorted, how had that gone undiscovered during the bitter election of 1864? Johnson's Unionism was unquestionable, Bain concluded, and, above all, God in his "mysterious providence" saw fit to elevate him. He was God's choice for the hour of Reconstruction.[8]

Committed to being "most things to most people," Johnson's immediate actions also seemed to please evangelicals.[9] He astutely cultivated clerical support by initiating an April 17 meeting with a group of sixty Washington-area clergymen. Lincoln's former pastor Phineas Gurley, speaking for the group, promised to pray for Johnson just as they had for Lincoln, while assuring him that they also looked ahead to that day "when the nation shall emerge from its trials with augmented purity and vigor, and be reestablished upon . . . the foundation of liberty and righteousness, of unity and peace." Johnson expressed seemingly humble gratitude for "the countenance, the assistance, and the prayers of such a body," in addition to confidence in God "that our beloved country will pass through the trouble of the present . . . to a better and higher life."[10] He generated further goodwill by requesting that the country's churches gather on April 19 to solemnize the state funeral in Washington, and subsequently, on April 25, Johnson used covenantal and Unionist language to designate May 25 as a day of humiliation and mourning; referring to Lincoln as "the head of the family," Johnson recommended "humbling ourselves before Almighty God, in order that the bereavement might be sanctified to the nation." Only "communion with the Father in Heaven" could assuage the country's grief. In response, Henry Boardman applauded Johnson's "high dignity" and stated that he "has already shown himself so worthy of the cordial respect and confidence of the country."[11]

Johnson did precipitate a minor controversy by changing the day of humiliation and mourning from May 25 to June 1, and the episode reveals much about evangelical priorities and attitudes as Reconstruction began. As Johnson put it, "My attention has since been called to the fact that [May 25] is sacred to large numbers of Christians as one of rejoicing for the ascension of the Savior." Given that most evangelicals disregarded the traditional liturgical calendar and were typically jealous for the symbolism of presidential actions, some reacted bitterly. Their scorn, however, was directed at those deemed responsible—Episcopalians and Roman Catholics, rather than Johnson. Putatively rooted in democratic-republican concern for the common weal and belief in majority rule, those angry about the switch implicitly questioned the fitness of Roman Catholics and Episcopalians within the Protestant republic. One man from Jamestown, New York, claiming to speak for "thousands upon thousands of others, all over the land," protested to Johnson, "If there are any days in the Episcopal or Catholic calendar too sacred [to commemorate Lincoln], they had better be expunged, or at least not allowed to interfere with the arrangements of an entire people." Focusing solely on the Episcopal Church, the *National Baptist* angrily insisted that the government should not "conform to the customs and wishes of a small minority." This was particularly true of those whose hierarchical "principles of church government are less in harmony with the spirit of our national government, than those of other churches." To the critics, those favoring the change were defiantly and selfishly refusing to conform themselves to the prevailing ethos of evangelical and republican America.[12]

Despite the controversy, Johnson's shibboleth promising to make treason "odious" and punish traitors garnered further support, particularly from radicals.[13] Even George Cheever expressed cautious approval. "Our new President's speeches recently thus far give assurance that so far as the [secessionists] are concerned, he will deal justly, not letting them off." One Illinois evangelical, promising "furvant prayer" and hoping that "the Lord will keep you from all harm and give you Wisdom and Bless you," urged the president to remain true to his promise. The Methodist William Studley enjoyed a play on 1 Kings 12:10: "In dealing with traitors, Andrew Johnson's little finger will be thicker than Abraham Lincoln's loins. If the OLD president chastised them with whips, the NEW president will chastise them with scorpions."[14]

It is helpful to recall at this point the distinction between southern leadership and the southern masses that enabled many northerners to maintain two seemingly contrary desires—an angry demand for justice and a strong and often merciful desire for a harmoniously restored Union.[15] One week after Lincoln's death, Henry Martyn Dexter, a Congregationalist pastor, editor, and future historian, emphasized the former as the key to achieving the latter. Contending that he was one in "spirit" with Johnson and threatening covenant-breaking consequences if northerners failed in their duty, Dexter advocated trying "all prominent surviving rebels," but only hanging "a few . . . in vindication of outraged justice, and in perpetual demonstration to the future that the powers that be in this land are ordained of God"; others, although deserving of the "halter," should be banished. Then the country could begin functioning again as a unified whole. Nearly simultaneously, the Philadelphia Baptist George Dana Boardman argued similarly, although advocating only banishment. He remarked, "If ever the halter was a fit instrument . . . , it is in the case of these murderous, fiendish traitors, who inaugurated and guided this colossal and gory treason. But let us be careful how we permit these miscreants to become martyrs." Like dealing with Cain, Themistocles, or Napoleon, "Establish a rigorous passport system, and make it . . . impossible for [southern leaders] to enter this purified Republic." To the rest of the South, "I would speak words of forgiveness and good cheer. . . . Come back, come back into this disenthralled, regenerated, transfigured Republic." Gordon Hall, the Congregationalist pastor of the First Church in Northampton, Massachusetts, also sharply distinguished between "the influential, responsible conspirators in this great rebellion and their deluded instruments." Punish the former, while treating the latter "tenderly," thereby inducing them "to return to allegiance and live comfortably again under the old flag of the union." He was ready "to overlook the past and call such my southern brethren."[16]

By late May, Johnson appeared to be following a course reflective of that general distinction between the southern few and the southern many, while seeking a middle course between "universal forgiveness and universal punishment."[17] On May 29, he formally commenced his restoration plan with two proclamations, one intending to address the status of individual rebels, the other intending to reestablish functioning governments within the ex-Confederate states. In tandem, the two proclamations aimed to speedily restore the Union.

The first was a general amnesty for ex-rebels, excepting a host of military and civilian officials and those possessing taxable property valued at twenty thousand dollars. Upon taking an oath of future loyalty to the Constitution and Union, along with support for any future slavery-related laws, those amnestied would have all civil and political rights and property, excluding slaves, restored. However, if the excepted individuals personally requested pardon, Johnson promised to "liberally" extend it, which he did. Despite a strong fear of dishonor that many southern gentlemen undoubtedly felt in petitioning their conquerors, Johnson personally met with delegations of southerners during June and July, and by 1866 he had issued at least 15,000 pardons. Although amnestied white southerners, which included evangelicals of course, may have recognized that secession was no longer possible and that emancipation was permanent, that recognition did not mean that they had come to believe that secession and race-based slavery were wrong. Nor did they necessarily believe that God had abandoned the South. As one southern Baptist reflected on matters late in 1865, "There is nothing in the issues of our late and unhappy and ruinous war to change our views as to the rectitude of the Southern struggle for independence." Despite that apparent lack of heartfelt submission or acceptance of guilt for secession or slavery, the act of suing for pardon demonstrated sufficient repentance to Johnson. Though his liberality surprised observers in both sections, particularly given his well-publicized anti-elitist rhetoric, he was personally gratified that southern leaders petitioned him, while ultimately intending that such actions serve the end of harmoniously restoring the Union.[18]

Johnson's initial policy appeared to mesh well with the expectations of many northern evangelicals, who underestimated the breadth and depth of southern belief in the rightness of their cause while continuing to overestimate southerners' heartfelt desire for reunion. The influential Charles Hodge maintained the distinction between southern leaders and the masses with a conciliatory essay in the July *Biblical Repertory and Princeton Review*. Human motivation, he insisted, was far too mysterious and complex to indiscriminately sweep away the bulk of the rebels. "Men forget what a strange anomalous thing human nature is," and thus some might be tempted to assume "that every man who aided the rebellion was in heart a reprobate." Hodge's opinion differed from that of other northern evangelicals discussed above more in tone and emphasis than in substance. With them he assumed that a core group of southerners was responsible for secession in defense of slavery; he acknowledged so-called southern atrocities committed during the war; and he had no objection to the arrest, trial, and conviction of "the authors of such offenses." However, rather than focusing on the group to be punished, Hodge focused on the much larger group to be received back into the Union. Furthermore, he believed that the war itself constituted substantial judgment, for slavery was abolished, southern property, industry, and agriculture were devastated, and hundreds of thousands were dead or wounded. Such judgment, he insisted, would efficaciously bring about sufficient southern humility. Thus, in the spirit of Christ, past evil must be met with present good. This would head off future national troubles and convert "enemies into friends." In substance, then, evangelicals generally agreed with Johnson's advocacy of leniency for most southerners.[19]

Under presumed war powers and again ostensibly following Lincoln, Johnson issued a second proclamation on May 29. He appointed the Unionist William Holden as provisional governor of North Carolina and outlined a plan for the state's restoration. Johnson, having recognized Lincoln's Unionist governments in Louisiana, Arkansas, and Tennessee, in addition to Virginia's so-called loyalist government, used this proclamation as a template for subsequent proclamations issued during the summer for the six remaining states. Provisional governors would meet in convention with delegates, who would be selected by an electorate consisting of those who had been amnestied and eligible to vote on the day of their respective state's secession, in order to draw up new state constitutions. Johnson's minimal requirements included the abolition of slavery, nullification of secession ordinances, and repudiation of all state debts incurred in supporting the Confederacy. Johnson's appointees were generally moderate nonplanters, but they nevertheless tended to represent traditional southern white interests. In conjunction with his amnesty program, Johnson envisioned that the Union's restoration would be nearly completed by December 1865. At that point Congress would assemble to begin a new session and the president would deliver his first annual message.[20]

As anger over the assassination subsided in the months following, northerners began to settle into their postwar lives impelled by a "back to normal urge."[21] Symbolically important to northerners and southerners alike was Jefferson Davis's capture on May 10, which resulted in rumors circulating that he was caught disguised as a woman. One Philadelphia acquaintance of O. O. Howard saw the episode as a fitting end to the Civil War and wrote, "He must be blind who cannot see God's hand in every event of the past four years." At nearly every turn, as was true of southern evangelicals, providential thinking had been and would continue to be heard. For southerners, God's mysterious chastisement continued, while for northerners, God was bringing the crisis of the Union to completion. The *National Baptist* relished Davis's capture as the culmination of a series of providential events. "Thus has God been our friend in disaster and delay," the paper commented, "as he has been in victory, in all this war; and he has brought it to a close by means tending, more than we could have hoped, to a speedy and harmonious Union, so that we may know no North, no South, no East, no West." The last clause, most knew, hearkened back to Henry Clay's Union-saving efforts during the Compromise of 1850. With Davis imprisoned, perhaps the book could be closed on the entire era of sectional dispute. "Now that peace is restored," another evangelical remarked, "we must love those who have been enemies."[22]

Returning to Normalcy

In general agreement with Johnson during the summer, many evangelicals continued to perceive and portray postwar circumstances positively and thereby provided tacit approval of his desire for the Union's speedy restoration. A prominent example of this came in June from "Philadelphia's most famous citizen," the long-time pastor of the city's First Presbyterian Church (New School) and the former antislavery reformer Albert Barnes. The nation, he proclaimed, had accomplished its "purposes" in war; slavery had ended, while confederation had given way to an actual Union and nationality—"one people" with "one government" overseeing a land wherein "all the inhabitants shall be free." Though "anarchy . . . *seems* to reign over so large a part of our land," the deeper reality, he proclaimed, was that "our country is not ruined," despite the death and destruction. He insisted that the war had not substantially affected their "civil and social institutions" or fundamentally altered the American way of life.[23] From nearby Princeton, Charles Hodge observed similarly: "The work . . . has been done; the Union is restored; the constitution is preserved; the rights of property, the liberty of speech and of the press remain intact. . . . We are as free a people at this moment as when the war began." Such reflections glossed over a very destructive war and the post-Appomattox attitudes of white southerners, while paying slight attention to the ex-slaves' future and place in postwar America. Still, such thoughts should not be too striking. Although the war directly touched hundreds of thousands of northern lives, southern death, devastation, and ex-slaves could be remote abstractions to northerners eager for a return of normalcy. It might also be unsurprising, then, for Barnes to pronounce that the South would soon be "among the richest gardens of the world."[24]

Of course, such a transformation required northern assistance, and just as slavery was the linchpin for antebellum sectional differences, so northerners believed that its demise was the linchpin for the realization of a new Union. New York's well-known Congregationalist pastor Joseph Parrish Thompson foresaw the masses of both southern "races" being raised "up to the point of self-support in freedom." That which had previously transformed the Midwest—a mix of free labor, republican, and evangelical ideals inculcated through schools, the press, and churches—would do its work on the South. Soon the ex-slave would be known "only as a *man*," while "the ignorance of the poor whites," those "who furnished fighting material to the rebellion," would disappear. With the end of slave-based plantation agriculture and the "slavocracy's" hegemony, southern states would be primed to become fit members of the restored Union. As Pliny Day stated, while counseling leniency toward most white southerners, "If we encourage intelligence, universal freedom, free schools, and an untrammeled gospel; if we will help [southern whites] to elevate the freedmen, and bring them up to citizens with equal rights, we shall do our country an unspeakable favor." Rather than treating the South as "a subjugated colony," the South could be slowly transformed through tried and true northern means. "Our school-masters are already [there], by hundreds, among the people; our presses are at work on their soil; northern men are already in their pulpits; loyal merchants are in their cities, and good seed is sown all along their thoroughfares, which will spring up and bear an hundred fold."[25]

Indeed, many northern evangelicals saw the South as a mission field in need of a pro-Union, free-labor gospel, regardless of the government's Reconstruction policy. But what seemed so clear and reasonable to northern evangelicals was anything but to white southern evangelicals, who arguably became even more deeply committed to the southern way of life after the war. Having feared and resented the intrusion of Yankees into their pulpits and schools during the antebellum period, stepped-up northern efforts by all major evangelical denominations during the war and Reconstruction—which often included the literal occupation of southern churches—heightened the Yankee threat and exacerbated sectional tensions. In addition to the interdenominational American Missionary Association, which received significant Congregationalist support, Presbyterians, Baptists, and Methodists engaged in missionary and educational work in the

South. Unsurprisingly, those most radical had long supported and worked in various freedmen's aid societies, and the Civil War and Reconstruction era appeared as an opportunity not only to increase such activity but to transform the South. The success of such efforts in relation to both whites and blacks remains debatable, however. Many southern whites resented the ex-slaves' autonomy, both religiously and politically, and this often became violently manifest. The ex-slaves, for their part, "viewed with varying degrees of marvel, gratitude, and suspicion" the northern missionaries and teachers "who came into their midst carrying Bibles and spelling books instead of rifles." Undoubtedly, when it came to religious matters, the freedmen sought a great degree of autonomy, given their long experience of forging a distinctive African American evangelicalism. It was a different matter regarding education; the ex-slaves understood that it was crucial to attaining and experiencing actual freedom, and they were more receptive to northern assistance in that regard.[26]

Although northern evangelicals worked with the Freedmen's Bureau in the South, they generally insisted that the federal government give the ex-slaves little in the way of special treatment in their transition to freedom. Henry Ward Beecher revealed as much in an early May letter to Secretary of War Stanton recommending General Oliver Otis Howard to head the Freedmen's Bureau. One biographer contends that Howard's overarching preoccupation was not the ex-slaves per se, but America itself, and this contention comports with Beecher's characterization of the "very truly Christian" Howard as one who would please both "the Christian public" and "secular" philanthropists. Beecher insisted that Howard would give no thought to self-interest or that of "any section, party, or sect." Beecher also added that because he himself feared "too much northern managing for the negro," he was "anxious" for the moderate Howard to lead the bureau. "The black man is just like white in . . . that he should be left, and obliged, to take care of himself," Beecher wrote, "and suffer and enjoy, according as he creates the means of either." Besides vaguely allowing for protection from "imposition" by southern whites, hinting at some involvement in education, and conceding federal provision for "a small start, in tools, seed, etc.," the federal government must disavow "nursing" the ex-slave. Doing so would "only pauperize him." Wary of those desiring to "dandle the black man, or at least, to recite his suffering so as to gain sympathy and money from the public," Beecher believed that Howard would be resistant to such efforts and thus ideal to head up the bureau.

The Congregationalist Frederic Abbe similarly downplayed the federal government's role, though he more explicitly argued that equality before the law should be militarily enforced. That would support northern evangelicals' private efforts to usher the freedmen into their new meritocratic "manhood" and ensure that "justice is satisfied." Still, with an eye toward the larger goal of a restored Union, he was also focused on white southerners. "These men of rebellion are our brethren, whether we will or not, our fellows under one roof, and heirs of a common heritage," and northerners must therefore act "to ensure a hearty and fraternal union." Alluding to Lincoln's second inaugural address, he said further, "We have gained their respect by hard blows; let us gain their love by binding up their wounds." In the summer of 1865, both goals, care for the ex-slaves—if not full civic, political, and social inclusion—and kindness toward the ex-rebels, were ultimately in the service of restoring the Union with minimal government oversight.[27]

In that context Barnes rehashed manifest destiny–type arguments for Union that had been a staple of the Federalist-Whig-Republican tradition, some of which could have come straight from the *Federalist* papers. Portraying disunion as unnatural and irrational, he said, "Nature, or the God of nature . . . made us to be one." With no natural sectional boundary, and given shared waterways, limited ocean access, and diverse agricultural and industrial production, the nation's economic interdependence was evident and gave the whole country a manifest empirical reality. Furthermore, Barnes appealed to pragmatic self-interest: National oneness was essential to the sections' "common prosperity" and mutual defense needs. Finally, adding a romantic-nationalist layer, he said, "In . . . origin, in language, in literature, in civilization, in religion, we are made to be one." Pointing to the country's "Anglo-Saxon," if not specifically Puritan, roots, he asserted that the people who originally came to America, along with the institutions they established and the ideas they propagated, were "essentially one people." The subsequent historical character and development were almost like "magic"—further evidence "that the nation was destined to be one." By implication it was fruitless for white southerners to resist reintegration into the Union.[28]

His emphasis on a historically forged common people and culture was the most significant factor. "Our history is one," Barnes stated matter-of-factly. "The struggles for independence were the struggles of one people, not many." Bostonians and Charlestonians together had defended their "common liberties," culminating in a Constitution governing one whole people. Sounding like Henry Ward Beecher at Fort Sumter, he was confident that southerners would not forget their common historical origins. "When passion subsides, and reason resumes her sway, they will be recalled fresh to memory." Barnes had essentially portrayed disunion as emotional and irrational, but he insisted that the South knew deep down that its true interests and affection lay in oneness with the North.

Consequently, the South should readily understand the North's noble intention in fighting. "It was not," he said, reiterating a common theme, "from any spirit of enmity to the South that this war was waged. . . . It was not because the North wished to conquer the South, to exterminate them, to break up their constitutional governments." Yes, he admitted it was true, "an overruling providence" saw to "the removal of slavery," but, he reminded his audience, emancipation had never been the North's avowed aim. The reason for the bitter war was "*only* because the North regarded the Union as of inestimable worth to the whole nation, North and South alike." Surely there were many southerners whose anger would melt away through heartfelt recognition of their shared past.[29]

In addition to appealing to romantic, southern affection for the historic Union, Barnes sought to calm fears regarding consolidationist tendencies that had emerged during the war. Undeniably, he admitted, the Lincoln-led government had expanded and encroached upon the states, giving even a patriot such as himself "pause." The size and power of the military, the ability to finance the war through taxation and bond issues, and "the power to reach, arrest, and imprison individuals" throughout the country were unprecedented. Though saving the Union perhaps necessitated such measures, Lincoln's noble character ensured that they were neither long-term nor intended for evil. However, with the return of peace, vigilance once again became necessary. American and classical history both warned of "the danger" of centralized power, and thus he seconded the desire to restrain that which might "destroy the very idea of a Union of States." Striving to find a conciliatory, middle way, he said that while the government "is not a mere confederation of independent States," neither is it "a great central power having no relation to the States, and at liberty to pursue its great purposes regardless of the States." State and federal power must exist in tension, and although secession was and must remain dead, that death must not result in consolidation. Conscious of southern concerns, Barnes found himself animated by a near-Jeffersonian spirit that envisioned "communities managing their own affairs, endowing their institutions of learning and religion, making laws to regulate their own domestic institutions, [and] granting titles to property."[30]

Barnes's Old-School Presbyterian counterpart in Philadelphia, Henry Boardman, certainly would have agreed with the overall argument, but Boardman still believed that something more was needed. Grateful that "we" emerged from the war "still one people, under one government, and with an undivided country," he nevertheless insisted that "our trials" and "work" are not finished. "The question, 'Can the North and South ever become one again in affection?' is heard on every side." A political Union was not a real Union, which southern Protestants knew just as well. William Nelson Pendleton, Lee's former chief of artillery and an Episcopal rector following the war, provided emblematic expression of this. Having refused to restore prayer for the President of the United States at his church in Lexington, Virginia, he was arrested by Union troops in July and consequently likened southerners' relationship "towards the government and Northern people somewhat as were our Blessed Lord and the Apostles towards the Roman authorities and population; submission but without other ties than general good inte[rest] and the common brotherhood of humanity." Of course, southerners for several decades had not granted northerners much respect when it came to religion, and in the postwar context they were even less inclined to do so. Nevertheless, Boardman insisted that the responsibility of achieving a true, affective Union rested with northern evangelical churches, the repository of true Christianity in America. Northern evangelicals were obligated to heal "our country's wounds; to repair its desolations; to soothe its sorrows; to allay its enmities; to replace prejudice, discord, and confusion, with candor, respect, and kindness; and to resuscitate the various agencies, moral and material, which may cement the Union, and renew its prosperity."[31]

Ever the evangelical, Boardman accentuated the problem in order to place the cure in stark relief. Although "the formal union . . . may be invigorated and cemented by the wholesome tendencies of commerce, of education, and of social intercourse," these were "only co-efficients." Having expressed approval of Andrew Johnson, he left the specifics of political reunion to the government, while insisting that only the gospel could "reach the seat of the malady to be cured"; only it was "strong enough to cope with the human heart"; and only it was "God's appointed instrumentality for subduing and re-moulding human nature." Ignoring the reality that white southerners would not appreciate the comparison, he remarked, "Men who but yesterday were cannibals, are to-day sitting at the feet of Jesus, clothed, and in their right mind." Furthermore, Boardman pointed to the historical animosity between the "two races," Jew and Gentile, as paralleling the animosity between North and South. Just as Jews and Gentiles "felt their mutual enmity turn to love" at the cross, so could alienated Americans. "Such is the Union *we* need, and such the means by which it can be effected." Adapting Saint Paul's Epistle to the Romans, Boardman promised that "the wall of partition" between North and South would fall if the gospel were to pervade the country. Though ex-Confederates must "return without delay," the onus continued to be on northern evangelicals to induce heartfelt repentance. They must not be like a "stern" and "unforgiving" Jonah. Nor should they be like the priest and Levite "passing by on the other side"; rather, they were to be like the Good Samaritan and not "harbor vindictive feelings." If that sentiment prevailed, he said, "The land will soon be healed of its deadly wounds." The "love of Christ" would constrain northern evangelicals "to repress in ourselves, and discountenance in others, 'all bitterness, and wrath, and anger, and clamor, and evil speaking, and all malice,'" and the country would "find the promised Messiah to be our Peace: every wall of partition will be broken down; and our restored civil Union will but typify that deeper, holier union which has made us 'ALL ONE IN CHRIST JESUS.'"[32]

Several things might be striking to twenty-first-century readers, aside from the near-conflation of nation and church. First, Boardman's emphasis is almost exclusively on cultivating a certain sentiment toward the South. Second, Boardman was focused primarily on white Americans, saying nothing about removing racial enmity when citing inherently racial scriptural passages. In speaking of overcoming "prejudice, discord, and confusion," he meant that which existed between whites North and South, and in citing the story of the Good Samaritan, Boardman was not concerned that northern white Christians might "pass by" the African American ex-slaves lying in "the ditch." Rather, he was concerned that white northerners would avoid reconciling with white southerners. Boardman's postwar preoccupation with restoring an affective Union, when considered alongside the opinions of Beecher, Barnes, Hodge, and others, suggests that not all evangelicals were thinking in abolitionist, civic-nationalist terms about the meaning of the just-completed war and what Reconstruction entailed.[33]

Still, it is obviously true that nineteenth-century radicals had been attuned to racial injustice for decades, with most simply assuming that full civil and political equality necessarily accompanied abolition and would be guaranteed by the federal government.[34] Despite the widely shared early optimism regarding Johnson, George Cheever was among those who saw early on that the president's promise to make treason "odious" would become an empty one and that his desire for a speedy restoration would eventuate in a powerful reassertion of the former slaveholders' authority in southern society and politics. By mid-June Cheever believed that the country was courting divine judgment. Holding Johnson responsible, Cheever argued that restoration without ensuring full citizenship rights, particularly suffrage, amounted to "giving [the ex-slaves] over into the power of traitors to be trampled as at their pleasure." By fall Cheever felt as though he were swimming against the tide and confessed that he felt like "weeping." Believing that he and his church were being "proscribed" by prevailing public opinion, he angrily asked, "Where are the churches or ministers that speak out in defense of the poor whose faces are thus ground by the nation because of their colour?" None possessed the courage to "rebuke" Johnson, he complained, and the person who "pursues a different course and speaks out in God's name" received "nothing but rebuke and wrath." To Cheever, evangelicals were approving of "a blaspheming Ahab in the President's chair."[35]

Perhaps, then, he and fellow abolitionists did have "their fingers on the nation's pulse," as one historian says of them, but not because abolitionism represented widespread northern opinion. It is an overstatement to say that during 1865 "northern Protestantism was swept up in and helped nurture a revolutionary tide in which racial prejudice was in retreat." Cheever certainly did not believe that, and for plenty of other evangelicals the ex-slaves were clearly lower in importance than Cheever-like abolitionists would have desired. It is more accurate to view figures such as Cheever and Gilbert Haven, the latter of whom explicitly thought in terms of racially inclusive civic nationalism, as prophetic voices outside the mainstream. Although most evangelicals were not unmindful of the "four millions of emancipated slaves to be cared for," Cheever might be closer to the truth in believing that many were implicitly, if not explicitly, supporting Johnson's restoration plan.[36]

Henry Boardman, who surely hoped slavery-related issues would not interfere with reunion, regarded the ex-slaves with a trepidation similar to Johnson's. The president had told soon-to-be-discharged black troops that the United States "is your country as well as anybody else's," but in doing so he revealed much anxiety about their presence. It was their patriotic and Christian duty, he instructed them, to ensure that "resentments should cease, that angry feelings should subside, and that every man should . . . be prepared for what is before him." What lay ahead was a test by which they could demonstrate their fitness for liberty. Would they be "industrious" and "economical," or would liberty become license? Their future conduct would shed light on his larger question: "Can four millions of people . . . be made to work harmoniously and congruously in our system?" Hopefully racial harmony will result, Johnson said, but "if we have to become a separate and distinct people," then Providence, which "works mysteriously but unerringly and certainly, will point out the way." Although Boardman gave no indication of belief in the colonization implied by Johnson, he did view the ex-slaves as a problem to be solved and a potential hindrance to achieving national Christian oneness. Having prescribed rebuilt "churches and schoolhouses" for southern whites, Boardman prescribed only religion for the ex-slaves. Even though many were evangelicals, and even though he vaguely called for "justice" and "humanity" from the white South, he urged that "this great mass of ignorant people must be brought under the influence of thorough religious training. . . . Without it, there can be neither tranquility nor safety for either race," the "American" or the

"African." Given his conservative theological views and temperament, Boardman could only hope that "the two races may, by God's blessing, thread this perilous labyrinth, and come forth at length into a 'wealthy place.'" That wealthy place was likely to remain in the South, where most northerners plainly expected the slaves to continue laboring.[37]

Even the less conservative Henry Martyn Dexter expressed ambivalence about the ex-slaves' presence. For all intents and purposes, he informed his audience, they were stuck with them, since emancipation was a near-certainty and colonization was not realistic. Dexter advocated a relatively radical program—land reform, suffrage, and federally funded education—in the expressed hope that the freedmen would become "intelligent, virtuous, and useful copartners with us in the nation"; however, so as not to be misunderstood, he assured his audience that the sort of equality he had in mind should not be confused with radical social equality. "We need not marry [blacks]," Dexter said, "nor . . . walk arm in arm with them in the streets; we need not prefer them in any respect to our own color." Rather, he continued, those in his circle of influence should "respect and honor and love them, in their appropriate place, just as we do our Irish and German fellow-citizens in *their* place." He made it clear that the ex-slaves' "place" was where they had always labored.[38]

Citing their supposed affinity for the South, based on a climatic theory of races, Dexter reassured his white audience that most blacks would not come north.[39] This was fortunate, because a revived international commerce depended on their laboring in the South, where whites would find it difficult to do the necessary work. "Those tropical cotton-fields, and sugar-plantations, and rice swamps, where [blacks] have for generations delved sadly under the lash, must lie waste, or freedmen must take up the shovel and the hoe with the new elasticity and enthusiasm of a personal interest in their labor," he said. There in the South, "where they can do what needs to be done, and what they need to do, and long to do, and what the world needs to have them do, is surely the place for them. Let them live at home." Saying nothing about northern blacks, but implying much about their place in society, Dexter left no doubt that the ex-slaves were instrumental to the future well-being of the nation—primarily as agricultural workers in the South. The nation's economy would soon be humming along, with the ex-slaves taking their place in the reinvigorated and restored Union.[40]

If Dexter and prominent nonradicals such as Henry Ward Beecher, Albert Barnes, Charles Hodge, and Henry Boardman are any indication, northern evangelicals were not quite thinking in twenty-first-century terms of civic-nationalist inclusion. Rather, they were wrestling, alongside the president, with what to do with the freedmen while desiring an end to decades-long sectional hostilities. To be sure, many evangelicals realized that there was long-term work to be done in the South, as evidenced by their missionary and educational efforts. Nevertheless, more than a few likely agreed with Johnson's assessment that the nation was nearing a return to normalcy in July. Treason had been defeated; ports were reopened; domestic and international commerce were flowing uninhibited; Union soldiers and sailors had resumed their civilian pursuits; the flag flew over the entire country; "and the only barrier to our national progress—human slavery—is forever at an end." Moreover, Johnson announced in a millennial vein, "I believe that God sent this people on a mission among the nations of the earth, and that when He founded our nation, He founded it in perpetuity. . . . I feel that whatever the means He uses, the Almighty is determined to preserve us as a people."[41] Despite nervous glances south, some evangelicals were similarly proclaiming the reality they so earnestly desired. Theirs was no radical vision for the Union; rather, it was something approximating the status quo antebellum, minus slavery and the threat of secession. Buffalo's New School Presbyterian Joel Bingham penned a song for the nation's first postwar Fourth of July, giving expression to this sense of moving on in anticipation of better days ahead for God's republic:

> Bright Republic, white and gleaming
> In the robes of joy to-day!
> Brothers' hate and red blood streaming
> And the slave are passed away.
> Silver music
> Merrily proclaims thy sway.
> Her blood-ransomed flag glitters bright as her daughters,
> Unshorn of a star it shall glitter for aye,
> And each gallant ship riding o'er the blue waters
> Shall grand old "*E Pluribus Unum*" display.
>
> Grand Republic, States united
> By the smiling grace of God,
> And the Constitution plighted—
> Once defied—now sealed with blood!
> Freedom's martyrs
> Sleep in glory 'neath thy sod . . . .

Mighty Union, one forever!
On thy borders oceans roll,
And we swear that men shall never
Sunder that which God made whole!
Mighty Union!
Stand while earthly ages roll.[42]

Pronouncing the Union Restored

This optimism and "trust-Johnson" sentiment continued through the fall, culminating in Johnson's annual message to Congress in December. Following the address, the Congregationalist pastor and former Vermont state legislator Clark Elam Ferrin spoke to a gathering of Vermont Baptists, Methodists, and Congregationalists and exalted Johnson for exemplifying America's republican possibilities. Having risen from obscurity and poverty to become president, Johnson embodied the greatest American dream possible. Ferrin also celebrated the Christian republic's survival and transition to peace, symbolized by the soon-to-be-ratified Thirteenth Amendment. He thus announced, "The conquered rebels with one voice admit that all they started to get is lost, and that these points are settled: Negro slavery is to have no more guaranties from the National Constitution and laws, and their doctrine of State rights, the right of secession, is gone forever." The two problems that had saddled the nation since its beginning were resolved. "Thank God," he concluded, "we are one, and the ties that unite us are stronger than before." Alongside the president, many evangelicals were eager to believe that Reconstruction was over and the Union was secure.[43]

During the fall run-up to Johnson's message, Henry Ward Beecher was among the president's most visible and exuberant backers. On October 23 Beecher wrote Johnson an obsequious letter, lauding his nonpartisan, patriotic wisdom, expressing thanks that "God has raised you up for such a crisis," and proclaiming that Johnson would be "intimately associated with a Nation the Grandeur of whose History even the most lively imagination cannot estimate or conceive." Beecher also assured Johnson that "the religious men of the north and west are rapidly growing into a confidence in [you] second only to that which they felt for Mr. Lincoln; a confidence which I am sure will increase." Six days later, on October 29, Beecher delivered a sermon pleading that his congregation and readers support Johnson's southern policy.[44] The significance of receiving support from Beecher—of whom a contemporary said, "few preachers . . . have greater power with the people"—could not have been lost on Andrew Johnson, who fundamentally saw himself as a Jacksonian man of the people.[45]

What precipitated Beecher's fulsome support was a friendly October 3 interview of Johnson by the Boston radical George Stearns. Defending his amnesty policy, Johnson said, "I did not expect to keep out all who were excluded . . . , or even a large number of them, but I intended they should sue for pardon, and so realize the enormity of the crime they had committed." Their punishment was essentially having to grovel before Johnson (even if by letter) and pledge loyalty to the Union. Johnson's amnesty program was crucial, for although he said the federal government possessed the power to actually "reconstruct State governments," he desired that pardoned southerners do the actual work of restoration for readmission to the Union. Seeking a mediating position between "giving the States too much power" and a "consolidation of power in the central government," he refused to impose black suffrage on the ex-Confederate states; that should be left to the states, and, moreover, if he insisted on suffrage in the South, he would have to do the same in the North. Better to leave it to the states "than to force them to it; for if they go wrong, the power is in our hands and we can check them at any stage." With radicals loudly insisting that a federal guarantee of suffrage necessarily accompanied freedom, Johnson believed that prudence and deference to America's federal system dictated an experimental, cautious, and conciliatory course.[46]

It was this approach that Beecher supported. The southern state conventions, Beecher insisted, were acting sufficiently by abolishing slavery and renouncing secession. The southern states, he said, "are now . . . brought to our feet; and they ask to be our equals again." Calling for their readmission "at the earliest practicable moment," Beecher gladly advocated "lenity, charity, sympathy, and, as far as I may in consistency with duty, forgetfulness." He also praised Johnson for his "clear perception that the welfare of the freedmen depends far more upon the good will of their white neighbors than it does upon northern philanthropy or Governmental protection" and for resisting "the temptation to use the Federal Government to meddle with State affairs" by foisting suffrage on southern states. Beecher's support came despite his theoretical disagreement with Johnson that suffrage was a natural right, not merely a political one. Northerners should get their own racial house in order prior to dictating to the South on the matter: "When black men can ride without being insulted and ejected from our streetcars; when they can sit undisturbed in our sanctuaries; when they can work in shops with foreigners without being vomited out; when they can vote as white men do," then the North may justly "rebuke the South on this subject." As with the Irish, however, it would be "absurd" to insist that "because I claim for the black man the right to be a man, . . . I am bound to like him . . . [or] hold that he is socially on a level with the man that is educated or refined." Instead of insisting on equity throughout the Union, Beecher "heartily" thanked Johnson for his "statesman like caution" regarding the South. Although "state sovereignty is a heresy," Beecher reiterated, "state-rights, is a reality of transcendent value." A slave-free re-Union should not be sacrificed on the altar of black suffrage or full equality.[47]

Skilled at reducing the complex to the simple, and advocating a sentimental and optimistic version of evangelicalism, Beecher portrayed sectional readjustment as a matter of common sense and warm, Christian reconciliation.[48] In doing so he echoed and added to the arguments made by other prominent figures, such as Barnes, Hodge, and Boardman. But to Beecher, emancipation was the key. During the 1850s, when the slave power had sought to use the federal government to extend slavery, he said that northerners "were obliged to be stern and unflinching. There was no room permitted us for charity." In 1865, however, with slavery being replaced by the transformative system of free labor, Beecher said, northerners must "adapt ourselves to the new state of things, and perform now, though in a reverse manner, the duties which we sought hitherto to perform—then by opposition to the South; now by kindness toward them, and concord with them." The exercise of kindness and forgiveness was the only possible Christian stance. And because northerners could not expect "that in one hour [white southerners] will get over their enmities, their life-long prejudices and their humiliation," magnanimity was, a fortiori, required. Christ did not wait until sinners were in their "right mind" before accepting them; therefore, neither should northerners be tardy in extending forgiveness to the South. "We must take them as they are," he said. "If we wait to have them become what we would have them to be, we shall wait in vain." Finally, Beecher stressed, white southerners had suffered and been humiliated enough, inescapably conscious as they were that all of the death and destruction had occurred for a lost cause. "For my own part," he announced, "I think it to be the great need of the nation to save the self-respect of the South. . . . I do not wish to see the South humbled any more than the war has humbled them."[49]

Beecher was not alone in this particular sentiment in the fall. For example, the Congregationalist Samuel Giles Buckingham said that his "indignation" at the South had changed to "compassion." For starters, he cited the massive death and destruction from the war, and, moreover, evidently retaining a great degree of faith in Johnson, Buckingham believed that confiscation of southern property and the political proscription of ex-Confederates were more extensive than they actually were and that they would likely continue if necessary. Furthermore, he pointed to a punishment even more "terrible and eternal." Ironic to us, perhaps, he suggested that the war would haunt southerners at every turn, for there would be few places where an ex-rebel or his descendant could travel "without coming upon battle-fields, and the scene of naval engagements, and battle-flags, and trophies, and paintings, and statues, and the verdict of history, and the sentiment of mankind, and the world's admiration at our triumph over this accursed conspiracy, and its inspiring cause."[50] The South had suffered enough.

During the same late-October week that Beecher had written to Johnson and preached about Reconstruction, Secretary of State Seward penned a Thanksgiving proclamation for Johnson to deliver. The proclamation deferred to "Almighty God" as the source of the nation's prosperity, peace, and harmony, and, implicitly, of emancipation. Furthermore, the proclamation explicitly reflected a covenantal understanding of the nation's obligation to God. Quoting Proverbs 14:34—"righteousness exalteth a nation, while sin is a reproach to any people"—the president recommended that "the whole people make confession of our national sins against His infinite goodness, and with one heart and one mind implore the Divine guidance in the ways of national virtue and holiness." Despite the strikingly formulaic nature of such proclamations, northern evangelicals continued to relish their issuance from the president. Henry Hopkins of South Williamstown, New York, announced, "How significant and hopeful is the fact that the nation is . . . , through its legally constituted head, called to an act of solemn, religious homage to the great ruler of all." The New Hampshire Congregationalist Theophilus Sawin packed the first postwar Thanksgiving proclamation with auspicious meaning: "Our Moses," he said, "was permitted to lead us to the borders of our promised land. . . . Our Joshua succeeded him, with no interruption to the wheels of government." Just as the original Joshua "taught his people that the 'Lord their God had given them rest from war,'" Andrew Johnson "exalts the agency of God," and nothing he could do as president was more fitting than recommending to the "whole people" a national Thanksgiving. Theoretically at least, when confronting the problems of Reconstruction, recognizing God's primary agency and entrusting the country's future to God remained the crucial starting point. Sawin said further, "The value of the peace achieved and the future of our country depend upon the depth to which this sentiment penetrates the hearts of the people." Only with this sentiment in place, he said, could postwar Americans legitimately and satisfactorily "go home to their friends, their lands, [and] their industrial pursuits." Peace essentially meant, then, a return to antebellum lifestyles, albeit within a firmer and freer God-delivered Union.[51]

Following Johnson's proclamation, Granville Moody, the Methodist pastor and former regimental commander who had visited Lincoln along with George Peck in 1864, informed Johnson that he was particularly pleased with the president's Reconstruction policy. Moody, who had met Johnson in Nashville during the war and believed that the then-governor had converted to evangelical Christianity following a pious session of prayer together, assured Johnson that all lovers of the Union esteemed the president greatly. Moody even speculated that were a presidential election to take place, Johnson would win easily. Johnson's pardon of Moody's brother George, who had been captured with Jefferson Davis, probably colored Moody's positive forecast, while his words and relationship with Johnson likely did nothing but affirm the president in his desire for a quick restoration of the Union and his intention to forge a middle path between Republican radicals to his left and defiant southerners on his right.[52] Receiving encouragement from men such as Moody and Beecher, Johnson returned the favor with his first annual message to Congress on December 5.

Of course, with more on his mind than speaking to evangelicals, the address was still well suited to their ears. Obliged, he said, to express "gratitude to God in the name of the people" for preserving the Union, Johnson also praised "the hand of Divine Providence" in creating the American Constitution. With the Thirteenth Amendment set to be ratified the following day, Johnson suggested that evidence of God's oversight was there to be seen in the unwitting brilliance of those who subjected the document to amendment. Furthermore, he expressed great optimism for the future. Alluding to the Scottish philosopher Adam Smith, Johnson urged the nation to thank "the invisible hand" which preserved the country through dark times and which will "guide us onward to a perfect restoration of fraternal affection"; just as an invisible hand causes a harmonious equilibrium to emerge from competing economic decisions in a free market, so too would an invisible hand produce a harmonious, restored Union of states from among competing visions for postwar America. And the Thirteenth Amendment was the crucial step in that process. Making emancipation legal throughout the Union would "efface the sad memory of the past." Acceptance of the amendment would pave the way for southern states to rejoin "the family of the Union" and also serve as a "pledge of perpetual loyalty and peace." Sounding like Lincoln, Beecher, and many others, he continued, "The adoption of the amendment reunites us beyond all power of disruption; it heals the wound that is still imperfectly closed; it removes slavery, the element which has so long perplexed and divided the country;

it makes us once more a united people, renewed and strengthened, bound more than ever to mutual affection and support."[53]

Two days later, northern evangelicals responded to Johnson's annual message and his earlier Thanksgiving proclamation with their own pronouncements regarding the state of the Union.[54] The Philadelphia Presbyterian Elias Beadle, a renowned preacher and former missionary who occasionally filled Henry Boardman's pulpit, commended Johnson and reminded his audience that Americans had "a goodly heritage" to protect. Theirs was a country "blessed" by God and one that held "the graves of our fathers, who counted not their lives dear unto them, and the graves of their sons, who followed . . . , and fell . . . in defending their country's honor and weal." Protecting that heritage following civil war necessitated remembering that Christ's love alone overcomes "alienation," converts enemies into friends, "cements afresh all diversified bonds, and joins tribes and tongues and nationalities into one household of faith: so that there shall be but one fold and one Shephard." With slavery gone, such oneness seemed attainable. The San Francisco Presbyterian Henry Scudder, another former missionary, seconded Johnson's belief that sectional reunion would soon follow the Thirteenth Amendment; slavery created a culture that had "miseducated" southerners, but with its removal northerners could welcome their "brethren" back. "War," he said, "has not made [northerners] rigorous, and exacting, and tyrannical, and savagely vindictive"; no Carthaginian Peace or French reign of terror awaited the South. Though slavery indeed had been "a cancer" and was removed by "the sword of the North," Scudder extolled the former tailor occupying the White House. He is presently "stitching the wound—you know he is good at stitching—and the wound will heal."[55]

The abolitionist Congregationalist Charles Smith chose to scold radical critics of Johnson following the annual message. "[The president] may not think or act as Mr. Sumner or Mr. Phillips or Mr. Douglass, or as you or I would have him," he admitted. "What then? Is he for this to be accounted as unworthy of trust? Is he for this to be denounced, held up as a prospective traitor? Oh, shame on such despicable meanness [and] cowardly baseness!" During the secession crisis, Smith reminded, it was Johnson who "stood up alone among Southern men in the senate . . . and denounced treason with fiery tongue"; it was he who sacrificed property, home, and friends for the Union. Recalling Johnson's 1864 "Moses Speech" and pointing to his present insistence that southern states ratify the Thirteenth Amendment, repudiate their war debt, and provide "legal protection for the free men" before reentering the Union, Smith said it "is almost impious" to criticize the president. Americans must "trust Andrew Johnson,—reason with him if need be, and pray for him,—and there is not the remotest danger of his proving recreant to any vital interest trusted to his hands." In light of "God's marked kindness towards us as a people," Americans must retain "faith in [Johnson's] continued wise management of our national affairs, till, upon the broad basis of 'equal rights and exact justice to all men,' we shall, as a nation, become as harmonious as it is possible for a people occupying such a broad space on the map of the world." Undoubtedly, Smith and others were accentuating the positive, alongside Johnson, in early December.[56]

And once again evangelicals brought forth glorious narrations of America's providential and historic Union, but now with emancipation interwoven. George Duffield Jr., the pastor of the Second Presbyterian (New School) Church in Galesburg, Illinois, did just that in addressing a meeting of the city's Baptist and Old and New School Presbyterians. "The tremendous problem that has so long been perplexing us, how to tear the poison-vine from the tree without destroying the tree itself, is now solved," he said, in reference to Lincoln's "House Divided" speech. "Mr. Lincoln's great alternative of a free Republic or a slave Republic, at length has come. The inevitable conflict between free labor and slave labor has been fought, and the victory been won!" Vigilantly aware that some Americans might be inclined to celebrate the state of affairs "in the spirit of a Roman triumph," Duffield made haste to compare their situation to the Passover celebration following King Josiah's recovery of the Mosaic Law. The United States was no mere republic; rather, it had been chosen, formed, and preserved through civil war by God, and "but for [his mercy] to us as a nation, it would not, and could not, have been as well with us as it is." In December 1865 it was well in the minds of plenty. The Union had been preserved, and the slaves had been emancipated. The American flag, Duffield said, "waves over the happiest nation now on the face of the earth, and happiest of all among them, over four million once slaves, but who this day look up to its brighter stars and still redder stripes as the symbol of *their* freedom, as well as our own." Consequently, of "the Great Thanksgiving that we celebrate . . . , will it be said hereafter, that there was none like to it in all our history."[57]

One Whole People

Northern evangelicals were once again proclaiming the reality of that which they so earnestly desired. Finally it was time to leave behind the bitterness of civil war and look ahead to peace, emancipation, and prosperous national wholeness.[58] From coast to coast, pronouncements came forth. The Chicago Congregationalist Harvey Denison Kitchel, who would shortly become president of Vermont's Middlebury College, gloriously announced, "We are a Union now—a nation at last, . . . a nation of the American people!" San Francisco's Henry Scudder further appreciated Johnson for having called together the "unbroken Republic" to celebrate "the oneness of a great, consolidated people"; Americans were again "a whole people—a people chastened by many sorrows, humbled and softened by many bereavements—a people disciplined in war [but] touched with the sense of divine deliverances." The Civil War was being buried and forgotten; a transformed Union was emerging slowly, almost imperceptibly. Long Island's Presbyterian James McDougall waxed lyrical as he recounted the end of bloodshed, soldiers coming home, families being reunited, and the nation's industry humming again. Memory of the war would be consigned to "the musket over the mantel for coming generations to gaze upon," while battlefields would be replaced by fields of grain and "kindly Nature" would obscure "the mementoes of the deadly shock, absorbing the wrecked and broken material, filling up the trench and rifle-pit, leveling the fortification, and growing flowers over the long rows of nameless graves." There was in December 1865 "hope on every face, the cloud gone from every brow, sunshine in every eye, vigor and courage in every step.[59]

McDougall could not help but emphasize the sovereignty of God in the process. It was God, he said, who had limited northern arms so that Lincoln would unwittingly issue the Emancipation Proclamation "under the guise of a 'war measure.'" Following emancipation it was God who used what McDougall perceived to be blacks' docility as the means of keeping "this land from the predicted horrors of a servile insurrection." That is, it was God who "restrained and kept from waking the fierce animal, the tiger that sleeps in the negro's nature." Most notably, it was God who brought the nation through Democrats' near-treasonous behavior in 1864 and then Lincoln's assassination in order to enlarge and solidify the "spirit of union." Finally, it was God who ensured a seamless transition to Johnson's presidency. "No crash ensues, no stopping of the wheels of Government, no cessation or interruption of the task of exterminating treason. A successor, as eminently chosen of God, silently and reverently assumes the vacated chair. The nation moves on, steadier, soberer, wiser, stronger, to finish the great work." The "God of nations" had ordained peace for "his people" under the leadership of Andrew Johnson.[60]

Evangelicals, like other northerners, wanted to believe that Reconstruction was over. However, they soon would be hard-pressed to sustain such hopeful attitudes. Johnson would reveal himself to be a Judas rather than a Joshua, turning out to be no friend of the ex-slave and stubbornly at odds with Congress.

Moreover, intransigent white southerners, with Johnson seemingly enabling them, would provide unambiguous evidence that they were not terribly interested in heartfelt reconciliation with the North. Such events would force moderate evangelicals to the left, just as they had been moved during the war, even while they continued to long for national Christian oneness. Johnson would become the latest threat to their Christian republic, and evangelicals would ultimately support congressional Republicans in their impeachment of him. They would also agree to increased federal intervention in the South on behalf of the ex-slaves in order to challenge unrepentant southerners. Finally, they would welcome Ulysses S. Grant as a two-time savior of the Union during the election of 1868.

5 The Union Saved Again

> That same special providence that made you the successful leader of our army will now make you the Savior of Our Country. . . . There is no possible excuse now for any further bickerings between Radicals and Conservatives. Let us fall into line, while God leads you on, and we follow you to peace prosperity and Union.
>
> —George C. Bates to Ulysses S. Grant, May 21, 1868

On March 28, 1868, with Andrew Johnson's impeachment trial scheduled to commence in two days, New England Methodists issued a report on "the state of the country." They sent copies to various officials, including Secretary of War Edwin Stanton, House Speaker Schuyler Colfax, Supreme Court Chief Justice Salmon Chase, and General of the Army Ulysses S. Grant. After thanking "our Lord and Saviour" for preserving the Union and ending slavery, the authors applauded Congress's efforts to protect those fruits of victory over the past few years. The committee then portrayed Johnson as having been hostile to "the will of the people" and, by implication, the will of God, due to his struggles with Congress since 1866. The report "heartily and solemnly" supported impeachment and declared Johnson a lawbreaker because of his dismissal of Stanton in violation of the Tenure of Office Act. Furthermore, the report juxtaposed Johnson's actions with Grant's seemingly sterling behavior in the controversy. Although the Senate did not convict Johnson, Grant, who would receive the Republican nomination for the fall presidential election, was well situated to receive the support of evangelicals who were anxious over the state of the country under Johnson.[1]

The president had gone from a "Joshua" set to gloriously restore the Union to a "Judas" betraying the Christian republic. Clearly plenty of evangelicals had regarded Johnson highly, and for most that esteem derived from their affection and hopes for the Union and their allegiance to the Republican Party that had saved it. During 1866 and 1867, however, Johnson's defiance of Congress over its Reconstruction policy, his amicable relationship with Democrats, and his refusal to guarantee minimal justice to the ex-slaves in the face of racial violence compelled former allies, which included many evangelicals, to forsake him. They saw Johnson ungratefully joining hands with treasonous enemies—northern Democrats and unrepentant white southerners. "It was not what the people expected," Brooklyn's New School Presbyterian Samuel Spear wrote in early 1867. In deserting Johnson northern evangelicals never abandoned their desire for national oneness, but Johnson's disagreement with Congress became the latest threat to the Union. George Prentiss, pastor of New York City's Presbyterian Church of the Covenant and a future professor at Union Theological Seminary, described it as "a political crisis as momentous as any [the country] has ever known."[2]

Dismayed by the turn of events, Henry Boardman longed for a Christianized "Cincinnatus" to leave his plow and save the republic. Boardman typified the continuing habit among evangelicals of packing the presidency with immense meaning. This was not as much about patronage, appointments, and access to power, as much as it was the fact that the particular occupant symbolized, however vaguely and subjectively, whether the country was on the right track or not. Although it is true that there was something generally American about this symbolism, particularly given the importance of Greco-Roman antiquity to American political culture, there was also something evangelical about it, given the Bible's emphasis on the significance of leaders submitting to (or resisting) God. Drawing on both the classical and the biblical, Boardman desired to see "the wounds of war" healed in the next president and to see Americans living "once more as one people, united in the bonds of true brotherhood. Whoever comes upon this mission, we will welcome him as an ambassador of the Prince of Peace." Following their brief flirtation with Andrew Johnson, evangelicals would indeed welcome Ulysses S. Grant, with his motto of "let us have peace," as a two-time savior of the Union. Against the backdrop of Johnson's threatening presidency, evangelicals perceived in Grant a Christian president, chosen by God to save the Union once again. Sectional difficulties could be left behind once and for all.[3]

Breaking with Congress

In December 1865 Congress exercised its constitutional prerogative and refused to seat representatives from Johnson's provisional southern governments. To ex-Confederates Congress's refusal amounted to "bad faith," since they had laid down their arms and, in their view, were thus "entitled" to rejoin the Union. But Congress felt fully justified, since many of those representatives turned out to be ex-Confederate military officers and government officials, while various states had refused to ratify the Thirteenth Amendment, nullify secession ordinances, or repudiate Confederate war debt. Nevertheless, despite the controversy, a split between Congress and Johnson was not a foregone conclusion. The period between December 4, 1865, and February 23, 1866, was the first phase of a "critical period," when an "accommodation" between the two remained possible and which a majority in Congress and the public likely still desired.[4] Perceiving this in January 1866, Gilbert Haven lumped "prejudiced Republicans" in with "traitors" and "copperheads," portraying them all as "mean enough, and wicked enough, to declare that this is a white man's government." Only Congress could impede Johnson, and though Haven held out hope that the president might yet become a liberating Moses to the ex-slaves, he implored readers to pray that Congress would act courageously and justly.[5]

Johnson's actions would soon disappoint Haven and many others, as the simmering dispute between the executive and legislative branches began to heat up on February 19, 1866. Having received conflicting advice from his cabinet, Johnson vetoed an appropriations bill that would have continued funding the Freedmen's Bureau, thereby initiating a series of events that eventually culminated in his break with Congress and the Republican Party. "The country has returned, or is returning," he said, "to a state of peace and industry, and the rebellion is in fact at an end." With slavery "effectually and finally abrogated throughout the whole country," having received reports from the South of alleged corruption and overreach by the bureau's agents, and predisposed to see the bureau as an expensive, meddlesome, and potentially tyrannical hindrance to restoration, Johnson believed that it was time for the ex-slaves to fend for themselves, for Congress to seat southern representatives, for the ex-Confederate states to rejoin the federal family, and for government oversight of the South to cease.[6]

Although he was criticized by most Republicans, the rupture remained incomplete, and, in many respects, Johnson's veto message highlighted familiar themes that continued to garner support. Shortly thereafter George Peck referred to emancipation and associated wartime problems with a satisfied sense of finality, while the New School Presbyterian William Adams, having championed slavery's providential end and secession's defeat, alluded to Henry Clay in hopefully forecasting "universal gladness" throughout "the whole land, North, South, East, [and] West." Regarding emancipation in particular, he repeated what had become a commonplace: "God has wrought more than man had devised." Though recognizing that problems remained, Adams nevertheless communicated a desire to leave the war behind. Paraphrasing Saint Paul, he advised, "Let us put away all wrath, all bitterness, all party willfulness, and devise things which look to the good of the whole country."[7] Furthermore, despite radicals' displeasure with the veto—Oliver Johnson referred to the moment "as about the darkest day in our history"—Johnson's message drew praise from some northern evangelicals.[8] The Chicago Old School Presbyterian pastor David Xavier Junkin, for instance, encouraged and assured Johnson that the wisest and most patriotic men of the country were still behind him, while others from throughout the North wrote Johnson in praise of his moderation and devotion to the Union. Such support only encouraged his sense of being a Jacksonian man of the people.[9]

Perhaps most influentially, Henry Ward Beecher once again vocally supported Johnson. Optimistically proclaiming that southern blacks and whites were adapting well to their new relationship, Beecher assumed that whites in need of labor would pragmatically treat ex-slaves as partners seeking to restore the southern economy. Additionally, taking Johnson at his word that the disagreement with Congress concerned means and not ends, such that Johnson also sought the long-term well-being of both the country and the ex-slaves, Beecher depicted Johnson's veto as legitimately resisting a federal usurpation of state power. There was a "danger," Beecher warned, that those "who think only of the black man may be warped by their sympathies and tempted to resort to [extreme] measures for his relief and protection." Patience and "forgetfulness of the old past" were more needful than undermining the federal system with a centralized bureaucracy. Permitting the South to work out the new social arrangements would not only uphold federalism, doing so would also benefit the freedmen in the long run. By analogy, in the same way that many Israelites were lost along the way to the Promised Land, Beecher unflinchingly allowed for great loss in the short term for "the black race." If in ten years half of the ex-slaves "stand strong on the platform of liberty, I shall feel that the price paid was cheap." Clearly "pains and trouble and disappointment" will mark the exodus from slavery, "but one-half of them free and strong are worth four times as many groveling in bondage." Above all, delaying readmission and the return of local control meant delaying the restoration of the Union to its proper condition. Echoing the remarks that he had made the previous fall, Beecher proclaimed that defeat in war and the removal of its material cause—slavery—had transformed the South. "It is not the South of old that we look at to-day, but a wholly new South," and that new South, he said, must be welcomed back, for "we want again a full-rounded Union, a whole and undivided country." Let "kindness, commerce, school-houses and churches" do their work, and "an era of good feeling will prevail, when hand in hand with the North she will seek a common prosperity, a nobler future, a destiny unmoved by sectional bitterness, unhindered by passion or misrule."[10]

Despite Beecher's efforts, Johnson was in the process of losing moderate northern support. Three days after the veto, on February 22, he delivered an undignified address to supporters on Washington's Birthday, and then, on March 27, he surprisingly vetoed the moderate Congress's Civil Rights Bill. The law overturned the *Dred Scott* decision, by granting birthright citizenship, and it aimed to ensure equal protection of the law for the ex-slaves.[11] In his "Washington's Birthday Address," Johnson broke openly with congressional radicals, who he incorrectly believed dominated the Republican Party, and revealed himself as vindictive, self-absorbed, and perhaps paranoid. Cheever appreciated the episode's potential to unite Republicans and sarcastically commented, "Here is a model President for you, American Citizens." Although Americans had caught previous glimpses of the crass Johnson, that day they arguably saw Andrew Johnson's true character as fully manifest as ever. He implied that congressional radicals were traitorous opponents of the Union's restoration, no different than southerners who refused to accept defeat. He also outlandishly compared himself to Christ, first counseling forgiveness of southerners, and then casting himself as a potential martyr by hinting that radicals had designs to assassinate him: "Are they not satisfied with one martyr in this place? Does not the blood of Lincoln appease their vengeance and wrath? Do they still want more blood?" If so, "Let them have the courage to strike like men"; then erect "an altar to the Union" and "take me and lay me upon it, and [my] blood . . . shall be poured out as the last libation as a tribute to the union of the States." Conjuring the third-century church father Tertullian, he threatened, "Let the opponents of this Government remember . . . that the blood of the martyrs is the seed of the Church."[12]

The speech, though praised by Secretary of State Seward, left many northerners shocked, including some of those evangelicals who shared his devotion to the Union and earlier had supported him. For example, one New Haven Methodist, after expressing appreciation for the Freedmen's Bureau Bill veto and telling Johnson that he loved, voted, and prayed for him, informed the president that the ensuing address "mortified" him and that probably "all your real friends feel mortified." George Prentiss, though explicitly distancing himself from radicals, said it pained him "exceedingly" to even discuss "the deplorable scene and speech." Six months later, with the benefit of more perspective, he said the speech marked "the final rupture" between Congress and the president. The Congregationalist *New Englander*, though also quick to disclaim radicalism, particularly regarding suffrage, described the speech as a "harangue to the Washington mob." Unlike at Lincoln's inauguration, Johnson likely was not drunk—though some suggested otherwise—and given very different circumstances than the previous year, many found it impossible to excuse the president. Johnson's conduct and his subsequent veto of the Civil Rights Bill set the tone for the next two years, and outrage from that moment forward formed the center of Congress's case for impeachment in 1868. The tenth article of impeachment would declare Johnson's behavior "peculiarly indecent and unbecoming" of the president; Johnson had brought the presidential office "into contempt, ridicule, and disgrace." The *New Englander* would refer to Johnson's "imbecility" and "gross party spirit" since 1866 as substantial grounds for supporting impeachment. In contrast to the optimism engendered through December 1865, his actions and words beginning in February 1866 indicated that the Union's much-hoped-for restoration had stalled. This proved particularly vexing to evangelicals looking ahead to a "new era" of oneness and prosperity under the leadership of Andrew Johnson.[13]

The Rupture Complete

George Prentiss admitted that Johnson's dispute with Congress surprised many northerners. Until the "Washington's Birthday Address," Prentiss said, "thousands of patriotic and thoughtful citizens" had upheld Johnson. In April Prentiss observed "that a very different feeling . . . is now pervading the minds of a vast majority of [Johnson's] countrymen, to whose favor and suffrage he owes his great office." A glorious and "honorable" outcome still awaited the country, but they would have to wait a while longer.[14] Perhaps previously eager evangelicals were embarrassed by their support of Johnson, for it was true that radicals had vocally criticized his amnesty policy and brought attention to unrepentant southern attitudes since the summer of 1865, and the simple fact that Jefferson Davis and other leaders had not been brought to justice raised the hackles of plenty.[15] Furthermore, northern media reported on horrific racial violence that occurred in parts of the South during 1865 and early 1866 and on the Black Codes, legislation passed by several southern states that blatantly discriminated against the ex-slaves and relegated them to society's margins as little more than agricultural laborers.[16] Hoping to explain Johnson's course and the public approval he received, Prentiss speculated that Lincoln's assassination had so "filled the public mind with religious thoughts, hushed the voice of faction, and knit all true hearts together in patriotic and awe-struck feeling," that most people hesitated to advise Johnson. Or, perhaps it was all providentially permitted "for the nation's good," though what that good might be, only time would tell. With a tone of tragic fatalism, Prentiss concluded, "We were ready to believe that he did so from deliberate conviction, and with the best motives." Nevertheless, Prentiss wondered if things could have turned out differently "had congress been in session," while lamenting that "the golden hour had passed." Indeed, in retrospect, the initial phase of Johnson's presidency now appeared as a squandered opportunity for the government to have dictated terms of settlement, terms that might have guaranteed protection and assistance for the ex-slaves, if not a firm and stable reunion with southern whites.[17] Hoping primarily for the latter, northerners received neither.

The important point here is that evangelicals were among those supporting Johnson. Besides Beecher and the encouragement of miscellaneous letter writers, Johnson knew that others, like his old friend Granville Moody, were in his corner. The non-Methodist Johnson attended a service at Washington's Foundry Methodist Church when Moody was a visiting preacher in January 1866, and he donated one thousand dollars to the church's building fund. Writing Johnson five days later, Moody said, "My daily prayer and the prayer of *Millions* is that you may be momentarily guided and guarded by Almighty God in the discharge of your great responsibilities at this great *crisis*!" Most likely, such words heartened Johnson while he sought to create a bipartisan coalition of northern and southern Unionists, a coalition that he confidently believed would position him to ignore both radical Republicans and unrepentant ex-rebels and then be elected president in 1868. His desire to forge a centrist alliance was clearly manifest by late-summer 1866, when Johnson supported a Unionist political convention meeting in Philadelphia just prior to his notorious "swing around the circle" that followed.[18]

By that point, however, many evangelicals had turned against him. As the *New Englander* portrayed events, Johnson's policy had turned out to be "simply a plan for *smuggling back* into the Union the late Confederate States." Moreover, his "improper rebukes of Congress . . . and his undignified abuse of 'the radicals,' have done great mischief at the South, by awakening the old defiant, insolent spirit which the events of the war had humbled and silenced, and which might have been exorcised forever." Irrespective of the accuracy of such an analysis, plenty were convinced that Johnson had mysteriously deceived and betrayed his Republican supporters and the country in his refusal to work with Congress. Prentiss implied this in quoting Matthew 18:7 (which Lincoln had also quoted in his second inaugural address in counseling leniency toward the South): "If it must needs be that offences come, woe to that man by whom the offense cometh!" Although Johnson's actual "motive and influences" were unclear, he was the culpable human agent, a tragic, Judas-like figure. Inexplicable and diabolical though the process might have been, Johnson's veto of the Freedmen's Bureau Bill, his "Washington's Birthday Address," his veto of Congress's Civil Rights Bill, and then his apparent cooperation with Democrats and ex-rebels during the summer all made the betrayal manifest. Johnson was now apostate, which was the real rub. The *New Englander* perceived the "swing around the circle" as the bald attempt "to break down the patriotic Republican party, and build up on its ruins a new party to be composed of the enemies of the country and its lukewarm friends—a party that would be sure to use all its power in undoing the great work of the last five years."[19]

Even Granville Moody paused upon hearing of Johnson's support for the August National Union convention in Philadelphia. Pleading with his "honored friend," Moody warned, "I am *amongst the people*, day by day. . . . And I know that if you identify yourself with *that party* you will be ruined!" He provided Johnson a host of reasons to stick by Republicans and work with Congress: Moody reminded Johnson of his earlier commitment to make treason odious; he implicitly invoked their friendship and common cause in defeating the rebellion; he appeared to promise on behalf of Ohio's congressmen that those men would work with Johnson; he appealed in pious evangelical terms that Johnson could yet receive great honor as God's agent in maintaining "the integrity of our glorious Country," indicating that Johnson's significance would surpass Andrew Jackson's or Abraham Lincoln's if he chose correctly; and above all, Moody used Christological language to suggest that Johnson could be "*the Mediator of the New Covenant founded on better promises*" between North and South. And if Johnson remained unpersuaded, perhaps an ominous allusion to Caesar would convince him: "My dear Sir, let me beg you to pause and think and Pray and decide to abide with the friends who elevated you to power with the assurance of your cooperation, in securing the Nationality of our land on a just—and lasting foundation. The eyes of Millions are upon you, and you must soon pass the Rubicon!"[20]

Despite Moody's pleading, Johnson crossed the Rubicon, and nonradical evangelicals would have even less difficulty siding with Congress after his late summer electioneering that found Democrats welcoming him in some of the cities on his trip through the Northeast and Midwest. And once again, Johnson could not resist the urge to respond to hecklers with intemperate extemporaneous remarks. In St. Louis on September 8, for instance, Johnson acknowledged that some regarded him as a Judas, but he asked, "If I have played the Judas, who has been my Christ that I have played the Judas with? Was it Thad. Stevens? Was it Wendell Phillips? Was it Charles Sumner?" The trip only worsened his relationship with former allies, and the *Independent*'s account of Johnson's "pilgrimage" provided a succinct summary of the perception that prevailed among many: "What an opportunity for a great career was offered to this man, before the nation suspected that he was a trickster!" Johnson could have "restored the Union in thirty days after Lee's surrender by simply dictating Impartial Justice." Instead, he chose "to reanimate the rebellion and to reimperil the country. Though he might have won a proud title as the uplifter of the lowly, he chose instead to remand the oppressed to be crushed by the oppressor." Johnson had gone over to the other side and had enabled defiant southerners, thus making it necessary to oppose him. The "swing around the circle," in Samuel Spear's view, reinforced the perception that had been growing since February. Johnson's speeches "were any thing but fitting in one who was the Chief Magistrate of a great nation. The vanity, weakness, indiscretion, and bad temper of the man, no one could fail to perceive."[21]

It is instructive to recall that evangelicals remained at home in a political tradition whose roots were identifiably Whig. The party itself was born in opposition to the perceived tyranny of Andrew Jackson, while they championed deference to Congress. Consequently, it only became easier to depart from the Jacksonian Johnson over the next two years. The *New Englander*, overlooking Lincoln's frequent independent actions and skipping right past Jackson, associated Johnson's actions with czarist Russia. Plainly, by summer 1866, it was up to "Congress to fix the terms and the manner of the restoration of the rebel States." Nonradicals had once again been compelled by circumstances to move closer to those such as abolitionist Oliver Johnson, who expressed the sentiment of many when he said the country would now be wise to permit Congress to "keep all the enemies of our national family out . . . until we can get to housekeeping on sound and correct principles, and then see what their temper is and whether we can let them come in and live with us safely."[22]

Defending Congress and its own move leftward, some moderates insisted that Reconstruction legislation during 1866 was not radical.[23] In particular, ensuring civil equality did not necessitate ensuring social or political equality. Daniel Whedon, editor of the *Methodist Quarterly Review*, supported the Civil Rights Bill, though he allowed for "social separateness," or the "spontaneous preference for [one's] own color." The *New Englander* also left the door open to social inequality, in addition to siding with Johnson and against radicals by arguing that suffrage was merely a political—and not a natural—right. However, the journal did argue that the federal government was obligated to protect the ex-slaves in their natural "civil rights," which were being abused and denied through the Black Codes, intimidation, and violence. Highly publicized race riots, one in Memphis in May and another in New Orleans in July—in which whites wantonly murdered and raped blacks, killed white Unionists, and destroyed black churches, homes, and schools, shocked northerners and led to a congressional investigation of the latter riot. Amid heightened dismay over Johnson, whom many Republicans held responsible for the violence, the country could afford to wait a little while longer "until the disaffected whites shall become reconciled to the new order of things, and learn to treat their former slaves as freemen."[24]

John L. Smith, a Methodist minister and federal tax collector from Stockwell, Indiana, revealed a familiar mix of personal, civic-religious, and political feelings in his about-face regarding Johnson. Smith began a letter of resignation by fondly recalling the "feelings of adoration" that had prevailed among "the American people" for Johnson. Particularly following the president's 1865 annual message, Smith said, "I regarded myself (however humble) as one of your friends and sincere supporters. I looked upon you as the visible head and standard bearer of the great Union party, which, under God, had so far saved the country from hopeless ruin." However, by August 1866, Smith saw Johnson turning his back on those "who elevated you" and then encouraging and enabling ex-rebels who "hate" the federal government. Finding inexcusable Johnson's response to the New Orleans riot, during which a Methodist friend of Smith's was murdered, Smith confessed, "I have lost all hope in the future of your administration."[25]

Johnson's actions, in conjunction with white southern behavior, had compelled moderate evangelicals to see the necessity of slowing restoration long enough to ensure adequate protection for the freedmen and the federal government's supremacy in a restored Union. Likening the South to a prodigal son in the "national family," Prentiss insisted on clearer indications of southern repentance than had been forthcoming. Ex-Confederates "would be welcomed back to the ancestral hearth-stone" when they came "with frank and manly acknowledgment of error . . . ; let them return to their Country—that benignant Parent who nourished and brought them up as children, and against whose august Majesty they lifted up their unfilial hands." If white southerners ever provided tangible evidence of contrition, he said, "the hardest 'Radicals,' even Mr. Sumner and Mr. Garrison, would not be a whit behind . . . Mr. Beecher, or the President himself, in willingness to forget the past and restore them to the full communion and enjoyment of the National life and patrimony." Prentiss insisted that his stance required no radical-like vindictiveness, "extreme measures," or "sweeping confiscation" of property.[26]

In practice, such moderation required southern states to ratify a proposed Fourteenth Amendment prior to readmission. Though having overturned Johnson's veto of the Civil Rights Bill, Congress sought firmer constitutional ground and a guarantee that southern states (or the Supreme Court) could not circumvent future federal legislation. As an election-year compromise, the amendment, which was sent to the states on June 13, would legally guarantee citizenship and equal protection, but it would not mandate suffrage; furthermore, although the amendment proscribed some ex-Confederate officials, repudiated Confederate war debt, and authorized Congress to enforce the amendment, nothing was forthcoming to satisfy radicals' desire for land redistribution. The amendment seemed to protect federalism sufficiently and promise Reconstruction's end; thus it received the support of all but the most radical Republicans. Johnson's attempt to marginalize radicals and enlist moderate support, then, had failed. Although Johnson campaigned against the amendment on behalf of Democratic congressional candidates during the fall elections and encouraged southerners not to ratify, many northerners supported the Republican Party and, in essence, the Fourteenth Amendment.[27]

Once again, however, Henry Ward Beecher supported Johnson, writing well-publicized letters defending the president's unabated desire to quickly restore southern congressional representation. "The first demand of our time," Beecher wrote to soldiers and sailors meeting in Cleveland on August 30, "is entire reunion." Reiterating themes he had championed since war's end, he insisted with Johnson that southerners must participate in a government whose actions touched them directly. Thus Beecher advocated restoration with no strings attached, insisting with Johnson that southern states could rightfully reject the amendment. Professing that he had no qualms with the amendment's details, Beecher still believed that the wisest, long-term tack with the South was "moral agitation" rather than legislative coercion. It was unjust to insist that southern states ratify an amendment (or submit to federal legislation) whose creation emerged from a national legislature lacking southern representation, a contention that formed the gist of Johnson's opposition to Congress. In addition, Beecher argued, speedy restoration would avoid the appearance, and perhaps reality, of a consolidated government that threatened America's federal tradition. Beecher also continued to argue that local control over labor and racial matters would induce self-interested whites to kindly treat the ex-slaves. Finally, Beecher suggested that it was primarily his Republican brethren, and not Andrew Johnson, who were acting out of partisan self-interest to keep the country divided.[28]

Beecher's remarks touched a raw nerve among some, including members of his congregation and family.[29] The *New Englander* regarded him as "sincere, noble, and courageous," but also as one "betrayed by his over trustful temperament and constitutional good-nature." Although the *Independent* continued to print his sermons, the paper likened him to Clement Vallandigham and said of Beecher, "Under the spell of an unhappy blindness . . . , he has done more injury to the

American Republic than . . . any other citizen except Andrew Johnson." Prentiss responded particularly to Beecher's claim that engaging in "moral agitation" was wiser than demanding ratification of the Fourteenth Amendment as a condition for readmission. Notably, however, Prentiss also engaged Beecher in an apparent contest over who most desired reunion: "We yield nothing to these eminent men [notably Beecher] in our desire for a speedy and complete restoration of the Union." In fact, Prentiss contended that his support of Congress best combined "wise and genuine conservatism" with "Christian mercy and magnanimity." Laboring to distance himself from both radical Republicans and Beecher, Prentiss remarked, "The loyal heart of the Nation is still disposed, as it has ever been, to the largest possible exercise of mercy and magnanimity towards those lately in arms against its life, that is consistent with the claims of public order, righteousness and good faith." The South, he believed, would shortly realize that nothing less than Lincoln's second inaugural address informed Congress's actions.[30]

Just as with the issue of emancipation as a war aim, the desire to establish conditions for restoration was reactive, or, as Samuel Spear put it, born of "the exigence of the times and [a concern] for the future of the nation."[31] Although Beecher had remained on the same trajectory since early 1865, others who supported the Fourteenth Amendment were being carried along by events just as they had been during the war and were possibly acting as a drag on Radical Reconstruction. Even if they envisioned a restored Union in which the Thirteenth Amendment would not be a dead letter, most were not principled advocates of blacks' full inclusion into the American body politic.

This interpretation meshes with that of George Cheever. Alongside other radicals, he opposed the Fourteenth Amendment because he believed that citizenship without suffrage was meaningless; white southerners would never willingly grant the ex-slaves anything more than nominal freedom, thus leaving African Americans at the mercy of their former masters. Consequently, Cheever mocked the pretensions of his country to the title of "Christian republic." Its refusal to grant suffrage was utter "wickedness," and, as always, Cheever could not comprehend fellow evangelicals' inability to see matters as he did. It was a plain matter of justice: African Americans merited suffrage as a reward for loyalty, but more important, it was a natural right—not simply a political right that "the white government may please to bestow upon them." It was nothing short of "robbery" for white citizens to retain suffrage for themselves while withholding it from blacks who would become citizens. Perhaps suffrage was not a necessity "in a monarchy, but it is in a republic." Without suffrage, "citizenship is legalized serfdom." Similar to his critique of Lincoln's preliminary Emancipation Proclamation, Cheever portrayed the amendment as a conciliating bribe to southern states to rejoin the Union in exchange for the ability to exclude the ex-slaves from full citizenship.[32]

Thus, unlike Beecher, who saw the amendment threatening federalism, Cheever and other radicals found the amendment preserving too much of it. Frederick Douglass's criticism is emblematic of what Beecher found disconcerting; the amendment was meaningless, Douglass insisted, "unless . . . the government is changed from a government by States to something like a despotic central government, with power to control even the municipal regulations of States, and to make them conform to its own despotic will." Knowing that no such change was immediately forthcoming and recognizing the widespread support for the amendment, he bemoaned, "There remains such an idea as the right of each State to control its own local affairs,—an idea, by the way, more deeply rooted in the minds of men of all sections of the country than perhaps any one other political idea." Undoubtedly this included many evangelicals, and the amendment was, in fact, a compromise respectful of federalism. Accordingly, Cheever viewed his fellow evangelicals as "dead asleep" when it came to racial justice.[33]

Insofar as it recognized the amendment's moderate nature, Cheever's analysis was on target. Prentiss touted the amendment "as an eminently wise, just, and magnanimous basis for the settlement of the questions arising out of the rebellion," embodying "national leniency and moderation, containing nothing vindictive, nothing harsh, even." The ex-Confederate states had their terms; they could be readmitted and the Union restored. "Where," he asked, "do the records of history afford another instance of a great and high-spirited nation dealing with a conquered rebellion, which had assailed and almost destroyed its life, on terms so considerate and merciful?" Admitting that he was unbothered by the lack of suffrage, Prentiss suggested that only radicals would complain of "its extreme mildness." He did not anticipate white southerners balking, and he believed that equal suffrage would naturally follow the amendment because it threatened to reduce a state's congressional representation in proportion to the population that was being denied suffrage. Most important, a return to normalcy was near. As so many evangelicals had been accustomed to doing, he proclaimed the reality of that which was so desired: A "new era" was dawning, when

> bitter memories . . . would gradually fade away, the antipathies and rivalries of North and South would cease, and the whole nation, revering the merciful hand of God in the past, even in the bloody conflicts of the battle-field, would march forward on the line of its great destiny with exultant hope, trusting still to the guidance of that merciful and almighty Hand.[34]

Despite such comforting rhetoric, reconciliation between North and South remained elusive. After Johnson's Tennessee ratified the amendment and reentered the Union in July 1866, the remaining Confederate states, urged on by Johnson, refused to ratify. Nonradical Republicans, against both their temperament and principles, would again be pulled leftward. Sensing that sectional reunion might not be at hand, Samuel Spear remarked in early 1867, "We have no spite to gratify against the Southern people; we do not wish to protract the ordeal of their sufferings, or unnecessarily delay their representation in Congress; yet we have no idea of submitting to their dictation in fixing the final terms of settlement." Spear then threatened the South: "The next trial, if there be one, will . . . be very much more radical." Though insisting that the North remained "magnanimous," suffrage would be imposed if southerners rejected the Fourteenth Amendment. With an apparent mandate from voters following congressional elections, Congress did take increasingly "radical" measures in 1867 to control Reconstruction, even while the aim was not fundamentally to reshape the South. Rather, the aim was to establish and then enforce conditions for readmission and southern self-government. Congress had taken the reins from Johnson, but moderate legislators were only slightly less impatient than the president in seeking the Union's restoration. Under its Reconstruction Acts Congress reorganized the ten remaining ex-Confederate states into five military districts, though leaving the provisional state governments intact. Congress also set terms for readmission and representation in Congress, which required that new state constitutional conventions (with full black participation) ratify the Fourteenth Amendment and permit universal adult male suffrage.[35] Despite Congress's halting and moderate course, Johnson and white southerners continued to defy and obstruct.

By 1867, with criticism of Johnson increasing and talk of impeachment emerging, evangelicals would close ranks. Unsurprisingly the A.M.E.'s *Christian Recorder* angrily thrashed Johnson—"a greater reprobate, and, consequently, more unworthy being, never filled the presidential chair"—and hinted that Johnson was plotting with the "Slave Power" to control the federal government. The *New Englander*, in the guise of theorizing about the executive's proper role in a republic, insultingly portrayed Johnson as a classical tyrant, but derived consolation from Aesop's fables—Johnson probably could not play the part well: "A weak, low minded braggart . . . will excite only ridicule and disgust. The crow could not carry off the sheep in imitation of the eagle, and the frog, which assumed to be an ox, only burst himself in the effort." George Cheever, however, feared such complacency. He was infuriated by Johnson's southern policy and thus accused congressional moderates of "treason" for their perceived lackadaisical response.

Democratic success in the 1867 fall congressional elections found Cheever speculating, however, that the results "may turn out to be the best possible thing through the mercy of Divine Providence. . . . Perhaps it is a permitted lure to draw our Pharaoh booted and spurred into the Red Sea, in which case nobody will be very sorry to see him drowned, along with boasted rebel chivalry." Although Johnson maintained a low profile into 1868, he was in fact lured out, as it were, and managed to unify most Republicans—which, of course, included many evangelicals—when he attempted to remove Secretary of War Stanton. The *Independent*, referring to Johnson as "the criminal in the White House," said his actions "have at last reached a point beyond which forbearance, even in the estimation of Conservative Republicans, ceases to be a virtue." Johnson's now former friend Granville Moody simply referred to him with a Republican commonplace, "his accidency." Although many knew that impeachment was as much about politics as it was principle, Cheever saw it as more than merely a human political struggle. In his view, the God of all nations was once again mercifully interposing to save the country.[36]

The hope that Reconstruction might end under Congress's wise direction fueled broad support for impeachment. Although the Senate failed to convict, much to Cheever's dismay—acquittal, he said, vindicated Johnson's policy, while revealing "hatred of the negro and a determination that this shall be a white man's government"—the president was effectively removed and Congress was undoubtedly controlling Reconstruction. Still, Cheever recognized Republicans' continuing moderation, insofar as they did not want the radical Senator Benjamin Wade (next in the line of succession) to take Johnson's spot. Most were content with a lame duck president, and for those who did not necessarily hate the "negro," but who had indeed desired Reconstruction to end, perhaps they would finally get their wish with a Grant presidency.[37]

An Evangelical President

Republicans met in Chicago on May 20 and 21, 1868, to nominate the taciturn Ulysses S. Grant for president. The two-day event found evangelicals euphoric at the prospect of the Union hero occupying the White House. "No man since Washington has been nominated . . . by such universal acclaim," the *Zion's Herald* reported. It would have been tough to miss evangelicals' sanctifying presence at the convention, with the Methodist bishop Matthew Simpson delivering the opening prayer and then leading all in a recitation of the Lord's Prayer following the nomination. Conflating religion, party, and country, the *Zion's Herald* concluded, "The Ruler of nations will we trust bless and prosper this choice of the nation."[38]

Regardless of the Democratic candidate opposing Grant, the Republicans were, in effect, running against Johnson and seeking to capitalize on strong public opinion against him. The Republican platform expressed "regret" over his presidency and declared that he had acted "treacherously to the people who elected him and the cause he was pledged to support," and Grant's acceptance speech emphasized that the executive is bound "to execute the will of the people," which, "I always have respected . . . and always shall."[39] Echoing such language that drew a clear contrast with Johnson, evangelicals, like many others, foresaw Grant restoring the presidential office's proper function and dignity: He would be "an Executive whose highest duty and pride it will be, to learn and respect the will of the people, and an Administration whose chief honor it will be to make the Republic an honor at home and respected abroad."[40] Respecting the will of the people meant, negatively, that he was not an ambitious office seeker in the mold of a Johnsonian tyrant, while positively it meant that he would be particularly cognizant of that will as expressed through the people's congressional representatives. Reconstruction had become a problem that called for an apparently apolitical candidate like Grant, even if he was not quite the political innocent he presented himself as being, and he closed his acceptance letter with the unassuming phrase, "Let us have peace." As one historian has said, those words expressed "the innermost desires of many Americans" and would become "an ideal campaign slogan."[41]

Within the immediate context of Johnson's presidency, then, Grant could not have been better situated to receive a wide swath of evangelical support. The war's end "ought to have been the end of all anxiety," but instead protracted squabbling over Reconstruction had heightened the perception that the Christian country's very existence was again threatened. Evangelicals seemed ready-made for what Granville Moody called "the grand crisis," and, insisting that "the Lord is on our side," they eagerly supported Grant.[42] He was the man for the hour, perhaps even more than Lincoln had been for his. The former soldier Grant, it appeared, was a more fitting Joshua than the former tailor Andrew Johnson possibly could have been; Grant was the one finally to lead the country into the promised land of a harmoniously restored Union. The Methodist editor Daniel Curry proclaimed that the "Divine Hand" of God was "leading us now" through the unexpected crisis that Reconstruction had become. "Our Moses," Curry said in reference to Lincoln, "who under God had brought us through the wilderness of rebellion and intestine war, fell just as the nation was passing its Jordan; but our Joshua lives, and through him, we trust, our God will soon give rest to his people." It was as though Johnson's presidency had never been.[43] A Grant presidency portended sectional peace, but that peace relied on peace between Congress and the executive and likely deference by the latter to the former. As one evangelical publication said, "With General Grant we longingly desire peace. And because we desire it we are tenacious of the conditions essential to peace. Among these at this moment must be included and made prominent the letting alone, to work out its completed course, the Congressional scheme of Reconstruction." Grant unified the Republican Party and left evangelicals optimistic about the prospects of achieving national Christian oneness in a Union once and for all restored.[44]

Support for Grant should be understood also within the larger context of a nineteenth-century antiparty tradition, habitually cherished by evangelicals, which called for a reluctant, humble, and nonpartisan servant of the Christian republic. Late in 1867, the *New Englander* implicitly denounced Johnson in describing a virtuous executive, thereby helping to pave the way for a candidate like Grant: "An honest man of sound sense, and firm resolution to do his simple duty plainly and well, makes a far safer chief magistrate than a talented, ambitious party chief, who will be tempted to use his high position for the aggrandizement of himself, his party, or even of the presidential office." Washington and Lincoln fit that bill, and now Grant would be included on a short list of great, seemingly apolitical republicans. The Pennsylvania coal dealer J. B. Corey, responding to Grant's acceptance speech in "the strong bond of Christian love," praised the candidate precisely because he was not a politician and then warned Grant about the dangerous world awaiting him. Because Grant was one of the people and "the People's Choice," he must "beware the detested Politician" while seeking the presidency. Grant, an ostensible outsider, was an ideal American citizen on this view. Though not really leaving the plow like Cincinnatus had done—Grant had failed at farming after all and was more politically savvy than his constituency might have liked to believe—he was coming to the rescue once again. He had saved the Union the first time, one Methodist said, by being "incapable of any thought save for the good of the country," and if he could avoid the corrupting influences of the capital, he would save it a second time as president.[45]

Evangelicals were among those who accepted and promoted an image of Grant as the truest embodiment of the Union's republican ideals and possibilities. This was despite the fact that Johnson, the self-educated tailor from the mountains of East Tennessee, arguably embodied them as much or more than the West Point–educated Grant. Regardless, numerous campaign biographies and newspaper articles publicized Grant's inspiring story of humble beginnings, financial struggles, and various failures prior to his heroic emergence during the war. "Less than ten years ago the people of America had never heard of Ulysses S. Grant. He was poor, he was disappointed. He had neither social position nor political influence," the *Independent* said of the "certain-to-be President of the United States." Referring to Grant's antebellum residence in the lead-mining community of Galena, Illinois, Gilbert Haven fondly praised him as "the humble merchant of a country town."[46]

That image meant a great deal to evangelicals, who readily integrated free labor and republican ideals into their Christian American dream, and when they looked at Grant, they also saw a religious image of themselves. This would only increase during the White House years. Despite scant evidence of substantial belief, alongside persistent, unsettling rumors that called some aspects of his behavior and character into question, Grant was apparently evangelical enough. Like Lincoln, he regularly attended church services—in his case Methodist rather than Presbyterian—his parents were devoted Methodists, and the piety of his wife, Julia Dent, was unquestioned and widely known. Furthermore, throughout his presidency Grant publicly recognized America as a Protestant republic, gave clear preference to Methodists for patronage appointments, and his connections with the prominent Methodist ministers John P. Newman and Matthew Simpson were well known.[47] Finally, as will be explored in the next chapter, his rhetoric and policies regarding Native Americans and Roman Catholics did nothing but affirm his evangelical credentials.

Given Grant's ostensible faith, and faced with another crisis of the Union, questions regarding his character would not deter evangelicals from supporting him. Rumors existed that Grant had fathered children with an Indian woman when he was an antebellum soldier, and the image of him as a simpleton who wanted nothing more than to smoke and drink circulated widely. Though such a perception of Grant never disappeared entirely, it was not going to derail his candidacy, since the stories on which it was based related to long-past events or had originated within the context of his very successful generalship in defense of the Union. Moreover, apologists could make counterassertions and marshal evidence of upright behavior, knowing there was no unambiguous way of settling most matters. For example, an anonymous woman, reporting for the *Independent* following Grant's seemingly honorable behavior during the dispute with Johnson over the office of secretary of war, passed along her impressions of the general while she attended a reception at Grant's home in Washington. She conjured an image of Grant in republican simplicity greeting the crowd, while reassuringly testifying that "no fumes of wine or tobacco" were detectable. Such anecdotes likely dispelled the rumors sufficiently among those who already had deep affection for the man who had saved the Union.[48]

Moreover, the rumors were crowded out by more pressing concerns rooted in evangelicals' deeply entrenched regard for America as a Christian republic that always stood in particular need of faithful evangelical care and direction. One New York lawyer confidently envisioned Grant as the nation's proper covenant leader, one who would turn "the people's thoughts to their relations of dependence, for their welfare, upon God" more adequately than Andrew Johnson apparently ever had done. National dependence on God "is a grand historic fact," the man informed Grant; any nation ignored this to its peril, and following the Johnson interregnum, the lawyer hoped that Grant would resume a Lincolnian deference to providence. "The frankness and constancy with which Mr. Lincoln acknowledged this fact, was one of his elements of strength. We [the Republican Party] are, and have been called, a party of moral ideas, and while we maintain them, they will maintain us." Following the election, another evangelical, John McClean, informed Grant that God had chosen him to be president specifically because of his faith and its importance for the republic. "At the head of a civil government which embraces forty millions of people," McClean advised, "your influence and responsibility will be measureless. *In such a position a thoroughgoing Christian is a mighty power.*" Optimistically, and in a characteristically evangelical way, he believed that the "Christian" Grant, in leading the nation out of the problem that was Reconstruction and into "genuine peace," would also influence increasing numbers of Americans to become evangelicals themselves. Though not alone sufficient to achieve the republic's proper Christianization, transformed individuals were a necessary aspect of that process. With a similar goal in mind, a group of Methodist bishops, most notably including Matthew Simpson and Edward Ames, informed Grant of the executive's powerful ability to influence the nation to "steadily rise to [a] higher, nobler, more Christian civilization."[49] Northern evangelicals had high hopes for their Christianized Cincinnatus.

In addition to Grant's positive appeal as a Christian republican, and regardless of evangelicals' antiparty disposition, he was a Republican Party candidate running against a Democratic Party that could not have chosen a worse candidate than they had in former New York governor Horatio Seymour. With no evangelical credentials to boast of, most opponents remembered him as the Copperhead coddler of New York's 1863 draft rioters, and his candidacy guaranteed unity among Republican factions, while solidifying, if not increasing, evangelical allegiance to the party.[50] For instance, George Cheever, referring to Grant as "the salvation of the country," returned to the fold after not voting in 1864, and Grant's apparent evangelical faith, combined with Cheever's heightened disdain for the Democratic Party—a party where "all the wickedness of this modern age seems concentrated"—evidently sufficed for him to support Grant in a way he never had Lincoln.[51] In comparison to 1864, the overall enthusiasm was palpable. To most, Seymour simply appeared to be more clearly traitorous than McClellan; the election thus found evangelicals waving the "bloody shirt" with the best of northerners, ready to portray Democrats, in the words of Drew Theological Seminary professor Bernard Nadal, as "enemies of the country."[52] Furthermore, perhaps because of unrealistic expectations about a speedy restoration of the Union in the first place, the noncontroversial Grant promised relief from Johnson and the wearisome struggle over Reconstruction, thus producing a more acute feeling of the election's importance. And finally, there was no substantial history of tension between radicals and Grant. This was partly because Grant's public record regarding slavery-related issues was meager when compared to that of Lincoln. The upshot found Horatio Seymour serving as the catalyst for Republican unity. "Let there be in 1868," the *Independent* beckoned, "as there was in 1861, an uprising of the loyal masses . . . , who, with patriotic forgetfulness of past differences, shall reunite their forces for the suppression of a rebellion which was supposed to be crushed at Appomattox Court House, but which has broken out anew at Tammany Hall." Seymour was one "who made patriots his enemies and rioters his friends," and aside from Clement Vallandigham, "no Democrat in the North is more cordially hated by Republicans." Horatio Seymour had entered the divine drama as the latest threat to the Christian republic.[53]

Evangelicals were habituated to think that way. Their proprietary and covenantal regard for the historic Union had long overlapped with traditional republicanism to provide a potent and deeply ingrained "paranoid style," a predisposition that found their country constantly threatened by malevolent forces and groups. It was a stance whose vitality almost depended on the periodic appearance of crises and God's meeting those crises. John Delany, a private citizen from Detroit, revealed the persistent, conspiratorial fears when he warned Grant of a dangerous threat from the "Slave Power." That still-powerful minority of southern rebels and northern sympathizers, Delany said, "does not intend that the general [to] whose loyal blows it was forced to yield—shall ever occupy the Executive Chair." Referring to Grant's acceptance speech, Delany urged him to realize that "a nation's hope of liberty—order and 'Peace' with consequent prosperity is to-day centered in you." Delany also urged Grant in covenantal terms to realize that "only in the keeping of the Lord who holds the destinies of Nations in

His hands is your life safe." And when Grant realized this, the Christian republic would be safe.[54]

But he had to win the election, and, to that end, Granville Moody portrayed the Republican Party as running against Andrew Johnson, Horatio Seymour, ex-Confederates, and a sordid history of Democratic treason all rolled into one. Moody transformed and appropriated those Democrats who remained acceptably American, such as Andrew Jackson and Stephen Douglas, for a sort of nonpartisan, consensus history that necessarily excluded many contemporary Democrats. One wonders if there were any good Democrats left in 1868, as Moody reminded voters that "this party has produced all the State sovereignty, nullification conspiracy and civil war, and furnished all the traitors in the United States." Democrats, he continued, were the ones who "fought in six hundred battles in the South for the purpose of destroying our Government, whilst the same party rendered aid and comfort to their cause in the North." Finally, it was northern Democrats who "steadily opposed the war, resisted the draft, denounced President Lincoln for keeping his heaven-recorded oath, and did all they could to embarrass him in the discharge of his bounden duties." In Moody's rhetoric, which other Republicans echoed, to side with Seymour in 1868 was to side with a party that had announced the war a "failure" back in 1864, and, were he to be elected, the country would be asked to surrender once again to the South. "By the God of our fathers, this shame we won't share," Moody pronounced.[55] Grant did win, of course, as his candidacy and the Democratic threat caused Republican infighting to subside.

Gilbert Haven responded ecstatically by narrating the superintending hand of God on behalf of African Americans and the nation. In 1860, the election of the first Republican president halted slavery's extension; in 1864, Lincoln's reelection vindicated emancipation as a war aim; and now, in 1868, Grant's election intended "Peace and Equal Rights." Just four years before, who could have imagined that "this campaign would have turned on the political amalgamation of blacks and whites. But God pushes us forward faster than we wish to go." In a sense, Haven was right, for ex-slaves in several southern states voted for Grant, and many nonradicals would have agreed that God had been moving reluctant northerners along for some time. Such providential motion, Haven continued, would also produce widespread approval of Grant, North and South, which would then give way to sectional and racial peace. As a divine instrument, Grant was no Andrew Johnson; white southerners would submit to Grant, just as they had at Fort Donelson, Shiloh, Vicksburg, Chattanooga, the Wilderness, and

Richmond. Under President Grant a free-labor and racially harmonious Union would emerge, when "complexion shall not imperil life, but shall be a bond of mutual affection." In other words, Grant would usher the ex-slaves—and all African Americans—into a fuller and more equal place in America. This would finally include universal suffrage for men, which, a few months later, Congress did seek to guarantee through its proposed Fifteenth Amendment prohibiting states from denying suffrage based on race or former slave status. Above all, Haven's civic-nationalist vision forecast increased social equality and amalgamation—bringing an end to what he called "the Satanism of caste," which "makes us [whites] look on our [black] brother with loathing" and "separate him from ourselves as an abhorred thing. [Satan] makes us exclude [blacks] from our table, our pulpit, our pew, our shop, our store, our homes, our hearts." The day was fast approaching, Haven proclaimed, "when the white-hued husband shall boast of the dusky beauty of his wife, and the Caucasian wife shall admire the sun-kissed countenance of her husband." In a repetition of his exuberant reaction to the election of 1864, Haven's civic-nationalist, amalgamationist hope had gotten the better of him.[56]

Perhaps tellingly, some abolitionists greeted Grant's victory differently. Most prominently, Wendell Phillips—who never forgot Grant's prewar Democratic affiliation or his participation in Johnson's "swing around the circle," had harped on Grant's conservatism since 1866, and had opposed his nomination—thus responded to the election results with sarcasm. Phillips was unconvinced that the election of Grant meant anything close to what Haven was imagining. The *Independent*, striving to remain positive, nevertheless discerned the meaning of Grant's election as a "demand for Union and Peace" rather than "a demand for Justice and Equality." The paper expressed cautious optimism that Grant would prove as "teachable" as he appeared to be. "Patriots believe that the nation is saved," a Washington correspondent said. "Let us trust that two years hence our present hopes will be justified." Possibly pleading too much, the writer continued, "I confess that I have full confidence in Gen. Grant's principles. He is not going to play Andrew Johnson over again. It is sufficient to restate the well-known fact that he was in favor of the impeachment." Following such faint praise, the writer said further, "He is more like Lincoln than Sumner; but [he] is a genuine Republican, in spite of his constitutional tendencies to conservatism."[57] Such an analysis was close to the mark, for Grant was temperamentally conservative and would prove to be politically moderate.

As had been the case during the war, racial justice still followed in the wake of the Union's preeminence. Thus any perceived gains in that regard resulted as much from partisan expediency and fear for the Union's survival as from principle. Furthermore, it is clear that African American ex-slaves remained a problem to some simply by their presence. In late 1867 Henry Boardman had predicted a relapse into "barbarism" by them if white Americans did not respond prudently to the southern situation. Believing that both philanthropy and government legislation had proven inadequate, his new suggestion was to channel northern assistance directly to southern churches, whose task would be to care for and educate the ex-slaves. The threat of their "barbarism" and perceived lack of fitness for republican citizenship made reunion all the more necessary. The sooner whites North and South reestablished genuine national oneness, the sooner and more capably they could jointly solve the problem of four million ex-slaves that providence had presented. In 1868, the Methodist Daniel Curry referred to "the American negro" as "the disturbing ingredient in modern civilization" and, without predicting the future of American race relations, ominously announced, "Our nation is in the midst of an experiment of the most stupendous import, involving our exaltation or our overthrow." Sounding the death knell on any remaining sympathy for colonization, he continued, "It is quite certain that the colored element cannot be eliminated from our population. . . . The nation must prosper or perish with them." Curry looked vaguely but promisingly to Grant's presidency in the hope that it might somehow contain within it a solution to America's "negro problem."[58]

A Christianized Union

With the reflections of Boardman and Curry in mind, not only does a Haven-like interpretation of the election in civic-nationalist terms appear dubious, evidence suggests that it was far from representative of majority opinion at the time. Haven recognized that "the whole nation sighs for Peace," but the crucial question for him was whether or not the whole nation additionally "demands righteousness" for the black man. Just as during the war, when events pushed northern white evangelicals in a direction that they had not intended to go, Andrew Johnson's stunning behavior and white southern intransigence had slowed their ardor for restoration long enough for them to accept the Fourteenth Amendment and soon the Fifteenth Amendment. Such leftward movement was true of Republicans in general, of course, and for many evangelical Republicans, any interest in securing racial justice continued to be encompassed within the larger goal of securing a vital and stable Christianized Union. In the case of the San Francisco Presbyterian Charles Wadsworth, issues associated with Reconstruction did not even register with him in late 1868. Following Grant's election, he said, "I cannot see any great questions at issue in present political controversies." Moreover, he suggested that things could not have been much better than they presently were:

> And thus, to a truly Christian faith, our nationality rises to-day—a consolidated commonwealth, stretching from ocean to ocean athwart this broad continent; a nation of freemen, self-governed, governed by simple law, without police or soldiery—a nation . . . covering the land with great cities, and the sea with great fleets; first in arts and learning, and every true product of genius.[59]

With the ascension of Grant to the presidency, perhaps the period of postwar readjustment finally was over.

Whether a Joshua or a Cincinnatus, the war's one clear-cut military hero left many northerners relieved and grateful for God's manifest hand in America's exceptional history. It seemed obvious that providence had brought Grant east from humble obscurity to save the Union from the threatening George McClellan back in 1864 and had now, in 1868, brought Grant to Washington, D.C., in order to save the nation from the threatening Andrew Johnson and Horatio Seymour. In looking ahead, George Peck's brother Jesse again invoked the great Whig Daniel Webster. "We now know for ourselves," he said, "and the world understands, that, like 'liberty and union,' our great States are 'one and inseparable now and forever.'" A restored Union "aggregates our strength, bringing all our millions of people and wealth into one grand whole." This was no mere accident of history; the emergence of American wholeness was itself evidence of God's sanctifying activity on behalf of the American republic. "It is a unity . . . by the clearly expressed will of God, an organic, indissoluble unity." Jesse Peck, like so many others, had fused a Websterian Unionism with evangelical assumptions about America. "[The nation] has been 'tried, and comes forth as gold.' Now we love, not one town or one State merely, not the North or the South alone; but we love our whole country. . . . Every inch of this vast country is now sacred soil, —sacred to liberty and to God."[60]

6 *Pax Grantis*

The Great Protestant Republic

> I ask patient forbearance one towards another throughout the land, and a determined effort on the part of every citizen to do his share towards cementing a happy union, and I ask the prayers of the nation to Almighty God in behalf of this consummation.
>
> —Ulysses S. Grant, Inaugural Address, March 4, 1869

Jesse Peck finished his *History of the Great Republic, from a Christian Stand-Point* in time for the election of 1868, and he issued a second edition in time for the 1876 centennial. Describing the book as his life's "most important" endeavor, it began with the Puritans and culminated in the Union's preservation, slavery's end, and Grant's presidency. The book served as a covenant reminder, aiming to precipitate "devout recognition of God in the character, purposes, and history of this country" and thereby strengthen Americans' "loyalty" to God.[1] Though Peck believed that evidence of God's hand in American history abounded, northern evangelicals were particularly responsible to lead others in rightly understanding and acting within the unfolding drama.[2] In so doing, a homogeneous Christian American people would emerge more fully and securely during Grant's presidency.[3]

Although it is reasonable to contextualize the Christian American dream within the broader nineteenth-century phenomenon of romantic nationalism, stopping there overlooks the continuing importance of the Union ideal and its relevance to Reconstruction. Northern evangelicals were preoccupied during Grant's presidency with managing various cultural, social, and political forces centrifugally threatening the Union, and thus their romantic yearning for its affective oneness continued to subsume the ex-slaves.[4] This will become evident in several ways: First, many looked to the cohesive, homogenizing power that evangelicalism promised to provide for the large and growing republic; second, convinced that they had one of their own in the White House, evangelicals supported the nominally Methodist Grant during the 1872 election against the threat offered by the collection of disaffected Republicans, Democrats, and ex-rebels;

and third, they regarded Grant as an ally when it came to addressing the potential threat offered by Native Americans and Roman Catholics. By the end of Grant's presidency, the Union appeared restored; the nation had just celebrated its centennial; prosperity and oneness seemed to abound; and Americans felt generally at peace.

Civic-Religious Cohesion

Having survived the dissolution of "our own people," Americans would disregard God's historical superintendence at their peril, according to Jesse Peck. "We certainly cannot exist as a nation of atheists," he said, which functionally they would become if such disregard occurred. More specifically, this was a Christian nation, not "a Pagan or Mahometan" nation, and for those with eyes to see, the evidence was on full display in Peck's narrative.[5] One reviewer lauded it as the first American history modeled on the Bible, and as Jonathan Townley Crane, Stephen Crane's father and George Peck's son-in-law, approvingly said, Jesse Peck "sees the divine hand everywhere." Because people overlook, forget, or take for granted that hand, Peck's book should be read repeatedly by every "Christian patriot."[6] Analogous to Old Testament imperatives urging ancient Israel to remember its redemptive narrative, another Methodist implored, "Let us draw correct pictures of the past, that our children with us may recognize the goodness and wisdom of God." Accurately perceiving American history then obligated people to further Christianize the Union.[7]

That obligation also flowed from the continuing assumption that nations, unlike individuals, would not answer to God on Judgment Day. Instead, as one writer said, "The aggregated moral virtue or vice, truth or error . . . must be judged and rewarded or punished in this life only." Evangelicals thus remained preoccupied with collective behavior. When the Methodist Augusta Moore surveyed things in early 1869, she dejectedly asked, "Are we [even] a Christian nation?" Given their heritage they were supposed to be, and so she urged, let no one rest "until this our dear, troubled native land becomes [one]." Media reports of government corruption, however, meant that rest would not come easily. "Personal regeneration," Jesse Peck insisted, "must extend until political corruption shall become improbable, unpopular, impossible; until the only way to preferment shall be that of Christian patriotism, and an honest, broad, and noble philanthropy." Christian love must "permeate the nation, inspiring and exalting rulers, lifting up the poor and distressed, vitalizing all legislation and administration of law." Then "we are safe," he said in covenantal terms; there could be "absolute security" for "a nation ruled by a high and all-pervading sense of God—God everywhere; God in every thing, infusing life into the public organism, health and vigor into the nation's patriotism; giving intelligence, breadth, and efficiency to the nation's philanthropy."[8]

For some, this impulse meant combining evangelical piety with governmental power to battle alcohol production and usage. Speaking to the issue, the radical *Zion's Herald* provided a revealing glimpse of the transition away from federal Reconstruction. The "fires" of slavery were nearly out, but "this fire subsiding, only reveals another. . . . Hercules' work is that of every man and every age. One hydra-head smitten, another must be struck. Intemperance covers the land broader and deeper than slavery has done." In fact, "the whole nation is mad for rum. German, Irish, American, west, east and south, black and white, one wild demon possesses the land." A Union bound together by pervasive alcohol usage parodied a true, affective Union and even threatened its destruction. The temperance cause was in part, then, a Union-saving cause. Just as alcohol usage made Irish or German Catholics appear suspect to "American" evangelicals, it now threatened to envelop others.[9]

Evangelicals continued to believe, perhaps more intensely than others, that republics were inherently fragile. Although it remained a commonplace that republics were uniquely dependent on citizens' intelligent virtue, with virtue still carrying classical connotations of self-denial and a concern for the common good, just what contributed to or detracted from the common good was arguably broader for evangelicals. That is, although self-interested or self-indulgent behavior threatened the republic's continuance by breeding corruption or ripening it for tyranny, such behavior also invited God's judgment. Consequently, abstaining from alcohol and supporting its legal proscription were needful on both republican and covenantal grounds. Personal behavior always carried potential national ramifications.[10] Samuel Spear expressed this in early 1868 when he said, "Evils existing in the usages and habits of society that are detrimental to the interests of the body politic may and should be placed under legal restraint." Of course, in a democratized republic, where government "must follow the decrees of [public] sentiment," citizens must be properly molded. Though Spear's view seemingly stemmed from nonpartisan civic virtue, only one of the parties vying for citizens' allegiance threatened the republic. It was "the *Rum* party," he said, and that party, "though Democratic in name, is [also] the pro-slavery party of the country," a party selfishly continuing to seek its own welfare rather than the nation's.[11]

Evangelicals' desire to police the Union's political and moral culture brings to mind earlier discussions in American history. First, it evokes John Winthrop's

Massachusetts Bay and the problem of dissent. Like Winthrop's Puritans, Grant-era evangelicals aimed to produce a biblical commonwealth and therefore insisted on establishing uniform parameters within which Americans might act. But post–Civil War America dwarfed Winthrop's colony in size, and the eighteenth-century French political philosopher Montesquieu's axiom that only geographically small republics were viable remained a commonplace among evangelicals; large republics, the Methodist editor Daniel Whedon reiterated, tended "toward disintegration" due to the diversity of self-seeking "interests, tastes, and feelings." Though James Madison had argued that more variety diminished the likelihood of any particular faction dominating the whole, northern evangelicals remained uncomfortable with the proliferation of so-called factions, seeing them as potential sources of dissolution. Secession, civil war, and immigration seemingly necessitated a non-Madisonian solution: Namely, give "every citizen the same opinions, the same passions, and the same interests."[12]

Northern evangelicals wanted it both ways, since they desired a republic that was both homogeneous and large. Alongside President Grant, who announced in his first inaugural address, "It looks as if providence had bestowed upon us . . . the precious metals locked up in the sterile mountains of the far West," evangelicals envisioned a materially prosperous republic spanning the continent. Westward settlement remained America's manifest destiny, and the Congregationalist Joseph Thompson approvingly predicted that "the whoop of the savage" would increasingly give way "to the whistle of steam." In fact, the railroads binding the Union together served as further praiseworthy evidence of God's providential design. The Methodist bishop Matthew Simpson repeated Henry Clay's catchphrase while touring the Southwest: "The times indicate that we are soon to have 'no North, no South, no East, no West,' but one great nationality, its citizens in all part[s] commingling freely together, and by its growing internal commerce furnishing to every place the immense variety of its products." Just prior to Grant's inauguration, Simpson proclaimed, in fitting southwestern imagery, "That struggle through which we have passed was the darkness of the night, but the light is now breaking upon the mountain tops."[13]

Beneath the optimism, however, the Union's disparate elements were disconcerting. What kind of people would inhabit the expanding republic? Could the country remain coherently animated by Protestant evangelicalism?[14] Following Grant's election, Gilbert Haven's newspaper scolded "the Jews of Pennsylvania" for their "indignant" reaction to a Thanksgiving proclamation that had advised citizens "to pray 'that our paths through life may be directed by the example and instructions of the Redeemer, who died that we might enjoy the blessings which temporarily flow therefrom, and eternal life in the world to come.'" Implicitly questioning Jewish presence in America, the paper sarcastically remarked, "So incensed were they that they refused to shut up shop and eat turkey, a truly Jewish way of exhibiting rage, as it made them save a penny and gain one at the same time." Most infuriating, however, was the Philadelphia press's apparent approval of their response; Haven's paper rhetorically asked, "Are we a Christian or a Pantheistic nation?"[15] Farther west was the more troubling threat of Mormonism. "Utterly subversive of our Christian faith," the Presbyterian New York *Evangelist* pronounced in January 1870, Mormonism existed as "a separate and defiant political power," a "pestilent disease upon the vitals of the nation" because of polygamy. Equating the practice with adultery and assuming its intuitive wrongness, the paper urged Congress to regulate marriage. Polygamy cannot be the "cornerstone of one State in our Union" while being "a crime in every other," since the issue "concerns the entire moral welfare of the American people." In August Grant's pastor, John P. Newman, debated Mormon leader Orson Pratt in Salt Lake City over polygamy, and Grant later equated Mormonism with barbarism. The Presbyterian John Mears included Mormons among a large and "audacious anti-Protestant element" threatening the Union. Although Mormons, among others, were demanding "fuller recognition," Mears simply declared that because America was a Protestant nation, in its origins and by majority, evangelicals were not obligated to tolerate such groups.[16]

Evangelicals' long-standing desire to minimize or manage cultural and political differences intensified during Grant's presidency. Echoing others, and with ancient Rome in mind, the Methodist Dexter Hawkins ominously lectured, "History teaches that no nation, spread over a wide territory and composed of heterogeneous and discordant elements, can long preserve its integrity." With a sense of covenantal obligation to God, while haunted by historical republican failures, evangelicals rejected Madison's large republic of competing factions. Arguably, evangelicals' republican insecurity was more acute than that of others, since God's chastisement—or worse, judgment—always loomed. Their outlook insisted on a modicum of order, outward conformity to their moral assumptions, and apparent regard for the common good. George Cheever was typical in this regard, though his residence in New York City, the belly of the northern Democratic beast, probably exacerbated his fear of impending judgment. He was perpetually uncomfortable in both a city and a nation he loved, where circumstances and people were supposed to be other than they were.[17]

In the face of increasing ethnocultural pluralism, Cheever's fellow New Yorker Joseph Thompson wondered if America was destined to fail. "The Parthenon stands, . . . but there is no Greece," and "the Coliseum oppresses one with the vastness of a Rome that has ceased to be." The ancients had failed to ensure that a unified people could persist under one government, and, unlike some fellow evangelicals, he wondered whether modernization would help or hinder Americans' efforts to avoid repeating the failure. Through science and technology, Thompson said, modern human beings have "gained new control over material forces," but "can [they] at last build . . . a Nation that will endure?" With a mix of wariness and hope, Thompson reminded his audience that "confederation and nationality are irreconcilable terms." The ancient Greeks had "race, language, love of country, and similarity of institutions to identify them as one people," yet they "failed of becoming a nation" because of "the chronic jealousies and strifes" of various "tribes" within. "A nation," he continued with Lockean contract theory and southern secessionists in mind, "is not framed by statute or compact, but is properly an organism" having a collective life and will. In other words, a nation is not a swirl of competing individuals or groups, whether those groups were sectional or ethnocultural. Citing Lincoln's first inaugural address, Thompson reasserted that Americans had become "one people" prior to the Constitution. Nations were characterized by oneness.[18]

Others repeated Unionist arguments and advocated measures to ensure proper Christian American and republican formation. For example, in 1871 the Presbyterian E. P. Ree argued for a genuinely national military academy. Unlike what happened during the Civil War, when southern West Pointers followed their states out of the Union, an improved academy would produce officers "educated by the whole country, and upon their maps State boundaries should be blotted out." With a similar emphasis, the Congregationalist Sandford Cobb reasserted that "the Constitution is not an agreement, but a supreme law; that the Government is not a League, but a Power, and that the people are ONE PEOPLE." To Cobb, woeful constitutional ignorance permitted the "heresy" of states' rights to fester for decades, ultimately requiring "Sumter to convince multitudes of our people that the Federal Government was a *National* institution; that revolt even of a State must be stamped out under the foot of battle; and that constitutional law held within its clauses the elements of a supreme and irresistible authority and power." And to buttress proper constitutional thinking, repetitive recitation of what God had done historically to fashion one whole Christian and republican people was crucial.[19]

This was a practical and pious necessity in the making of Americans. Joseph Thompson, echoing Edmund Burke's notion of an implicit bond with one's forebears, insisted that Americans were obligated to actively remember the nation's revolutionary founders. "We strike hands across the century with the men of '76," he said, "feeling that our cause is theirs, and that the heroic past is part of our daily life. This organic identity should be cherished in perpetual growth." Reverent remembering—a sort of civic-religious liturgy involving recapitulation of American history through common, embodied practices regulated by the intentional use of space and time—promised to forge affective national oneness. As Thompson said:

> By histories, by orations, and by monuments, by sacred graves worthy of national pilgrimages, by memorial parks and statues, by storied pictures in public halls, by legends and mottoes, by commemorative services and martyr-days, and, above all, by a festival of the REDEMPTION OF LIBERTY, a day of flags and flowers, a day of prayers and thanksgivings, a day of requiem for our heroes—when all that music and ritual and eloquence can provide, shall celebrate the worth and glory of their sacrifice—by such pain-staking [*sic*] regard for the past, wrought into the habits of the people, let us keep ever bright the links of historic continuity that preserve the nation through all changes and all ages, ONE.

It is striking that evangelicals like Thompson, at home within a Protestant tradition that aimed to purify Christianity of analogous Catholic elements when it came to producing affective Christian oneness, had few qualms regarding the utility of such practices when it came to creating affective American oneness. American catholicity, it seemed, trumped Christian catholicity.[20] In that desire to foster American catholicity, Thompson no doubt perceived northern Democrats and unrepentant white southerners as disruptive elements, while his thoughts also make sense within the context of widespread memorializing activities being undertaken by ex-Confederates, Unionists, and African Americans.[21]

But Thompson was further burdened by a sense of ethnocultural crisis as Grant took office. Linking the Union war effort—and emancipation—to 1776 promised to Americanize various subgroups threatening national oneness. "Each immigrant race" would be naturalized "into the family of the American nation—no more strangers and foreigners, but fellow-citizens of the household of freedom, a commonwealth builded together into a holy temple, founded upon the apostles and confessors of '76, cemented with the blood of myriads of her native, her adopted, and her enfranchised sons."[22] On the surface, this appears to be of a piece with Gilbert Haven's civic nationalism, though it had its limits.[23] Thompson (and others) assumed that discrete peoples populated the world, that specific traits inhered within each, and that successful nations contained a core "RACE-STOCK sufficiently positive and vigorous to assimilate all foreign elements into its own individuality." Unsurprisingly, Thompson assumed that an "improved English stock" was historically central in America, and he asserted that the "permanence" of American national life rested on "this Anglo-American stock having enough of pith and pluck to give character and tone to the whole population." He conceded that "the original stock may be modified by climate, by culture, or even by intermarriage with other races," but any intermingling had to avoid overwhelming the dominant stock. In addition to ancient examples, contemporary Austria and Turkey revealed the threatening influence of unassimilated groups. Turning to the United States, he said, "Organized communities of Americans [the Anglo-Protestant core], Germans, Irish, Negroes, French, Scotch, Chinese, Jews, dwelling side by side upon the same soil and under the same laws, cannot constitute a nation." That situation made for an ethnocultural confederation of sorts, but not the kind of union—or Union—he and others desired following their civil war. There could be no national cohesion until "outside" groups ceased to exist as such and were "grafted" into the dominant Anglo-American stock. "We cease to be a nation," he insisted, "if German influence and Irish influence is to vie with American influence."[24]

Despite the apparent biological racialism, Thompson's in-grafting process was substantially cultural. Any particular group's limitations, even if carried in the blood, so to speak, were not insurmountable obstacles to Americanization. Transformation occurred by learning America's "One Language," a "language rich in the traditions of liberty," spoken "through the laws, through the press, through the schools, through the pulpits of the land," and "permeating all business and pleasure, all work and worship, all song and all sorrow, from the cradle to the grave." That "indispensable" language would create "a bond of nationality stronger than political constitutions." Regarding the ex-slaves, this implied that they needed to cease being culturally distinct, irrespective of two centuries of bondage that had contributed to the creation of a unique African American culture; Anglo-American Protestant culture must subsume African Americans.[25] For white evangelicals, then, a war that had been fought to preserve one Anglo-American Protestant people flowed seamlessly into a Reconstruction concerned with seeing a fuller, more secure realization of that people.

To reiterate, northern evangelicals sought to maintain two ideas in tension with one another—the viability of an inescapably large republic alongside belief in the necessity of ethnocultural homogeneity. Grant-era northern evangelicals cautiously believed that Americans could remain one people, but only if evangelical Protestantism pervaded the habits, morals, and minds of the republican populace within whom sovereignty resided. In the face of westward expansion and continuing immigration, Thompson preternaturally asked what might "hold together the people of this nation when they shall have become a hundred millions, occupying fifty states, and belting the continent with a line of cities—its extremities the depots where two oceans shall discharge the commerce of the world?" The most likely answer, he feared, would be a striving after material gain, which would pull together "the New Englander, the German, the Celt, the Chinese by one magnetic force." But that was an insufficient long-term bond of union; lasting cohesion—and thus "the fate of the American Republic"—depended on evangelical Christianity, which "must fuse together all sections, races, rivalries, in one vast commonwealth of peace and good-will." Without that unifying adhesive, the large republic would disintegrate. God had providentially created and cared for the American people, he had brought forth Ulysses S. Grant to save the Union in war and in peace, and he would continue to preserve and strengthen that Union in the face of ethnocultural strain, but only if evangelicals were faithful under their evangelical president to further Christianize their country.[26]

Ending Reconstruction and Backing Grant

The impulse to oneness carried with it a predisposition to be finished with Reconstruction, and for many evangelicals the Fifteenth Amendment signaled the end. Of course, the ex-slaves were never completely gone from view, especially in the face of Ku Klux Klan terror and Grant's well-publicized enforcement of Congress's Third Force Bill in 1871. Still northern evangelicals were inclined to leave it all behind, though they would not accept reconciliation on any terms. So when Liberal Republicans opposed Grant in 1872 and ran Horace Greeley as a candidate promoting sectional reunion—in addition to championing civil service reform and free trade—most evangelicals could not join in. Enthralled by Grant, they stood by him in opposition to a collection of Republican turncoats who had sided with Democrats and ex-rebels. Just as in 1864 and 1868, evangelicals desired reconciliation—but on their own terms and in relation to what was presumably best for the Christian republic. With Grant at the helm, Reconstruction could end and a fuller realization of national Christian oneness could emerge.

Jesse Peck suggested that Reconstruction was mostly completed by the time Grant was elected in 1868. Peck believed that the Freedmen's Bureau's minimal southern presence, when combined with northern philanthropic efforts and African American citizenship, would cause southern white hostility to dissipate.

Additionally, he said, the ex-slaves "are peaceable and loyal," wanting little more than "simple justice." Acknowledging that he and others had been compelled by providence to accept emancipation, Peck viewed suffrage—Congress sent the proposed Fifteenth Amendment to the states in February 1869—as the last significant piece in the divine plan relative to slavery. Proclaiming that the ex-slaves' "good behavior . . . has astonished both enemies and friends," he forecast harmonious race relations for the South. Adapting Daniel Webster's words for the evolving divine drama, Peck said, "We thought we could save the Union and concede 'the right' of property in man; but we learned that liberty and Union must stand or fall together."[27]

With the freedmen on the cusp of civic and political equality and with Grant as president, the desire to move on increased. Writing just prior to Congress's submission of the Fifteenth Amendment to the states and Grant's inauguration, Joseph Thompson reiterated his call for the ex-slaves to learn America's dominant cultural "language." Beyond that, however, white Americans must stop regarding the ex-slaves in terms of skin color or former enslaved condition. "We must no longer know him as a negro, no longer help him, protect him, care for him as a negro, nor even as a freedman, but only as a man merged in the one commonwealth of equal laws. Philanthropy must not perpetuate caste." President Grant, already predisposed toward reconciliation and aware of Republicans' tenuous position before a northern electorate desiring Reconstruction's end, also celebrated ratification in 1870 with a sense of completion. Although agreeing with the likes of Thompson, that the ex-slaves still needed education in American citizenship, federal reconstructive efforts could gradually cease. Later in 1870, in response to Grant's Thanksgiving proclamation, the *New York Evangelist* rested in the belief that sectional strife had ended. Never mentioning the amendment, the paper highlighted "the social and commercial intercourse which tends to knit together all the diverse elements of our national life. Heated passions have cooled down," and "the echoes of battle have died away, to give place to the hum of busy industries and the rivalships of peaceful enterprise."[28]

Although the desire to move on was widespread, some believed the government's actions on behalf of the ex-slaves made ending Reconstruction all the more urgent. Rather than the Fourteenth and Fifteenth Amendments having been necessary and just measures, they actually helped account for why the Union was not restored. The New England Methodist Nelson Cobleigh, who edited the *Zion's Herald* from 1863 until becoming president of East Tennessee Wesleyan University in 1867, was troubled that the South had not yet been "brought back into homogeneous relations" with the North. The "disease" of national disharmony "is not cured," he wrote in 1870, and in that respect the experiment that was Reconstruction had failed. Undoubtedly southern residency colored his viewpoint, and although he reproved white southerners for their "lost cause" attitude, he primarily criticized meddling Republicans who kept "irritating the minds we wish to soothe." It was "Reconstructionists" who had foisted black equality upon the South, thus precipitating fearful rage among white southerners; policy-makers underappreciated the depth and sincerity of white southern convictions, chief among them the idea that a black person was "by nature an inferior being" and perhaps "descended not from Adam, but from some federal head of the monkey tribe." If northerners had shown more foresight (and white southerners more repentance), perhaps, he implied, the Fourteenth and Fifteenth Amendments could have been avoided and the Union fully restored.[29]

Others voiced similar critiques, finding northern policy and activity partially responsible for the Ku Klux Klan's emergence. S. G. Arnold, a Methodist layman and Washington lawyer, though professing surprise at southern whites' defiance in the face of northern magnanimity, nonetheless castigated "Carpet-baggers." Their greatest "evil" was to encourage impudence in the ex-slaves, a desire to rise "above [their] condition" and "to lay aside their demeanor of deference, and to come forward and claim a share of the honors and offices hitherto enjoyed only by the white race." Arnold, like Cobleigh, primarily faulted northerners for having misunderstood the white South: "Emancipated, it was supposed that in time [the ex-slave] might grow into some intelligence and consideration. But to make him an equal at once, to put him in positions of honor and profit, to have him in the seats of authority, laying down the law to the white man, touched Southern pride to the quick, and aroused the most intense feeling of disgust." Though Arnold supported Grant's coercive efforts following Congress's Third Force Bill (passed on April 20, 1871), which empowered Grant to use the Army and suspend the writ of habeas corpus against offending individuals as a means of enforcing the Fourteenth and Fifteenth Amendments, Arnold nevertheless partly blamed the North for the Klan's appearance.[30] Similarly, just prior to the Third Force Bill, the *New York Evangelist* suggested that strong federal action would only "aggravate" matters and described enforcement as "foreign interference." The comment undoubtedly reflected some Republican Congressional opinion, while it also clearly resonated with southern and northern Democrats who saw Grant as a tyrannical oppressor. The paper concluded: "Let the reconstructed States feel that the duty and burden of maintaining civil order are left upon their own shoulders."[31] Two years later, stressing that southern whites resented black equality, the paper implied that granting citizenship and suffrage had been too hasty. Notably, the comments came following the Colfax Massacre in Louisiana, when, in one of the worst episodes of racial violence in American history, at least 105 blacks—and only three whites—were killed on Easter Sunday, April 13, 1873.[32]

Ex-Confederates throughout the South, including many evangelicals, were determined to resist or overturn—violently when necessary—what they regarded as an illegitimate, unnatural, and anarchical social (and racial) order being imposed on them, and consequently, as things stood in the early 1870s, the difficulty that Henry Boardman had identified late in the war—that of achieving affective national oneness—remained. The paramount issue for some northern evangelicals, more than the Union's mere political restoration and clearly more than racial justice, was, in Cobleigh's words, how to achieve sectional "peace, mutual good feeling and sympathy, social harmony, religious unity, and spiritual prosperity." Consequently, the question recurred, "How shall the wounds of war be healed; the animosities which the rebellion engendered rooted up and removed; and how shall the streams of brotherly love and Christian fellowship be made again to flow and fill their wonted channels?" White southerners, who refused to submit to "Black Republican" rule, were little interested in reconciliation based on anything other than their own self-governing terms.[33]

Nevertheless, despite that southern reality, northern evangelicals were still wont to portray the Union's long-term prospects optimistically. Arnold concluded that Grant's enforcement "has pretty much put an end" to the Klan's activities and "will probably prevent any general recurrence of these monstrous crimes." Cobleigh also concluded that sectional "bitterness is passing away," despite perceived northern missteps, while Southern whites and blacks were recognizing "their mutual dependence and their mutual interests." In a refrain heard since 1865, white southerners would treat their new employees "kindly" and educate them, while the freedmen—"so kind, so polite, so obliging"—would learn to "feel the binding force of a contract" and gladly work under the right conditions. "It will be impossible," Cobleigh surmised, "for the present generation to hand much [bitterness] down to the next." Utilizing the biblical imagery of Jews and Gentiles being reconciled in Christ, he concluded, "The middle wall of partition" between whites North and South "is tumbling down."[34]

Cobleigh, like others, continued to believe that a revival of southern evangelicalism, initiated by northern evangelicals, was the key to affective reunion. That belief again echoed Boardman's late-war sentiments, while also revealing the continuing inability to recognize white southerners' contemptuous lack of interest in oneness with Yankees—evangelical or otherwise. Southerners' uninterest in being a northern evangelical mission field in particular sometimes manifested itself in church burnings and vigilante violence against northern missionaries, in addition to disputes over property and pastoral supply. Clearly resenting northerners for stoking racial tensions, southern evangelicals also wished to exercise their religious liberty without northern interference. Cobleigh, observing the South from East Tennessee, where there was less violence and anti-Union sentiment than in other areas, continued to insist that white southerners, who, after all, had been victimized by "their leaders," would respond well to northerners' "Christlike" kindness and affection. Thus he held out hope that "the true Spirit of Christ" would yet pervade the South and "bring this work of religious and social reconstruction to a happy consummation."[35]

Echoing Cobleigh's hopeful gloss and sounding like Joseph Thompson from 1868, the Methodist editor Daniel Whedon proclaimed that national oneness was finally dawning by late 1873. Turning a blind eye to the South, he imperially predicted that "the great principle of indissoluble Federal Unity, enfibred in the national heart—a principle baptized with the blood of the great army of martyrs of the Republic—will rivet the bonds which unite the whole country." The cohesive force of evangelical and Anglo-Saxon culture would assimilate immigrants and further prevent the large republic from dissolving like ancient republics. Regarding "the negro element" in particular, Whedon assured readers that because of white population growth blacks would make up "less than one eleventh" of the nation's population by century's end and would therefore cease to be a problem element. Unlike Thompson, however, Whedon also eagerly linked emergent oneness to an integrated, modernizing economy. The wondrous complementarity of America's regional natural resources, its abundant waterways, impressive technological progress, and "the interlacing web of internal commerce" would all serve to "knit the remotest parts of the country together by the ties of a common interest"; common participation in the economy "will remove prejudice and exert a humanizing and affiliating influence which will be an antidote to disintegration." Whedon was particularly enchanted by the telegraph, which permitted the "whole country" to follow commercial and political happenings nearly simultaneously: "The fluctuations of the Gold Room in Wall-street are daily noted in every counting-house from New Orleans to St. Paul, from Eastport to San Francisco. A change in the cabinet at Washington is discussed the same evening in almost every hamlet in the Union." Remarkably, Whedon's glorious forecast appeared amid the panic of 1873 and less than a year after the Colfax Massacre. Concluding his essay with a paean to Grant, Whedon and others were continuing to see what they so deeply longed for, a united and great Christian American republic under an evangelical president.[36]

In sharp contrast, George Cheever did not so easily gloss over what was occurring during the Grant years, though his analysis had little to do with Reconstruction or the president. Rather, he marveled with disgust at American culture. The nation was not becoming the Christian America he had envisioned. "What a world it is! And it really seems as if science, refinement, and religion only made that whole portion of it worse and worse, that [which] does not really sit at the feet of Jesus." In words that come off as an antimodern diatribe, he continued, "Society seems a herd of highly cultivated swine, into which all the devils that have been cast out from believing souls have entered, and all their pride and luxury of knowledges and inventions, poetry, sciences and arts, avail nothing to restrain them from plunging into the abyss of sin and misery." Cheever was particularly astonished at perceived cultural changes following an 1872 Boston fire. Upon reading numerous published sermons following the conflagration, Cheever portrayed clergymen as having abandoned their covenantal responsibility to providentially interpret the event for the public. They were speaking, he said, "as if it were impossible that [the fire] could have been a disciplinary check or chastisement of pride and worldliness." Instead of repentance, Bostonians appeared determined to "make the city fire proof." But, he commented, "No city or nation, nor any generation of wise and princely merchants can ever insure their affairs against God's interference." In Cheever's analysis, Grant-era Americans, including some evangelicals, were blindly pursuing wealth and security independently of the God of nations.[37]

Despite the criticism, Cheever did not turn on Grant. In this Cheever was unlike many of those prominent public intellectuals and Republican reformers described at the time and since as the "best men."[38] Those such as Edwin L. Godkin, Carl Schurz, George William Curtis, Charles Eliot Norton, William Dean Howells, and Henry Adams gave great attention to Grant-era corruption and contributed to the formation of the Liberal Republican Party that nominated Horace Greeley in 1872.[39] However, Liberal Republican criticisms of Grant, although driving much of the campaign conversation and certainly reflecting some public opinion, do not appear to have caused evangelicals to forsake the party that had saved the Union and ended slavery. It is significant that Cheever and other evangelical radicals would not hold Grant responsible for the perceived cultural rot, cronyism, and scandals surrounding his administration. Gilbert Haven remarked that "Grant is one of the most incorruptible of men," even while criticizing him for two late-1870 cabinet dismissals. Haven insisted that Grant "would scorn a bribe, whether money or place." Although Cheever and Haven and others like them remained mindful of the ex-slaves, they appeared to be satisfied with the course of Reconstruction under Grant by 1872, with much of that satisfaction coming from the Fifteenth Amendment and Frederick Douglass's continuing support for Grant. Furthermore, the president could, as William McFeely puts it, realistically "point to a semblance of order" in the South. "The nation was not on the brink of war. Grant was safe and dependable. He seemed oblivious to the corruption in his administration."[40]

In a turnabout from 1864, when Cheever refused to support Lincoln, Cheever was furious at dissident Republicans who abandoned Grant. Many of them had helped found the party, possessed strong antislavery and abolitionist credentials, and had remained faithful through the war. Though some critics stood by Grant in the end, others stuck with Greeley, who also received the support of Democrats so demoralized by the war and Johnson that they did not even run a candidate. Besides the fact that Cheever and others positively liked Grant, it was Greeley's alliance with Democrats that was beyond the pale.[41] The New Yorker Cheever believed he knew Democrats' true nature; if one wanted to see corruption, look no further than Tammany Hall, he said, with its "ring of villains" who greedily "devour widows' houses" and its "lawyers that defeat justice and make rascality successful." To vote for Greeley was to treasonously side with Democrats, and Cheever was particularly angered when Charles Sumner supported Greeley: "What a deplorable betrayal . . . ! It is just as if Gideon instead of fighting the Philistines had attempted to carry over his regiment with their pitchers into the service of Baal, after having so nobly broken down his altars."[42]

Cheever was exceedingly thankful to God that Greeley was not elected, and the fact that Cheever remained loyal to Grant is significant. For as radical as Cheever had been regarding racial justice, he and others like him were moving on from federal Reconstruction.[43] There is no evidence that Cheever ever perceived Grant like he had Lincoln, and in 1875, for instance, he praised Grant for the same sort of Thanksgiving proclamation that evoked contempt when delivered by Lincoln. "It seems to me to be one of the best proclamations ever issued," Cheever commented, "and probably it raises not a little scorn and anger in the bosoms of our secularizing missionaries of infidelity." Somehow Grant's proclamation was efficacious in a way that Lincoln's proclamations never were. At the very least, circumstances had changed. Grant had taken office in 1868 as an apparent evangelical promising relief from the threat of Johnson; the Thirteenth and Fourteenth Amendments were in place, while the Fifteenth awaited ratification; and radical Republicans had more seeming influence over race-related issues than ever. Although Cheever continued to support freedmen's aid and education in the 1870s, any manifest frustration came in response to Democrats,

Catholics, and a growing secularism in what was supposed to be a Protestant nation.[44] To better understand Cheever's shift in focus, it is important to note that evangelicals in general were feeling pressure from biblical criticism and changing conceptions and findings of science, both of which were rendering Christianity increasingly implausible to many educated Americans. In that respect, Cheever was emblematic. He agreed to serve as "pastor emeritus" of New York's Second Presbyterian Church and deliver twelve lectures on "The Evidences of Christianity," deriving great joy and purpose in supporting laymen in the struggle against an "atheism" threatening Christianity and the republic. He was not agitating against Grant's moderate racial policies; instead, he was doing his duty as an evangelical and republican citizen, seeking to Christianize the country through proper thought and belief, one individual at a time.[45]

In so doing, he and other evangelicals gave little heed to Grant's "liberal" critics during the campaign of 1872. Regarding civil service reform in particular, Grant ably co-opted the issue by forming the Civil Service Commission in late 1870 and by naming *Harper's Weekly*'s editor-reformer George William Curtis as its commissioner in June 1871; when it came to corruption and reform, then, the issue lost some of its force as a criticism of Grant the individual. The *New York Evangelist* acknowledged administrative corruption but insisted that "no man doubted Grant's personal integrity."[46] Regardless, evangelicals were not content to defer to nonevangelical public intellectuals when it came to political culture and morality.[47] The paper professed gladness that reform was even being discussed, since, in covenantal terms, "righteousness exalteth a nation, and sin is a reproach to any people," and it lauded Scottish Presbyterian James McCosh, Princeton's new president, who had spoken about reform in late 1871: "He is able to speak with as much weight as any Senator or public man in this country, having had a large experience in . . . Great Britain." McCosh, who had invited Grant to speak at Princeton and publicly supported the Civil Service Commission, apparently envisioned some of Princeton's graduates serving in the government.[48] What the country needed, the paper continued, was men "who place party interests in the background of country," men governed by evangelical principles; without those principles, the reformer becomes "a social pest, and may prove a calamity." One cannot help but think that the paper had Greeley and, perhaps, liberal reformers in mind, especially when it joined former Yale president Theodore Dwight Woolsey in denouncing Greeley as a demagogue. The country needed "Christian statesmen" of the kind that evangelical institutions such as Princeton and Yale—rather than nonevangelical Harvard—aimed to produce. The solution to America's social and political problems was not to be found in a Greeley presidency backed by nonevangelical reformers.[49]

At bottom, even while decrying party spirit, proprietary evangelicals had no other political home besides the Republican Party, not when they saw Democrats and unrepentant ex-Confederates supporting Greeley. Although his candidacy was predicated on ending Reconstruction, evangelicals insisted on terms satisfying to the victors. Evangelicals were not going to turn on Grant; they were satisfied that his southern policy had engendered peace and had been effective, most recently regarding Klan violence, and they believed his reelection would secure "the fruits of the war."[50] Though Grant might not be "a brilliant statesman," according to the *New York Evangelist*, the country enjoyed a measure of prosperity in 1872 and he had been "a *safe* man"; as for the scandals, Americans "believed that he did not *mean* to make mistakes." Above all, as one Indiana woman remarked, Grant's victory was "decreed by a good Providence," while a man from Cincinnati pronounced, "God has granted us Grant." Grant was simply the Union's two-time savior, another George Washington: "First in War, First in Peace, and first in the hearts of your countryman."[51]

Following the election I. C. Wynn, a Baptist from Camden, New Jersey, implicitly responded to Grant's critics by bringing a covenant charge before his readers, urging them to fulfill their role as the nation's proprietors. Reiterating that "American history is peculiarly Christian history" and that "righteousness exalteth a nation," Wynn encased his exhortation in classical republican rhetoric. Not only had Americans forgotten that "our nation has been highly favored" of God, they fast were becoming a selfish, greedy people given over to an "idolatry of mammon." He too wondered if America would go the way of past republics, but he hopefully recalled the sacrificial spirit that had saved the Union: "The pursuit of wealth . . . and selfishness seemed as thoroughly to have dried the fountains of patriotism and humanity. . . . But when the national integrity was threatened, the seemingly sealed fountain of patriotism was reopened, the love of self was forgotten in the greater love of country." War was an unnecessary cure for the latest manifestation of un-Christian and un-republican behavior—if evangelical leaders fulfilled their responsibility. "Christian scholars," he proclaimed alongside university presidents McCosh and Woolsey, were obligated to morally form the citizenry so that the right sort of leaders—the kind who would not succumb to corruption—would be positioned throughout government.[52] "Our hope of reform," he said, "rests solely upon that class of citizens whose influence is now almost wholly ignored in political circles—the honest, the Christian men of the nation." America's "Christian men" were qualified by "heaven's commission," not the Civil Service Commission. Evangelicals, inspired by "the example, the spirit, and the faith of [their] fathers" and "the history of the past," would lead the nation in true reform.[53]

There had been no need to follow Liberal Republicans in rejecting Grant. He had secured peace; Reconstruction was ending; and the nation was headed toward fuller Christianization. In the minds of northern evangelicals, the bulk of necessary federal activity on behalf of the freedmen was completed with the Fifteenth Amendment, and Grant's use of troops suggested that he was capable of dealing with sporadic problems. Just as in 1864 and in 1868, evangelicals desiring sectional reconciliation had no intention of acquiring it outside the Republican Party. For radicals, Grant was their only choice, and apparently many were satisfied with diminished federal reconstructive efforts. Moreover, in relation to evangelicals' self-perception as the nation's true reformers, they generally had their eyes on more than just the ex-slaves and the South during Grant's eight years.

Further Protestantization under Grant

Grant's presidency promised to further the nation's proper Christianization concerning two nonsouthern "problem" groups—Indians and Roman Catholics. Grant's dealings with them resonated deeply, buttressing northern evangelicals' sense of responsibility for the Union and further solidifying their support for him. Following the 1872 election, one letter writer delightedly informed Grant that his reelection signified defeat for Catholics and that "Jesus Christ . . . is represented at the head of our nation, in you our beloved President." Another wrote, "You will now have due time to complete the noble work of Christian statesmanship. . . . You can complete the grand work of civil service reform [by] placing the right men and keeping them in the right places in the Federal Government." He was particularly enthused by Grant's "humane and Christian policy toward the Indians."[54]

Grant inaugurated his first term in March 1869 not with a discussion of the South and Reconstruction but of the West and its Indians. Hinting at inevitable collisions with "the original occupants of the land," he favored "any course toward them which tends to their civilization and ultimate citizenship." Grant's friend George H. Stuart, a wealthy Philadelphia Presbyterian, recalled that "nothing in General Grant's inaugural excited more attention . . . than his strong . . . desire and purpose to see full justice done to the Indian tribes of our country." The matter was deeply personal to Grant, due to his antebellum West Coast army experience and close friendship with his Seneca Indian aide-de-camp, Ely Parker. Consequently, Grant was committed to preventing the "extermination" of Native Americans.[55]

The president's inaugural comments initiated his "Peace Policy," which would come to receive substantial evangelical support. Against the backdrop of a half century of violence, greed, corruption, and broken treaties in dealing with Native Americans, and amid growing pressure to reform the Bureau of Indian Affairs, the policy's immediate catalyst was a January 1869 meeting between Grant and a Quaker delegation. He particularly appreciated Quakers' historic reputation for benevolence toward native groups, and some subsequently referred to his Indian policy as the "Quaker Policy." Its most important feature was the replacement of notoriously corrupt Indian agents with religious missionaries (and soldiers, who, Grant trusted, would perform their duty faithfully and honestly). The policy's second major aspect was a ten-man supervisory Board of Indian Commissioners, which Congress created in April 1869. Receiving substantial input from Stuart, Grant named three Presbyterians, two Episcopalians, two Methodists, one Congregationalist, one Baptist, only one Quaker, and no Roman Catholics to the board. With "honest"—and mostly evangelical—religious men implementing the policy, Grant hoped the Indians might become "civilized" and Christianized Americans like the Baptist-educated Ely Parker, whom Grant appointed Commissioner of Indian Affairs.[56]

Gilbert Haven commended Quaker involvement—and Parker's appointment—but the Quakers' initial prominence precipitated an angry response in August 1869 from W. G. Kephart, an Iowa Presbyterian who had served under Grant as a chaplain at Vicksburg and Chattanooga and who had labored for the American Missionary Association among New Mexico's Indians before the war. He protested to Grant that Quaker success during "the days of Wm Penn" was overblown, having little to do with their religion per se and much to do with Indians' limited experience with whites. The best chance of success, he advised, involved "apportioning to every man, woman and child a sufficient amount of land to constitute an ample farm." After that, "say to the Indians: now here is your land, you must cease your roving, hunting, predatory habits, *go to work*, and earn your living honestly, as all honest men do. . . . An Indian has no more right to be a vagabond, thief and murderer, than a white man." Demand law and order, and then "let the work of literature and evangelization be turned over to churches and [evangelical] missionary Societies." Kephart need not have worried, for Grant largely proceeded along those lines.[57]

Evangelicals responded enthusiastically to the Peace Policy, and Grant appointed scores of them as Indian agents.[58] Their support stemmed from a traditional Christian emphasis on evangelism, but it also flowed from evangelicals' desire to homogenize the large republic. Exemplifying these concerns, two Nebraska Congregationalist missionaries echoed Grant's inaugural remarks in a letter to him. Recommending patience alongside military-enforced law and order, the two men wrote: "As a powerful Christian people we should while giving them every just due, manifest such a spirit of true benevolence as to lift them up to a Christian civilization." Such sentiments cemented Grant's desire to use religious bodies, and the two men pledged themselves "to cooperate . . . in every effort for the evangelization and civilization of these Indians." Revealing evangelicals' continuing preoccupation with the presence of various ethnic groups, they also promised to pray "that the Lord would guide your Excellency to adopt and execute the best plans for the welfare of all races found within the borders of our nation, be they white, or black or red."[59]

Having cast the Indian problem as a choice between extermination and assimilation, Grant made supporting his policy easy, even if actual assimilation was a different matter. In that respect, the *Zion's Herald* proclaimed that at least Christian America had done right by the Indians: "If, after [Grant's efforts], the race should die out, the Republic may bow with submission to the dispensations of Providence, but without the blushing consciousness of guilt." However, "Should [the Indians] hold their own, in point of prosperity and numbers, none would have just cause of complaint. Or if they should disappear in the general national amalgam, there would then be nothing to evoke the wish that it were otherwise." In a best-case scenario, the republic benefited by the Indians' presence; in a worst-case scenario, Grant's policy meant the nation would not have blood on its hands if the Indians would not or could not be "civilized" and Christianized.[60]

The 1870 Presbyterian General Assembly, the first since the 1869 reunion of Old and New Schools, supported Grant's policy but did so apolitically. Expressing "deep concern" for "the unevangelized condition of the aboriginal population," Presbyterians "deprecated the increasing tendency among many of our citizens to treat them as a race to be exterminated, rather than as the proper objects of Christian effort, to be thereby civilized and gathered into the fold of Christ." The assembly thus authorized its missions board to exert "its utmost efforts to accomplish this humane and benignant purpose," although it rejected a proposed amendment from New York's outspoken wartime Unionist Howard Crosby to explicitly support Grant. The amendment's rejection was not disapproval of Grant, however; rather, it was the determined action of a recently reunited church, within a recently reunited Union, to appear aloof from politics. The assembly's report emphasized that the amendment's opponents were avowed "Republicans who voted for General Grant" and were in agreement "with every word." If the amendment passed, however, could the future introduction of some political matter—and "an endless wrangle on matters essentially secular, and heart-burnings, alienations, strifes, and divisions, and secessions"—be prevented? Presbyterians clearly supported Grant's policy, and they were not abandoning their prerogative and responsibility to address so-called political issues; but with slavery and civil war fresh in mind, it was prudent to keep Grant's name out of their resolution. As Princeton's James McCosh said, the safest route was to reject the idea that "inferior races ought to be exterminated."[61]

By the time Grant began his 1872 campaign, evangelicals regarded his policy as successful. With "honest and conscientious Christian men" endeavoring "to civilize and Christianize" the Indians, the *New York Evangelist* predicted their transformation from "wards of the nation" into productive members of society. In fact, "The success of the new system is all that could be expected, and if the experiment . . . is permitted to work itself out, our Indians will at no distant day be as valuable as any other class of our population." After painting a degrading picture of Indian life prior to Grant, the article closed with glowing news: "We have today more pious Christian Indians in Nebraska than we have of white people." Such reports, the paper claimed, could be multiplied many times over. "Hundreds of tribes have now settled down to civilized ways, and many are Christianized. Of the wild Indians under the new peace policy, [many tribes] are at peace. . . . This system, so humane and just . . . cannot fail."[62]

Despite reports of violence, then, some evangelicals could be as hopeful about the Indians as they were about the ex-slaves. Perhaps more so, since a civil war had not been fought over the Indians and no war-related issues inhibited Indians' full Christianization and Americanization. The secretary of the Presbyterian Board of Foreign Missions and a future professor at New York University, Francis Ellinwood, said as much in 1873. Admitting that although American Christians had not treated "enslaved Africans" well, they were now "citizens of the republic"; learning from experience, evangelicals should regard the Indians as "a golden opportunity" to do better. No other group besides the Chinese received such ill treatment as the Indians; would the government, he rhetorically asked, relocate Minnesota's Swedes? Or Missouri's Germans? And though "the Irish population is responsible for a larger proportion of crimes . . . than any other race," what American "would think of justifying the massacre of a whole Irish village?" Indians' occasional murderous behavior was born of an understandable "despair mingled with rage." Comparatively, they were little different than desperate Confederate soldiers, whose graves, he said, Americans rightfully mark and remember. Thanks to Grant, the nation finally had a just Indian policy and thus a sound basis for optimism about the Indians' place in the Christian republic.[63]

Just after Grant left office in 1877, the Methodist lawyer S. G. Arnold retrospectively examined and praised Grant's Indian policy as a successful example of civil service reform. Likely with Grant's intraparty critics in mind, Arnold said, "A hundred years of experience had not taught us how to tame these wild barbarians," and yet Grant's policy had "solved" the Indian problem precisely because it utilized religious men. Church involvement, Arnold said, was "an advantage that can hardly be overestimated. Besides securing better officers and better influences, it [brought] to the aid of the Government the sympathies and services of the best citizens of the nation, and enlist[ed] a kind of aid which no government can supply and no government can do without." Grant's policy demonstrated "that the Indian can be allured from his wild ways and taught 'to walk in the white man's road;' . . . that he can be induced to change his mode of life" and become "a successful farmer, mechanic, or tradesman" and ultimately "an independent citizen." In regarding themselves as the nation's proprietors, evangelicals periodically convinced themselves that problems associated with the Indians, as with the ex-slaves, were minimal or nonexistent.[64]

This proved to be far more difficult with Roman Catholicism. Even if the Civil War momentarily absorbed the bulk of evangelicals' energy, Roman Catholicism never ceased to be a threat. Not only did Catholics appear more determined to resist assimilation than any other "problem" group, evangelicals suspected them of acting at Rome's behest to overthrow the Protestant republic. Hiram Mattison, an antislavery Methodist, best remembered for his account of the "octoroon" slave Louisa Picquet, was alarmed by Roman Catholic leaders' "bold and defiant tone" following the war. With European immigration resuming, he believed that Rome was intentionally challenging the country's Protestant essence and evangelicals' proprietary responsibility for it. His account of New York Catholics' seemingly impudent insistence on holding a Sunday religious procession illustrates evangelical perceptions well. Catholic practices such as feast days and processionals, which Protestants had long rejected, violated evangelical conventions regarding Sabbath-keeping and the use of public space. Mattison angrily quoted a Catholic newspaper's opinion of the controversy to expose Catholics' brazenness: "The streets of the city are ours [Catholics'] as much as they are theirs [Protestants'], and we have as much right to march in procession through them . . . as they have." Mattison interpreted "the plain import of such language" as, "We shall do as we please," regardless of prevailing custom or law; such defiance clearly revealed Catholics as an anarchic threat.[65]

That perception took on renewed saliency during Grant's presidency. Catholicism was "confronting us without fear and with decided audacity," Boston's Congregationalist Edwin Harwood warned in a March 1869 lecture at Trinity Church. He provided a standard list of problems Protestants perceived in Catholicism: affinity for absolutism and authoritarianism; hostility to democratic republicanism; a confessional system that threatened the family; superstition; and opposition to lay Bible reading, popular education, and intellectual freedom. In addition, Harwood focused specifically on two issues—the papacy and the Mass—and contended that the fundamental dispute between Catholics and Protestants concerned theological authority. For Catholics it was the papacy and magisterium, whereas for evangelicals it was the individual's reading of the Bible. The implication found Protestant evangelicalism particularly well suited for an American republic that theoretically rested on popular sovereignty and individual liberty—and Catholicism thus particularly unsuited. Unsurprisingly, then, evangelicals were disconcerted by Pius IX's 1864 *Syllabus of Errors*—which condemned modern liberalism, including separation of church and state and non-Catholic education—and by the Vatican Council's 1870 declaration of papal infallibility. Historically deep-seated Protestant-Catholic tensions increased and merged with evangelicals' perception that Catholic activity in America was a particular manifestation of a worldwide—and, to some, apocalyptic—religious struggle.[66] George Cheever, having denounced "the blasphemous dogma of the Pope's Infallibility," thus celebrated the defeat by Protestant Prussia of Catholic Austria (1866) and Catholic France (1870), while the *Zion's Herald* conjoined the announcement of papal infallibility with Bismarck's victory over France and implored readers to "learn the connection between these startling events. . . . Learn that Bismarck is but a tool of the Lord Jesus Christ, and that Napoleon is only the tool of Antichrist."[67]

Like the Civil War, evangelicals' struggle with Roman Catholicism was deeply existential. Following Grant's inauguration in 1868, the *Zion's Herald* reminded readers of Catholicism's "fearful" history of dominating "rulers and people alike" through inquisitorial arrest, torture, imprisonment, and murder. Whereas the "Old World" was ridding itself of "Romanism," America "has been selected" to be "its future resting place." Granville Moody transitioned seamlessly from defending the Union to battling the new threat. Rather than a rebellion, he said in 1871, they faced "a foreign potentate, whose oath-bound priests and subjects are in our midst; and myriads more annually landing on our shores, with hearts alien to us. . . . Our controversy is with a system anti-American, anti-Republican, anti-Protestant." Quoting Patrick Henry, Moody concluded, "With us, 'Eternal vigilance is the price of liberty.'"[68]

In the struggle, perhaps no aspect of American life required more vigilance than public education. Continuous with antebellum beliefs and practices, the inculcation of nonsectarian (but Protestant) Bible reading, prayer, and hymn singing was a crucial aspect of proper American formation. Some evangelicals seemingly invited a contest with Catholics over education because of its unifying potential; the Philadelphia Presbyterian Elias Beadle remarked, "Our country is aroused, to watch and defend with . . . jealous care its . . . common school education. . . . Assaults . . . will be resisted, if need be, unto blood." Underscoring the point, he said, "Our country's flag shall float over [schools] as the sacred citadels of our liberty and our rights, and the command shall be echoed again, 'if any man attempts to pull it down, shoot him on the spot.'"[69] When Catholics protested against Protestant Bible reading and prayer, sought governmental proscription of such practices, requested that tax dollars be divided in order to establish separate schools, or asked to be exempted from paying taxes used to support non-Catholic schools, evangelicals met them not with bullets but interrelated proprietary, covenantal, and republican arguments. For instance, following the famous "Cincinnati Bible War" of 1869–70, the *Princeton Review* cast Roman Catholics as akin to secularists; according to the Presbyterian journal, opposing public schooling meant Catholics sought to prevent their children from receiving adequate moral instruction. In so doing Catholics also posed the same sort of centrifugal danger that secession had, and no issue "since the bombardment of Sumter" had so stirred Americans as the question of "morals and religion" in public education. The Union could not cohere without evangelical moral instruction. The journal thus offered the common argument on behalf of infusing state-financed common schools with Protestant belief and practice: Only a virtuous citizenry preserved the republic "from corruption and ruin"; religion is the only source of virtue; "and the only religion which the mass of our American States know, or can know, is the religion of the Bible." It went without saying that this excluded Roman Catholicism. Consequently, the aim of producing good citizens necessary for sustaining the Christian republic "is defeated by [Catholics'] extrusion of religion" from public education.[70]

Catholics, on this view, were being selfishly unrepublican and un-American. The *New York Evangelist* tendentiously construed Catholics' desire to divide tax-generated school funds as an effort to "destroy" the common schools. Using civic-nationalist language for arguably ethnocultural ends, the author insisted that in America "we recognize citizenship alone." Comparing America to the Christian church, he concluded, "The family likeness, American . . . obscures all distinctions." Catholic efforts "to separate the community into sects, or to array one portion of the community against another," the author said with a frightful wartime analogy, constituted "a mine run beneath the foundations of the republic." On entering the church that was America, one must shed all particularities, which especially applied to Catholics disinclined to submit their children to a culturally homogenizing Protestant education. Even those who conceded that explicit religious practices should be proscribed drew the line at dividing the school funds; for without a common education, according to Stanley Matthews, one of the attorneys in the Cincinnati decision, children "would grow up in isolation from each other, with blind and intense sectarian antipathies, such as would melt away if they were educated together in the public schools, where they would grow up with that sense of unity and brotherhood which would fit them for a common citizenship of our great republic."[71]

Others simply proclaimed that because America was a Protestant nation religious dissent need not be tolerated. In a majority Protestant country, the *Princeton Review* asserted, it was "out of the question" to attempt to please minority groups—which included "Mormons, Chinese, Jews, idolaters, atheists, and infidels," in addition to Roman Catholics.[72] The Methodist William H. Boole found it preposterous that a historic, Protestant republic, permeated with the knowledge that God holds nations morally responsible, would willingly remove the Bible from its schools. "This is a *Protestant Nation*," and it depends on Scripture as a "bulwark" against "foreign ignorance, superstition, and . . . the unbridled excesses of sensual and religious passion" that he believed underlay other religions. Adapting Daniel Webster's commonplace, Boole proclaimed, "Our Bible, Our Schools, and Our Flag: One and Inseparable."[73] The Presbyterian John Mears similarly underscored the country's Protestant origins and majority population but expressed fear that evangelicals' conciliatory "nature" might impel them to make dangerous concessions. To defer "to a bare seventh part of the population" would be suicidal, he said, while reminding his audience that just as they had not consented to national destruction back in 1861, neither should they in the 1870s.[74]

Sharing and voicing the common perceptions of Catholicism was Grant's pastor, John P. Newman.[75] Though possessing a typical proprietary regard for "our commonwealth," Newman was outspoken in his suspicion of Catholicism's presence, never more so than in November 1875. He ranked it with other "great evils" in history, such as the "rise of Mohammedanism" and "the late war for the

Union." Catholics' refusal to separate church and state, as modern Protestants presumably had done, meant that Catholics refused to "render unto Caesar the things which are Caesar's"; more specifically, in Newman's portrayal, it was axiomatic that "the citizen obeys the laws, pays his taxes, and if necessary, devotes his life for his country's good." By implication, Catholics were refusing such civic responsibilities. No religious group, Newman announced, whether Roman Catholic, Mormon, Muslim, or Hindu, may use American religious liberty as a basis for nonparticipation or nonconformity. Newman insisted, then, that Catholics send their children to the common schools for instruction in republican citizenship and the inculcation of those universal, and not merely Protestant, moral truths needed to sustain the republic; only when conscience was violated could one be excused. Unsurprisingly, Catholic parents' desire to form their children within their own tradition was not a legitimate conscientious objection. In Newman's view, Catholics selfishly sought to benefit from American citizenship while refusing to conform or contribute to the common good. By contrast, Newman proudly declared that no denomination "gave more men and money in the war to preserve the Union" than Methodists. Moreover, though Methodists were "ardent supporters" of the Methodist president, they were religious liberty's most vocal champions. Catholics, he said, were free to practice their religion—in their homes and churches—but they must otherwise Americanize. Staking out such a position was clearly easy to do when Protestantism seemed to fit hand in glove with America in a way that Roman Catholicism apparently could not.[76]

Newman's remarks came two months after Grant himself had weighed in on the schools issue. Although the president spoke within the context of simmering Protestant-Catholic tensions following the "Cincinnati Bible War," he was also cognizant of a weakening Republican Party and the reality of waning northern interest in southern Reconstruction. Back in February 1875, Congress had failed to authorize Grant further power to meet southern violence, and indicative of the so-called retreat from federal Reconstruction, formerly radical Connecticut congressman Joseph R. Hawley sounded a theme that many evangelicals had been expressing for some time: "There is a social, and educational, and moral reconstruction of the South needed that will never come from any legislative halls, State or national; it must be the growth of time, of education, and of Christianity." In the context of steadily declining northern will regarding Reconstruction, Grant addressed the Catholic problem in his now infamous speech to Union veterans in Des Moines, Iowa, in late September 1875.[77]

Having heard Newman preach on the schools issue for three successive Sundays, Grant cast Roman Catholic agitation over school funds as a new threat to the Union. With the nation's centennial around the corner, Grant alluded to the nation's revolutionary beginnings, echoed the Gettysburg Address, and unmistakably implied that the Union's dissolution was possible. "Let not the results of [soldiers'] sacrifices be destroyed," Grant urged. "The Union and free institutions for which they fell should be held more dear for these sacrifices." The war "will not have been fought in vain"—if the nation's common schools remained "free" and "unmixed with sectarian, pagan, or atheistical tenets." In a republic, where the people were sovereign, Grant continued, "the free school is the promoter of that intelligence which is to preserve us as a free nation." Perhaps relishing an esprit de corps with his former troops, Grant then raised the specter of war. "If we are to have another contest in the near future of our national existence," Grant warned, "the dividing line will not be Mason and Dixons but between patriotism . . . and intelligence on the one side and superstition, ambition and ignorance on the other." All knew Grant had Roman Catholics in mind, and nominal Methodist though he was, he was clearly speaking evangelicals' language. Furthermore, he held out an olive branch to former Confederates by suggesting they join patriotic northerners in a new common cause. "We will not deny to any of those who fought against us any privilege under the government which we claim for ourselves," he beckoned. "On the contrary we welcome all such who come forward in good faith to help build up the waste places, and perpetuate our institutions against all enemies, as brothers in full interest with us in a common heritage."[78]

Many others besides Newman responded enthusiastically to Grant's speech. A former soldier wrote: "The words you spoke . . . thrilled many Loyal Hearts throughout the Union. And if at any future time, the hated Jesuites [*sic*] should dare to show their hand, you have only to speak the word, and the Grand Army will rally around you." One Chicago Congregationalist assured Grant—by blending the Union hero's famous remark made during the battle of Spotsylvania with Henry Clay's Unionist language—that if he carried out "this 'line' of policy" he would "win the gratitude of every true patriot in our land, and will bring gladness into the heart of every Christian, North and South, East and West." Another Congregationalist referred to Grant's speech as the best news since 1864, when Grant had assumed command over all Union forces. Finally, James A. Briggs of Brooklyn wrote to Grant, "Our Pilgrim Fathers established free schools that their children might learn the Word of God. Let it be our duty and pleasure to perpetuate them, that '*Intelligence* may ever triumph over *ignorance*.'"[79]

In his December 1875 annual message, Grant again addressed the importance of common schooling. Attempting to elicit support for Maine congressman

James Blaine's proposed constitutional amendment to ban state aid to parochial schools, Grant argued that without common schooling "a large association of ignorant men . . . will inevitably sink into acquiescence to the will of intelligence, whether directed by the demagogue or by priestcraft. Hence the education of the masses becomes of the first necessity for the preservation of our institutions." Education must remain free of "religious, atheistic, or pagan tenets." Although admitting that no nation since "the fall of Adam" could completely escape threats to its "prosperity and happiness," such as that presently offered by Catholics, education remained a near-panacea for ethnocultural ills threatening the Union. Grant's foray into the schools issue had come "none too soon," according to one letter signed "*Vivat Respublica*." Giving thanks to God, the writer said that Grant's views would "command the applause of every Patriot in the Land."[80] Grant had certainly garnered evangelicals' applause—in this instance and throughout his presidency. He had been the savior of their Union in several contexts, on and off the battlefield; having solved the Indian problem, he was now saving the Union from Roman Catholics.

A Union Hero

Notably, Grant's annual message had little to say about Reconstruction beyond commenting that "the bondmen have been freed" and the country has thus "become possessed of the respect, if not the friendship, of all civilized nations." In September, around the time of his Des Moines speech, Grant had refused the Mississippi governor's request for troops to quell political and racial violence ahead of elections. He was a lame duck leaving both the White House and Reconstruction behind, despite calls for a third term, notably from Gilbert Haven and Frederick Douglass. And despite the economic depression that began in 1873, the country was extravagantly preparing for the upcoming Centennial Exhibition in Philadelphia, where "civilized" nations from around the world would celebrate with nearly ten million Americans from May to November 1876. When it opened on May 10, Mathew Simpson was present to ask God's blessings, as had been the case at Grant's nominating convention eight years before. The bishop particularly thanked God for the fulfillment of his providential intentions for the country. Southern problems could appear remote to northerners determined to congratulate themselves for one hundred years of republican liberty and a seemingly boundless future of political, technological, and economic progress.[81]

During a Memorial Day Service at Arlington Cemetery a few weeks later, with many senators and representatives present, Granville Moody delivered a lengthy discourse-like prayer that encapsulated the northern evangelical mood after seven years of Grant. Appearing in the style of an Old Testament priest on behalf of "a Christian nation," he rehearsed the now-typical narrative of God's providential care for the republic. God chose "a small people" in Europe, brought them to Plymouth, and then "didst rebuke kings for their sakes, saying, Touch not mine anointed." In 1776 that people, as Moody narrated events to God, himself, and the audience, "made declaration of their rights, their purposed independence of every power but thine; and 'pledged to each other . . . ' to achieve and maintain their supreme nationality, in firm and avowed dependence upon thine aid." God also saw fit to "raise them up a savior, and a great one, in thy servant Washington." What began as "a mere confederacy" became "indissolubly one" during the Civil War, "a government of and for and by the people," Moody continued in the words of Lincoln's Gettysburg Address. The American people had grown to fill the continent, under the watch of "Washington, Jackson, Lincoln, [Union General George H.] Thomas, and Grant, . . . men whom thou madest strong for thyself, and for our protection as a Nation, whose God is the Lord." As Moody spoke beside soldiers' graves, peace in a slave-free republic occasioned much thanksgiving, along with the assurance that "the blood of these martyrs [was] the seed of the Union!" Moody prayed further that God would care for the freedmen, possibly sensing that they were on their own in 1876. Finally, Moody prayed that God would visit the nation with "a spirit of reconciliation," hoping that the day would soon arrive when "all sectional feelings [are] merged in a common glory of a restored brotherhood."[82]

About a month after Moody's prayer, Grant proclaimed it "fitting that on the occurrence of the hundredth anniversary of our existence as a nation a grateful acknowledgement should be made to Almighty God for the protection and the bounties which He has vouchsafed to our beloved country." Thus he directed "the good people of the United States" to devoutly thank God and "humbly to invoke a continuance of His favor and of His protection." George Cheever welcomed the centennial proclamation with unparalleled praise, interpreting it as chiding Americans for their ingratitude amid plenty. Recognizing the proclamation's covenantal importance, he said the country owed Grant thanks for directing "us as a nation and people, amidst all the efforts of infidel and secularizing parties," to thank "God as the Author and Giver of all our country's prosperity and blessings." Surveying American culture in 1876, Cheever perceived thankless Americans busily seeking their own material well-being—though such a gilded age was apparently disconnected from Ulysses S. Grant. "It is certainly a remarkable and quite providential thing," Cheever said, "that at such a juncture the

President should have made this public explicit avowal and acknowledgement of our obligations to God and our dependence on him as a nation." It is unclear if he had Lincoln in mind, but Cheever said, "It quite rounds off and completes the preceding series of grateful references to God and his providence presented to the people by our best Presidents from Washington down." Suggestive of just how far Reconstruction had receded, he concluded, "Really, President Grant has done more for the turning of men's thoughts to God, as the author and Source of our country's life and greatness, and to remind us of our dependence upon him, in the few sentences . . . than all the Centennial self-applauding and congratulatory orations that I have yet seen."[83]

However, even as Cheever was praising Grant, news of two events reminded celebratory Americans of the Union's tenuous peace. First, news circulated that George Custer and his troops had been destroyed at Little Big Horn, Montana, in late June.[84] Perhaps pronouncements of peace with the Indians were premature. Meanwhile, South Carolina, one of three remaining southern states that had not reverted to white Democratic rule, served up a reminder that hopes did not always correspond with reality in the South either. On Independence Day, Hamburg's black militia paraded through the town, momentarily obstructing a buggy carrying two whites. This led to charges being filed against the militia leader for contempt of court and a trial set for July 8. After fighting between the militia and armed whites on the eighth, whites executed five African American prisoners overnight and looted blacks' homes and businesses. Although Grant responded to the Hamburg Massacre with strong words and directed troops to the area, charges against the whites were eventually dropped, and in the end Grant committed the South to God's mysterious providence. "How long these things are to continue, or what is to be the final remedy, the Great Ruler of the universe only knows," he said, "but I have an abiding faith that the remedy will come, and come speedily, and I earnestly hope that it will come peacefully. There has never been a desire on the part of the North to humiliate the South."[85] Of course, many ex-rebels had indeed found Reconstruction humiliating, and in October 1876 white South Carolinians would also turn to God—thanking him with potent biblical imagery for redeeming them from bondage to "Yankee and negro rule" by means of Democrat Wade Hampton's gubernatorial election. In response, the Baptist W. C. Lindsay said, "God has crowned the closing Centennial year with another blessing. We cannot doubt that 'every good and perfect gift (and this among them) cometh down from the Father of lights.' It is just like our God to do this for us." Grant and many northern evangelicals had consigned the South to God's hands, and many southern white evangelicals as well looked ahead to a new South redeemed by those hands.[86]

Despite the frustration of Reconstruction and even as Republicans turned to Rutherford B. Hayes following too many scandals and too much corruption, Grant remained a hero. "We are satisfied that the great mass of the American people still have confidence in the integrity of your motives," wrote a Minnesota Methodist, "and . . . we are satisfied that the Republic will yet be ever generous in its expressions of gratitude to her greatest soldier and faithful President U. S. Grant."[87] As it turned out, the contested election of 1876 provided one last opportunity for Grant to save the Union; by mediating between Democrats and Republicans, Grant defused the threat of another civil war.[88] And in December 1876, in his final message to Congress, he humbly acknowledged mistakes and political naïveté—further solidifying evangelical affection. He remained the humble "Christian Soldier and Patriot."[89] When Grant left office, the A.M.E.'s *Christian Recorder* effusively praised him as "a great man—as great as any the country has produced." He "has more decision of character than Washington and less pretentiousness than Lincoln." Grant "had the high honor of saving his country twice," first in winning the war and then holding the nation together through Reconstruction. "Grant and Grant alone is to be credited with the peace the country now enjoys."[90]

Conclusion: "The Nation Still in Danger"

Despite the optimistic gilding some were inclined to provide at various moments, Reconstruction had not proceeded the way many had hoped. As Grant's presidency wound down, "the alienation between North and South, growing out of negro slavery" remained dangerously apparent to those willing to look. That was the opinion of the American Missionary Association's Michael Strieby, whose observations appeared in a collection that included contributions by Frederick Douglass, Theodore Dwight Woolsey, and Washington Gladden. All were resigned to the fact that federal Reconstruction was essentially over, and, as part of a philanthropic appeal, Woolsey and Gladden raised the specter of racial war if the freedmen were not educated and "civilized."[1] As revolutionary as emancipating four million slaves and granting them citizenship and suffrage actually was, it is clear that Reconstruction had failed to fully produce what evangelical radicals had hoped for—a Christian America that ensured an equitable place for the ex-slaves. Though legally in possession of political and civil rights, those rights were tenuous at best under "redeemed" southern governments, and there was little cultural or political will at the national level to ensure much more beyond nominal freedom. As Frederick Douglass painfully asked Republicans at their presidential convention in June 1876, "What does it all amount to, if the black man, after having been made free by the letter of our law, is unable to exercise that freedom, and, having been freed from the slaveholder's lash, he is to be subject to the slaveholder's shot-gun?"[2] By 1877 the vision of northern evangelical radicals like Gilbert Haven and George Cheever, which had never been at the center of Whig-Republican evangelical culture in the first place, was fading even further into the past. For many white southerners, it appeared that providence, albeit by means of violence and intimidation, was beginning to restore the natural and divine order of things. And white southern evangelicals in particular would accept and, in some instances, actively support Jim Crow as it emerged during the last quarter of the century.[3]

For nonradical northern evangelicals such as George Peck and Henry Boardman, both of whom had long subordinated issues associated with racial justice to their overarching devotion to the Union, Reconstruction was also a failure—at least on their own terms—even if they did not perceive it as such. They and many others had entered Reconstruction hoping for more than the nominally restored Union they received following President Hayes's removal of the last federal troops from the South in 1877 and the redemption of the last three ex-Confederate governments.[4] Reality did not match the desire for heartfelt national oneness. White southerners had never been too keen on being made over in the North's Whig-Republican free-labor (or evangelical) image, no matter how reasonable or magnanimous northern evangelicals perceived the North's reconstructive actions to have been, and thus many southerners gladly reinstituted home rule when given the chance. Though northern evangelicals had helped ensure that slavery and secession would no longer mar the Union, the new era of national Christian oneness had not arrived.

Recognition by northern evangelicals that the restored Union was not actually marked by deep intersectional affection was particularly apparent following the melodrama surrounding President James Garfield's assassination in 1881. After he was shot by Charles J. Guiteau on July 2, Americans anxiously tracked the president's progress over the summer. Favorable news reports encouraged confidence that Garfield would recover, but the nation was stunned when he died on September 19. Afterward, the western Massachusetts evangelical Martin Stoddard Howard recounted expectations surrounding Garfield's election and, with yet another allusion to Daniel Webster, commented, "There was [a] confident looking forward to a general breaking up of old hostilities; to a subsidence of ancient bitterness; to a coming of the glad day when the Union should be in all parts, as of old, 'one and inseparable.'" Garfield, America's last log-cabin president, was "the noble Christian man whom the North and South trusted," the one whom they expected to affectively reunite the country.[5] On the heels of the eighty-day deathwatch, northern evangelicals not only eulogized the former Disciples of Christ minister and Union general for exemplifying the Christian republic's best qualities—for instance, the Philadelphia Presbyterian Henry McCook said Garfield "was the type of our American civilization, a typical product of our republican institutions"—they once again pondered God's dealings with the Union, while packing Garfield's travail and death with great conciliatory efficacy. On one level, then, the Garfield eulogies may be read collectively as a temporary acknowledgment that the Union was still marked by sectional tension, rather than national Christian oneness.[6]

Accordingly, Garfield's death precipitated the same sort of hopeful announcements of emergent unity that evangelical leaders had been offering in the face of threats to the Union since the antebellum period. McCook, who had been chaplain of the 41st Illinois Volunteer Infantry Regiment during the war, proclaimed:

> The great sections . . . so recently in civil war have melted into reconciliation before a common grief. We are looking upon the holy spectacle of a restored brotherhood. We see the North and the South clasping hands around the sick-bed and across the bier of the nation's dead, mingling their griefs and tears upon the face of a common woe, and burying their alienations in the grave of one whose memory is henceforth a common heritage.[7]

Charles Henry Parkhurst, the pastor of New York's Madison Square Presbyterian Church who subsequently became known for his caustic criticism of Tammany Hall, perceived Garfield's death struggle as "an immensely nationalizing event." Applying Henry Clay's commonplace, Parkhurst said, "Around Mr. Garfield's bedside, and now around his grave, is no North, no South, no East, no West. Not since the war, and not since a long time before the war, have all the sections of our country come so distinctly under the pressure of one heart-beat." Garfield's death had auspiciously driven the whole nation to bow "before our Christian God."[8] Similarly invoking Clay, Elias Nason went further, however. God, he said, was announcing to the country: "'Be still and know that I am God!' The United States of America belong to me. By creation, preservation and redemption they are mine; my own rightful property,—north, east, south, and west, all mine." Garfield's ordeal, then, promised to do more than simply bring an end to the sectional divide that had persisted since the days of Daniel Webster and Henry Clay.[9]

In light of intellectual challenges causing many educated Americans to question God's existence and providential oversight of all of creation and human history, the Bible's veracity, and cardinal beliefs regarding Jesus Christ, various eulogizers proclaimed that God was sending a signal to the nation's unbelievers in general and its liberalizing Protestants in particular for the purpose of thwarting secularization and theological modernism.[10] Henry McCook was especially pleased that "secular" Americans were forced to observe two months of public praying and mourning. God had providentially "seized the newspaper world," he said, and displayed "the gospel of His son through our martyred chieftain,—the martyred Preacher-President!"[11] The Lutheran Philip Strobel, in addition to perceiving Garfield's death as further evidence that God was sovereign over America and its history, explained that it was also a chastisement for "the liberal Christianity of the times" and its "poison of specious but destructive scepticism."[12]

The summer's drama was therefore particularly significant and gratifying, for, as Parkhurst commented, "These last years have been a season in which irreligion and unfaith have been displaying themselves with rather more than usual resoluteness and bravado." Although Christian scholars were diligently laboring "to dislodge this unfaith," God had bypassed them through an "event" intended to convince "the heart" rather than "the head." The emphasis on religious experience, though an essential feature of evangelicalism since its eighteenth-century beginnings, nevertheless reveals some defensiveness in the face of modern reason and science.[13] The Delaware Presbyterian Cyrus Huntington, marveling at the summer's events, is illustrative. "What a testimony," he announced, "has been borne by the prayers of the nation to the truth of Christianity, and to our belief in it—this too, just at a time when the blasphemer and scientist have joined their forces against the Church of God. Yes we are a Christian people." God had placed a suffering, Christlike Garfield—one who "accepted the Scriptures as the infallible rule of life"—before the nation for eighty days in order to providentially arrest encroaching unbelief.[14] Such reflections suggest an important link between Civil War–era evangelical devotion to the Union and what would become fundamentalism in the early twentieth century.

Northern evangelicals remained preoccupied with seeing a national Christian organism become more clearly manifest, and for a time such zeal could paper over a very real religious fissure developing. To most Protestants, theologically liberal or otherwise, America was still "our country"; many proudly recalled their defense of the Union and continued to reflexively presume responsibility for the country's proper Christianization. Four years after Garfield's death, the Presbyterian Byron Sunderland rehashed America's sacred narrative and announced through Daniel Webster's words once again: "We are a single people—'Union and liberty now and forever, one and inseparable!'"[15] In fact, by the 1880s some unity between northern and southern evangelicals had arisen around the use of federal governmental power to uphold aspects of individual Christian morality, in addition to participation in Dwight L. Moody's seemingly apolitical revivalism, cooperation in world missions and American imperialism, and even involvement in populist political activity; in general, however, achieving racial justice was not on the agenda, and the implication of any such intersectional activities was increasing acceptance of the Jim Crow South that was taking shape in a Christian America desirous of leaving behind war-related controversies, if not the glory of the war itself.[16] In late July 1885, just weeks after Sunderland's comments, Ulysses S. Grant died of cancer, and his death became yet another occasion for evangelicals to proclaim national Christian oneness. Eulogies for

Grant highlighted his ostensible evangelical Christian character and his heroic, Union-saving status, and his death became, as one historian puts it, "a vehicle for a religiously tinged emotional and political reconciliation of the North and South." In short, Grant was the symbolic and unifying head of a unified Protestant America—perhaps in death he could save the Union one final time.[17] In addition, 1885 was the year that the liberalizing Congregationalist Josiah Strong published *Our Country*. Strong's book, which gave attention to various perils threatening Christian America and its mission to spread beneficent Anglo-Saxon Christian civilization around the globe, was continuous with the proprietary Protestantism that stretched back to the early nineteenth century. Secularism and Roman Catholicism were among the perils he perceived; Civil War issues were not.[18] The cause of Christian America, championed in print by Strong and by all kinds of evangelicals during funerals for the two former Union generals, might obscure religious differences among white northern Protestants—but not for long.

Attaining a unified Christian American culture would remain elusive, as Protestants battled over theology and the sources of intellectual and theological authority at the turn of the century. From one angle, the fundamentalist-modernist controversy that arose primarily among northern Protestants may be viewed as a struggle over just what sort of Christianity would permeate and direct a national culture that both sides assumed was indeed supposed to be Protestant. The theologically conservative heirs of nineteenth-century northern evangelicals, known as fundamentalists by the 1910s and 1920s because of their militant defense of the so-called fundamentals of the faith, had little trouble perceiving their liberalizing opponents as threats to America. As evangelicals-turned-fundamentalists perceived matters, liberal Protestant zeal to harmonize Christianity with modernity meant emptying Protestantism of the very substance necessary to produce a virtuous and coherent American culture, the kind of culture that functioned to maintain their republic's cohesion and good standing before God. Fundamentalists thus militantly championed the type of religion that had made evangelical Protestants cultural "insiders" since the Civil War era, but which would leave them cultural "outsiders" by the 1920s. Crucially, even while fundamentalists retreated from America's dominant culture-shaping institutions and self-consciously rejected modern learning and cultural trends, they maintained and transmitted a proprietary regard for the nation that Union victory in the Civil War had seemingly vindicated.[19]

America remained "our country" to fundamentalists and the conservative evangelicals who followed in their wake, even while the discourse of Unionism fell away and new circumstances and issues arose to challenge their presumed responsibility for the nation. The historian Joel Carpenter, referring to fundamentalists after their symbolic cultural defeat in the 1925 Scopes trial, contends that "the mythic chords of 'Christian America' have played loudly in their memories, and their periodic public crusades have displayed their determination to regain lost cultural power and influence." Tellingly, Carpenter also stresses, "Even when fundamentalists have expressed their alienation toward American cultural trends and advocated separation from worldly involvement, their words have been more those of wounded lovers than true outsiders." Things were supposed to be otherwise—the way they had been in the Civil War era. During the 1930s and 1940s, fundamentalists were never "content to occupy the margins of American life," though occupy them they did. Instead, fundamentalists were "haunted," Carpenter says, "by the 'Christian America' of their memory and imagination," and thus they "could not shake the proprietary responsibility they felt for the nation's character. . . . Fundamentalists still felt called to be its guardians." It was still their country.[20]

Their successors, those World War II–era fundamentalist leaders who began the neo-evangelical movement during the late 1940s, maintained that ideal of Christian America. Throughout the 1950s and 1960s neo-evangelicals—led by the southerner Billy Graham and northerners Carl Henry and Harold John Ockenga, among others—sought to reform fundamentalism, which meant leaving behind its antimodern militancy in order to reengage with American culture. At the center of their reengagement efforts was the desire to renew America as a specifically Christian nation, though civil rights and racial justice were not a central part of that vision and garnered little active support. One could say that the cause of racial justice remained subordinate to the cause of Christian America. This was particularly true within the existential crisis of the Cold War, which found neo-evangelicals viewing their Christian country as the key to Western civilization's survival.[21] Their cultural reemergence, symbolized by Billy Graham's evangelistic efforts, would begin to include white southerners and comported well with the consensus ethos of the time that pitted a godly, free, and capitalist America against an atheistic, statist, and communist Soviet Union.[22]

In the wake of 1960s cultural disorder and struggle, the theme of a lost Christian America powerfully reemerged in conjunction with the nation's bicentennial, to become an important component of the Religious Right's response to so-called secular humanism's threatening sway over American society and politics. Needless to say, the Religious Right's influence is still felt and debated, especially after hotly contested presidential elections and disputes regarding rapidly changing cultural and moral norms since the early 1990s.[23] An important element in debates surrounding the Religious Right in the late twentieth century involved the telling of American history. Properly understanding and narrating America's story, so important to so many northern evangelicals during the nineteenth century, was crucial to white evangelicals during the 1980s, 1990s, and even into the new century.[24] In the 1860s and 1870s, getting the nation's history straight was part of a proper covenantal response to God's centuries-long beneficence toward the nation, and for some on the Religious Right, properly telling American history retains a similar covenantal meaning—likely in a vestigial and unconscious manner—vaguely promising to solve very real and complex social and moral problems facing the nation. Though such a stance has not dissipated entirely among white evangelicals, its force might be lessening in the face of dramatic political, cultural, and moral changes that have left evangelicals once again feeling as alienated cultural outsiders in what they regard as their own country. What George Marsden observed about early twentieth-century evangelicals—that they could not decide whether they resided in Israel or Babylon—likely holds true of their Religious Right descendants a hundred years later.[25]

Answering the question of "who owns" the country and its story is inextricably related to J. Hector St. Jean de Crèvecoeur's perennial question of what it means to be an American, and that question still permeates American political culture.[26] Although America never has been quite as secular as some twenty-first-century journalists, scholars, and politicians might like it to have been, neither has America ever been as unambiguously evangelical (or Christian) as some on the Religious Right longingly maintain.[27] While more secular-minded folks might be well served to think deeply about the ramifications of a history and culture shorn of religion, white evangelicals might be well served to reconsider America's meaning and history in relation to their more fundamental identity as a Christian. When Christians tell a historical tale that uncritically sanctifies much of America's past and blurs the distinction between the "city of man" and the "city of God," they put themselves at risk of violating the first and second greatest commandments—to love God above all competitors and their neighbors as themselves. When it comes to northern evangelicals and the Civil War era, the irony remains—love of the Union arguably contributed to its preservation and the slaves' emancipation, but in subsuming the ex-slaves to their vision for Christian America, northern evangelicals contributed to a Reconstruction that failed to ensure the ex-slaves' full freedom and equality as Americans.

Acknowledgments

Providentially or fortuitously, my parents and extended family are from Galena, Illinois, a small community just east of the Mississippi River. During the antebellum period, Galena was a booming lead-mining town, even surpassing Chicago in terms of economic importance for a time. In addition, the Galena area was the scene of fighting during the Black Hawk War of 1832, a conflict in which Abraham Lincoln briefly participated, and in 1856 Lincoln campaigned in Galena on behalf of the first Republican presidential candidate, John C. Frémont. However, Galena is perhaps best known as the town from which Ulysses S. Grant left for the Civil War and to which he briefly returned afterward. None of that was lost on me as a boy, especially because my maternal grandparents' home had once belonged to one of Grant's aides, William R. Rowley, and the home next door had been Civil War General John A. Rawlins's residence. I have vivid memories of wandering Galena's streets, wondering about Chief Black Hawk, Lincoln, Grant, and the Civil War. I am particularly grateful to my late grandparents, my parents, my siblings, and my aunts and uncles, each of whom in different ways encouraged my historical interests.

I am indebted to a large number of people for the completion of a book that has taken about as much time as the Civil War and Reconstruction did—or so it seems—and it is appropriate to begin with a number of individuals at the University of Notre Dame. Above all, I will always remember George Marsden with fondness and gratitude. He is a model of humility, kindness, and evenhandedness, and his scholarship continues to influence my thinking and teaching. I also will always be thankful for his generous concern for my family and me, which he exhibited in countless ways, large and small. Others deserve great thanks as well. I still own a large canoe given to me by James Turner, and thus invariably I find myself recalling with admiration and appreciation the breadth and depth of his knowledge and interests, in addition to his meticulous eye for syntax and style in his students' writing. John McGreevy's intensity, insights, and economy of thought also continue to inspire my own efforts to think, write, and teach about life in the modern world. Doris Bergen's energetic teaching, contagious passion for learning, and kindness toward my family and me never will be forgotten. Thomas Kidd, Dottie Pratt, and the late Remie Constable each assisted me in unique ways and deserve my gratitude. I also owe tremendous thanks to an anonymous donor who financed a summer research trip; constraints due to time, finances, and family commitments made research travel difficult and, without this person's generosity, nearly impossible. I am thankful to the Pew Foundation and Orville Burton for including me in a Civil War seminar held at Notre Dame a long time ago. I owe great thanks to Edward Blum, whom I met while he was visiting Notre Dame; though our interpretations differ, he steered me in a good direction and then graciously gave of his time to read the first few chapters and converse via email. Finally, I am deeply indebted to Ken Kinslow for his diligent, professional support as the interlibrary loan director at the Hesburgh Library; he regularly assured me that the budget could handle my inordinately high number of requests.

There are quite a few friends from Notre Dame who merit acknowledgment. Michael Lee, Jonathan Denhartog, and Margaret Abruzzo were continual sources of friendship, encouragement, and intellectual stimulation, and, although outside my immediate cohort, the same goes for Brian Pitts, Andrew Deliyannides, Daniel Kim, Peter Wallace, Jonathan Couser, David DiQuattro, Mitch Stokes, Michael DeGruccio, Darren Dochuk, and Thomas Kidd. I will always fondly remember Jarrett Carty, after whom our fifth child was named. Not only was Jarrett a steady source of encouragement, we had a great time playing hockey and discovering a fantastic double I.P.A. together.

Going further back in time, I must mention several folks from Boston and Gordon-Conwell. I am especially indebted to Richard Lints for looking out for me and specifically encouraging me to go to Notre Dame. Fabrice and Silvia Jotterand were always generous, faithful friends to us, never more so than when they gave us a car when we really needed one. Some of my deepest gratitude and affection goes to Peter and Doreen Butler for their kindness and friendship over two decades. I will never forget working at UPS for four years with Peter—arguing about the Blackhawks and Bruins, and occasionally moving packages. The Butlers also merit thanks for putting me up while I commuted back and forth to the American Antiquarian Society in Worcester.

I must thank a handful of others who also contributed in various ways to the book's completion. Gary Gallagher generously gave of his time to read a portion of the manuscript and encourage me to publish. Gabe Sink has been a dedicated, generous friend, to whom I owe great thanks for his steady encouragement and the countless diversionary conversations and activities we participated in over a long period of time—usually centered on hockey. Thanks also go to a long list of people in Florida. Much appreciation goes to Jim and Dayle Seneff, whose kind generosity to my family and me has been manifest in countless ways over the past decade. The same may be said of Bob Ingram, who has been unceasingly generous, while Jim Reynolds has been kindly supportive of my interests and efforts over the last several years. David and Lou Jones were particularly kind to make their vacated house available—the peace and quiet proved indispensable. I am deeply indebted to Megan Brown and Nathan Raley for their editorial assistance early on, and to Joe Moon, for reading the entire manuscript at a late stage. Joe's keen mind saved me from numerous mistakes—hopefully he caught them all. Jeremy Brown, Kevin Clark, Tim Michaud, my daughter, Sarah, and my son Eli deserve thanks for getting me books and articles at various moments. Edward Chandler, Kevin Clark, Nick DeGroot, Michael Miller, and David Petrak have been generous friends and inspiring conversation partners. Jordan Stewart, Lydia Francis, Madeline Miller, and Benjamin Reynolds, four former students, deserve special thanks for their constant encouragement and interest in the project.

Those at Fordham University Press have been nothing but professional, but that professionalism has been coupled with kindness, patience, and encouragement through the whole process. I am grateful. At every turn Fredric Nachbaur has exhibited all of those qualities in abundance; Andrew Slap's patient, critical readings and comments have encouraged excellence from the very beginning; and Will Cerbone and Katie Sweeney have exuded professional kindness in response to every email and question. Thanks also go to Fordham's anonymous reader for insightful and encouraging comments and to Teresa Jesionowski for her painstaking copyediting.

My wife and children deserve the most significant thanks. Sarah, Eli, Ethan, Thomas, and Jarrett have loved their dad, despite the fact that he seemed too tired, too busy, and too preoccupied all too often. Finally, I can only offer insufficient thanks to my wife, Kelli. She has patiently loved me and sacrificed more than I know to enable the book's completion.

Notes

Abbreviations

AHR — *American Historical Review*
AJP — Andrew Johnson Papers, Manuscripts Division, Library of Congress, Washington, D.C.
APR — *American Presbyterian Review*
APTR — *American Presbyterian and Theological Review*
AQ — *American Quarterly*
BQ — *Baptist Quarterly*
BRPR — *Biblical Repertory and Princeton Review*
CH — *Church History*
CR — *Christian Recorder*
CFP — Cheever Family Papers, American Antiquarian Society, Worcester, Massachusetts
CW — Roy P. Basler, ed., *The Collected Works of Abraham Lincoln*, 9 vols. New Brunswick, N.J.: Rutgers University Press, 1953–55.
CWH — *Civil War History*
FDP — John W. Blassingame and John R. McKivigan, eds., *The Frederick Douglass Papers*, Series One: Speeches, Debates, and Interviews, 5 vols. New Haven, Conn.: Yale University Press, 1979–92.
GHQ — *Georgia Historical Quarterly*
GPP — George Peck Papers, E. S. Bird Memorial Library, Special Collections, Syracuse University, Syracuse, New York
HBP — Henry Boardman Papers, Presbyterian Historical Society, Philadelphia
IHJ — *Illinois Historical Journal*
JAH — *Journal of American History*
JALA — *Journal of the Abraham Lincoln Association*
JCWE — *Journal of the Civil War Era*
JER — *Journal of the Early Republic*
JISHS — *Journal of the Illinois State Historical Society*
JNH — *Journal of Negro History*
JPH — *Journal of Presbyterian History*
JSH — *Journal of Southern History*
LWFD — Philip S. Foner, ed., *The Life and Writings of Frederick Douglass*, 5 vols. New York: International Publishers, 1950–55.
MQR — *Methodist Quarterly Review*
MSP — Matthew Simpson Papers, Manuscripts Division, Library of Congress, Washington, D.C.

NE	*New Englander and Yale Review*
NYE	*New York Evangelist*
OOHP	Oliver Otis Howard Papers, George J. Mitchell Department of Special Collections & Archives, Bowdoin College Library, Brunswick, Maine
PAJ	LeRoy P. Graf, Ralph Haskins, Paul H. Bergeron, et al., eds., *The Papers of Andrew Johnson*, 16 vols. Knoxville: University of Tennessee Press, 1967–.
PGP	Phineas Gurley Papers, Presbyterian Historical Society, Philadelphia
PQPR	*Presbyterian Quarterly and Princeton Review*
PUSG	John Y. Simon, ed., *The Papers of Ulysses S. Grant*, 28 vols. Carbondale: University of Southern Illinois Press, 1967–.
RKHS	*The Register of the Kentucky Historical Society*
USGP	Ulysses S. Grant Papers, Manuscripts Division, Library of Congress, Washington, D.C.
WMQ	*William and Mary Quarterly*
ZH	*Zion's Herald*

Introduction: "Long Live the Glorious Union"

1. George Peck, *Our Country: Its Trial and Its Triumph, a Series of Discourses Suggested by the Varying Events of the War for the Union* (New York: Carlton and Porter, 1865); idem, *The Life and Times of Rev. George Peck, D.D., Written by Himself* (New York: Nelson and Phillips, 1874), 384–85; Paul Sorrentino, *Stephen Crane: A Life of Fire* (Cambridge, Mass.: Belknap Press of Harvard University Press, 2014), 23–25. Peck's daughter Mary Helen, later a Women's Christian Temperance Union activist, married Methodist minister Jonathan Townley Crane, and Stephen Crane was the youngest of fourteen children; Peck's brother was Jesse Truesdell Peck, former college president, Methodist bishop, historian, and cofounder of Syracuse University.

2. G. Peck, *Life and Times*, 200; idem, *National Evils and Their Remedy* (N.p.: G. Lane and P. P. Sandford, 1841); Timothy L. Smith, *Revivalism and Social Reform: American Protestantism on the Eve of the Civil War* (Nashville, Tenn.: Abingdon Press, 1957; repr., New York: Harper and Row, 1965), 211; Richard J. Carwardine, *Evangelicals and Politics in Antebellum America* (New Haven, Conn.: Yale University Press, 1993), 183–85. Regarding Lincoln's Unionism, see William E. Gienapp, *Abraham Lincoln and Civil War America: A Biography* (New York: Oxford University Press, 2002), 72–203; William C. Harris, *With Charity for All: Lincoln and the Restoration of the Union* (Lexington: University Press of Kentucky, 1997), 258–64; idem, *Lincoln and the Border States: Preserving the Union* (Lawrence: University Press of Kansas, 2011); Brooks D. Simpson, *The Reconstruction Presidents* (Lawrence: University Press of Kansas, 1998), 9–64. Cf. George M. Fredrickson, *Big Enough to Be Inconsistent: Abraham Lincoln Confronts Slavery and Race* (Cambridge, Mass.: Harvard University Press, 2008); Eric Foner, *The Fiery Trial: Abraham Lincoln and American Slavery* (New York: W. W. Norton, 2010). Fredrickson and Foner accentuate Lincoln's "growth" regarding slavery, while revealing the Unionism within which emancipation emerged.

3. G. Peck, *Life and Times*, 9–12. Mark A. Noll, *America's God: From Jonathan Edwards to Abraham Lincoln* (New York: Oxford University Press, 2002), 362–63, downplays Methodist nationalism. Cf. Donald G. Jones, *The Sectional Crisis and Northern Methodism: A Study in Piety, Political Ethics, and Civil Religion* (Metuchen, N.J.: Scarecrow Press, 1979); Ralph E. Morrow, *Northern Methodism and Reconstruction* (East Lansing: Michigan State University Press, 1956); Richard J. Carwardine, "Methodists, Politics, and the Coming of the American Civil War," *CH* 69 (September 2000): 578–609.

4. G. Peck, *Our Country*, 8, 11, 18–19.

5. "Proprietary" comes from Mark A. Noll, *A History of Christianity in the United States and Canada* (Grand Rapids, Mich.: Wm. B. Eerdmans, 1992), 287. See also Robert T. Handy, *A Christian America: Protestant Hopes and Historical Realities*, 2nd ed. (New York: Oxford University Press, 1984); idem, "The Protestant Quest for a Christian America, 1830–1930," *CH* 22 (March 1953): 8–20; Mark A. Noll, Nathan O. Hatch, and George M. Marsden, *The Search for Christian America* (Westchester, Ill.: Crossway, 1983).

6. Richard J. Carwardine, *Lincoln* (Harlow, Eng,: Pearson Longman, 2003), xiii; idem, *Evangelicals and Politics*, 44; Noll, *History of Christianity*, 222.

7. This summary/definition rests on David Bebbington, *Evangelicalism in Modern Britain: A History from the 1730s to the 1980s* (London: Unwin Hyman, 1989), 2–17; Sydney E. Ahlstrom, *A Religious History of the American People* (New Haven, Conn.: Yale University Press, 1972), 263–329, 556; Mark A. Noll, *American Evangelical Christianity: An Introduction* (Oxford: Blackwell, 2001); idem, *The Rise of Evangelicalism: The Age of Edwards, Whitefield and the Wesleys* (Downers Grove, Ill.: InterVarsity, 2003), 13–21; idem, *America's God*, 5, 31–33, 227; idem, *History of Christianity*, 220–22, 243, 287; idem, "Common Sense Traditions and American Evangelical Thought," *AQ* 37 (Summer 1985): 216–38; Carwardine, *Evangelicals and Politics*, 1–6, 199–204; Donald G. Mathews, *Religion in the Old South* (Chicago: University of Chicago Press, 1977), xiv–xviii; Anne C. Loveland, *Southern Evangelicals and the Social Order, 1800–1860* (Baton Rouge: Louisiana State University Press, 1980); Christine Leigh Heyrman, *Southern Cross: The Beginnings of the Bible Belt* (Chapel Hill: University of North Carolina Press, 1997), 3–27; E. Brooks Holifield, *The Gentlemen Theologians: American Theology in Southern Culture, 1795–1860* (Durham, N.C.: Duke University Press, 1978); C. C. Goen, *Broken Churches, Broken Nation: Denominational Schisms and the Coming of the Civil War* (Macon, Ga.: Mercer University Press, 1985), 12–13, 43–63; George M. Marsden, *Fundamentalism and American Culture*, 2nd ed. (New York: Oxford University Press, 2006), 12–21.

8. Regarding denominational differences, see E. Brooks Holifield, *Theology in America: Christian Thought from the Age of the Puritans to the Civil War* (New Haven, Conn.: Yale University Press, 2003); idem, *Gentlemen Theologians*, 155–207; Richard J. Carwardine, "Religion and National Construction in the Age of Lincoln," *Journal of Mormon History* 36 (Spring 2010): 28–53; James D. Bratt, "Religious Anti-Revivalism in Antebellum America," *JER* 24 (Spring 2004): 65–106; Steve Longenecker, *Gettysburg Religion: Refinement, Diversity, and Race in the Antebellum and Civil War Border North* (New York: Fordham University Press, 2014), 80–98; John R. McKivigan, *The War against Proslavery Religion: Abolitionism and the Northern Churches, 1830–1865* (Ithaca, N.Y.: Cornell University Press, 1984), 24–29.

9. Mathews, *Religion in the Old South*, 39–80; Gaines M. Foster, "The End of Slavery and the Origins of the Bible Belt," in *Vale of Tears: New Essays on Religion and Reconstruction*, ed. Edward J. Blum and W. Scott Poole (Macon, Ga.: Mercer University Press, 2005), 149–50; Carwardine, *Evangelicals and Politics*, xvi–xvii; Daniel Walker Howe, *Making the American Self: Jonathan Edwards to Abraham Lincoln* (New York: Oxford University Press, 2009), 109, 115–17.

10. Ahlstrom, *Religious History*, 429–509; Noll, *America's God*, 73–92, 161–208; Nathan O. Hatch, *The Sacred Cause of Liberty: Republican Thought and the Millennium in Revolutionary New England* (New Haven, Conn.: Yale University Press, 1977); idem, *The Democratization of American Christianity* (New Haven, Conn.: Yale University Press, 1989); Mark A. Noll, *The Old Religion in the New World: The History of North American Christianity* (Grand Rapids, Mich.: Wm. B. Eerdmans, 2002), 48–71. Regarding antebellum reform, see Smith, *Revivalism and Social Reform*; Ronald G. Walters, *American Reformers, 1815–1860*, rev. ed. (New York: Hill and Wang, 1997); Robert H. Abzug, *Cosmos Crumbling: American Reform and the Religious Imagination* (New York: Oxford University Press, 1994); Alice Felt Tyler, *Freedom's Ferment: Phases of American Social History from the Colonial Period to the Outbreak of the Civil War* (Minneapolis: University of Minnesota Press, 1944; repr., New York: Harper and Row, 1962), 463–547; Charles C. Cole Jr., *The Social Ideas of the Northern Evangelists* (New York: Columbia University Press, 1954); John R. Bodo, *The Protestant Clergy and Social Issues, 1812–1848* (Princeton, N.J.: Princeton University Press, 1954); Loveland, *Southern Evangelicals*, 130–85; Donald G. Mathews, "The Second Great Awakening as an Organizing Process," *AQ* 21 (Spring 1969): 23–44; Daniel Walker Howe, "The Evangelical Movement and Political Culture in the North during the Second Party System," *JAH* 77 (March 1991): 1216–39; idem, *What Hath God Wrought: The Transformation of America, 1815–1848* (New York: Oxford University Press, 2007), 164–202, 285–327; George M. Marsden, *The Evangelical Mind and the New School Presbyterian Experience: A Case Study of Thought and Theology in Nineteenth-Century America* (New Haven, Conn.: Yale University Press, 1970); Leo P. Hirrel, *Children of Wrath: New School Calvinism and Antebellum Reform* (Lexington: University Press of Kentucky, 1998). Cf. Mark Y. Hanley, *Beyond a Christian Commonwealth: The Protestant Quarrel with the American Republic, 1830–1860* (Chapel Hill: University of North Carolina Press, 1994).

11. Commitment to the Union remained strong despite growing regional self-consciousness during the 1850s. Loveland, *Southern Evangelicals*, 109 (quote), 257–58; Bertram Wyatt-Brown, *The Shaping of Southern Culture: Honor, Grace, and War, 1760s–1880s* (Chapel Hill: University of North Carolina Press, 2001), 154–74; Charles F. Irons, *The Origins of Proslavery Christianity: White and Black Evangelicals in Colonial and Antebellum Virginia* (Chapel Hill: University of North Carolina Press, 2008), 211–46; George C. Rable, *God's Almost Chosen Peoples: A Religious History of the Civil War* (Chapel Hill: University of North Carolina Press, 2010), 27, 38; James W. Silver, *Confederate Morale and Church Propaganda* (Tuscaloosa, Ala.: Confederate, 1957; repr., New York: W. W. Norton, 1967), 23; Carwardine, *Evangelicals and Politics*, 279–318.

12. Regarding covenantalism, see Ahlstrom, *Religious History*, 124–50; Noll, *America's God*, 8–42; Marsden, *Evangelical Mind*, 198–211; idem, "America's 'Christian' Origins:

Puritan New England as a Case Study," in *The Search for Christian America*, ed. Mark A. Noll, Nathan O. Hatch, and George M. Marsden (Westchester, Ill.: Crossway, 1983), 28–47; Harry S. Stout, *The New England Soul: Preaching and Religious Culture in Colonial New England* (New York: Oxford University Press, 1986); idem, *Upon the Altar of the Nation: A Moral History of the Civil War* (New York: Viking, 2006), 38–52; Rable, *God's Almost Chosen Peoples*, passim; Loveland, *Southern Evangelicals*, 125–29; Mitchell Snay, *Gospel of Disunion: Religion and Separatism in the Antebellum South* (Cambridge: Cambridge University Press, 1993), 165–70; James O. Farmer Jr., *The Metaphysical Confederacy: James Henry Thornwell and the Synthesis of Southern Values*, 2nd ed. (Macon, Ga.: Mercer University Press, 1999), 261–63; Silver, *Confederate Morale and Church Propaganda*, 25–41; Gaines M. Foster, "A Christian Nation: Signs of a Covenant," in *Bonds of Affection: Americans Define Their Patriotism*, ed. John E. Bodnar (Princeton, N.J.: Princeton University Press, 1996), 120–38; Daniel W. Stowell, *Rebuilding Zion: The Religious Reconstruction of the South, 1863–1877* (New York: Oxford University Press, 1998), 33–79. Regarding millennialism, see Ernest Tuveson, *Redeemer Nation: The Idea of America's Millennial Role* (Chicago: University of Chicago Press, 1968); James Moorhead, *American Apocalypse: Yankee Protestants and the Civil War, 1860–1869* (New Haven, Conn.: Yale University Press, 1978); idem, "Between Progress and the Apocalypse: A Reassessment of Millennialism in American Religious Thought, 1800–1880," *JAH* 71 (December 1984): 524–42; Howe, *What Hath God Wrought*, 285–327; Orville Vernon Burton, *The Age of Lincoln* (New York: Hill and Wang, 2007), 139–41; George M. Fredrickson, "The Coming of the Lord: The Northern Protestant Clergy and the Civil War Crisis," in *Religion and the American Civil War*, ed. Randall M. Miller, Harry S. Stout, and Charles Reagan Wilson (New York: Oxford University Press, 1998), 110–30; Jack P. Maddex Jr., "Proslavery Millennialism: Social Eschatology in Antebellum Southern Calvinism," *AQ* 31 (Spring 1979): 46–62; Loveland, *Southern Evangelicals*, 159–62; Snay, *Gospel of Disunion*, 186–88.

13. Eugene D. Genovese, "Religion in the Collapse of the American Union," in *Religion and the American Civil War*, ed. Randall M. Miller, Harry S. Stout, and Charles Reagan Wilson (New York: Oxford University Press, 1998), 75. Regarding southern nationalism and sectional differences, see Rollin G. Osterweis, *Romanticism and Nationalism in the Old South* (New Haven, Conn.: Yale University Press, 1949), 132–41; William R. Taylor, *Cavalier and Yankee: The Old South and American National Character* (New York: G. Braziller, 1961); Emory M. Thomas, *The Confederate Nation: 1861–1865* (New York: Harper and Row, 1979), 17–36; John McCardell, *The Idea of a Southern Nation: Southern Nationalists and Southern Nationalism, 1830–1860* (New York: W. W. Norton, 1979); Drew Gilpin Faust, *The Creation of Confederate Nationalism* (Baton Rouge: Louisiana State University Press, 1988), 1–21; Gary W. Gallagher, *The Confederate War: How Popular Will, Nationalism, and Military Strategy Could Not Stave Off Defeat* (Cambridge, Mass.: Harvard University Press, 1997), 95–101; James M. McPherson, *Is Blood Thicker Than Water: Crises of Nationalism in the Modern World* (Toronto: Vintage Canada, 1998), 40–51; idem, *Drawn with the Sword: Reflections on the American Civil War* (New York: Oxford University Press, 1996), 3–23; Edward Pessen, "How Different from Each Other Were the Antebellum North and South?" *AHR* 85 (December 1980): 1119–49; Frank Towers, "Partisans, New History, and Modernization: The Historiography of the Civil War's Causes," *JCWE* 1 (June 2011): 237–64.

14. Charles Reagan Wilson, "Religion and the American Civil War in Comparative Perspective," in *Religion and the American Civil War*, ed. Randall M. Miller, Harry S. Stout, and Charles Reagan Wilson (New York: Oxford University Press, 1998), 385–407; Wyatt-Brown, *Shaping of Southern Culture*, 179–82; George M. Marsden, *Religion and American Culture*, 2nd ed. (Orlando, Fla.: Harcourt, 2001), 10–11, 16; Michael Fellman, *In the Name of God and Country: Reconsidering Terrorism in American History* (New Haven, Conn.: Yale University Press, 2010), 58; Sheldon S. Wolin, *Politics and Vision: Continuity and Innovation in Western Political Thought* (Boston: Little, Brown, 1960), 123–31.

15. I recognize that there was not a monolithic "South." See William W. Freehling, *The Road to Disunion*, vol. 1, *Secessionists at Bay, 1776–1854* (New York: Oxford University Press, 1990), 17–18. The paragraph relies on James M. McPherson, *Ordeal by Fire: The Civil War and Reconstruction*, 3rd ed. (Boston: McGraw Hill, 2001), 27–42; idem, *Drawn with the Sword*, 3–23; Bruce Levine, *Half Slave and Half Free: The Roots of the Civil War* (New York: Hill and Wang, 1992), 17–45, 95–120; Douglass C. North, *The Economic Growth of the United States, 1790–1860* (1961; New York: W. W. Norton, 1966), 122–34; James Oakes, *Slavery and Freedom: An Interpretation of the Old South* (New York: W. W. Norton, 1990); Kenneth Startup, "'A Mere Calculation of Profits and Loss': The Southern Clergy and the Economic Culture of the Antebellum North," in *God and Mammon: Protestants, Money, and the Market, 1790–1860*, ed. Mark A. Noll (New York: Oxford University Press, 2001), 217–35; Bertram Wyatt-Brown, *Southern Honor: Ethics and Behavior in the Old South*, 2nd ed. (New York: Oxford University Press, 2007); idem, *Shaping of Southern Culture*, 83–105; Edward R. Crowther, "Holy Honor: Sacred and Secular in the Old South," *JSH* 58 (November 1992): 619–36; Mathews, *Religion in the Old South*, 136–84; Loveland, *Southern Evangelicals*, 186–265; Albert J. Raboteau, *Slave Religion: The "Invisible Institution" in the Antebellum South* (New York: Oxford University Press, 1978), 96–210; Irons, *Origins of Proslavery Christianity*, 169–209; Gaines M. Foster, "Guilt over Slavery: A Historiographical Analysis," *JSH* 56 (November 1990): 665–94; William W. Freehling, *The Reintegration of American History: Slavery and the Civil War* (New York: Oxford University Press, 1994), 59–81; Farmer, *Metaphysical Confederacy*, 195–233; Elizabeth Fox-Genovese and Eugene D. Genovese, "The Divine Sanction of the Social Order: Religious Foundations of the Southern Slaveholders' World View," *Journal of the American Academy of Religion* 55 (Summer 1987): 211–33; idem, "The Religious Ideals of Southern Slave Society," *GHQ* (Spring 1986): 1–16; Snay, *Gospel of Disunion*, 151–218; McCardell, *Idea of a Southern Nation*, 177–276; Taylor, *Cavalier and Yankee*, 334–39; Arthur Bestor, "State Sovereignty and Slavery: A Reinterpretation of Proslavery Constitutional Doctrine, 1846–1860," *JISHS* 54 (Summer 1961): 117–80; idem, "The American Civil War as a Constitutional Crisis," *AHR* 69 (January 1964): 327–52.

16. Howe, "Evangelical Movement," 1216, 1222; idem, *Making the American Self*, 107–17; Wilfred M. McClay, *The Masterless: Self and Society in Modern America* (Chapel Hill: University of North Carolina Press, 1994), 46–50; McPherson, *Ordeal by Fire*, 5–26, 48–51; idem, *Drawn with the Sword*, 3–23; Eric Foner, *Free Soil, Free Labor, Free Men: The Ideology of the Republican Party before the Civil War*, 2nd ed. (New York: Oxford University Press, 1995); Levine, *Half Slave and Half Free*, 46–94.

17. Wyatt-Brown, *Shaping of Southern Culture*, 177 (quote); Mark A. Noll, *The Civil War as a Theological Crisis* (Chapel Hill: University of North Carolina Press, 2006), 31–74; idem, "The Bible and Slavery," in *Religion and the American Civil War*, ed. Randall M. Miller, Harry S. Stout, and Charles Reagan Wilson (New York: Oxford University Press, 1998), 43–73; Holifield, *Theology in America*, 494–504; Genovese, "Religion in the Collapse of the American Union"; Farmer, *Metaphysical Confederacy*, 195–233; Snay, *Gospel of Disunion*, 53–150; Loveland, *Southern Evangelicals*, 257–65; Mathews, *Religion in the Old South*, 136–84; Stephen R. Haynes, *The Biblical Justification of American Slavery* (New York: Oxford University Press, 2002); Goen, *Broken Churches, Broken Nation*, 65–107; Carwardine, *Evangelicals and Politics*, 133–74; idem, "Trauma in Methodism: Property, Church Schism, and Sectional Polarization in Antebellum America," in *God and Mammon: Protestants, Money, and the Market, 1790–1860*, ed. Mark A. Noll (New York: Oxford University Press, 2001), 195–216; Rable, *God's Almost Chosen Peoples*, 22–32; Marsden, *Evangelical Mind*, 59–87; Lewis G. Vander Velde, *The Presbyterian Churches and the Federal Union, 1861–1869* (Cambridge, Mass.: Harvard University Press, 1932), 3–17. Old and New School Presbyterians divided in 1837 primarily over doctrinal differences, but slavery-related issues were involved. In 1857 New School Presbyterians split along sectional lines, followed by Old School Presbyterians in 1861. Episcopalians never split.

18. Faust, *Creation of Confederate Nationalism*, 22; Edward L. Ayers, *What Caused the Civil War? Reflections on the South and Southern History* (New York: W. W. Norton, 2005), 55; William J. Cooper Jr., *Liberty and Slavery: Southern Politics to 1860* (New York: McGraw-Hill, 1983), 267–69; Wyatt-Brown, *Shaping of Southern Culture*, 154–202; idem, *Yankee Saints and Southern Sinners* (Baton Rouge: Louisiana State University Press, 1985), 183–213. Regarding the path to secession, see William W. Freehling, *The Road to Disunion*, vol. 2, *Secessionists Triumphant, 1854–1861* (New York: Oxford University Press, 2007).

19. Snay, *Gospel of Disunion*, 151–56, 199–200, 215–16; Rable, *God's Almost Chosen Peoples*, 33–50, 62–63; Mark E. Neely Jr., *Lincoln and the Triumph of the Nation: Constitutional Conflict in the American Civil War* (Chapel Hill: University of North Carolina Press, 2011), 253–60, 277–78; Marshall L. DeRosa, *The Confederate Constitution of 1861: An Inquiry into American Constitutionalism* (Columbia: University of Missouri Press, 1991), 53–55. The Confederate Constitution, unlike the U.S. Constitution, invoked "the favor and guidance of Almighty God."

20. Michael F. Holt, *The Political Crisis of the 1850s* (New York: W. W. Norton, 1983), 183–217; idem, *The Fate of Our Country: Politicians, Slavery Extension, and the Coming of the Civil War* (New York: Hill and Wang, 2004), 26–28, 115–27; William W. Freehling, "Reviving State Rights," in *A Political Nation: New Directions in Mid-Nineteenth-Century American Political History*, ed. Gary W. Gallagher and Rachel A. Shelden (Charlottesville: University of Virginia Press, 2012), 112–14; Leonard L. Richards, *The Slave Power: The Free North and Southern Domination, 1780–1860* (Baton Rouge: Louisiana State University Press, 2000).

21. Loveland, *Southern Evangelicals*, 263–64; Snay, *Gospel of Disunion*, 164–98.

22. Alexander H. Stephens, "Cornerstone Address," in *Southern Pamphlets on Secession, November 1860–April 1861*, ed. Jon L. Wakelyn (Chapel Hill: University of North

Carolina Press, 1996), 402–12; Neely, *Lincoln and the Triumph of the Nation*, 237–74; Charles B. Dew, *Apostles of Disunion: Southern Secession Commissioners and the Causes of the Civil War* (Charlottesville: University of Virginia Press, 2001).

23. Cooper, *Liberty and Slavery*, 267; Freehling, *Road to Disunion*, 2:346–47; Faust, *Creation of Confederate Nationalism*, 14; Taylor, *Cavalier and Yankee*, 261–76; James M. McPherson, "American Victory, American Defeat," in *Why the Confederacy Lost*, ed. Gabor S. Boritt (New York: Oxford University Press, 1992), 30.

24. See Benjamin Morgan Palmer, *Thanksgiving Sermon* (New York: George F. Nesbitt, 1861). Snay, *Gospel of Disunion*, 188–96, portrays the New Orleans Presbyterian's sermon as representative of evangelicals' defense of the South and secession.

25. Carwardine, *Evangelicals and Politics*, xv–xvi, 51, 98; Robert P. Swierenga, "Ethnoreligious Political Behavior in the Mid-Nineteenth Century: Voting, Values, Cultures," in *Religion and American Politics: From the Colonial Period to the Present*, 2nd ed., ed. Mark A. Noll and Luke E. Harlow (New York: Oxford University Press, 2007), 145–68; Ronald P. Formisano, "The Invention of the Ethnocultural Interpretation," *AHR* 99 (April 1994): 453–77; Michael F. Holt, *The Rise of the American Whig Party: Jacksonian Politics and the Origins of the Civil War* (New York: Oxford University Press, 1999), 117–19; Richard Jensen, *The Winning of the Midwest: Social and Political Conflict, 1888–1896* (Chicago: University of Chicago Press, 1971); Paul Kleppner, *Cross of Culture: A Social Analysis of Midwestern Politics, 1850–1900* (New York: Free Press, 1970); idem, *The Third Electoral System, 1853–1892: Parties, Voters, and Political Cultures* (Chapel Hill: University of North Carolina Press, 1979). Cf. Eric Foner, "The Causes of the American Civil War: Recent Interpretations and New Directions," *CWH* 20 (September 1974): 197–214.

26. Boardman graduated from Yale and Princeton and pastored Tenth Presbyterian Church (1833–76). He preached a typical evangelical message of sin, salvation, and piety. See Henry A. Boardman, Undated Sermons, "Spiritual Declensions," HBP; idem, *The Great Question: Will You Consider the Subject of Personal Religion* (Philadelphia: American Sunday School Union, 1855 [?]); idem, *Earthly Suffering and Heavenly Glory* (Philadelphia: J. B. Lippincott, 1878); Allen C. Guelzo, "The First Three 'B's,'" in *Tenth Presbyterian Church of Philadelphia: 175 Years of Thinking and Acting Biblically*, ed. Philip Graham Ryken (Phillipsburg, N.J.: Presbyterian and Reformed, 2004), 49–67; A. A. Hodge, *Address at the Funeral of Rev. Henry Augustus Boardman, D.D.* (Philadelphia: Chandler Printing House, 1881); John DeWitt, *A Sermon Commemorative of the Life and Work of the Rev. Henry Augustus Boardman, D.D.* (Philadelphia: Chandler Printing House [?], 1881).

27. Cheever graduated from Bowdoin College and Andover Seminary and was a classmate of Nathaniel Hawthorne, Henry Longfellow, and Franklin Pierce at Bowdoin. He pastored New York's aptly named Church of the Puritans (1846–70) and involved himself in numerous controversies over Indian removal, temperance, Unitarianism, Roman Catholicism, education, and capital punishment. During the 1850s he was a nationally known abolitionist gadfly. Because of religious differences, he maintained formal distance from prominent abolitionists such as William Lloyd Garrison, Wendell Phillips, Parker Pillsbury, and Oliver Johnson; in 1859 he and his brother, Henry, founded the Church Anti-Slavery Society as the evangelical counterpart to the American Anti-Slavery Society. See Robert M. York, *George B. Cheever: Religious and Social Reformer,*

1807–1890 (Orono, Maine: University Press, 1955); Wyatt-Brown, *Yankee Saints and Southern Sinners*, 42–75; James M. McPherson, *The Struggle for Equality: Abolitionists and the Negro in the Civil War and Reconstruction* (Princeton, N.J.: Princeton University Press, 1964), 5, 78, 83–84; George B. Cheever, *God's Hand in America* (New York: M. W. Dodd, 1841); idem, *The Elements of National Greatness* (New York: John S. Taylor, 1843); idem, *Right of the Bible in Our Public Schools* (New York: Robert Carter and Brothers, 1854); idem, *God against Slavery* (New York: Joseph H. Ladd, 1857).

28. The terms *conservative*, *moderate*, and *radical* indicate wartime differences regarding the importance of the Union vis-à-vis emancipation, while suggesting differing attitudes toward blacks and the South afterward. Although many conservatives and moderates came to oppose slavery, they were not abolitionists, that small, vocal, and less-than-unified group of radicals calling for federal action to accomplish several things: abolish slavery immediately; ensure civil, political, and (perhaps) social equality for ex-slaves; redistribute confiscated southern land; harshly punish and proscribe southern leadership; and keep southern states out of the Union as long as necessary. See Harris, *With Charity for All*, 5–6; McPherson, *Struggle for Equality*; James Brewer Stewart, *Holy Warriors: The Abolitionists and American Slavery* (New York: Hill and Wang, 1976); Carwardine, *Evangelicals and Politics*, 139–43; McKivigan, *War against Proslavery Religion*, 29–35; Anne C. Loveland, "Evangelicalism and 'Immediate Emancipation' in American Antislavery Thought," *JSH* 32 (May 1966): 172–88; Eric Foner, *Reconstruction: America's Unfinished Revolution, 1863–1877* (New York: Harper and Row, 1988), 60–62; Simpson, *Reconstruction Presidents*, 37; Michael Les Benedict, *Compromise of Principle: Congressional Republicans and Reconstruction, 1863–1869* (New York: W. W. Norton, 1974), 21–58.

29. Note Freehling, *Reintegration of American History*, viii; Holt, *Fate of Our Country*, xi; Simpson, *Reconstruction Presidents*, ix; Glenn C. Altschuler and Stuart M. Blumin, *Rude Republic: Americans and Their Politics in the Nineteenth Century* (Princeton, N.J.: Princeton University Press, 2000); idem, "'Where Is the Real America?': Politics and Popular Consciousness in the Antebellum Era," *AQ* 49 (June 1997): 225–67; William E. Gienapp, "'Politics Seem to Enter into Everything': Political Culture in the North, 1840–1860," in *Essays on American Antebellum Politics, 1840–1860*, ed. William E. Gienapp et al. (College Station: Texas A & M University Press, 1982), 15, 66; Joel H. Silbey, *The American Political Nation, 1838–1893* (Stanford, Calif.: Stanford University Press, 1991); Ronald P. Formisano, "The 'Party Period' Revisited," *JAH* 86 (June 1999): 93–120; Mark E. Neely Jr., *The Boundaries of American Political Culture in the Civil War Era* (Chapel Hill: University of North Carolina Press, 2005).

30. Gary Scott Smith, *Faith and the Presidency: From George Washington to George W. Bush* (New York: Oxford University Press, 2006); Richard V. Pierard and Robert D. Linder, *Civil Religion and the Presidency* (Grand Rapids, Mich.: Academie, 1988); Caroline Winterer, *The Culture of Classicism: Ancient Greece and Rome in American Intellectual Life, 1780–1910* (Baltimore: Johns Hopkins University Press, 2002), 44–76.

31. Martin Marty, Foreword to Pierard and Linder, *Civil Religion and the Presidency*, ix.

32. Note Brooks D. Simpson, "Consider the Alternatives: Reassessing Republican Reconstruction," in *A Political Nation: New Directions in Mid-Nineteenth-Century*

American Political History, ed. Gary W. Gallagher and Rachel A. Shelden (Charlottesville: University Virginia Press, 2012), 214–30; Ayers, *What Caused the Civil War*, 145–66; James L. Huston, "Reconstruction as It Should Have Been: An Exercise in Counterfactual History," *CWH* 51 (December 2005): 358–63; Roger L. Ransom, "Reconstructing Reconstruction: Options and Limitations to Federal Policies on Land Distribution in 1866–67," *CWH* 51 (December 2005): 364–77; Heather Cox Richardson, "A Marshall Plan for the South? The Failure of Republican and Democratic Ideology during Reconstruction," *CWH* 51 (December 2005): 378–87; William Alan Blair, "The Use of Military Force to Protect the Gains of Reconstruction," *CWH* 51 (December 2005): 388–402; James L. Huston, "An Alternative to the Tragic Era: Applying the Virtues of Bureaucracy to the Reconstruction Dilemma," *CWH* 51 (December 2005): 403–15; Michael Vorenberg, "Imagining a Different Reconstruction Constitution," *CWH* 51 (December 2005): 416–26.

33. Note Jon Butler, "Jack-in-the-Box Faith: The Religion Problem in American History," *JAH* 90 (March 2004): 1357–78; David Hollinger, "The 'Secularization' Question and the United States in the Twentieth Century," *CH* 70 (March 2001): 132–43. Paul Harvey rightly indicates that although religion "has been left largely on the sidelines" of Reconstruction historiography, "religious historians have . . . tended to ignore the implications of their work for the larger Reconstruction story" (Paul Harvey, "That Was about Equalization after Freedom: Southern Evangelicalism and the Politics of Reconstruction and Redemption, 1861–1900," in *Vale of Tears: New Essays on Religion and Reconstruction*, ed. Edward J. Blum and W. Scott Poole [Macon, Ga.: Mercer University Press, 2005], 76). See the following that inadequately integrate religion: Eric Foner, "Reconstruction Revisited," *Reviews in American History* 10 (December 1982): 82–100; idem, *Reconstruction*; John Hope Franklin, "Mirror for Americans: A Century of Reconstruction Historiography," *AHR* 85 (February 1980): 1–14; Kenneth M. Stampp, *The Era of Reconstruction, 1865–1877* (New York: Alfred A. Knopf, 1965); Heather Cox Richardson, *The Death of Reconstruction: Race, Labor, and Politics in the Post–Civil War North, 1865–1901* (Cambridge, Mass.: Harvard University Press, 2001); Benedict, *Compromise of Principle*; William Gillette, *Retreat from Reconstruction, 1869–79* (Baton Rouge: Louisiana State University Press, 1979); Eric L. McKitrick, *Andrew Johnson and Reconstruction* (Chicago: University of Chicago Press, 1960); Brooks D. Simpson, *Let Us Have Peace: Ulysses S. Grant and the Politics of War and Reconstruction, 1861–1868* (Chapel Hill: University of North Carolina Press, 1991); idem, *Reconstruction Presidents*; Eric Anderson and Alfred A. Moss Jr., eds., *The Facts of Reconstruction: Essays in Honor of John Hope Franklin* (Baton Rouge: Louisiana State University Press, 1991); McPherson, *Ordeal by Fire*, 533–661; David Herbert Donald, Jean Harvey Baker, and Michael F. Holt, *The Civil War and Reconstruction* (New York: W. W. Norton, 2001), 477–644.

34. For works addressing religion, see Stowell, *Rebuilding Zion*; Edward J. Blum, *Reforging the White Republic: Race, Religion, and American Nationalism, 1865–1898* (Baton Rouge: Louisiana State University Press, 2005); Edward J. Blum and W. Scott Poole, eds., *Vale of Tears: New Essays on Religion and Reconstruction* (Macon, Ga.: Mercer University Press, 2005); Victor B. Howard, *Religion and the Radical Republican Movement, 1860–1870* (Lexington: University Press of Kentucky, 1990), 90–214; Joe M. Richardson,

Christian Reconstruction: The American Missionary Association and Southern Blacks, 1861–1890 (Athens: University of Georgia Press, 1986); William S. McFeely, *Yankee Stepfather: General O. O. Howard and the Freedmen* (New York: W. W. Norton, 1968); John A. Carpenter, *Sword and Olive Branch: Oliver Otis Howard* (Pittsburgh: University of Pittsburgh Press, 1964); Charles Reagan Wilson, *Baptized in Blood: The Religion of the Lost Cause, 1865–1920* (Athens: University of Georgia Press, 1980); Gaines M. Foster, *Moral Reconstruction: Christian Lobbyists and the Federal Legislation of Morality, 1865–1920* (Chapel Hill: University of North Carolina Press, 2002); Ward M. McAfee, *Religion, Race, and Reconstruction: The Public School in the Politics of the 1870s* (Albany: State University of New York Press, 1998).

35. In addition to Moorhead, Stout, and Blum, the following inform the paragraph: Carwardine, *Evangelicals and Politics*, 169–90, 279–318, 457 (quote); Fredrickson, "Coming of the Lord"; Stowell, *Rebuilding Zion*, 49–64; Peter J. Parish, "The Instruments of Providence: Slavery, Civil War, and the American Churches," in *The Church and War: Papers Read at the Twenty-First Summer Meeting and the Twenty-Second Winter Meeting of the Ecclesiastical History Society*, ed. W. J. Sheils (London: Basil Blackwell, 1983), 291–320; Chester Forrester Dunham, *The Attitude of the Northern Clergy toward the South, 1860–1865* (Toledo, Ohio: Gray, 1942), 35–109; Noll, *Civil War as a Theological Crisis*, 31–94; Howard, *Religion and the Radical Republican Movement*; McKivigan, *War against Proslavery Religion*; Phillip Shaw Paludan, "Religion and the American Civil War," in *Religion and the American Civil War*, ed. Randall M. Miller, Harry S. Stout, and Charles Reagan Wilson (New York: Oxford University Press, 1998), 21–40; idem, *"A People's Contest": The Union and Civil War, 1861–1865* (Lawrence: University Press of Kansas, 1988), 339–74; Allen C. Guelzo, *The Crisis of the American Republic* (New York: St. Martin's, 1995), 322–27. Works that emphasize Union include Rable, *God's Almost Chosen Peoples*; Sean A. Scott, *A Visitation of God: Northern Civilians Interpret the Civil War* (New York: Oxford University Press, 2011); David Rolfs, *No Peace for the Wicked: Northern Protestant Soldiers and the American Civil War* (Knoxville: University of Tennessee Press, 2009); Vander Velde, *Presbyterian Churches and the Federal Union*; William A. Clebsch, "Christian Interpretations of the Civil War," *CH* 30 (June 1961): 212–22; C. C. Goen, "Broken Churches, Broken Nation: Regional Religion and North–South Alienation in Antebellum America," *CH* 52 (March 1983): 28; idem, *Broken Churches, Broken Nation*, 120; Marsden, *Evangelical Mind*, 199–211.

36. Theodore Dwight Bozeman, *To Live Ancient Lives: The Primitivist Dimension in Puritanism* (Chapel Hill: University of North Carolina Press, 1988); Jeffrey K. Jue, "Puritan Millenarianism in Old and New England," in *The Cambridge Companion to Puritanism*, ed. John Coffey and Paul C. H. Lim (Cambridge: Cambridge University Press, 2008), 259–76.

37. Carwardine, "Religion and National Construction," 38; idem, *Lincoln*, 268; Rable, *God's Almost Chosen Peoples*, 376; McKivigan, *War against Proslavery Religion*, 183–201; Harry S. Stout, "'Baptism in Blood': The Civil War and the Creation of an American Civil Religion," *Books and Culture* (July/August 2003): 17.

38. Alexander Saxton, *The Rise and Fall of the White Republic: Class Politics and Mass Culture in Nineteenth-Century America* (New York: Verso, 1990).

39. See Andrew L. Slap and Michael Thomas Smith, eds., *This Distracted and Anarchical People: New Answers for Old Questions about the Civil War–Era North* (New York: Fordham University Press, 2013), 1–10. Pointing to James McPherson's and Eric Foner's scholarly predominance, Slap and Smith suggest that it has become orthodox to view slavery, emancipation, and black experience as central to the war's meaning; however, they contend, this "Freedom School" of Civil War interpretation potentially obscures or distorts historical reality and forestalls research and debate. See also Gary W. Gallagher, *The Union War* (Cambridge, Mass.: Harvard University Press, 2011).

40. Gallagher, *Union War*, 42–43. Cf. Eric Foner, "Why the North Fought the Civil War," *New York Times Book Review*, 1 May 2011, p. 18. Foner helpfully warns against being "excessively schematic" regarding Union and emancipation as separate war aims; nevertheless, Union encompassed emancipation, and the latter cannot be understood apart from the former. See also Edward L. Ayers, "Worrying about the Civil War," in *Moral Problems in American Life: New Perspectives on Cultural History*, ed. Karen Halttunen and Lewis Perry (Ithaca, N.Y.: Cornell University Press, 1998), 145–65; idem, *In the Presence of Mine Enemies: The Civil War in the Heart of America, 1859–1863* (New York: W. W. Norton, 2003), 216–19; Dorothy Ross, "Lincoln and the Ethics of Emancipation: Universalism, Nationalism, Exceptionalism," *JAH* 96 (September 2009): 379–99.

41. Note Foster, *Moral Reconstruction*; McAfee, *Religion, Race, and Reconstruction*. On Whig-Republican political culture, see Howe, *What Hath God Wrought*, 570–612; idem, *The Political Culture of the American Whigs* (Chicago: University of Chicago Press, 1979), 69–75; Carwardine, *Evangelicals and Politics*, 302–3, 305–7; idem, *Lincoln*, 272. Cf. Byron C. Andreasen, "'As Good a Right to Pray': Copperhead Christians on the Northern Civil War Home Front" (PhD diss., University of Illinois, 1998); idem, "Lincoln's Religious Critics: Copperhead Christian Reactions to the President and the War," in *Politics and Culture of the Civil War Era: Essays in Honor of Robert W. Johannsen*, ed. Daniel McDonough and Kenneth W. Noe (Selinsgrove, Pa.: Susquehanna University Press, 2006).

42. Josiah Strong, *Our Country: Its Possible Future and Its Present Crisis* (New York: Baker and Taylor, 1885), stressed "perils" such as immigration, "Romanism," secularization, Mormonism, alcohol, socialism, greed, and urbanization. Strong's was the last in a series following *Our Country, Its Capabilities, Its Perils, and Its Hope: Being a Plea for the Early Establishment of Gospel Institutions in the Destitute Portions of the United States* (New York: American Home Missionary Society, 1842); *Our Country No. 2: A Plea for Home Missions* (New York: American Home Missionary Society, 1858). See Josiah Strong, *Our Country*, ed. Jurgen Herbst (Cambridge, Mass.: Belknap Press of Harvard University Press, 1963), ix–xxvi; Handy, *Christian America*, 57–100; Elizabeth Varon, *Disunion! The Coming of the American Civil War, 1789–1859* (Chapel Hill: University of North Carolina Press, 2008). Varon portrays a mentality that found the Union constantly threatened, and evangelicals were no exception to this.

43. Paul C. Nagel, *One Nation Indivisible: The Union in American Thought, 1776–1861* (New York: Oxford University Press, 1964), v; idem, *This Sacred Trust: American Nationality, 1798–1898* (New York: Oxford University Press, 1971); Dorothy Leeds Werner, "The Idea of the Union in American Verse" (PhD diss., University of Pennsylvania, 1932);

Alpheus Thomas Mason, "The Nature of Our Federal Union Reconsidered," *Political Science Quarterly* 45 (December 1950): 502–21.

44. "The True Sources of Our National Strength," *Harper's New Monthly Magazine* 9 (November 1854): 835.

45. Nicholas Onuf and Peter Onuf, *Nations, Markets, and War: Modern History and the American Civil War* (Charlottesville: University of Virginia Press, 2006), 278–307.

46. Neely, *Lincoln and the Triumph of the Nation*, 29.

47. Freehling, *Road to Disunion*, 2:501, 528–29; Faust, *Creation of Confederate Nationalism*, 14.

48. Abraham Lincoln, "A House Divided": Speech at Springfield, Illinois, 16 June 1858, *CW*, 2:461–69; idem, Annual Message to Congress, 1 December 1862, *CW*, 5:537. On Lincoln's argument for a perpetual Union, see idem, First Inaugural Address—Final Text, 4 March 1861, *CW*, 4:264–65; Kenneth M. Stampp, *The Imperiled Union: Essays on the Background of the Civil War* (New York: Oxford University Press, 1980), 3–36; Neely, *Lincoln and the Triumph of the Nation*, 29–61. On Lincoln's vision for America, see Michael Burlingame, *Abraham Lincoln: A Life*, 2 vols. (Baltimore: Johns Hopkins University Press, 2008), 1:71–73, 438–66; David Herbert Donald, *Lincoln* (New York: Simon and Schuster, 1995), 94–141, 162–229; idem, *Lincoln Reconsidered: Essays on the Civil War Era* (New York: Alfred A. Knopf, 1956), 187–208; Michael Thomas Smith, "Abraham Lincoln, Manhood, and Nineteenth-Century American Political Culture," in *This Distracted and Anarchical People: New Answers for Old Questions about the Civil War–Era North*, ed. Andrew L. Slap and Michael Thomas Smith (New York: Fordham University Press, 2013), 29–41; Laura Smith Porter, "'The Last, Best Hope of Earth': Abraham Lincoln's Perception of the Mission of America, 1834–1854," *IHJ* 78 (Autumn 1985): 207–16; Mark E. Neely Jr., *The Last Best Hope of Earth: Abraham Lincoln and the Promise of America* (Cambridge, Mass.: Harvard University Press, 1993); Allen C. Guelzo, *Abraham Lincoln: Redeemer President* (Grand Rapids, Mich.: Wm. B. Eerdmans, 1999), 26–63; Carwardine, *Lincoln*, 1–42; Howe, *Making the American Self*, 136–56; idem, "Why Abraham Lincoln Was a Whig," *JALA* 16 (Winter 1995): 27–38; idem, *Political Culture of the American Whigs*, 263–98; William J. Cooper Jr., "Where Was Henry Clay? President-Elect Abraham Lincoln and the Crisis of the Union, 1860–1861," in *New Directions in Mid-Nineteenth-Century American Political History*, ed. Gary W. Gallagher and Rachel A. Shelden (Charlottesville: University of Virginia Press, 2012), 126–40; Foner, *Fiery Trial*, 33–91; idem, *Free Soil, Free Labor, Free Men*, 225, 309–10. Regarding Civil War deaths, see J. David Hacker, "A Census-Based Count of the Civil War Dead," *CWH* 57 (December 2011): 306–47; Nicholas Marshall, "The Great Exaggeration: Death and the Civil War," *JCWE* 4 (March 2014): 3–27.

49. Henry A. Boardman, *The American Union* (Philadelphia: Lippincott, Grambo, 1851), 43.

50. Charles Taylor, *A Secular Age* (Cambridge, Mass.: Belknap Press of Harvard University Press, 2007), 171–72. Regarding transgenerational political beliefs, see Jean Baker, *Affairs of Party: The Political Culture of Northern Democrats in the Mid-Nineteenth Century* (Ithaca, N.Y.: Cornell University Press, 1983), 27–107; Swierenga, "Ethnoreligious Political Behavior in the Mid-Nineteenth Century."

51. Boardman, *American Union*, 43–44. See also Carwardine, *Evangelicals and Politics*,

180–91, 279–318; Kenneth M. Stampp, *And the War Came: The North and the Secession Crisis, 1860–1861* (Baton Rouge: Louisiana State University Press, 1950), 253–54.

52. Washington Gladden, *Recollections* (Boston: Houghton Mifflin, 1909), 124.

53. Rogan Kersh, *Dreams of a More Perfect Union* (Ithaca, N.Y.: Cornell University Press, 2001). Debate centers on eighteenth-century republicanism's centrality vis-à-vis liberalism and on its nineteenth-century form. See Bernard Bailyn, *The Ideological Origins of the American Revolution* (Cambridge, Mass.: Harvard University Press, 1967); Gordon S. Wood, *Creation of the American Republic, 1776–1787* (Chapel Hill: University of North Carolina Press, 1969); Robert E. Shalhope, "Toward a Republican Synthesis: The Emergence of an Understanding of Republicanism in American Historiography," *WMQ* 29 (January 1972): 49–80; J. G. A. Pocock, *The Machiavellian Moment: Florentine Political Thought and the Atlantic Republican Tradition* (Princeton, N.J.: Princeton University Press, 1975); Joyce Appleby, "Republicanism and Ideology," *AQ* 37 (Autumn 1985): 461–73; James T. Kloppenberg, "The Virtues of Liberalism: Christianity, Republicanism, and Ethics in Early American Discourse," *JAH* 74 (June 1987): 9–37; Isaac Kramnick, "The 'Great National Discussion': The Discourse of Politics in 1787," *WMQ*, 3rd ser., 45 (January 1988): 3–32; Daniel T. Rodgers, "Republicanism: The Career of a Concept," *JAH* 79 (June 1992): 11–38; John M. Murrin, "Fundamental Values, the Founding Fathers, and the Constitution," in *To Form a More Perfect Union: The Critical Ideas of the Constitution*, ed. Herman Belz, Ronald Hoffman, and Peter J. Albert (Charlottesville: University Press of Virginia, 1992), 1–37; Noll, *America's God*, 53–92 447–51; Carwardine, *Evangelicals and Politics*, 18–30, 199–234; Holt, *Political Crisis of the 1850s*.

54. Gary W. Gallagher, *Causes Won, Lost, and Forgotten: How Hollywood and Popular Art Shape What We Know about the Civil War* (Chapel Hill: University of North Carolina Press, 2008), 92, 46. See also James E. Lewis Jr., *The American Union and the Problem of Neighborhood: The United States and the Collapse of the Spanish Empire, 1783–1829* (Chapel Hill: University of North Carolina Press, 1998); Peter Knupfer, *"The Union as It Is": Constitutional Unionism and Sectional Compromise, 1787–1861* (Chapel Hill: University of North Carolina Press, 1991); George M. Fredrickson, *The Inner Civil War: Northern Intellectuals and the Crisis of the Union* (New York: Harper and Row, 1965); Samuel H. Beer, *To Make a Nation: The Rediscovery of American Federalism* (Cambridge, Mass.: Harvard University Press, 1993), 341–77; Wilson Carey McWilliams, *The Idea of Fraternity in America* (Berkeley: University of California Press, 1973); Forrest McDonald, *States' Rights and the Union:* Imperium in Imperio, *1776–1876* (Lawrence: University Press of Kansas, 2000); John Lauritz Larson, *Internal Improvements: National Public Works and the Promise of Popular Government in the Early United States* (Chapel Hill: University of North Carolina Press, 2001); Peter S. Onuf, "Anarchy and the Crisis of the Union," in *To Form a More Perfect Union: The Critical Ideas of the Constitution*, ed. Herman Belz, Ronald Hoffman, and Peter J. Albert (Charlottesville: University Press of Virginia, 1992), 272–302; Harold M. Hyman, *A More Perfect Union: The Impact of the Civil War and Reconstruction on the Constitution* (New York: Alfred A. Knopf, 1973).

55. The etymology of *nation* (from the Latin *natio*, meaning people, stock, or tribe) and *ethnic* (from the Greek *ethnos*, meaning nation or people) suggests to some that nations are necessarily ethnic. McPherson, *Is Blood Thicker Than Water*, 32; Liah Greenfeld,

Nationalism: Five Roads to Modernity (Cambridge, Mass.: Harvard University Press, 1992), 3–87.

56. Steven Grosby, *Nationalism: A Very Short Introduction* (New York: Oxford University Press, 2005), 11–12, 47–48.

57. George M. Fredrickson, *The Black Image in the White Mind: The Debate on Afro-American Character and Destiny, 1817–1914* (New York: Harper and Row, 1971), 138. "Imagining" comes from Benedict Anderson, *Imagined Communities: Reflections on the Origin and Spread of Nationalism*, rev. and enl. ed. (London: Verso, 1991). Nations are imaginary in that most citizens never see each other, though they imagine a community due to features of modernization facilitating the transcendence of space and time.

58. See Allan Nevins, *The War for the Union*, vol. 4, *The Organized War to Victory, 1864–1865* (New York: Charles Scribner's Sons, 1971), 393–404; David R. Goldfield, *America Aflame: How the Civil War Created a Nation* (New York: Bloomsbury Press, 2011); Richard Franklin Bensel, *Yankee Leviathan: The Origins of Central State Authority in America, 1859–1877* (Cambridge: Cambridge University Press, 1990); Heather Cox Richardson, *The Greatest Nation of the Earth: Republican Economic Policies during the Civil War* (Cambridge, Mass.: Harvard University Press, 1997); Paludan, *"People's Contest,"* 105–169; idem, "What Did the Winners Win? The Social and Economic History of the North during the Civil War," in *Writing the Civil War: The Quest to Understand*, ed. James M. McPherson and William J. Cooper Jr. (Columbia: University of South Carolina Press, 1998), 174–200; Fredrickson, *Inner Civil War*, 98–112, 183–216; Susan-Mary Grant, *North over South: Northern Nationalism and American Identity in the Antebellum Era* (Lawrence: University Press of Kansas, 2000), 153–72; idem, "'The Charter of Its Birthright': The Civil War and American Nationalism," in *Legacy of Disunion: The Enduring Significance of the American Civil War*, ed. Susan-Mary Grant and Peter J. Parish (Baton Rouge: Louisiana State University Press, 2003), 188–206; idem, "From Union to Nation: The Civil War and the Development of American Nationalism," in *Themes of the American Civil War: The War between the States*, 2nd ed., ed. Susan-Mary Grant and Brian Holden Reid (New York: Routledge, 2010), 295–316; Melinda Lawson, *Patriot Fires: Forging a New Nationalism in the Civil War North* (Lawrence: University Press of Kansas, 2002); Mark R. Wilson, *The Business of Civil War: Military Mobilization and the State, 1861–1865* (Baltimore: Johns Hopkins University Press, 2006).

59. See Kersh, *Dreams of a More Perfect Union*, 199; Gallagher, *Union War*, 153, 161; Slap and Smith, *This Distracted and Anarchical People*, 1–10.

60. George Duffield Sr., *Our Federal Union a Cause for Gratitude to God* (Detroit: Harmon, Broadhead, 1850), 9–11, quoted in Carwardine, *Evangelicals and Politics*, 181.

61. Charles Hodge, "The State of the Country," *BRPR* 33 (January 1861): 2–3.

62. "The Test-Hour of Popular Liberty and Republican Government," *NE* 21 (April 1862): 244.

63. David Waldstreicher, *In the Midst of Perpetual Fetes: The Making of American Nationalism, 1776–1820* (Chapel Hill: University of North Carolina Press, 1997).

64. Blum's *Reforging the White Republic* hinges on his assertion that the Civil War transformed Protestants into civic nationalists.

65. Note Jack N. Rakove, *The Annotated U.S. Constitution and Declaration of Independence* (Cambridge, Mass.: Belknap Press of Harvard University Press, 2009), 22–23.

66. David Hollinger, *Postethnic America: Beyond Multiculturalism*, rev. ed. (New York: Basic Books, 2000), 134.

67. McPherson, *Is Blood Thicker Than Water*, 31.

68. James M. McPherson, *Battle Cry of Freedom: The Civil War Era* (New York: Oxford University Press, 1988), 861; Kersh, *Dreams of a More Perfect Union*, 168–97; James H. Kettner, *The Development of American Citizenship, 1608–1870* (Chapel Hill: University of North Carolina Press, 1978), 334–51; Hans Kohn, *The Idea of Nationalism: A Study in Its Origins and Background* (New York: Macmillan, 1944), 3–24; idem, *American Nationalism: An Interpretive Essay* (New York: Macmillan, 1957), 93–131; Greenfeld, *Nationalism: Five Roads to Modernity*, 399–484; Garry Wills, *Lincoln at Gettysburg: The Words That Remade America* (New York: Touchstone, 1992), 37–38, 121–47; Ayers, "Worrying About the Civil War."

69. Gary Gerstle, "Theodore Roosevelt and the Divided Character of American Nationalism," *JAH* 86 (December 1999): 1280–1307; idem, *American Crucible: Race and Nation in the Twentieth Century* (Princeton, N.J.: Princeton University Press, 2001).

70. Rogers M. Smith, *Civic Ideals: Conflicting Visions of Citizenship in U.S. History* (New Haven, Conn.: Yale University Press, 1997), 197–346.

1. "The Uprising of a Great People": A Providential Union

1. Alexander H. Stephens, *A Constitutional View of the Late War between the States; Its Causes, Character, Conduct and Results*, 2 vols. (Philadelphia: National, 1868–70), 2:447–48.

2. Mark E. Neely Jr., *The Fate of Liberty: Abraham Lincoln and Civil Liberties* (New York: Oxford University Press, 1991), xi, 231–32. See also Edmund Wilson, *Patriotic Gore: Studies in American Literature of the American Civil War* (New York: Oxford University Press, 1962), 91–127; Garry Wills, *Lincoln at Gettysburg: The Words That Remade America* (New York: Touchstone, 1992), 125; Rogan Kersh, *Dreams of a More Perfect Union* (Ithaca, N.Y.: Cornell University Press, 2001), 169–97. Cf. Mark E. Neely Jr., *Lincoln and the Triumph of the Nation: Constitutional Conflict in the American Civil War* (Chapel Hill: University of North Carolina Press, 2011), 50–51.

3. Abraham Lincoln, Speech at Lafayette, Indiana, 11 February 1861, *CW*, 4:192; idem, Reply to Oliver P. Morton at Indianapolis, Indiana, 11 February 1861, *CW*, 4:193–94. Regarding evangelicalism as "romantic," see David W. Bebbington, "Evangelical Christianity and Romanticism," *Crux* 26 (March 1990): 9–15; Daniel Walker Howe, *Making the American Self: Jonathan Edwards to Abraham Lincoln* (New York: Oxford University Press, 1997), 107–17; James Turner, *Without God, without Creed: The Origins of Unbelief in America* (Baltimore: Johns Hopkins University Press, 1985), 73–113; Anne C. Rose, *Victorian America and the Civil War* (Cambridge: Cambridge University Press, 1992); Paul Kjoss Helseth, "'Right Reason' and the Princeton Mind: The Moral Context," *JPH* 77 (Spring 1999): 13–28. Regarding Lincoln's awareness of evangelical sensibilities, see Richard J. Carwardine, "Lincoln, Evangelical Religion, and American Political Culture,"

JALA 18 (Winter 1997): 27–55; idem, *Lincoln* (Harlow, Eng.: Pearson, Longman, 2003), x–xi, 274–82, 313.

4. Regarding actual arguments for perpetuity, see Kenneth M. Stampp, *The Imperiled Union: Essays on the Background of the Civil War* (New York: Oxford University Press, 1980), 3–36; Neely, *Lincoln and the Triumph of the Nation*, 37–51. See also Daniel Farber, *Lincoln's Constitution* (Chicago: University of Chicago Press, 1993), which generally defends the constitutionality of Lincoln's actions. Henry A. Boardman, *What Christianity Demands of Us at the Present Crisis* (Philadelphia: J. B. Lippincott, 1860), 6, 8, 27.

5. Lincoln, Reply to Oliver P. Morton, *CW*, 4:194; Washington Gladden, *Recollections* (Boston: Houghton Mifflin, 1909), 103–13; Oliver Otis Howard, *Autobiography of Oliver Otis Howard, Major General United States Army*, 2 vols. (New York: Baker and Taylor, 1907), 1:107–8, 112.

6. William Peter Strickland, "Methodism and the War," *MQR* 45 (July 1863): 448. Moody's son died as a Union soldier, and Moody's brother, a Confederate captain, was captured with Jefferson Davis's escape party. See Granville Moody, *A Life's Retrospect: Autobiography of Granville Moody, D.D. (Brigadier General by Brevet)*, ed. Sylvester Weeks (Cincinnati: Cranston and Stowe, 1890); Chester Forrester Dunham, *The Attitude of the Northern Clergy toward the South, 1860–1865* (Toledo, Ohio: Gray, 1942), 141.

7. Henry Ward Beecher, *Patriotic Addresses: America and England, from 1850 to 1885, on Slavery, the Civil War, and the Development of Civil Liberty in the United States*, ed. John R. Howard (New York: Fords, Howard, and Hulbert, 1887), 276; Debby Applegate, *The Most Famous Man in America: The Biography of Henry Ward Beecher* (New York: Doubleday, 2006); William G. McLoughlin, *The Meaning of Henry Ward Beecher: An Essay on the Shifting Values of Mid-Victorian America, 1840–1870* (New York: Alfred A. Knopf, 1970); Clifford E. Clark Jr. *Henry Ward Beecher: Spokesman for a Middle-Class America* (Urbana: University of Illinois Press, 1978); Abraham Lincoln, Remarks at Poughkeepsie, New York, 19 February 1861, *CW*, 4:228.

8. Henry A. Boardman, *Thanksgiving in War* (Philadelphia: C. Sherman and Son, 1861), 13–14. See also George Duffield Jr., *Courage in a Good Cause: The Lawful and Courageous Use of the Sword* (Philadelphia: T. B. Pugh, 1861); Andrew Leete Stone, *The War and the Patriot's Duty* (Boston: Henry Hoyt, 1861); Daniel Denison Whedon, "The State of the Country," *MQR* 43 (April 1861): 312–22; Charles Hodge, "The State of the Country," *BRPR* 33 (January 1861): 1–36; L. P. Brocket, "Philanthropy in War Time," *MQR* 47 (January 1865): 65–81; Joseph Horner, "Christianity and the War Power," *MQR* 47 (April 1865): 185.

9. Regarding southern evangelicals and the Confederate cause, see Daniel W. Stowell, *Rebuilding Zion: The Religious Reconstruction of the South, 1863–1877* (New York: Oxford University Press, 1998), 33–48; George C. Rable, *God's Almost Chosen Peoples: A Religious History of the American Civil War* (Chapel Hill: University of North Carolina Press, 2010), passim; Harry S. Stout, *Upon the Altar of the Nation: A Moral History of the Civil War* (New York: Viking, 2006), 47–58, 73–81, 95–99; James W. Silver, *Confederate Morale and Church Propaganda* (Tuscaloosa, Ala.: Confederate, 1957; repr., New York: W. W. Norton, 1967), 25–81; Jason Phillips, "Rebels in War and Peace: Their Ethos and Its Impact," in *The Great Task Remaining before Us: Reconstruction as America's Continuing*

Civil War, ed. Paul A. Cimbala and Randall M. Miller (New York: Fordham University Press, 2010), 154–72; Daniel W. Stowell, "Stonewall Jackson and the Providence of God," in *Religion and the American Civil War*, ed. Randall M. Miller, Harry S. Stout, and Charles Reagan Wilson (New York: Oxford University Press, 1998), 187–207. Having transferred covenantalism to the Confederacy, southern evangelicals would become Christian Americans again through participation in various national reform efforts and the Spanish-American War and World War I; re-Americanization occurred despite their contribution to a sectionalized civic religion of the Lost Cause. See Daniel W. Stowell, "Why 'Redemption'? Religion and the End of Reconstruction, 1869–1877," in *Vale of Tears: New Essays on Religion and Reconstruction*, ed. Edward J. Blum and W. Scott Poole (Macon, Ga.: Mercer University Press, 2005), 133–46; Gaines M. Foster, *Moral Reconstruction: Christian Lobbyists and the Federal Legislation of Morality, 1865–1920* (Chapel Hill: University of North Carolina Press, 2002); idem, *Ghosts of the Confederacy: Defeat, the Lost Cause, and the Emergence of the New South* (New York: Oxford University Press, 1987), 145–79; idem, "A Christian Nation: Signs of a Covenant," in *Bonds of Affection: Americans Define Their Patriotism*, ed. John E. Bodnar (Princeton, N.J.: Princeton University Press, 1996); Charles Reagan Wilson, *Baptized in Blood: The Religion of the Lost Cause, 1865–1920* (Athens: University of Georgia Press, 1980), 161–82; Lloyd Hunter, "The Immortal Confederacy: Another Look at Lost Cause Religion," in *The Myth of the Lost Cause and Civil War History*, ed. Gary W. Gallagher and Alan T. Nolan (Bloomington: Indiana University Press, 2000), 185–218; Edward J. Blum, *Reforging the White Republic: Race, Religion, and American Nationalism, 1865–1898* (Baton Rouge: Louisiana State University Press, 2005), 174–243; David W. Blight, *Race and Reunion: The Civil War in American Memory* (Cambridge, Mass.: Belknap Press of Harvard University Press, 2001), 258–64, 291; Caroline E. Janney, *Remembering the Civil War: Reunion and the Limits of Reconciliation* (Chapel Hill: University of North Carolina Press, 2013), 146, 222–31, 280; David Goldfield, *Still Fighting the Civil War: The American South and Southern History* (Baton Rouge: Louisiana State University Press, 2002), 43–61. The covenantal outlook also appeared in the nationalism of the southern Presbyterian Woodrow Wilson. See John M. Mulder, *Woodrow Wilson: The Years of Preparation* (Princeton, N.J.: Princeton University Press, 1978); Thomas J. Knock, *To End All Wars: Woodrow Wilson and the Quest for a New World Order* (Princeton, N.J.: Princeton University Press, 1992).

10. Edward McPherson, *The Political History of the United States of America during the Great Rebellion*, 2nd ed. (Washington, D.C.: Philip and Solomons, 1865), 475.

11. Abraham Lincoln, Second Inaugural Address, 4 March 1865, *CW*, 8:332; Douglas L. Wilson, *Lincoln's Sword: The Presidency and the Power of Words* (New York: Alfred A. Knopf, 2006), 101, 254; Amory Dwight Mayo, *The Nation's Sacrifice* (Cincinnati: Robert Clarke, 1865), 22. Regarding Lincoln's beliefs, see Allen C. Guelzo, "Abraham Lincoln and the Doctrine of Necessity," *JALA* 18 (Winter 1997): 57–81; idem, *Abraham Lincoln: Redeemer President* (Grand Rapids, Mich.: Wm. B. Eerdmans, 1999), 148–60, 409–21, 445–47; Wilson, *Lincoln's Sword*, 249–63; Carwardine, *Lincoln*, 37–40; Samuel W. Calhoun and Lucas E. Morel, "Abraham Lincoln's Religion: The Case for His Ultimate Belief in a Personal, Sovereign God," *JALA* 33 (Winter 2012): 38–74; Mark Noll, "'Both . . . Pray to the Same God': The Singularity of Lincoln's Faith in the Era of the Civil War," JALA 18

(Winter 1997): 1–26; idem, "Lincoln's God," *JPH* 82 (Summer 2004): 77–88; idem, *The Civil War as a Theological Crisis* (Chapel Hill: University of North Carolina Press, 2006), 88; idem, *America's God: From Jonathan Edwards to Abraham Lincoln* (New York: Oxford University Press, 2002), 430–32. Regarding the second inaugural in particular, see Ronald C. White Jr., *Lincoln's Greatest Speech: The Second Inaugural* (New York: Simon and Schuster, 2002), 60–80; idem, *The Eloquent President: A Portrait of Lincoln through His Words* (New York: Random House, 2005), 277–303; idem, *A. Lincoln: A Biography* (New York: Random House, 2009), 661–66; Wilson, *Lincoln's Sword*, 263–77; Michael Burlingame, *Abraham Lincoln: A Life*, 2 vols. (Baltimore: Johns Hopkins University Press, 2008), 2:767–72; David Herbert Donald, *Lincoln* (New York: Simon and Schuster, 1995), 565–68; Carwardine, *Lincoln*, 240–42.

12. Lincoln, Reply to Oliver P. Morton, *CW*, 4:193–94; idem, Address to the New Jersey Senate at Trenton, New Jersey, 21 February 1861, *CW*, 4:236; idem, Meditation on the Divine Will, 2 September 1862 [1864?], *CW*, 5:404; idem, To Albert G. Hodges, 4 April 1864, *CW*, 7:282. Regarding the Meditation on the Divine Will's date, see Calhoun and Morel, "Abraham Lincoln's Religion, 62n63; Ronald C. White Jr., *A. Lincoln: A Biography* (New York: Random House, 2009), 622–27; Rable, *God's Almost Chosen Peoples*, 370; Wilson, *Lincoln's Sword*, 254–56.

13. Abraham Lincoln, Farewell Address at Springfield, Illinois [B. Version], *CW*, 4:190. Though not as widely distributed, the third version is perhaps more accurate and most attuned to evangelical ears. Villard quoted in Wilson, *Lincoln's Sword*, 13. See also Albert Barnes, *The Love of Country* (Philadelphia: C. Sherman and Son, 1861), 31–32; Gladden, *Recollections*, 106–7.

14. George Peck, *The Life and Times of Rev. George Peck, D.D., Written by Himself* (New York: Nelson and Phillips, 1874), 252–62, 369–72; idem, *Our Country: Its Trials and Its Triumph, a Series of Discourses Suggested by the Varying Events of the War for the Union* (New York: Carlton and Porter, 1865), 39; Richard J. Carwardine, *Evangelicals and Politics in Antebellum America* (New Haven, Conn.: Yale University Press, 1993), 185; George Peck, *Formation of Manly Character: A Series of Lectures to Young Men* (New York: Phillips and Hunt, 1853), 184; Loring Grant to George Peck, 11 June 1865, GPP; James Rusling, "The War for the Union," *MQR* 46 (April 1864): 307; Ronald P. Formisano, "Political Character, Antipartyism, and the Second Party System," *AQ* 21 (Winter 1969): 683–709; idem, "The Party Period Revisited," *JAH* 86 (June 1999): 98–102; Richard Hofstadter, *The Idea of a Party System: The Rise of Legitimate Opposition in the United States, 1780–1840* (Berkeley: University of California Press, 1969); Daniel Walker Howe, *The Political Culture of the American Whigs* (Chicago: University of Chicago Press, 1979), 50–55; Peter B. Knupfer, *The Union as It Is: Constitutional Unionism and Sectional Compromise, 1787–1861* (Chapel Hill: University of North Carolina Press, 1991); Adam I. P. Smith, *No Party Now: Politics in the Civil War North* (New York: Oxford University Press, 2006).

15. Edward L. Ayers, "Worrying about the Civil War," in *Moral Problems in American Life: New Perspectives on Cultural History*, ed. Karen Halttunen and Lewis Perry (Ithaca, N.Y.: Cornell University Press, 1998), 150; James M. McPherson, *Drawn with the Sword: Reflections on the American Civil War* (New York: Oxford University Press, 1996), 55–65.

16. Eliza Gilmore to O. O. Howard, 23 December 1860, 17 February 1861, O. O. Howard to Eliza Gilmore, 12 January, 11 February, 6, 30 March 1861, OOHP.

17. "American Nationality," *BRPR* 33 (October 1861): 641. See also Joel F. Bingham, *National Disappointment* (Buffalo: Breed, Butler, 1865), 4.

18. Frederick Douglass, "The New President," *Douglass Monthly*, March 1861, in *LWFD*, 3:67. Douglass's outlook encompassed several evangelical themes, including belief in providence, American exceptionalism, and millennialism. See David W. Blight, *Frederick Douglass' Civil War: Keeping Faith in Jubilee* (Baton Rouge: Louisiana State University Press, 1989), 59–79, 101–21; William S. McFeely, *Frederick Douglass* (New York: W. W. Norton, 1991), 206–37. Regarding varied responses to secession and war, see James M. McPherson, *The Struggle for Equality: Abolitionists and the Negro in the Civil War and Reconstruction* (Princeton, N.J.: Princeton University Press, 1964), 29–51; William T. Dwight, *The Nationality of a People: Its Vital Element* (Portland, Maine: N. A. Foster, 1861), 24–25; Andrew Leete Stone, *The Divineness of Human Government* (Boston: Henry Hoyt, 1861), 9–10, 49; Barnes, *Love of Country*, 32–35; James H. Moorhead, *American Apocalypse: Yankee Protestants and the Civil War, 1860–1869* (New Haven, Conn.: Yale University Press, 1978), 39; Stout, *Upon the Altar of the Nation*, 18.

19. Eliza Gilmore to O. O. Howard, 21 April 1861, OOHP.

20. Charles Hodge, "The Church and the Country," *BRPR* 33 (April 1861): 336.

21. Wheelock Craig, quoted in Henry K. Craig, *Toil and Triumph* (New Bedford, Mass.: Taber Brothers, 1870), 55.

22. Silver, *Confederate Morale and Church Propaganda*, 31; Rable, *God's Almost Chosen Peoples*, 51–52; Stowell, *Rebuilding Zion*, 34–35; Freehling, *The Road to Disunion*, vol. 2: *Secessionists Triumphant, 1854–1861* (New York: Oxford University Press, 2007), 528; O. O. Howard to his brother [Charles?], 27 April 1861, OOHP.

23. Sherman B. Canfield, *The American Crisis* (Syracuse, N.Y.: Journal Book and Job Office, 1865), 19, 21. See also idem, *The Indications of a Divine Purpose to Make Our Country a Model Christian Republic* (Syracuse, N.Y.: W. T. Hamilton, 1855); George Duffield Jr., *The God of Our Fathers* (Philadelphia: T. B. Pugh, 1861). Some nonevangelicals appropriated and attached a general, even secularized, form of Protestantism to their own narrative of American history. See Charles Eliot Norton, "American Political Ideas," *North American Review* 101 (Oct 1865): 550–66; James Turner, *The Liberal Education of Charles Eliot Norton* (Baltimore: Johns Hopkins University Press, 1999), 200–206.

24. Note Rable, *God's Almost Chosen Peoples*, 75; Sean A. Scott, *A Visitation of God: Northern Civilians Interpret the Civil War* (New York: Oxford University Press, 2011), 12–13; Loveland, *Southern Evangelicals and the Social Order, 1800–1860* (Baton Rouge: Louisiana State University Press, 1980), 264–65; Nicholas Guyatt, *Providence and the Invention of the United States, 1607–1876* (Cambridge: Cambridge University Press, 2007). Cf. Lewis O. Saum, *The Popular Mood of Pre-Civil War America, 1830–1860* (Westport, Conn.: Greenwood Press, 1980), 3–26; idem, *The Popular Mood of America, 1860–1890* (Lincoln: University of Nebraska Press, 1990), 13–39.

25. Reuben Jeffery, *The Mission of Abraham Lincoln* (Philadelphia: Bryson and Son, 1865), 4.

26. George B. Cheever to Henry T. Cheever, 28 February 1863, George B. Cheever to Elizabeth Cheever, 15 December 1863, CFP; Robert M. York, *George B. Cheever, Religious and Social Reformer, 1807–1890* (Orono, Maine: University Press, 1955), 189, 197; McPherson, *Struggle for Equality*, 5.

27. Nathaniel West, *Victory and Gratitude* (New York: E. B. Clayton's Sons, 1864), 24; Henry A. Boardman, The War (2), 28 April 1861, HBP.

28. Elizabeth Washburn to Elizabeth Cheever, 17 May 1864, CFP; Cadford Mellen Dinsmore, *Our Country* (Claremont, N.H.: Press of the Claremont Manufacturing Company, 1864), 18; Gary W. Gallagher, *Union War* (Cambridge, Mass.: Harvard University Press, 2011), 129–31; Neely, *Lincoln and the Triumph of the Nation*, 19–25; Henry A. Boardman, Christians and the War, HBP; Gilbert Haven, *National Sermons: Sermons, Speeches, and Letters on Slavery and Its War: From the Passage of the Fugitive Slave Bill to the Election of President Grant* (Boston: Lee and Shepard, 1869), 394.

29. Joseph Henry Gilmore, *"Hath God Forgotten to Be Gracious"* (Concord, N.H.: P. B. Cogswell, 1864), 13; "Washington Correspondence," *CR*, 21 May 1864, p. 81; N. Grossmayer to Edwin M. Stanton, 10 September 1864, USGP. See also Herrick Johnson, *God's Ways Unsearchable* (Pittsburgh: W. G. Johnston, 1865), 4; Joseph P. Thompson, *Peace through Victory* (New York: Loyal Publication Society, 1864), 1–4.

30. Luther Peck to George Peck, 27 July 1864, Loring Grant to George Peck, 1 November 1864, GPP; Jesse T. Peck, *The Great Republic from the Discovery of America to the Centennial, July 4, 1876* (New York: Nelson and Phillips, 1876), 14.

31. Howard Crosby, *God's View of the Rebellion* (New York: E. French, 1864), 5. Crosby publicly disagreed with Cheever over the latter's radicalism. *Encyclopaedia Britannica*, 11th ed., s.v. "Crosby, Howard"; York, *George B. Cheever, Religious and Social Reformer*, 143–46.

32. Henry Smith, *God in the War* (Buffalo: Wheeler, Matthews, and Warren, 1863), 15. See also idem, *The Truly Christian Pulpit: Our Strongest National Defense* (New York: American Home Missionary Society, 1854).

33. Silver, *Confederate Morale and Church Propaganda*, 25–41; Rable, *God's Almost Chosen Peoples*, 147–49, 270–76.

34. "Our Failures and Their Cause," *CR*, 27 February 1864, p. 33. See also "Our Country," *CR*, 19 March 1864, p. 44; "Representatives from All Nationalities to Be Combined into One Great Family upon This Continent," *CR*, 9 April 1864, p. 57; "Our Duty in the Crisis," *CR*, 7 May 1864, p. 73; "Why the Present Great Southern Rebellion Has Not Been Long Since Crushed," *CR*, 30 July 1864, p. 121.

35. Henry A. Boardman, Christians and the War, HBP.

36. Henry A. Boardman, Sermon Outline on 2 Kings 19:32–34, idem, Christians and the War, HBP; idem, *Healing and Salvation for Our Country from God Alone* (Philadelphia: William S. and Alfred Martien, 1864), 7–8; idem, *The Sovereignty of God, The Sure and Only Stay of the Christian Patriot in Our National Troubles* (Philadelphia: William and Alfred Martien, 1862), 7–8. See also idem, *A Sermon Occasioned by the Death of William Henry Harrison* (Philadelphia: William S. Martien, 1841); idem, *God's Providence in Accidents* (Philadelphia: Parry and McMillan, 1855). Regarding the Reformed tradition, see "The Doctrine of Providence," *BRPR* 34 (April 1862): 277–86; Charles Hodge,

"Providence," in *Systematic Theology*, vol. 1, *Theology* (New York: Charles Scribner, 1871), 575–616; James O. Farmer, *The Metaphysical Confederacy: James Henry Thornwell and the Synthesis of Southern Values*, 2nd ed. (Macon, Ga.: Mercer University Press, 1999), 126–34.

37. See Henry A. Boardman, *A Discourse on the Life and Character of Daniel Webster* (Philadelphia: Joseph M. Wilson, 1852). Boardman's views were similar to those of his friend Charles Hodge. See Lewis G. Vander Velde, *The Presbyterian Churches and the Federal Union, 1861–1869* (Cambridge, Mass.: Harvard University Press, 1932), 236; Richard J. Carwardine, "The Politics of Charles Hodge," in *Charles Hodge Revisited: A Critical Appraisal of His Life and Work*, ed. John W. Stewart and James H. Moorhead (Grand Rapids, Mich.: Wm. B. Eerdmans, 2002), 247–97; John W. Stewart, *Mediating the Center: Charles Hodge on American Science, Language, Literature, and Politics* (Princeton, N.J.: Princeton Theological Seminary, 1995). Cf. the critical series in Cheever's *Principia*, titled "'The War,' or *The Princeton Review* Reviewed" (March–June 1863), which contended that God's moral governance entailed liberty and equality for all.

38. Henry A. Boardman, Sermon on Romans 9:20, HBP. Boardman was critical of emergent industrial capitalism and decried the selfish pursuit of wealth. See idem, *The Bible in the Counting-House: A Course of Lectures to Merchants*, 7th ed. (Philadelphia: American Sunday School Union, 1877). He corresponded regularly with Binney, who staunchly supported Lincoln. See Horace Binney letters to Henry A. Boardman, 21 July 1853 to 9 March 1874, HBP; Henry A. Boardman, *The Federal Judiciary* (Philadelphia: William S. and Alfred Martien, 1862); Neely, *Lincoln and the Triumph of the Nation*, 71–80; George M. Fredrickson, *The Inner Civil War: Northern Intellectuals and the Crisis of the Union* (New York: Harper and Row, 1965), 56, 114. Of course, theological conservatism and social conservatism do not necessarily coincide; Horace Bushnell maintained the latter in tandem with a liberalizing theology, as did many New Englanders with theological views more liberal than Bushnell's. See James Turner, *Language, Religion, Knowledge: Past and Present* (Notre Dame, Ind.: University of Notre Dame Press, 2003), 44–47; Horace Bushnell, "The Doctrine of Loyalty," *NE* 22 (July 1863): 560–82; Robert Bruce Mullin, *The Puritan as Yankee: A Life of Horace Bushnell* (Grand Rapids, Mich.: Wm. B. Eerdmans, 2002); Howard A. Barnes, *Horace Bushnell and the Virtuous Republic* (Metuchen, N.J.: Scarecrow Press, 1991).

39. Note his two-part sermon series "The War," delivered in April 1861. HBP.

40. Lincoln issued proclamations on 12 August 1861, 10 April 1862, 30 March, 15 July, 3 October 1863, 9 May, 7 July, 3 September, 20 October 1864, found respectively in *CW*, 4:482–83, 5:185–86, 6:155–57, 6:332–33, 6:496–97, 7:333, 7:431–32, 7:533–34, 8:55–56. Seward wrote all but those issued 9 May and 3 September 1864.

41. Davis issued proclamations on 13 June, 15 November 1861, 28 February, 16 May, 18 September 1862, 27 March, 21 August 1863, 8 April, 16 November 1864, 3 March 1865. See Silver, *Confederate Morale and Church Propaganda*, 64–65; Stout, *Upon the Altar of the Nation*, passim; Rable, *God's Almost Chosen Peoples*, passim; Drew Gilpin Faust, *The Creation of Confederate Nationalism* (Baton Rouge: Louisiana State University Press, 1988), 24–33; William J. Cooper Jr., *Jefferson Davis, American* (New York: Alfred A. Knopf, 2000), 532 (quote).

42. Carwardine, *Lincoln*, 289.

43. Abraham Lincoln, Proclamation of a National Fast Day, 12 August 1861, *CW*, 4:482.

44. Phineas D. Gurley, Sermon Delivered by Dr. Gurley at the Funeral of Willie Lincoln at the White House at Washington, 24 February 1862, PGP. See also idem, God Never Forsakes His People, PGP. Note that Gurley was a colonizationist, and Lincoln's colonizationist beliefs persisted until at least 1863, if not longer. See John H. B. Latrobe and Phineas D. Gurley, *American Colonization: Addresses Delivered at Its Late Annual Meeting* (Washington, D.C.: T. R. Dawley, 1864), 13–16; George M. Fredrickson, "A Man but Not a Brother: Abraham Lincoln and Racial Equality," *JSH* 41 (February 1975): 56–57; idem, *Big Enough to Be Inconsistent: Abraham Lincoln Confronts Slavery and Race* (Cambridge, Mass.: Harvard University Press, 2008), 113; Mark E. Neely Jr., "Abraham Lincoln and Black Colonization: Benjamin Butler's Spurious Testimony," *CWH* 25 (1979): 77–83; Eric Foner, *The Fiery Trial: Abraham Lincoln and American Slavery* (New York: W. W. Norton, 2010), 258–61. Regarding Gurley and Lincoln, see David Rankin Barbee, "President Lincoln and Doctor Gurley," *Abraham Lincoln Quarterly* 1 (March 1948): 3–24; Guelzo, *Abraham Lincoln*, 318–37; Donald, *Lincoln*, 336–38; White, *Lincoln's Greatest Speech*, 131–41; Carwardine, *Lincoln*, 220–26.

45. See the following sermons: Phineas D. Gurley, My Soul Thirsteth for God, the Living God, Consecrated to Christ, Sermon on Job 13:15, Preparation to Die, PGP; idem, *Man's Projects and God's Results* (Washington, D.C.: Wm. Ballantyne, 1863).

46. Nathan Lewis Rice, *Sermon on the Death of Abraham Lincoln, Late President of the United States, Preached on the Occasion of the National Funeral* (New York: Wm. C. Bryant, 1865), 6.

47. Gurley, *Man's Projects and God's Results*, 5, 17, 15.

48. *The Little Mac Campaign Songster* (New York: T. R. Dawley, 1864), 24.

49. Henry Smith, *God in the War*, 5–7; John W. Bain, *National Lessons from the Life and Death of President Lincoln* (Pittsburgh: W. S. Haven, 1865), 9; John Woart, *Thanksgiving Discourse* (Philadelphia: King and Baird, 1864), 8. See also "The Gospel in the Army," *CR*, Thanksgiving Supplement, 26 November 1864, p. 1; William Blackburn, *The Crime against the Presidency* (Trenton, N.J.: Murphy and Bechtel, 1865), 8; Jeffery, *Mission of Abraham Lincoln*, 21.

50. G. Peck, *Life and Times*, 379–81; Abraham Lincoln, Response to Methodists, 18 May 1864, *CW*, 7:350–51. Several papers reported the meeting, and Methodists took great pride in their defense of the Union and connection to Lincoln. See Moody, *Life's Retrospect*, 441–45; idem, *Memorial Days: A Centennial Sermon* (Cincinnati: Hitchcock and Walden, 1875), 53–54; Lucius C. Matlack, "Our Past and Present Relations to Slavery," *MQR* 50 (April 1868): 262; Daniel Steele, "Politics and the Pulpit," *MQR* 52 (April 1870): 190; Erastus Otis Haven, "The Approaching Centennial of American Independence," *MQR* 56 (October 1874): 535; Jonathan K. Peck, *Luther Peck and His Five Sons* (New York: Eaton and Mains, 1897), 138–39; J. T. Peck, *Great Republic*, 653; George R. Crooks, *The Life of Bishop Matthew Simpson of the Methodist Episcopal Church* (New York: Harper and Brothers, 1890), 368–95. Hartford Baptist Cephas B. Crane, who also accompanied the delegation, echoed Peck: "The President looks thin and care-worn. I believe with all my

heart that he bears this great nation like a burden on his life." Cephas B. Crane, *Sermon on the Occasion of the Death of President Lincoln* (Hartford, Conn.: Case, Lockwood, 1865), 8.

51. See William R. Gordon, *The Sin of Reviling, and Its Work* (New York: John A. Gray and Green, 1865), 13. Note Moody's recollection of a September 1864 meeting that found Lincoln praising Methodists for their support of the Union and revealing the circumstances surrounding the Emancipation Proclamation's issuance. Moody's account jibes with others, which had the president vowing to God that if Lee's invasion were thwarted he would issue the proclamation, but Moody also attributed the following to Lincoln: "Lord, if thou wilt discomfit, dismay, and defeat Lee . . . , I will abolish slavery as a military necessity. So help me God! I will. I ask this in the name and for the sake of Jesus Christ, our Lord." Moody, *Life's Retrospect*, 448. Cf. Allen C. Guelzo, *Lincoln's Emancipation Proclamation: The End of Slavery in America* (New York: Simon and Schuster, 2004), 148–56.

52. C. W. Heisley to Matthew Simpson, 5 July 1864, W. H. Black to Matthew Simpson, 3 August 1864, O. M. Spencer to Matthew Simpson, 13 January 1865, J. L. G. McKown to Matthew Simpson, 21 February 1865, MSP.

53. Crooks, *Life of Bishop Matthew Simpson*, 374–75.

54. Gordon Hall, *Divine Mercy a Cause for Humiliation* (Northampton, Mass.: Trumbull and Gere, 1865), 9.

55. Letters to Simpson indicate a widespread perception that he had influence with Lincoln and later Grant. Simpson cultivated relationships with many Washington insiders, including Presidents Johnson and Hayes, and he became embroiled in controversy over patronage. See Robert D. Clark, *The Life of Matthew Simpson* (New York: Macmillan, 1956), 221–35; Carwardine, *Lincoln*, 271.

56. J. T. Peck, *Great Republic*, 15; Boardman, *Sovereignty of God*, 7; Dinsmore, *Our Country*, 8, 29; Woart, *Thanksgiving Discourse*, 8–9; Caspar R. Gregory, *A Thanksgiving Sermon* (Bridgeton, N.J.: G. F. Nixon, 1865), 6; G. Peck, *Our Country*, 117, 238 (quote); J. P. C., "The War and Its Design," *CR* 8 October 1864, p. 162; Joseph Smiley Grimes, *The Nation's Last Hope* (New Castle, Pa.: E. S. Durban, 1864), 13; Duffield, *God of Our Fathers*; "The Mill of God," *Independent*, 3 March 1864, p. 4; Nathaniel Hall, *The Moral Significance of the Contrasts between Slavery and Freedom* (Boston: Walker, Wise, and Company and Ebenezer Clapp, 1864), 10–11; Thomas Laurie, *Three Discourses* (Dedham, Mass.: John Cox Jr., 1865), 18. Cf. Charles Hodge, "The War," *BRPR* 35 (January 1863): 140–69. Although most understood national life in covenantal terms, Hodge contended that not all suffering and hardship—individual or corporate—was divine punishment; rather, God uses "trials" to try men's faith and patience, to develop character, or simply to manifest divine existence, strength, and glory (143–44).

57. James Madison Hoyt, *The Suicide of Slavery* (Cleveland: Fairbanks, Benedict, 1864), 5. See also Henry Darling, *Chastened but Not Killed* (Albany, N.Y.: Van Benthuysen's Steam Printing House, 1864), 32; Henry W. Lee, *The Great Deliverance* (Davenport, Iowa: Luse and Griggs, 1865), 9–10.

58. This call coincided with the November Thanksgiving, thus beginning the tradition of a national holiday called by the president. Subsequent presidents followed suit until 1941, when Congress designated November's fourth Thursday as the annual national day. See Anne Blue Wills, "Pilgrims and Progress: How Magazines Made Thanksgiving,"

CH 72 (March 2003): 138–58; Elizabeth H. Pleck, "The Making of the Domestic Occasion: The History of Thanksgiving in the United States," *Journal of Social History* 32 (June 1999): 773–89; Janet Siskind, "The Invention of Thanksgiving: A Ritual of American Nationality," *Critique of Anthropology* 12 (June 1992): 167–91.

59. Joseph G. Symmes, *National Thanksgiving* (Philadelphia: William S. and Alfred Martien), 1864), 6, 30. More specifically, Symmes believed the nation's "greatest sin" was its inadequate recognition of Jesus: "As sinners will perish who refuse to believe on him, so nations that refuse to acknowledge his authority shall be 'dashed in pieces like a potter's vessel'" (31). Symmes joined others in seeking a Constitutional amendment explicitly recognizing that authority. See Stewart Olin Jacoby, "The Religious Amendment Movement: God, People and Nation in the Gilded Age" (PhD diss., University of Michigan, 1984), 78–230; Morton Borden, "The Christian Amendment," *CWH* 25 (June 1979): 156–67; Isaac Kramnick and R. Laurence Moore, *The Godless Constitution: The Case against Religious Correctness* (New York: W. W. Norton, 1996), 131–49; Foster, *Moral Reconstruction*, 27–30; idem, "Christian Nation." See also Thomas Nelson Haskell, *Christian Patriotism: A Medium of God's Power and Purpose to Bless Our Land* (Boston: Hollis and Gun, 1863), 27; James Renwick Wilson Sloane, "Amendments to the Constitution," *Independent*, 17 March 1864, p. 1.

60. Theodore Tilton, "Proclamation by Horatio Seymour, Governor of the State of New York," *Independent*, 19 November 1863, p. 4; "Our Thanksgiving Hymn," *Independent*, 19 November 1863, p. 1; William [?] Muhlenberg, "The President's Hymn: Give Thanks All Ye People," *Independent*, 19 November 1863, p. 6; Symmes, *National Thanksgiving*, 6; Samuel Bell, *Sermon* (New York: Baptist and Taylor, 1864), 3. See also Gilmore, *"Hath God Forgotten to Be Gracious,"* 3–4; "Thanksgiving," *CR*, 3 December 1864, p. 194; Haven, *National Sermons*, 390–91. Haven emphasized that God had joined Union military victories to national holidays—Vicksburg on July 4, 1863, and Chattanooga during Thanksgiving week 1863.

61. Silver, *Confederate Morale and Church Propaganda*, 27; Mitchell Snay, *Gospel of Disunion: Religion and Separatism in the Antebellum South* (Cambridge: Cambridge University Press, 1993), 188–90; Rable, *God's Almost Chosen Peoples*, 73; Stout, *Upon the Altar of the Nation*, 47–52.

62. Edward Norris Kirk, "Psalms XLVI, 10," in *Sermons Preached in Boston on the Death of Abraham Lincoln* (Boston: J. E. Tilton, 1865), 45–46; idem, *Only One Human Race* (1865); David O. Mears, *Edward Norris Kirk* (Boston: Lockwood, Brooks, 1877); Timothy L. Smith, *Revivalism and Social Reform: American Protestantism on the Eve of the Civil War* (Nashville, Tenn.: Abingdon Press, 1957; repr., New York: Harper and Row, 1965), 50–51.

63. Frederic Dan Huntington, *Personal Humiliation Demanded by the National Danger* (Boston: E. P. Dutton, 1864), 5; Henry A. Boardman, The War (1), HBP. See also Haven, *National Sermons*, 394–95; Haskell, *Christian Patriotism*, 12–18, 24–32; Andrew Leete Stone, *Emancipation* (Boston: Henry Hoyt, 1862), 4; Levi Paine, *Political Lessons of the Rebellion* (Farmington, Conn.: Samuel Cowles, 1862), 5.

64. Henry Augustus Boardman, *The American Union* (Philadelphia: Lippincott, Grambo, 1851), 30.

65. Gurley, *Man's Projects and God's Results*, 16; G. Peck, *Our Country*, 8–9, 12–14. Moorhead, *American Apocalypse*, 54–56, 72–77, emphasizes that evangelicals often were "millennial" in the sense that they raised American republicanism to a level of cosmic significance. See Bernard H. Nadal, *The War in the Light of Divine Providence* (New Haven, Conn.: Tuttle, Morehouse and Taylor, 1863), 19; Beecher, *Patriotic Addresses*, 245; Joel F. Bingham, *The Hour of Patriotism* (Buffalo: Franklin, 1862), 23–24.

66. G. Peck, *Life and Times*, 372, 375; idem, *Our Country*, 38.

67. Byron Sunderland, *The Crisis of the Times* (Washington D.C.: National Banner Press, 1863), 7, 23, 34–35. See also G. Peck, *Our Country*, 107–8, 117; Duffield, *God of Our Fathers*, 13–29; Lee, *Great Deliverance*, 3–10; Rable, *God's Almost Chosen Peoples*, 81; Silver, *Confederate Morale and Church Propaganda*, 31; Stowell, *Rebuilding Zion*, 37–38; Stout, *Upon the Altar of the Nation*, 92–93. Stout indicts the habituated jeremiad for stifling serious reflection and "rhetorical creativity" and fostering a Stoic-like acceptance of the war. Cf. George B. Cheever [?], "The Guilt and Consequences of National Covenant Breaking," *Principia*, 16 April 1863, p. 1097. Regarding the theme generally, see Sacvan Bercovitch, *The American Jeremiad* (Madison: University of Wisconsin Press, 1978).

68. Grimes, *Nation's Last Hope*, 5–7, 16. The full text of 2 Chronicles 7:14 reads: "If my people, which are called by my name, shall humble themselves, and pray, and seek my face, and turn from their wicked ways; then will I hear from heaven, and will forgive their sin, and heal their land." Unsurprisingly, southern ministers appropriated the same text. See Silver, *Confederate Morale and Church Propaganda*, 66n11.

69. Grimes, *Nation's Last Hope*, 5.

70. Bernard Harrison Nadal, *A Christian Nation's Ordeal* (Washington D.C.: M'Gill and Witherow, 1864), 16. Nadal went on to become a theology professor and president of Drew Theological Seminary. See idem, *The New Life Dawning, and Other Discourses*, ed. Henry A. Butz (New York: Nelson and Phillips, 1873), 7, 37; Ezra Squier Tipple, ed., *Drew Theological Seminary: A Review of the First Half Century* (New York: Methodist Book Concern, 1917), 53–4.

71. Huntington, *Personal Humiliation*, 9–10.

72. George B. Cheever to Henry T. Cheever, 28 February 1863, CFP. Cheever spoke to the Senate on 15 February 1863 urging the government to strike at slavery wholeheartedly. See also George B. Cheever, *The Proposed Return into Egypt, and Its Consequences* (Washington, D.C. [?]: n.p., 1863); idem, "The Proposed Return into Egypt and Its Consequences," *Principia*, 2 April 1863, p. 1089; idem, "The War Power," *Principia*, 12 March 1863, p. 1077; idem, "The War Power as Ordained of God," 19 March 1863, p. 1081; "The War Power as Ordained of God," 26 March 1863, p. 1085. Cheever feared Lincoln's proclamation meant very little in terms of changing the war's actual aim. George B. Cheever to Elizabeth Cheever, 14 June 1863, George B. Cheever to Elizabeth Washburn, 7 July 1863, 7 May 1864, CFP. Blight, *Frederick Douglass' Civil War*, 107.

73. George B. Cheever to Elizabeth Washburn, 15 July 1863, 5 August 1863, CFP; Abraham Lincoln, Proclamation of Thanksgiving, 15 July 1863, *CW*, 6:332–33.

74. Abraham Lincoln, Proclamation Appointing a National Fast Day, 30 March 1863, *CW*, 6:155–56.

75. Haskell, *Christian Patriotism*, 26–27, 38; H. Smith, *God in the War*, 5; John K. Plitt,

God's Doings for the Nation (Easton, Pa.: L. Gordon, 1864), 5; Thompson, *Peace through Victory*, 3; Abraham Lincoln, Proclamation of Thanksgiving and Prayer, 3 September 1864, *CW*, 7:533–34; idem, Order of Thanks to David G. Farragut and Others, 3 September 1864, *CW*, 7:532–33.

2. 1864: *Annus Mirabilis*

1. Gilbert Haven, *National Sermons: Sermons, Speeches, and Letters on Slavery and Its War: From the Passage of the Fugitive Slave Bill to the Election of President Grant* (Boston: Lee and Shepard, 1869), 489, 493; idem, "The Great Election," *MQR* 47 (April 1865): 253–75; William Gravely, *Gilbert Haven, Methodist Abolitionist: A Study in Race, Religion, and Reform, 1850–1880* (Nashville, Tenn.: Abingdon Press, 1973); David W. Blight, *Frederick Douglass' Civil War: Keeping Faith in Jubilee* (Baton Rouge: Louisiana State University Press, 1989), 73–79, 101–21, 182–87; James M. McPherson, *The Struggle for Equality: Abolitionists and the Negro in the Civil War and Reconstruction* (Princeton, N.J.: Princeton University Press, 1964), 260–86. James Oakes, *The Radical and the Republican: Frederick Douglass, Abraham Lincoln, and the Triumph of Antislavery Politics* (New York: W. W. Norton, 2007), views Lincoln as being morally transformed to become more like Douglass (and thus more like Haven). Cf. Eric Foner, *The Fiery Trial: Abraham Lincoln and American Slavery* (New York: W. W. Norton, 2010); George M. Fredrickson, *Big Enough to Be Inconsistent: Abraham Lincoln Confronts Slavery and Race* (Cambridge, Mass.: Harvard University Press, 2008); Larry E. Nelson, "Black Leaders and the Presidential Election of 1864," *JNH* 63 (January 1978): 42–58; William C. Harris, "The Hampton Roads Peace Conference: A Final Test of Lincoln's Presidential Leadership," *JALA* 21 (Winter 2000): 53–55; Allen C. Guelzo, *Abraham Lincoln: Redeemer President* (Grand Rapids, Mich.: Wm. B. Eerdmans, 1999), 408–9; Adam I. P. Smith, "The Challenge of Biography: What Do They Know of Lincoln Who Only Lincoln Know?," review of *Abraham Lincoln*, by Michael Burlingame, *JALA* 31 (Summer 2010): 61–75; Colin McCoy, "Review Essay," review of *The Radical and the Republican: Frederick Douglass, Abraham Lincoln, and the Triumph of Antislavery Politics*, by James Oakes, *JALA* 29 (Summer 2008): 73–79. See also "The Union War," *NB*, 12 January 1865, p. 3; Increase Niles Tarbox, "Universal Suffrage," *NE* 24 (January 1865): 154; Joel Foote Bingham, *National Disappointment* (Buffalo: Breed, Butler, 1865), 4–6, 30; Albert Barnes, *The State of the Country* (Philadelphia: Henry B. Ashmead, 1865), 14, 22–24; William M. Blackburn, *The Crime against the Presidency* (Trenton, N.J.: Murphy and Bechtel, 1965), 8, 18.

2. Frederick Douglass to Theodore Tilton, 15 October 1864, *LWFD*, 3:422, 424; McPherson, *Struggle for Equality*, 26; Blight, *Frederick Douglass' Civil War*, 184–85; Michael Vorenberg, "'The Deformed Child': Slavery and the Election of 1864," *CWH* 47 (September 2001): 240–57; Nelson, "Black Leaders and the Presidential Election of 1864"; Louis S. Gerteis, "Salmon P. Chase, Radicalism, and the Politics of Emancipation, 1861–1864," *JAH* 60 (June 1973): 42–62.

3. James M. McPherson, "No Peace without Victory," *AHR* 109 (February 2004): 10–11; Stephen W. Sears, "McClellan and the Peace Plank: A Reappraisal," *CWH* 36 (March 1990): 57–64; Harold M. Hyman, "Election of 1864," in *History of American*

Presidential Elections, 1789–1968, ed. Arthur M. Schlesinger Jr. (New York: Chelsea House, 1985), 3:1167; William C. Harris, "Conservative Unionists and the Presidential Election of 1864," *CWH* 38 (December 1992): 298–318; Larry E. Nelson, *Bullets, Ballots, and Rhetoric: Confederate Policy for the United States Presidential Contest of 1864* (Tuscaloosa: University of Alabama Press, 1980); Ludwell H. Johnson, "Lincoln's Solution to the Problem of Peace Terms, 1864–1865," *JSH* 34 (November 1968): 576–86; Harriet Chappell Owsley, "Peace and the Presidential Election of 1864," *Tennessee Historical Quarterly* 18 (March 1959): 3–19.

4. Frederick Douglass to Theodore Tilton, 15 October 1864, *LWFD*, 3:424. On northern racism, see Leon Litwack, *North of Slavery: The Negro in the Free States, 1790–1860* (Chicago: University of Chicago Press, 1961); George M. Fredrickson, *The Black Image in the White Mind: The Debate on Afro-American Character and Destiny, 1817–1914* (New York: Harper and Row, 1971); Jean H. Baker, *Affairs of Party: The Political Culture of Northern Democrats in the Mid-Nineteenth Century* (Ithaca, N.Y.: Cornell University Press, 1983), 212–58; Alexander Saxton, *The Rise and Fall of the White Republic: Class Politics and Mass Culture in Nineteenth-Century America* (New York: Verso, 1990); Rogers M. Smith, *Civic Ideals: Conflicting Visions of Citizenship in U.S. History* (New Haven, Conn.: Yale University Press, 1997), 197–289.

5. My understanding also has been informed by Michael Burlingame, *Abraham Lincoln: A Life*, 2 vols. (Baltimore: Johns Hopkins University Press, 2008), 2:581–730; David Herbert Donald, *Lincoln* (New York: Simon and Schuster, 1995), 493–545; Ronald C. White Jr., *A. Lincoln: A Biography* (New York: Random House, 2009), 632–45; William E. Gienapp, *Abraham Lincoln and Civil War America: A Biography* (New York: Oxford University Press, 2002), 151–76; John C. Waugh, *Reelecting Lincoln: The Battle for the 1864 Presidency* (New York: Crown, 1997); David E. Long, *The Jewel of Liberty: Abraham Lincoln's Re-Election and the End of Slavery* (Mechanicsburg, Pa.: Stackpole Books, 1994); Mark E. Neely Jr. and Harold Holzer, *The Union Image: Popular Prints of the Civil War North* (Chapel Hill: University of North Carolina Press, 2000), 129–59; James A. Rawley, *The Politics of Union: Northern Politics during the Civil War* (Lincoln: University of Nebraska Press, 1974), 154–63; Frank William Zornow, *Lincoln and the Party Divided* (Norman: University of Oklahoma Press, 1954), 213–14; Larry T. Balsamo, "'We Cannot Have Free Government without Elections': Abraham Lincoln and the Election of 1864," *JISHS* 94 (Summer 2001): 181–99; Harold M. Dudley, "The Election of 1864," *Mississippi Valley Historical Review* 18 (March 1932): 514; Sidney Kaplan, "The Miscegenation Issue in the Election of 1864" *JNH* 34 (July 1949): 274–343; Leonard Newman, "Opposition to Lincoln in the Election of 1864," *Science and Society* 8 (Fall 1944): 305–27; Michael Kleen, "The Copperhead Threat in Illinois: Peace Democrats, Loyalty Leagues, and the Charleston Riot of 1864," *JISHS* 105 (Spring 2012): 69–92; Jennifer L. Weber, *Copperheads: The Rise and Fall of Lincoln's Opponents in the North* (New York: Oxford University Press, 2006), 135–217; Jonathan W. White, "'For My Part I Don't Care Who Is Elected President': The Union Army and the Election of 1864," in *This Distracted and Anarchical People: New Answers for Old Questions about the Civil War–Era North*, ed. Andrew L. Slap and Michael Thomas Smith (New York: Fordham University Press, 2013), 104–22.

6. William A. Stearns, *A Sermon Delivered before the Executive and Legislative Departments of the Government of Massachusetts, at the Annual Election, Wednesday, Jan. 6, 1864* (Boston: Wright and Potter, 1864), 7, 45. See also idem, *A Discourse on Educated Manhood* (Springfield, Mass.: Samuel Bowles, 1859); Haven, *National Sermons*, 374; John Knox, *Sermon for the Times* (Baltimore, 1864), 7; Andrew Leete Stone, *National Godliness* (Boston: T. R. Marvin and Sons, 1864).

7. Abraham Lincoln, Speech to Ulysses S. Grant, 9 March 1864, *CW*, 7:234; Ulysses S. Grant, Speech, 9 March 1864, *PUSG*, 10:195; "The New Lieutenant-General," *Independent*, 17 March 1864, p. 1; Brooks D. Simpson, *Let Us Have Peace: Ulysses S. Grant and the Politics of War and Reconstruction, 1861–1868* (Chapel Hill: University of North Carolina Press, 1991), 51–55; idem, *Ulysses S. Grant: Triumph Over Adversity, 1822–1865* (New York: Houghton Mifflin, 2000), 258–61. William S. McFeely, *Grant: A Biography* (New York: W. W. Norton, 1981), 155, excludes the remark about providence. Note Grant's *Memoirs*, wherein he repeated Thomas à Kempis's commonplace from *Imitation of Christ*, 1:19: "'Man proposes and God disposes.' There are but few important events in the affairs of men brought about by their own choice." See Ulysses S. Grant, *Personal Memoirs of U. S. Grant*, with an introduction by William S. McFeely (Cleveland: World, 1952; repr., New York: Da Capo, 1982), vii; John Y. Simon, "The Paradox of Ulysses S. Grant," *RKHS* 81 (Autumn 1983): 370–72.

8. George Duffield Jr., *The Dark Night and the Glorious Morning* (Galesburg, Ill.: Free Press Book and Job Office, 1866), 19–20; George M. Marsden, *The Evangelical Mind and the New School Presbyterian Experience: A Case Study of Thought and Theology in Nineteenth-Century America* (New Haven, Conn.: Yale University Press, 1970), 52, 182. See also Marvin R. Vincent, *The Lord of War and of Righteousness* (Troy, N.Y.: A. W. Scribner, 1864), 17.

9. Jesse T. Peck, *The Great Republic from the Discovery of America to the Centennial, July 4, 1876* (New York: Nelson and Phillips, 1876), 641.

10. "Our Washington Correspondence," *Independent*, 17 March 1864, p. 1; J. T. Peck, *Great Republic*, 642. Matthew Simpson, "Our National Conflict," *New York Daily Tribune*, 7 November 1864, p. 7, compared Grant to a Union-saving Andrew Jackson. Most cast him as another Washington, a humble, unpretentious Christian republican. McFeely, *Grant*, 165, perhaps underappreciates Grant's heroic status. Cf. Oliver Otis Howard, "Washington and Grant Compared," ca. 1890, OOHP; Horace Porter, *Campaigning with Grant* (1897; New York: Century, 1906), 18–22, 181; Brooks D. Simpson, "Great Expectations: Ulysses S. Grant, the Northern Press, and the Opening of the Wilderness Campaign," in *The Wilderness Campaign*, ed. Gary W. Gallagher (Chapel Hill: University of North Carolina Press, 1997), 1–35; Joan Waugh, *U. S. Grant: American Hero, American Myth* (Chapel Hill: University of North Carolina Press, 2009); John Y. Simon, "Ulysses S. Grant One Hundred Years Later," *IHJ* 79 (Winter 1986): 245–56; James A. Ramage and Kristopher A. Teters, "Public Reactions to Ulysses S. Grant's Vicksburg Campaign in Kentucky, Cincinnati, and across the Union," *RKHS* 103 (Autumn 2005): 627–60.

11. Haven, *National Sermons*, 402–3, 544. See also Jesse Winegar Hough, *Our Country's Mission; or, The Present Suffering of the Nation Justified by its Future Glory* (Burlington, Vt.: Free Press, 1864), 9–11; George M. Randall, *Sermon before the Ancient and*

Honorable Artillery Co., on Its CCXXVII Anniversary, June 5, 1865 (Boston: Wright and Potter, 1865), 29–32; James G. Vose, *"The Decisive Battle"* (Boston: T. R. Marvin and Son, 1865), 18; T. Sandford Doolittle, *A Sermon* (Schenectady, N.Y.: Young and Graham, 1866), 20; Duffield, *Dark Night*, 27; James McDougall, *God's Blessing of Peace* (Brooklyn: Daily Times, 1866), 10.

12. Haven, *National Sermons*, 398. McClellan also spoke of the providential Union cause—in terms that met approval when uttered by others. See George C. Rable, *God's Almost Chosen Peoples: A Religious History of the American Civil War* (Chapel Hill: University of North Carolina Press, 2010), 95–96, 138–39; Harry S. Stout, *Upon the Altar of the Nation: A Moral History of the Civil War* (New York: Viking, 2006), 136–38.

13. Erastus Wright to Ulysses S. Grant, 4 April 1864, USGP. On Wright, see Abraham Lincoln to Mrs. Eliza Hamilton, 29 October 1860, *CW*, 4:134n2; Burlingame, *Abraham Lincoln*, 1:236, 349; Richard E. Hart, "Lincoln's Springfield: The Underground Railroad, Part 2," *For the People: A Newsletter of the Abraham Lincoln Association* 8 (Summer 2006): 1. Grant's views were similar to Lincoln's. See Simpson, *Let Us Have Peace*, 35–67. Wright eventually supported Lincoln. See Erastus Wright, "From the Home of Mr. Lincoln," *Principia*, 26 May 1864, p. 42; "A Religious Argument in Favor of Voting for Mr. Lincoln, Examined," *Principia*, 30 June 1864, p. 81.

14. Stone, *National Godliness*, 15–16, 23; McPherson, *Struggle for Equality*, 227; Andrew Leete Stone, *Memorial Discourses* (Boston: Henry Hoyt, 1866); idem, *Leaves from a Finished Pastorate* (New York: Anson D. F. Randolph, 1882).

15. George Peck, *Our Country: Its Trial and Its Triumph: A Series of Discourses Suggested by the Varying Events of the War for the Union* (New York: Carlton and Porter, 1865), 227; idem, *The Life and Times of Rev. George Peck, D.D., Written by Himself* (New York: Nelson and Phillips, 1874), 378. See also Sabin Smith, *Our Country* (New York: John A. Gray and Green, 1865), 26.

16. New York *Tribune*, 13 May 1864, quoted in Simpson, "Great Expectations," 23; "Our Country," *CR*, 21 May, 1864, p. 83. See also "Washington Correspondence," *CR*, 14 May 1864, p. 77; "Washington Correspondence," *CR*, 21 May 1864, p. 81. By 1863 A.M.E. leaders eventually supported the war effort, although they criticized inequities regarding pay and treatment of black soldiers. See "Colored Troops of the United States," *CR*, 2 April 1864, p. 54; "A Soldier's Interesting Letter," *CR*, 16 April 1864, p. 61; "Our Duty in the Present Crisis," *CR*, 7 May 1864, p. 73; "The President's Call for Five Hundred Thousand More Troops, *CR*, 23 July 1864, p. 118; Clarence Walker, *Rock in a Weary Land: The African Methodist Episcopal Church during the Civil War and Reconstruction* (Baton Rouge: Louisiana State University Press, 1982), 30–45; Blight, *Frederick Douglass' Civil War*, 148–174; McPherson, *Struggle for Equality*, 192–220.

17. Abraham Lincoln, To the Friends of Union and Liberty, 9 May 1864, *CW*, 7:333; G. Peck, *Life and Times*, 380–81; Abraham Lincoln, Response to Serenade, 9 May 1864, *CW*, 7:334.

18. Noah A. Trudeau, *Bloody Roads South: The Wilderness to Cold Harbor, May–June 1864* (Boston: Little, Brown, 1989), 172–85; Robert K. Krick, "An Insurmountable Barrier between the Army and Ruin: The Confederate Experience at Spotsylvania's Bloody Angle," in *The Spotsylvania Campaign*, ed. Gary W. Gallagher (Chapel Hill: University of

North Carolina Press, 1998), 80–126; James M. McPherson, *Battle Cry of Freedom: The Civil War Era* (New York: Oxford University Press, 1988), 730–31. Holmes's reflections precipitated claims regarding larger intellectual changes; see Louis Menand, *The Metaphysical Club: A Story of Ideas in America* (New York: Farrar, Straus and Giroux, 2001), 49–69; Anne C. Rose, *Victorian America and the Civil War* (Cambridge: Cambridge University Press, 1992), 17–67; Drew Gilpin Faust, *This Republic of Suffering: Death and the American Civil War* (New York: Vintage, 2008), 24, 193–94, 270; George M. Fredrickson, *The Inner Civil War: Northern Intellectuals and the Crisis of the Union* (New York: Harper and Row, 1965), 166–72; Edmund Wilson, *Patriotic Gore: Studies in the Literature of the American Civil War* (New York: Oxford University Press, 1962), 747–53.

19. Haven, *National Sermons*, 393–94. See also Byron Sunderland, *A Sermon in Memory of Colonel Ulrich Dahlgren* (Washington, D.C.: McGill and Witherow, 1864), 44; David Rolfs, *No Peace for the Wicked: Northern Protestant Soldiers and the American Civil War* (Knoxville: University of Tennessee Press, 2009), 167–96.

20. Thomas Nast, "The Union Christmas Dinner," *Harper's Weekly*, 31 December 1864. http://www.harpweek.com/09Cartoon/BrowseByDateCartoon.asp?Month=December&Date=31. Accessed 16 March 2015. Note William J. Cooper Jr., "Where Was Henry Clay? President-Elect Abraham Lincoln and the Crisis of Union, 180660–1861," in *New Directions in Mid-Nineteenth-Century American Political History*, ed. Gary W. Gallagher and Rachel A. Shelden (Charlottesville: University of Virginia Press, 2012), 131: "[Lincoln] appears to have had no understanding either of the widespread ownership of slaves among whites or how deeply slavery had become embedded in Southern society. . . . Lincoln thought of [southern whites] as conservative Unionists with little attachment to slavery." See also William C. Harris, *With Charity for All: Lincoln and the Restoration of the Union* (Lexington: University Press of Kentucky, 1997); Brooks D. Simpson, *The Reconstruction Presidents* (Lawrence: University Press of Kansas, 1998), 9–64; Gienapp, *Abraham Lincoln and Civil War America*, 152–55.

21. Ulysses S. Grant to J. Russell Jones, 5 July 1864, *PUSG*, 11:176; Henry A. Boardman, The War (1), HBP; Howard Crosby, *God's View of the Rebellion* (New York: E. French, 1864); William Barrows, *Honor to the Brave* (Boston: John M. Whittemore, 1863); Chester Forrester Dunham, *The Attitude of the Northern Clergy toward the South, 1860–1865* (Toledo, Ohio: Gray, 1942), 118–26. Most denominations issued statements of support in 1864.

22. Henry Darling, *Chastened, But Not Killed* (Albany, N.Y.: Van Benthuysen's 1864), 21–24. See also idem, *Slavery and the War: A Historical Essay* (Philadelphia: J. B. Lippincott, 1863); Richard W. Darling, ed., *Memorial of President Henry Darling* (Utica, N.Y.: L. C. Childs and Son, 1893).

23. Ulysses S. Grant to Edwin M. Stanton, 11 May 1864, *PUSG*, 10:422; McPherson, *Struggle for Equality*, 282; idem, *Battle Cry of Freedom*, 735–42; David Herbert Donald, Jean Harvey Baker, and Michael E. Holt, *The Civil War and Reconstruction* (New York: W. W. Norton, 2001), 378; Trudeau, *Bloody Roads South*, 265–99, 341; *CR*, "Our Country," 21 May 1864, p. 83; Duffield, *Dark Night*, 20.

24. Elizabeth Washburn to Elizabeth Cheever, 17 May 1864, George B. Cheever to Elizabeth Cheever, 29 April 1864, George B. Cheever to Elizabeth Washburn, 7 May 1864, CFP; Hough, *Our Country's Mission*, 6; Rable, *God's Almost Chosen Peoples*, 344.

25. Mrs. James Harlan to George B. Cheever, 22, 30 March 1864, George B. Cheever to Elizabeth Cheever, 29 May 1864, CFP. See also William Henry Channing to George B. Cheever, 26 April 1864, George B. Cheever to Elizabeth Washburn, 7 May 1864, George B. Cheever to Elizabeth Cheever, 29 April 1864, CFP; George B. Cheever [?], "The Claims of Colored Soldiers," *Principia*, 10 March 1864, p. 1285, 17 March 1864, p. 1289.

26. George B. Cheever to Elizabeth Cheever, 5 August 1863, Elizabeth Washburn to George B. Cheever, 20 July 1864, George B. Cheever to Elizabeth Cheever, 1 July 1864, Salmon P. Chase to George B. Cheever, 17 October 1863, George B. Cheever to Elizabeth Cheever, 31 May 1864, CFP.

27. George B. Cheever [?], "The Next President: Our Position Defined," *Principia*, 24 March 1864, p. 1294; idem [?], "Reasons for a Change of Administration," "An Appeal to the People, For the Country's Salvation," *Principia*, 21 April 1864, p. 2; idem [?], "The President's Veto," *Principia*, 14 July 1864, p. 100; idem, *A Change of Administration, for the Security of the Government, a Christian Duty and a National Necessity* (New York: J. W. Alden, 1864), 3–4; idem, "A Change of Administration for the Security of the Government: A Christian Duty and a National Necessity," *Principia*, 21 July 1864, p. 105, 28 July 1864, p. 113, 4 August 1864, p. 121; McPherson, *Struggle for Equality*, 264–75. The *Principia* was unceasingly critical of Lincoln; see "The Union of the Future and the Future of the Union," *Principia*, 6 November 1862, p. 1006; "The Destruction of Slavery the Ground of Our Salvation," *Principia*, 13 November 1862, p. 1009; "The Purpose and Results of God's Chastening Discipline with Us as a Nation. Which Will We Choose, Slavery or Freedom," *Principia*, 28 November 1862, p. 1017; "The Consequences of a Policy Half Sin and Half Righteousness," *Principia*, 4 December 1862, p. 1021, 11 December 1862, p. 1025; "The Mercy of God in Our Chastisements," *Principia*, 25 December 1862, p. 1033, 1 January 1863, p. 1037; "The President's Proclamation," *Principia*, 8 January 1863, p. 1042; "Consequences of the Right of Slavery, as a Pretended Right of State Sovereignty," *Principia*, 21 May 1863, p. 1117; "The Career of Pres. Lincoln and Its Consequences," *Principia* 26 May 1864, p. 41; "Summary of Reasons against Voting for Mr. Lincoln," *Principia*, 25 August 1864, p. 25.

28. George B. Cheever, *A Change of Administration for the Security of the Government: A Christian Duty and a National Necessity* (New York: J. W. Alden, 1864), 10, 16; George B. Cheever to Elizabeth Washburn, 22 September 1864, CFP; Lincoln to Hodges, *CW*, 7:282; Abraham Lincoln, To Horace Greeley, 22 August 1862, *CW*, 5:388–89; Thomas Nelson Haskell, *Christian Patriotism: A Medium of God's Power and Purpose to Bless Our Land* (Boston: Hollis and Gun, 1863), 27; Smith, *Our Country*, 26–28; Phineas Densmore Gurley, *Man's Projects and God's Results* (Washington, D.C.: Wm. Ballantyne, 1863), 14–15; Alfred Taylor, *Our Nation Not Dead Yet* (Philadelphia: Henry B. Ashmead, 1863), 14–15; Joseph G. Symmes, *National Thanksgiving* (Philadelphia: William S. and Alfred Martien, 1864), 15–17.

29. Joseph Henry Gilmore, *"Hath God Forgotten to Be Gracious"* (Concord, N.H.: P. B. Cogswell, 1864), 12–13; James Madison Hoyt, *The Suicide of Slavery* (Cleveland: Fairbanks, Benedict, 1864); Cheever, *Change of Administration*, 3, 16–17; George B. Cheever to Elizabeth Cheever, 17 June 1863, George B. Cheever to Elizabeth Washburn, 7 May, 22 September 1864, CFP; McPherson, *Struggle for Equality*, 221–37.

30. Cheever, like unyielding radicals such as Wendell Phillips, Elizabeth Cady Stanton, and Susan B. Anthony, probably did not vote. See George B. Cheever to Elizabeth Washburn, 10, 22 September, 1 November 1864, Elizabeth Washburn to George B. Cheever, 16 September 1864, CFP; Robert M. York, *George B. Cheever, Religious and Social Reformer, 1807–1890* (Orono, Maine: University Press, 1955), 200; McPherson, *Struggle for Equality*, 285.

31. Abraham Lincoln, Proclamation of a Day of Prayer, 7 July 1864, *CW*, 7:431–32; Haven, *National Sermons*, 474; Hough, *Our Country's Mission*, 9–11. See also Elisha Lord Cleaveland, *The Patriot's Song of Victory* (New Haven, Conn.: Thomas H. Pease, 1864), 8–9.

32. Henry Conkling, *An Inside View of the Rebellion, and the American Citizens' Textbook* (Chicago: Tribune Book and Job Printing Establishment, 1864), 21–22.

33. *The Little Mac Campaign Songster* (New York: T. R. Dawley, 1864), 53; *Trial of Abraham Lincoln by the Great Statesmen of the Republic: A Council of the Past on the Tyranny of the Present* (New York: Office of the Metropolitan Record, 1863), 28; Baker, *Affairs of Party*, 281–311; Joel H. Silbey, *A Respectable Minority: The Democratic Party in the Civil War Era* (New York: W. W. Norton, 1977), 140–76.

34. Quoted in Weber, *Copperheads*, 159.

35. Hyman, "Election of 1864," 1179–80.

36. *Little Mac Campaign Songster*, 28–29.

37. Edward Crosby, *Our Country versus Party Spirit: Being a Rejoinder to the Reply of Prof. Morse* (Poughkeepsie, N.Y.: Platt and Schram, 1863), 9.

38. Quoted in *Spirit of the Chicago Convention* (Chicago: Chicago Tribune, 1864), 5; John T. McGreevy, *Catholicism and American Freedom: A History* (New York: W. W. Norton, 2003), 68–90.

39. *Little Mac Campaign Songster*, 70, 64.

40. George McClellan to Mary Ellen McClellan, 16 August, 11 October, 17 November 1861, in *The Civil War Papers of George B. McClellan, Selected Correspondence, 1860–1865*, ed. Stephen W. Sears (New York: Ticknor and Fields, 1989), 85, 106, 135; Vincent, *Lord of War and of Righteousness*, 17; Hough, *Our Country's Mission*, 7; Haven, *National Sermons*, 389, 543; M. A. Blanchard to Matthew Simpson, 16 November 1864, MSP; Henry Hopkins, *Peace in Our Borders* (Troy, N.Y.: A. W. Scribner, 1866), 12; Harvey Denison Kitchel, *A Thanksgiving Sermon* (Chicago: Republican Book and Job Printing Office, 1865), 12; James Rusling, "The War for the Union," *MQR* 46 (April 1864): 313; Rable, *God's Almost Chosen Peoples*, 355. Stephen W. Sears, *George B. McClellan: The Young Napoleon* (New York: Ticknor and Fields, 1988), contends that McClellan arrogantly believed he was "God's chosen instrument for saving the Union" (xi) and was alone working for "the good of the country" (72). Cf. Stout, *Upon the Altar of the Nation*, 69, 281, which portrays McClellan's caution as "humane" opposition to Lincoln's "total war."

41. Darling, *Chastened*, 32; Joseph Smiley Grimes, *The Nation's Last Hope* (New Castle, Pa.: E. S. Durban, 1864), 6; Abraham Lincoln, Memorandum concerning His Probable Failure of Re-election, 23 August 1864, *CW*, 7:514. Stout, *Upon the Altar of the Nation*, 72, 145–46, 170, 185, 242, contends that Lincoln was beginning to transcend the civic-religious/covenantal mind-set by late 1862. Cf. Richard J. Carwardine,

Lincoln (Harlow, Eng.: Pearson Longman, 2003), 287–91; idem, "Religion and National Construction in the Age of Lincoln," *Journal of Mormon History* 36 (Spring 2010): 50–51.

42. Various northerners voiced some idea of war as a chastening means of revivifying society. See "*E Pluribus Unum*," *Atlantic Monthly* 7 (February 1861): 235–46; "Adequacy of the Constitution," *NE* 21 (January 1862): 60; Charles Eliot Norton, "The Advantages of Defeat," *Atlantic Monthly* 8 (September 1861): 360–65; Fredrickson, *Inner Civil War*, 73–112; Horace Bushnell, *Reverses Needed* (Hartford, Conn.: L. E. Hunt, 1861); Matthew Simpson, "Our National Conflict," *New York Daily Tribune*, 7 November 1864, p. 7; G. Peck, *Our Country*, 69–89; Charles Wadsworth, *War a Discipline* (San Francisco: H. H. Bancroft, 1864).

43. Gilmore, *"Hath God Forgotten to Be Gracious,"* 5, 8, 11. See also Joseph S. Ropes, "Financial Aspects of the Rebellion," *NE* 22 (January 1863): 66–78; Alfred H. Guernsey, "The Indivisibility of the Nation," *Harper's New Monthly Magazine* 26 (February 1863): 413–18; Dwight K. Bartlett, *The Philosophy of the Rebellion* (Albany, N.Y.: Weed, Parsons, 1864), 17; "The War and National Wealth," *BRPR* 36 (July 1864): 449–83; William M. Grosvenor, "The Law of Conquest the True Basis of Reconstruction," *NE* 24 (January 1865): 111–32.

44. Horace Bushnell, "The Doctrine of Loyalty," *NE* 22 (July 1863): 569–72. Bushnell is primarily remembered as a precursor to Protestant liberalism, though he was socially conservative and shared mainstream evangelicals' concern over what the Civil War—and slavery—meant for Christian America. See William R. Hutchison, *The Modernist Impulse in American Protestantism* (Cambridge, Mass.: Harvard University Press, 1976), 43–48; Robert Bruce Mullin, *The Puritan as Yankee: A Life of Horace Bushnell* (Grand Rapids, Mich.: Wm. B. Eerdmans, 2002), 208–33. See chapter 1, note 38.

45. H. Crosby, *God's View of the Rebellion*, 12; E. Crosby, *Our Country versus Party Spirit*, 6–7. See also Mark E. Neely Jr., *The Fate of Liberty: Abraham Lincoln and Civil Liberties* (New York: Oxford University Press, 1991), 202–9; Henry Smith, *God in the War* (Buffalo: Wheeler, Matthews, and Warren, 1863), 26–27; Herrick Johnson, *The Banners of a Free People Set Up in the Name of their God* (Pittsburgh: W. S. Haven, 1864), 19–22; Barrows, *Honor to the Brave*, 11.

46. Bernard H. Nadal, *A Christian Nation's Ordeal* (Washington, D.C.: M'Gill and Witherow, 1864), 15; Cadford Mellen Dinsmore, *Our Country* (Claremont, N.H.: Press of the Claremont Manufacturing Company, 1865), 5–9.

47. Haven, *National Sermons*, 474; Theodore Tilton [?], "The Political Situation," *Independent*, 15 September 1864, p. 4; idem [?], "Chicago," *Independent*, 1 September 1864, p. 4; idem [?], "An Appeal to the People," *Independent*, 8 September 1864, p. 4; H. Crosby, *God's View of the Rebellion*, 7, 13; Herrick Johnson, *The Shaking of the Nations* (Pittsburgh: W. S. Haven, 1864), 8, 22–23; Charles E. Robinson, *Herrick Johnson: An Appreciative Memoir* (New York: Fleming H. Revell, 1914), 36.

48. George B. Cheever to Elizabeth Washburn, 10, 22 September 1864, CFP; Richard E. Beringer, Herman Hattaway, Archer Jones, and William N. Still Jr., *Why the South Lost the Civil War* (Athens: University of Georgia Press, 1986), 351–54; Joseph Parrish Thompson, *Peace through Victory* (New York: Loyal Publication Society, 1865).

49. Theodore Tilton [?], "The Last Word," *Independent*, 3 November 1864. See also John Austin Howard to Henry T. Cheever, 14 September 1864, CFP. Frederick Douglass supported Lincoln only after the Democratic Convention. Frederick Douglass to Theodore Tilton, 15 October 1864, *LWFD*, 3:424.

50. Haven, *National Sermons*, 478–82; Cleaveland, *Patriot's Song of Victory*, 12–15.

51. G. Peck, *Our Country*, 170, 174–76. Because most understood civil government as ordained of God, it followed that, in the words of Henry Boardman, "all factious opposition to government bears the taint of criminality"; Christians in particular "may do nothing, especially in the presence of a great rebellion, wilfully to embarrass the government in re-establishing its authority." See Henry A. Boardman, *The Peace-Makers* (Philadelphia: James S. Claxton, 1865), 19; Samuel T. Spear, *Our Country and Its Cause* (Brooklyn: "The Union" Steam Presses, 1864); George Dana Boardman, *Civil Government, a Divine Ordinance* (Philadelphia: Ringwalt and Brown, 1864).

52. Simpson, "Our National Conflict." Simpson delivered the speech under various titles and received more invitations to speak than he could accept. See "Bishop Simpson's Lecture," *Pittsburgh Christian Advocate*, 22 October 1864, A. G. Byers to Matthew Simpson, 20 September 1864, Ruth Marshall to Matthew Simpson, 4 October 1864, S. W. Thomas to Matthew Simpson, 7 October 1864, L. A. Chase to Matthew Simpson, 2 November 1864, J. H. Robinson to Matthew Simpson, 9 November 1864, M. A. Blanchard to Matthew Simpson, 10 November 1864, E. Clark to Matthew Simpson, 18 November 1864, MSP; Robert D. Clark, *Life of Matthew Simpson* (New York: Macmillan, 1956), 240–42; George B. Crooks, *The Life of Bishop Matthew Simpson of the Methodist Episcopal Church* (New York: Harper and Brothers, 1890), 379 (quote); James E. Kerby, "Matthew Simpson and the Mission of America," *CH* 36 (September 1967): 299–307.

53. Simpson, "Our National Conflict"; C. C. Leigh to Matthew Simpson, 7 November 1864, MSP. Lincoln stopped publicly advocating colonization by December 1862, although how African Americans fit within his vision for the Union remains debatable. See Foner, *Fiery Trial*, 258–61, 312; Fredrickson, *Big Enough to Be Inconsistent*, 113; Lerone Bennett Jr., *Forced into Glory: Abraham Lincoln's White Dream* (Chicago: Johnson, 2000), 469–609.

54. Harold M. Hyman, *A More Perfect Union: The Impact of the Civil War and Reconstruction on the Constitution* (New York: Alfred A. Knopf, 1973), 5–7. Note particularly Joel Parker, *Constitutional Law and Unconstitutional Divinity: Letters to Rev. Henry M. Dexter and to Rev. Leonard Bacon, D.D.* (Cambridge, Mass.: H. O. Houghton, 1863). My understanding has been informed by Kenneth M. Stampp, *Imperiled Union: Essays on the Background of the Civil War* (New York: Oxford University Press, 1980), 3–36; Arthur Bestor, "The American Civil War as a Constitutional Crisis," *AHR* 69 (January 1964): 327–52; idem, "State Sovereignty and Slavery: A Reinterpretation of Proslavery Constitutional Doctrine, 1846–1860," *JISHS* 54 (Summer 1961): 117–80; Mark E. Neely Jr., *Lincoln and the Triumph of the Nation: Constitutional Conflict in the American Civil War* (Chapel Hill: University of North Carolina Press, 2011), 5–7, 29–61, 237–74; Herman Belz, "Secession, Revolution and Social Contract Theory in American Political Thought," *Good Society* 6 (Fall 1996): 11–15; Forrest McDonald, *States' Rights and the Union: Imperium in Imperio* (Lawrence: University Press of Kansas, 2000); Daniel Farber, *Lincoln's Constitution*

(Chicago: University of Chicago Press, 1993), 7–44; Michael Les Benedict, "A Constitutional Crisis," in *Writing the Civil War: The Quest to Understand*, ed. James M. McPherson and William J. Cooper Jr. (Columbia: University of South Carolina Press, 1998), 154–73; James H. Kettner, *The Development of American Citizenship, 1608–1870* (Chapel Hill: University of North Carolina Press, 1978), 334–40; Edward Countryman, "The Creation of the United States," in *What Did the Constitution Mean to Early Americans?*, ed. Edward Countryman (Boston: Bedford/St. Martin's, 1999), 17–29; Jack N. Rakove, *Original Meanings: Politics and Ideas in the Making of the Constitution* (New York: Alfred A. Knopf, 1996), 161–202; Gordon S. Wood, *The American Revolution: A History* (New York: Modern Library, 2002), 42–44, 158–66; idem, *The Creation of the American Republic, 1776–1787* (Chapel Hill: University of North Carolina Press, 1969), 593–618.

55. G. Peck, *Our Country*, 72–73, 77. See also Bartlett, *Philosophy of the Rebellion*, 6–9; Haven, *National Sermons*, 499–502; Joel F. Bingham, *Great Providences toward the Loyal Part of this Nation* (Buffalo: Breed, Butler, 1864), 14–17; Rusling, "War for the Union," 308–10; Wadsworth, *War a Discipline*, 12.

56. G. Peck, *Our Country*, 70. Cf. Charles Eliot Norton, "American Political Ideas," *NAR* 101 (Oct 1865): 550–66; Joseph A. Conforti, *Jonathan Edwards, Religious Tradition, and American Culture* (Chapel Hill: University of North Carolina Press, 1995), 145–85. Nonevangelicals also could begin the American narrative with the Puritans, but what was important to evangelicals was that the Puritans initiated "Christian America"—not simply that Puritans were the first "Americans" or the precursors of liberty. See also Barrows, *Honor to the Brave*, 8–9; Bartlett, *Philosophy of the Rebellion*, 16–17; Albert Barnes, "Presbyterianism: Its Affinities," *APTR* 1 (October 1863): 547–48.

57. G. Peck, *Our Country*, 89, 97. Webster's actual words were, "Liberty *and* Union, now and forever, one and inseparable!" *Speeches of the Hon. Robert Y. Hayne, and the Hon. Daniel Webster, Delivered in the Senate of the United States, Jan. 21 and 26, 1830. With a Sketch of the Preceding Debate on the Resolution of Mr. Foot, Respecting the Sale, &c, of Public Lands* (Boston: Carter and Hendee, 1830), 131. See also John Woart, *Thanksgiving Discourse* (Philadelphia: King and Baird, 1864), 11; Gilmore, *"Hath God Forgotten to Be Gracious,"* 14. Prior to quoting Webster, Gilmore added, "Let us turn a deaf ear to the demon of captious criticism. Let us subordinate the claims of self and party to the more sacred demands of the Fatherland."

58. Lincoln, First Inaugural Address—Final Text, *CW*, 4:264–65; idem, Message to Congress in Special Session, 4 July 1861, *CW*, 4:433–34. See Donald, *Lincoln*, 302.

59. Gurley, *Man's Projects and God's Results*, 16. See also Wadsworth, *War a Discipline*, 12; Sherman B. Canfield, *The American Crisis* (Syracuse, N.Y.: Journal Book and Job Office, 1865), 13–32; "Principles of Church Union, and the Reunion of the Old and New-school Presbyterians," *BRPR* 37 (April 1865): 277; Joseph Horner, "Christianity and the War Power," *MQR* 47 (April 1865): 183–84; "The Federalist," *Independent*, 28 January 1864, p. 3; Samuel B. Bell, *Sermon* (New York: Baptist and Taylor, 1864), 20; H. Crosby, *God's View of the Rebellion*, 8–10; Bingham, *Great Providences*, 12–13.

60. Barnes, *State of the Country*, 16–17.

61. Horace Bushnell, *Popular Government by Divine Right* (Hartford, Conn.: L. E. Hunt, 1864), 4; idem, "Doctrine of Loyalty," 581. See also William A.

Clebsch, "Christian Interpretations of the American Civil War," *CH* 30 (June 1961): 215–18.

62. Rusling served as a quartermaster and experienced many of the war's major battles; he unsuccessfully ran for Congress as a New Jersey Republican, and was a federal pension agent during both of Grant's terms. He is also remembered for reporting President McKinley's pious decision to invade the Philippines during the Spanish-American War. James F. Rusling, *The Rusling Family* (Philadelphia: J. B. Lippincott, 1907), 80–92; idem, "Interview with President William McKinley," *Christian Advocate*, 22 January 1903, 17. See also idem, *Men and Things I Saw in Civil War Days* (New York: Eaton and Mains, 1899), 14–18, 355–59, which provides a retrospective portrait of Lincoln, highlighting his love of the Union and his ostensible religious faith; Rusling claimed that Lincoln said, "I . . . got down on my knees and prayed [to] Almighty God for victory at Gettysburg. I told Him that this was His country, and the war was His war. . . . I made a solemn vow with my Maker, that if He would stand by [Union troops] at Gettysburg, I would stand by Him" (17).

63. Rusling, "War for the Union," 308, 311. Garry Wills, *Lincoln at Gettysburg: The Words That Remade America* (New York: Touchstone, 1992), 125, stresses Lincoln's reaching behind the Constitution to the Declaration of Independence in order to locate a preexistent, sovereign people. See also White, *A. Lincoln*, 608, which provides an "evangelical" interpretation of the Gettysburg Address: The old Union, which had merely sought slavery's containment, must die and experience a "new birth of freedom" more in keeping with the Declaration of Independence.

64. Wadsworth, *War a Discipline*, 12; Haven, *National Sermons*, 499.

65. Oliver Johnson to George B. Cheever, 1 November 1864, George B. Cheever to Elizabeth Washburn, 1 November 1864, CFP.

66. Tarbox, "Universal Suffrage," 154; Nathaniel West, *Victory and Gratitude* (New York: E. B. Clayton's Sons, 1864), 25, 29.

67. On the election as a referendum, see Abraham Lincoln, Annual Message, 6 December 1864, *CW*, 8:149; Victor B. Howard, *Religion and the Radical Republican Movement, 1860–1870* (Lexington: University Press of Kentucky, 1990), 68–89; Stout, *Upon the Altar of the Nation*, 377–92; Burlingame, *Abraham Lincoln*, 2:745; Carwardine, *Lincoln*, 287–96; idem, "Lincoln, Evangelical Religion, and American Political Culture," *JALA* 18 (Winter 1997): 53–55; Rable, *God's Almost Chosen Peoples*, 335–36, 353–69; James McPherson, *Abraham Lincoln and the Second American Revolution* (New York: Oxford University Press, 1991), 41.

68. Haven, *National Sermons*, 504, 506.

69. Canfield, *American Crisis*, 23. Note idem, *The Indications of a Divine Purpose to Make Our Country a Model Christian Republic* (Syracuse, N.Y.: T. S. Truair, 1855). Cf. Stout, *Upon the Altar of the Nation*, 78–79, 170–75, 460.

70. Wadsworth, *War a Discipline*, 15. See also Darling, *Chastened*, 34–35. Wadsworth was an effective and affective preacher, exemplifying Old School Presbyterianism; he pastored Philadelphia's Arch Street Presbyterian Church (1850–1862) before taking a pastorate at San Francisco's Calvary Church. Rumors persist that the married Wadsworth had a romantic relationship with Dickinson, that he was the subject of her "Master"

letters, and that their relationship contributed to his move west. See Roger Lundin, *Emily Dickinson and the Art of Belief* (Grand Rapids, Mich.: Wm. B. Eerdmans, 1998), 85–86, 101, 171, 248–49; Charles Wadsworth, *Sermons* (New York: A. Roman, 1869).

71. Henry Augustus Boardman, *Healing and Salvation for Our Country from God Alone* (Philadelphia: William S. and Alfred Martien, 1864), 12–14.

72. Ibid., 16–18, 20–21, 23–24.

73. Bingham, *Great Providences*, 44–45; Dinsmore, *Our Country*, 27; Hoyt, *Suicide of Slavery*; Johnson, *Banners of a Free People*, 10; John K. Plitt, *God's Doings for the Nation* (Easton, Pa.: L. Gordon, 1864), 16–19; Vincent, *Lord of War and of Righteousness*, 36–38; West, *Victory and Gratitude*, 15–20.

74. Duffield, *Dark Night*, 21–22; Aaron Merrick Colton, *God's Dealings with Our Nation* (Northampton, Mass.: Trumbull and Gere, 1866), 13. See also Alexander H. Vinton, *The Duties of Peace* (New York: John A. Gray and Green, 1865), 4; Hopkins, *Peace in Our Borders*, 12–13; McDougal, *God's Blessing of Peace*, 7.

3. "The Harvest of Death Is Complete": Imagined Unity

1. O. O. Howard to Elizabeth Howard, 27 January 1865, OOHP.

2. Quoted in Chester Forrester Dunham, *The Attitude of the Northern Clergy toward the South, 1860–1865* (Toledo, Ohio: Gray, 1942), 207. See also Elizabeth Howard to O. O. Howard, 26 March 1865, O. O. Howard to Eliza Gilmore, 17 April 1865, OOHP.

3. William M. Grosvenor, "The Law of Conquest the True Basis of Reconstruction," *NE* 24 (January 1865): 113–15. Lincoln overruled the court-martial due to insubstantial evidence. During the 1870s, Grosvenor was involved in the liberal republican movement opposing Grant and mainstream Republicans. See Edwin C. Bearss, *Historic Resource Study, Ship Island, Harrison County, Mississippi, Gulf Islands National Seashore, Florida/Mississippi* (Denver: U.S. Department of the Interior, National Park Service, Denver Service Center, 1984), 219–30; Andrew L. Slap, *The Doom of Reconstruction: The Liberal Republicans in the Civil War Era* (New York: Fordham University Press, 2006), 6–9, 51, 206–8. National rebirth was a prominent theme, especially after Lincoln's assassination. See Samuel Johnson, *A Discourse Preached on the Day of the National Funeral, Wednesday, April 19, 1865* (Lynn, Mass., 1865), 8; David Goldfield, *America Aflame: How the Civil War Created a Nation* (New York: Bloomsbury, 2011), 1–16; David W. Blight, *Race and Reunion: The Civil War in American Memory* (Cambridge, Mass.: Belknap Press of Harvard University Press, 2001), 38–39; Rogan Kersh, *Dreams of a More Perfect Union* (Ithaca, N.Y.: Cornell University Press, 2001), 208–11. Kersh classifies Grosvenor's remarks as "the first sustained appearance in the United States of union ideology in organicist dress," while asserting that "organic unionists drew on Darwinist thought to identify a 'natural' connection among all Americans" (209). Though Kersh may be correct in some instances, "organicism" was present among evangelicals before, during, and after the war, and, moreover, it did not stem directly from Darwinian theory.

4. Grosvenor, "Law of Conquest," 116–21. Lincoln also proved willing to pardon those from the excluded classes. See Abraham Lincoln, Annual Message to Congress, 8 December 1863, *CW*, 7:49–53; idem, Proclamation of Amnesty and Reconstruction,

8 December 1863, *CW*, 7:53–55; William C. Harris, *With Charity for All: Lincoln and the Restoration of the Union* (Lexington: University Press of Kentucky, 1997), 131–42; William E. Gienapp, "Abraham Lincoln and the Border States," *JALA* 13 (1992): 13–46; Eric Foner, *Reconstruction: America's Unfinished Revolution, 1863–1877* (New York: Harper and Row, 1988), 35–50; Michael Burlingame, *Abraham Lincoln: A Life*, 2 vols. (Baltimore: Johns Hopkins University Press, 2008), 2:594–601.

5. Abraham Lincoln, Last Public Address, 11 April 1865, *CW*, 8:403; Grosvenor, "Law of Conquest," 122.

6. Harris, *With Charity for All*, 241; Grosvenor, "Law of Conquest," 118.

7. Grosvenor, "Law of Conquest, 113, 124, 127, 131. Regarding Stevens and Sumner, see Eric L. McKitrick, *Andrew Johnson and Reconstruction* (Chicago: University of Chicago Press, 1960), 99–101, 110–13. Aiming to check ex-Confederates and thereby place the restored Union on a surer republican footing, Grosvenor advocated black suffrage; however, by November 1866, he supported universal amnesty for ex-rebels in his state of Missouri. See Slap, *Doom of Reconstruction*, 9.

8. Caroline Janney, *Remembering the Civil War: Reunion and the Limits of Reconciliation* (Chapel Hill: University of North Carolina Press, 2013), contends that affective reconciliation with former enemies was more difficult than political restoration and not something easily achieved or necessarily embraced widely. Plenty of northern evangelicals understood the distinction, and it left them anxious to achieve reconciliation. See also Nina Silber, "Reunion and Reconciliation, Reviewed and Reconsidered," *JAH* 103 (June 2016): 59–83.

9. Lincoln, Second Inaugural Address, *CW*, 8:332; Edwin M. Stanton to Ulysses S. Grant, 3 March 1865, *CW*, 8:330–31; Harris, *With Charity for All*, 247–49; Charles Royster, *The Destructive War: William Tecumseh Sherman, Stonewall Jackson, and the Americans* (New York: Alfred A. Knopf, 1991), 18–33. Note George Peck, *Our Country: Its Trial and Its Triumph, a Series of Discourses Suggested by the Varying Events of the War for the Union* (New York: Carlton and Porter, 1865), 203–30. Like others, Peck feared that Lincoln's February 3 meeting with Confederate peace commissioners at Hampton Roads might forge a settlement permitting southern independence and slavery's continuance; however, by March the "threat" of peace had passed. See William C. Harris, "The Hampton Roads Peace Conference: A Final Test of Lincoln's Presidential Leadership," *JALA* 21 (Winter 2000): 30–61; Michael Vorenberg, "'The Deformed Child': Slavery and the Election of 1864," *CWH* 47 (September 2001): 240–57; James M. McPherson, "No Peace without Victory, 1861–1865," *AHR* 109 (February 2004): 1–18.

10. Abraham Lincoln, Response to a Serenade, 1 February 1865, *CW*, 8:254. See Michael Vorenberg, *Final Freedom: The Civil War, the Abolition of Slavery, and the Thirteenth Amendment* (Cambridge: Cambridge University Press, 2001); Burlingame, *Abraham Lincoln*, 2:745–51; Harris, *With Charity for All*, 237–39; Foner, *Reconstruction*, 66–70.

11. See Paul A. Cimbala, *The Freedmen's Bureau: Reconstructing the South after the Civil War* (Malabar, Fla.: Krieger, 2005); Paul A. Cimbala and Randall M. Miller, eds., *The Freedmen's Bureau and Reconstruction: Reconsiderations* (New York: Fordham University Press, 1999); William S. McFeely, *Yankee Stepfather: General O. O. Howard and the Freedmen* (New Haven, Conn.: Yale University Press, 1968).

12. Charles Hodge, "President Lincoln," *BRPR* 37 (July 1865): 450. Frederick Douglass, among many, commented on the address's sermonic nature. See William B. Hesseltine, *Lincoln's Plan of Reconstruction* (Tuscaloosa, Ala.: Confederate, 1960), 136; Ronald C. White Jr., *Lincoln's Greatest Speech: The Second Inaugural* (New York: Simon and Schuster, 2003); idem, *A. Lincoln: A Biography* (New York: Random House, 2009), 657–76; Douglas L. Wilson, *Lincoln's Sword: The Presidency and the Power of Words* (New York: Alfred A. Knopf, 2006), 262–63; Burlingame, *Abraham Lincoln*, 2:767–72. Note the discussion in Brooks D. Simpson, *Let Us Have Peace: Ulysses S. Grant and the Politics of War and Reconstruction, 1861–1868* (Chapel Hill: University of North Carolina Press, 1991), 78, around Lincoln's March 24 meeting with Generals Grant and Sherman and Admiral Porter, when Lincoln emphasized his desire for a lenient peace predicated on nothing more than emancipation and reunion. Harris, *With Charity for All*, contends that Reconstruction—or restoration, to use Lincoln's preferred term—began for the president with his first inaugural address.

13. G. Peck, *Our Country*, 214; Lincoln, Second Inaugural Address, *CW*, 8:333. See also Henry W. Foote, "Address Spoken at King's Chapel," in *Sermons Preached in Boston on the Death of Abraham Lincoln* (Boston: J. E. Tilton, 1865), 181–82.

14. Reuben Jeffery, *The Mission of Abraham Lincoln* (Philadelphia: Bryson and Son, 1865), 22, 25; Kersh, *Dreams of a More Perfect Union*, 171; Hesseltine, *Lincoln's Plan of Reconstruction*, 12; David Montgomery, *Beyond Equality: Labor and the Radical Republicans, 1862–1872* (New York: Alfred A. Knopf, 1967), 14–16, 26–31; Allen C. Guelzo, *Abraham Lincoln: Redeemer President* (Grand Rapids, Mich.: Wm. B. Eerdmans, 1999), 372, 413. For a contemporary emphasis on Lincoln's Whig understanding of the republic, see Samuel L. Crocker Jr., *Eulogy upon the Character and Services of Abraham Lincoln, Late President of the United States* (Boston: John Wilson and Son, 1865), 12–15.

15. Andrew Leete Stone, *Fasting and Feasting* (Boston: Henry Hoyt, 1865), 7; Lincoln, Second Inaugural Address, *CW*, 8:333; Pliny Butts Day, *A Memorial Discourse on the Character of Abraham Lincoln* (Concord, N.H.: McFarland and Jenks, 1865), 12; "Congregational Necrology," *Congregational Quarterly* 13 (July 1871): 431.

16. William M. Blackburn, *The Crime against the Presidency* (Trenton, N.J.: Murphy and Bechtel, 1865), 23.

17. Seth Reed, *A Discourse Delivered on the Occasion of the Funeral Obsequies of President Lincoln* (Boston: Geo. C. Rand and Avery, 1865), 14. See also Henry Fowler, *Character and Death of Abraham Lincoln* (Auburn, N.Y.: Wm. J. Moses' Steam Press Establishment, 1865), 12.

18. Alexander H. Bullock, *Abraham Lincoln: The Just Magistrate, the Representative Statesman, the Practical Philanthropist* (Worcester, Mass.: Charles Hamilton, Palladium Office, 1865), 8, 20; Charles Devens, *Memoir of Alexander H. Bullock* (Cambridge, Mass.: John Wilson and Son, 1887), 15–18.

19. Gilbert Haven, *National Sermons: Sermons, Speeches, and Letters on Slavery and Its War: From the Passage of the Fugitive Slave Bill to the Election of President Grant* (Boston: Lee and Shepard, 1869), 528; idem, *The Uniter and Liberator of America* (Boston: James P. Magee, 1865), 27; idem, "The Last Word and Deed of Abraham Lincoln," *Independent*, 4 May 1865, p. 1. See also Rufus Spalding Cushman, *Resolutions and Discourse,*

Occasioned by the Death of Abraham Lincoln, President of the United States, Who Died at Washington City, April 15, 1865 (Manchester, Vt., 1865), 15; William R. Gordon, *The Sin of Reviling, and Its Work* (New York: John A. Gray and Green, 1965), 12; George Hepworth, "Matthew IX: 15," in *Sermons Preached in Boston on the Death of Abraham Lincoln* (Boston: J. E. Tilton, 1865), 116; Cyrus Bartol, "Address," in *Sermons Preached in Boston on the Death of Abraham Lincoln* (Boston: J. E. Tilton, 1865), 55; Oliver Ellsworth Daggett, *A Sermon on the Death of Abraham Lincoln, April 15th, 1865* (Canandaigua, N.Y.: N. J. Milliken, 1865), 15. For a survey of public reaction to the address, see Benjamin Barondess, *Three Lincoln Masterpieces* (Charleston: Education Foundation of West Virginia, 1954), 51–109.

20. Wilson, *Lincoln's Sword*, 271; Mark A. Noll, "'Both . . . Pray to the Same God': The Singularity of Lincoln's Faith in the Era of the Civil War," *JALA* 18 (Winter 1997): 1–26; idem, *America's God: From Jonathan Edwards to Abraham Lincoln* (New York: Oxford University Press, 2002), 426–38; Harry S. Stout, *Upon the Altar of the Nation: A Moral History of the Civil War* (New York: Viking, 2006), 425–28; Sean A. Scott, *A Visitation of God: Northern Civilians Interpret the Civil War* (New York: Oxford University Press, 2011), 240–43; Lincoln, Meditation on the Divine Will, *CW*, 5:403–4; Abraham Lincoln, Reply to Emancipation Memorial Presented to Chicago Christians of All Denominations, 13 September 1862, *CW*, 5:419–25; Abraham Lincoln, To Eliza P. Gurney, 4 September 1864, *CW*, 7:535; Wilson, *Lincoln's Sword*, 249–77.

21. Phineas D. Gurley, "Burial Service," in *Sermons Preached in Boston on the Death of Abraham Lincoln* (Boston: J. E. Tilton, 1865), 21–23. The following inform this paragraph: Burlingame, *Abraham Lincoln*, 2:767–72; Guelzo, *Abraham Lincoln*, 412–21; George C. Rable, *God's Almost Chosen Peoples: A Religious History of the American Civil War* (Chapel Hill: University of North Carolina Press, 2010), 371–74; Richard J. Carwardine, *Lincoln* (Harlow, Eng.: Pearson Longman, 2003), 238–42; idem, "Religion and National Construction in the Age of Lincoln," *Journal of Mormon History* 36 (Spring 2010): 45–51; Harris, *With Charity for All*, 244–75; James M. McPherson, *Tried by War: Abraham Lincoln as Commander in Chief* (New York: Penguin, 2008); Geoffrey Perret, *Lincoln's War: The Untold Story of America's Greatest President as Commander in Chief* (New York: Random House, 2004).

22. G. Peck, *Our Country*, 211, 239; James G. Vose, "*The Decisive Battle*" (Boston: T. R. Marvin, 1965), 20–21. Paul Buck, *The Road to Reunion, 1865–1900* (Boston: Little, Brown, 1937), 11, was not wrong to suggest that Lincoln contributed to the notion that northerners "had been chosen as God's agents first in overthrowing and then in chastising an iniquitous opponent. . . . Lincoln had no suspicion of becoming another Cromwell. He merely saw God's hand in the conflict." By 1865 the major evangelical denominations publicly supported emancipation as a necessary and providential means of saving the Union, but, as McKivigan emphasizes, abolitionists "had failed to make northern churches into firm friends of blacks" (John R. McKivigan, *The War against Pro-slavery Religion: Abolitionism and the Northern Churches, 1830–1865* [Ithaca, N.Y.: Cornell University Press, 1984], 199–201). Timothy Smith, pointing to similarities between evangelicals' antislavery position and Lincoln's "enigmatic stand on slavery," concludes, "Vested interests combined with pious dreams and ties of brotherly sentiment to make the unity

of both church and nation a thing more precious than the freedom of the Negro" (Timothy L. Smith, *Revivalism and Social Reform: American Protestantism on the Eve of the Civil War* [Nashville: Abingdon Press, 1957; repr., New York: Harper and Row, 1965], 201).

23. Villeroy Dibble Reed, *The Conflict of Truth* (Camden, N.J.: S. Chew, 1865), 23–24; Henry A. Boardman, *Peace-Makers* (Philadelphia: James S. Claxton, 1865), 23, 27–28. See also Herrick Johnson, *God's Ways Unsearchable* (Pittsburgh: W. S. Haven, 1864), 5; Stone, *Fasting and Feasting*, 9; Wheelock Craig, *A Key to Our Joy* (New Bedford, Mass.: E. Anthony and Sons, 1865), 10–18; idem, *A Sermon on the Fruits of Our Bereavement* (New Bedford, Mass.: E. Anthony and Sons, 1865), 7–9; Hodge, "President Lincoln," 436–40, 444.

24. Haven, *National Sermons*, 529–31; Alonzo H. Quint, *Three Sermons Preached in the North Congregational Churches, New Bedford, Mass., Fast Day, April 13, and Sunday, April 16, 1865* (New Bedford, Mass.: Mercury Job Press, 1865), 7–8. See also Amory Dwight Mayo, *The Nation's Sacrifice* (Cincinnati: Robert Clarke, 1865), 25–26; Gordon Hall, *Divine Mercy a Cause for Humiliation* (Northampton, Mass.: Trumbull and Gere, 1865), 12–14; Albert Barnes, *The State of the Country* (Philadelphia: Henry B. Ashmead, 1865), 24–25. Moderately antislavery, Barnes referred to the second inaugural address and insisted that it was "fit" that the North also suffered because of slavery.

25. Stone, *Fasting and Feasting*, 9; G. Peck, *Our Country*, 239; Nathan Lewis Rice, *Sermon on the Death of Abraham Lincoln, Late President of the United States* (New York: Wm. C. Bryant, 1865), 12–13; Quint, *Three Sermons*, 14. Rice provides an early example of one who indicted the entire nation for slavery in covenantal terms; moderately antislavery, he regarded abolitionism as dangerously extremist. Born in Kentucky and educated at Princeton, he is remembered for his 1845 debate with the abolitionist Jonathan Blanchard and for his defense of Old School Presbyterianism. See Nathan Rice, *Our Country and the Church* (New York: Charles Scribner, 1861); Luke Harlow, *Religion, Race, and the Making of Confederate Kentucky, 1830–1880* (Cambridge: Cambridge University Press, 2014), 56; Mark A. Noll, *The Civil War as a Theological Crisis* (Chapel Hill: University of North Carolina Press, 2006), 41–42; George M. Marsden, *The Evangelical Mind and the New School Presbyterian Experience: A Case Study of Thought and Theology in Nineteenth-Century America* (New Haven, Conn.: Yale University Press, 1970), 132–35.

26. Haven, *National Sermons*, 538–39. Haven, like many Americans, located his conspiratorial fears for the Christian republic in an individual or a small group. Exempting the masses promised a smoother reconciliation with southerners. Regarding the events of 1–2 April, see Nelson Lankford, *Richmond Burning: The Last Days of the Confederate Capital* (New York: Viking, 2002), 49–69; Noah Trudeau, *Out of the Storm: The End of the Civil War, April–June 1865* (Boston: Little, Brown, 1994), 14–85.

27. William Solomon Leavitt, *A Sermon Preached April 9, 1865, the Sunday after the Capture of Richmond* (Hudson, N.Y.: Bryan and Webb, 1865), 17; Pliny Butts Day, *A Discourse on Victory and Its Dangers* (Concord, N.H.: McFarland and Jenks, 1865), 6–7; Alonzo A. Miner, "Psalms LXXXIX:18," in *Sermons Preached in Boston on the Death of Abraham Lincoln* (Boston: J. E. Tilton, 1865), 279–80.

28. Vose, *"Decisive Battle,"* 18, 16. Russell Conwell, the future Baptist minister who became famous for his "Acres of Diamonds" speech, lamented the relative disregard of the

Petersburg-area battlefields by 1869. How odd, he said, that "while hundreds of Americans visit the battlefield of Waterloo weekly," so few travel to the Petersburg area, "where at least one of the world's greatest battles was fought!" Russell H. Conwell, *Magnolia Journey: A Union Veteran Revisits the Former Confederate States*, ed. Joseph C. Carter (1869; University: University of Alabama Press, 1974), 21. See also Andrew Leete Stone, *The Work of New England in the Future of the Country* (Boston: Wright and Potter, 1865); idem, *Memorial Discourses* (Boston: Henry Hoyt, 1866), 14–45; F. R. Abbe, *"Wisdom Better Than the Weapons of War"* (Boston: T. R. Marvin and Son, 1865), 5–8.

29. Quoted in Dunham, *Attitude of the Northern Clergy*, 165.

30. Henry C. Badger, *The Humble Conqueror: A Discourse Commemorative of the Life and Services of Abraham Lincoln* (Boston: William V. Spencer, 1865), 11. See also Rollin H. Neale, "Matthew, IX:15," in *Sermons Preached in Boston on the Death of Abraham Lincoln* (Boston: J. E. Tilton, 1865), 169; Haven, *Uniter and Liberator*, 28–31; John W. Adams, *National Thanksgiving Sermon* (Manchester, N.H.: Mirror Steam Job Printing Establishment, 1866), 5.

31. This summary rests on Gary W. Gallagher, *The Confederate War: How Popular Will, Nationalism, and Military Strategy Could Not Stave Off Defeat* (Cambridge, Mass.: Harvard University Press, 1997), 157–72 (quote on 163–64); Daniel W. Stowell, *Rebuilding Zion: The Religious Reconstruction of the South, 1863–1877* (New York: Oxford University Press, 1998), 33–48 (quote on 39); Gaines M. Foster, *Ghosts of the Confederacy: Defeat, the Lost Cause, and the Emergence of the New South* (New York: Oxford University Press, 1987), 11–15; Jason Phillips, "Rebels in War and Peace: Their Ethos and Its Impact," in *The Great Task Remaining before Us: Reconstruction as America's Continuing Civil War*, ed. Paul A. Cimbala and Randall M. Miller (New York: Fordham University Press, 2010), 154–72; Michael Perman, *Reunion without Compromise: The South and Reconstruction, 1865–1868* (Cambridge: Cambridge University Press, 1973), 28–30; James L. Roark, *Masters without Slaves: Southern Planters in the Civil War and Reconstruction* (New York: W. W. Norton, 1977), 120–21, 132; George C. Rable, *But There Was No Peace: The Role of Violence in the Politics of Reconstruction*, 2nd ed. (Athens: University of Georgia Press, 2007), 1–15; Janney, *Remembering the Civil War*, 43–44, 53–55, 84–87.

32. Boardman, *Peace-Makers*, 6–7, 11, 27, 29.

33. Ibid., 23; Gary W. Gallagher, *Union War* Cambridge, Mass.: Harvard University Press, 2011, 151; Perman, *Reunion without Compromise*, 3–6.

34. Washington Gladden, *Recollections* (Boston: Houghton, Mifflin, 1909), 147; Samuel B. Babcock, *A Discourse on the Death of President Lincoln* (Dedham, Mass.: John Cox Jr., 1865), 4; Henry Ward Beecher, "Trip to South Carolina," *Independent*, 11 May 1865, p. 2.

35. William H. Boole, *Our Bible, Our Schools, and Our Flag: One and Inseparable* (Brooklyn: L. Darbee and Son, 1870), 9; Hall, *Divine Mercy*, 9–10; Thomas Laurie, *Three Discourses* (Dedham, Mass.: John Cox Jr., 1865), 6; Warren Hathaway, *A Discourse Occasioned by the Death of Abraham Lincoln* (Albany, N.Y.: J. Munsell, 1865), 7; David Waldstreicher, *In the Midst of Perpetual Fetes: The Making of American Nationalism, 1776–1820* (Chapel Hill: University of North Carolina Press, 1997), 6–7. See also A. D. Gillette, *God Seen Above All National Calamities* (Washington, D.C.: McGill and Witherow, 1865),

9–11; Daggett, *Sermon on the Death of Abraham Lincoln*, 3; Neale, "Matthew, IX:15," 164; Edwin Bonaparte Webb, "Isaiah XXI: 11, 12," in *Sermons Preached in Boston on the Death of Abraham Lincoln* (Boston: J. E. Tilton, 1865), 145; Gladden, *Recollections*, 145–49; Nina Silber, *The Romance of Reunion: Northerners and the South, 1865–1900* (Chapel Hill: University of North Carolina Press, 1993), 14.

36. Stone, *Fasting and Feasting*, 4–7. To some extent this mirrored expectations of white southerners, thus laying the groundwork for northern surprise, frustration, and anger. Perman, *Reunion without Compromise*, sees this approach to the South as the key to understanding subsequent white southern intransigence.

37. W. Craig, *Key to Our Joy*, 6–7, 11–12; idem, *A Sermon on the Fruits of Our Bereavement* (New Bedford: Mass.: E. Anthony and Sons, 1865), 11–12; Henry K. Craig, *Toil and Triumph* (New Bedford: Mass.: Taber Brothers, 1970), 32–3, 41–2, 55, 132–34; Wheelock Craig, *The Invalid's Sabbath in Florence* (New Bedford, Mass.: Taber Brothers, 1869); George Lewis Prentiss, ed., *The Life and Letters of Elizabeth Prentiss* (New York: Anson D. F. Randolph, 1882), 287–88; Wheelock Craig, *An Address on the Occasion of the Twenty-Seventh Anniversary of the New Bedford Port Society* (New Bedford, Mass.: Executive Board of the Port Society, 1857); Kathryn Grover, *Fugitive's Gibraltar: Escaping Slaves and Abolitionism in New Bedford, Massachusetts* (Amherst: University of Massachusetts Press, 2001).

38. W. Craig, *Key to Our Joy*, 10, 17–19.

39. Ibid., 19; Day, *Discourse*, 14.

40. "The Old Flag at Sumter!" *Independent*, 27 April 1865, p. 2. The four Psalms were 126, 47, 98, and 20. To some evangelicals Robert Anderson embodied an ideal mix of piety and patriotism. See Charles H. Howard to O. O. Howard, 22 April 1865, OOHP; George Dana Boardman, *Addresses Delivered in the Meeting-House of the First Baptist Church of Philadelphia, April 14th, 16th, and 19th, 1865* (Philadelphia: Sherman, 1865); Samuel Giles Buckingham, *A Sermon* (Springfield, Mass.: Samuel Bowles, 1866), 12–13; Jesse T. Peck, *The Great Republic from the Discovery of America to the Centennial, July 4, 1876* (New York: Nelson and Phillips, 1876), 673. On the day's events, see Abraham Lincoln to Edwin M. Stanton, 26, 27 March 1865, *CW*, 8:375–76; Robert C. Mills, *The Southern States Hardened until Ruined* (Boston: J. M. Hewes, 1865), 3–4; William A. Spicer, *The Flag Replaced: A Personal Narrative* (Providence, R. I.: Providence Press Co., 1885); David Detzer, *Allegiance: Fort Sumter, Charleston, and the Beginning of the Civil War* (New York: Harcourt, 2001), 317–19; Blight, *Race and Reunion*, 67–68.

41. Beecher, "Trip to South Carolina," 2; idem, *Oration at Raising the Old Flag over Fort Sumter, April 14th, 1865* (New York: Schermerhorn, Bancroft, 1865), 2–3. See also Babcock, *Discourse on the Death of President Lincoln*, 10.

42. Haven, *National Sermons*, 547–48.

43. Joseph F. Tuttle, "The College and the New Country," *APTR* 3 (July 1865): 460; Day, *Discourse*, 17.

44. Carlton Chase to Abraham Lincoln, 16 March 1865. Available at Abraham Lincoln Papers at the Library of Congress, Manuscript Division (Washington, D.C.: American Memory Project, [2000–01]), http://memory.loc.gov/ammem/alhtml/alhome.html, accessed August 10, 2005. See also Carlton Chase, *A Discourse, Delivered in Trinity Church, Claremont, January 4, 1861, Being the Day Appointed by the President of the United States,*

for General Fasting and Prayer, on Account of the Distracted State of the Country (Claremont, N.H.: George G. and Lemuel N. Ide, 1861).

45. G. D. Boardman, *Addresses Delivered in the Meeting-House of the First Baptist Church of Philadelphia*, 13–15. Baptists often presented themselves as essentially apolitical, emphasizing that the Christian's primary citizenship is in heaven; nevertheless, typical covenantal arguments about the nation's collective responsibility to God and his forging of a unified national people were heard. See "The Opening Era," *NB*, 27 April 1865, p. 2; "A Lesson of the War," *NB*, 8 June 1865, p. 1; "The Providences of the War," *NB*, 29 June 1865, p. 1; "Providences and the War," *NB*, 24 August 1865, p. 1; "The National Thanksgiving," *NB*, 7 December 1865, p. 2.

46. Elizabeth Howard to O. O. Howard, 15 April 1865, OOHP; Webb, "Isaiah XXI: 11, 12," 147; John E. Todd, "President Lincoln," in *Sermons Preached in Boston on the Death of Abraham Lincoln* (Boston: J. E. Tilton, 1865), 76; George Peck, *The Life and Times of Rev. George Peck, D.D., Written by Himself* (New York: Nelson and Phillips, 1874), 385; Gurley, "Burial Service," 18.

47. Historians generally have not emphasized this point; rather, understandably they have stressed northern bitterness. See Edward J. Blum, *Reforging the White Republic: Race, Religion, and American Nationalism, 1965–1898* (Baton Rouge: Louisiana State University Press, 2005), 11, 21–50; Dunham, *Attitude of the Northern Clergy*, 170–91; Janney, *Remembering the Civil War*, 58–61. Blum portrays a "deeply fractured" white America, contending that northerners viewed southerners as alien, near nonhuman "others." For surveys of public reaction, both religious and nonreligious, see David B. Chesebrough, *"No Sorrow Like Our Sorrow": Northern Protestant Ministers and the Assassination of Lincoln* (Kent, Ohio: Kent State University Press, 1994); Thomas Reed Turner, *Beware the People Weeping: Public Opinion and the Assassination of Abraham Lincoln* (Baton Rouge: Louisiana State University Press, 1982).

48. William Hague, "2 Samuel III: 38," in *Sermons Preached in Boston on the Death of Abraham Lincoln* (Boston: J. E. Tilton, 1865), 132–34; *A Souvenir of Our Pastor, the Rev. William Hague, D.D.* (Boston: Covenant Band of the Shawmut Avenue Baptist Church, 1869), 15–16; Gurley, "Burial Service," 18–19; Warren H. Cudworth, "Daniel IV: 35," in *Sermons Preached in Boston on the Death of Abraham Lincoln* (Boston: J. E. Tilton, 1865), 204, 201; Cephas B. Crane, *Sermon on the Occasion of the Death of President Lincoln* (Hartford, Conn.: Case, Lockwood, 1965), 6. Note Jeremiah Eames Rankin, *Moses and Joshua* (Boston: Dakin and Metcalf, 1865), 15. Rankin thought it fitting that the funeral was held on April 19, four years to the day of the war's first bloodshed at Baltimore and on the anniversary of the 1775 Battle of Lexington.

49. See Janney, *Remembering the Civil War*, 61–68 (quote on 64).

50. David Banks to George B. Cheever, 21 April 1865, CFP; Gordon, *Sin of Reviling*, 20–21.

51. George Cheever, quoted in "Church of the Puritans," *New York Daily Tribune*, 21 April 1865, 7; Barnes, *State of the Country*, 15–17. See David B. Chesebrough, "'His Own Fault': Rev. Charles H. Ellis of Bloomington Sermonizes on the Assassination of Abraham Lincoln," *IHJ* 86 (Autumn 1993): 146–58, which explores a radical sermon that voiced many Cheever-like themes and led to the pastor's expulsion from town.

52. Henry Boynton Smith, quoted in Lewis F. Stearns, *Henry Boynton Smith* (Boston: Houghton, Mifflin, 1892), 251; Henry Ward Beecher, "Punishment of the Rebel Leaders," *Independent*, 20 July 1865, p. 1. In the interest of reunion, Joseph P. Thompson, *Abraham Lincoln* (New York: Loyal Publications Society, 1865), 30–36, notably called for punishing leaders, in the form of exile or political proscription, alongside extending kindness toward the rest.

53. George Cheever, quoted in "Church of the Puritans," *New York Daily Tribune*, 21 April 1865, p. 7; George B. Cheever to Elizabeth Washburn, 24 April 1865, CFP.

54. Charles Backman, *Abraham Lincoln: The World's Great Martyr* (Jamaica, N.Y.: Charles Welling, 1865), 9–10. In 1862 Congress's Joint Committee on the Conduct of the War heard testimony of alleged atrocities and eventually published several reports. See T. Harry Williams, *Lincoln and the Radicals* (Madison: University of Wisconsin Press, 1941), 254–62; Dunham, *Attitude of the Northern Clergy*, 150–59; Simon Harrison, *Dark Trophies: Hunting and the Enemy Body in Modern War* (New York: Berghahn, 2012), 95–102; Mark E. Neely Jr., *The Civil War and the Limits of Destruction* (Cambridge, Mass.: Harvard University Press, 2007), 180–81; Michael J. Bennett, "The Black Flag and Confederate Soldiers: Total War from the Bottom Up," in *This Distracted and Anarchical People: New Answers for Old Questions about the Civil War–Era North*, ed. Andrew L. Slap and Michael Thomas Smith (New York: Fordham University Press, 2013), 142–58.

55. Leonard Swain, *A Nation's Sorrow* (Providence, 1865), 7, quoted in Dunham, *Attitude of the Northern Clergy*, 168; Edward S. Atwood, *The Nation's Loss* (Salem, Mass.[?]: The Office of the Salem Gazette, 1865), 9–10, 14.

56. Frederick Douglass, "Our Martyred President: An Address Delivered in Rochester, New York, on April 15, 1865," in *FDP*, 4:76–78. Blum, *Reforging the White Republic*, 21–24, recognizes that Douglass and like-minded evangelicals were not representative of widespread northern opinion, referring to them as "a cadre of Yankee preachers" envisioning "a new nation" that included blacks and whites as fully equal citizens.

57. Jonathan L. Jenkins, "Retribution," *Independent*, 20 July 1865, p. 1; Henry Ward Beecher, "Sermon on the Death of the President," *Independent*, 4 May 1865, p. 4; Joel Foote Bingham, *National Disappointment* (Buffalo: Breed, Butler, 1865), 29, 32; S. Reed, *A Discourse*, 15; Jeffery, *Mission of Abraham Lincoln*, 25–27; Hodge, "President Lincoln," 445.

58. Henry E. Parker, *Discourse the Day after the Reception of the Tidings of the Assassination of President Lincoln* (Concord, N.H.: McFarland and Jenks, 1865), 12; "Necrology," *Granite Monthly* 21 (December 1896): 373.

59. George Duffield Sr., *The Nation's Wail* (Detroit: Advertiser and Tribune, 1865), 5, 8; Adams, *National Thanksgiving Sermon*, 5, 8.

4. From Moses to Joshua

1. Jeremiah Eames Rankin, *Moses and Joshua* (Boston: Press of Dakin and Metcalf, 1865), 5, 7, 16. See also idem, "The Sources of New-England Civilization," in *Addresses Delivered before the Vermont Historical Society in the Representative Hall, Montpelier,*

October 16, 1866 (Montpelier, Vt.: Walton's Steam Printing, 1866), 49–72, which reveals an organicist understanding of America. Matthew Simpson, Phineas Gurley, Henry Ward Beecher, and Charles Hodge all employed the same analogy. See Phineas Densmore Gurley, "Burial Service," in *Sermons Preached in Boston on the Death of Abraham Lincoln* (Boston: J. E. Tilton, 1865), 3–29; Henry Ward Beecher, "Sermon on the Death of the President," *Independent*, 4 May 1865, p. 4; Charles Hodge, "President Lincoln," *BRPR* 33 (July 1865): 458.

2. Although historians may be imprecisely divided between "revisionists" or "post-revisionists," depending on how they view Reconstruction with respect to racial justice, all agree that Johnson was centrally important. See Edward L. Ayers, *What Caused the Civil War: Reflections on the South and Southern History* (New York: W. W. Norton, 2005), 161; Eric Foner, *Reconstruction: America's Unfinished Revolution, 1863–1877* (New York: Harper and Row, 1988), 176–227; Eric L. McKitrick, *Andrew Johnson and Reconstruction* (Chicago: University of Chicago Press, 1960), 7–41, 85–92, 135–213; Michael Les Benedict, *A Compromise of Principle: Congressional Republicans and Reconstruction, 1863–1869* (New York: W. W. Norton, 1974), 100–16; Michael Perman, *Reunion without Compromise: The South and Reconstruction, 1865–1868* (Cambridge: Cambridge University Press, 1973), 3–181; Dan T. Carter, *When the War Was Over: The Failure of Self-Reconstruction in the South, 1865–1867* (Baton Rouge: Louisiana State University Press, 1985), 24–95; Kenneth M, Stampp, *The Era of Reconstruction, 1865–1877* (New York: Vintage Books, 1965), 65–82; Brooks D. Simpson, *The Reconstruction Presidents* (Lawrence: University Press of Kansas, 1998), 67–99. Cf. Paul H. Bergeron, *Andrew Johnson's Civil War and Reconstruction* (Knoxville: University of Tennessee Press, 2011), 65–98, which portrays Johnson as an effective leader and points to 1865 as his "finest hour" (98).

3. William W. Holden to Andrew Johnson, 6 December 1865, *PAJ*, 9:487; Foner, *Reconstruction*, 184.

4. McKitrick, *Andrew Johnson and Reconstruction*, 20; Cf. James H. Moorhead, *American Apocalypse: Yankee Protestants and the Civil War, 1860–1869* (New Haven, Conn.: Yale University Press, 1978), 178–83; Paul C. Brownlow, "The Northern Protestant Pulpit and Andrew Johnson," *Southern Speech Communication Journal* 39 (Spring 1974): 248–59; Victor B. Howard, *Religion and the Radical Republican Movement, 1860–1870* (Lexington: University Press of Kentucky, 1990), 90–127; Edward J. Blum, *Reforging the White Republic: Race, Religion, and American Nationalism, 1865–1898* (Baton Rouge: Louisiana State University Press, 2005), 38–50.

5. Andrew Johnson, Remarks on Assuming the Presidency, 15 April 1865, *PAJ*, 7:554; Benjamin B. French to Andrew Johnson, 16 April 1865, AJP.

6. Andrew Johnson, Remarks to Illinois Delegation, 18 April 1865, *PAJ*, 7:582–84; Herrick Johnson, *God's Ways Unsearchable* (Pittsburgh: W. G. Johnson, 1865), 4. The president later said that if he had any creed at all, it was "that all things should be done with the approval of Him who controls the events and destinies of the world." Andrew Johnson, Speech to Washington Sunday School Union, 29 May 1865, *PAJ*, 8:139. Johnson had been ill and apparently drank heavily prior to delivering a blustery inaugural speech about his plebeian origins, devotion to the "people," and secession. Andrew Johnson, "Remarks at Vice-Presidential Swearing In," 4 March 1865, *PAJ*, 7:502–7; Howard K.

Beale, *The Critical Year: A Study of Andrew Johnson and Reconstruction* (New York: Harcourt, Brace, 1930), 12–16; Hans L. Trefousse, *Andrew Johnson: A Biography* (New York: W. W. Norton, 1989), 188–92; Bergeron, *Andrew Johnson's Civil War*, 65–67.

7. Cephas B. Crane, *Sermon on the Occasion of the Death of President Lincoln* (Hartford, Conn.: Case, Lockwood, 1865), 23–26; Edward Norris Kirk, "Psalms XLVI: 10," in *Sermons Preached in Boston on the Death of Abraham Lincoln* (Boston: J. E. Tilton, 1865), 41. See also James Cooper, *The Death of President Lincoln* (Philadelphia: Jas. B. Rodgers, 1865), 22; Elizabeth Howard to O. O. Howard, 15 April 1865, OOHP; Samuel K. Lothrop, "2 Samuel XIX: 2," in *Sermons Preached in Boston on the Death of Abraham Lincoln* (Boston: J. E. Tilton, 1865), 262. Regarding Johnson's religion, he attended Methodist services in Tennessee, and in Washington he attended St. Patrick's Church (Roman Catholic). See Albert J. Menendez, *Religion and the U.S. Presidency: A Bibliography* (New York: Garland, 1985), 59; John S. Bonnell, *Presidential Profiles: Religion in the Life of American Presidents* (Philadelphia: Westminster, 1971), 116–19; Edmund Fuller and David E. Green, *God in the White House: The Faiths of American Presidents* (New York: Crown, 1968), 117–24; Vernon B. Hampton, *The Religious Background of the White House* (Boston: Christopher, 1932), 234–41; William J. Hampton, *The Religion of the Presidents* (Somerville, N.J.: Somerville Press, 1925), 58–60; Bliss Isely, *Presidents, Men of Faith* (Boston: Wilde, 1953), 131–36.

8. Wheelock Craig, *A Sermon on the Fruits of Our Bereavement* (New Bedford, Mass.: E. Anthony and Sons, 1865), 11–12; Resolutions of the New York Methodist Episcopal Conference, 19 April 1865, *PAJ*, 7:588; John W. Bain, *National Lessons from the Life and Death of President Lincoln* (Pittsburgh, Pa.: W. S. Haven, 1865), 8–9. See also Letter from Ottawa, Illinois, Clergyman to Andrew Johnson, 17 April 1865, AJP; Elizabeth Washburn to George B. Cheever, 27 April 1865, CFP; Resolutions of the Essex North Association of Clergymen, 18 April 1865, Resolutions of the Ministers of Lewiston, Maine, 18 April 1865, Resolutions of the Baptist Ministers of Philadelphia, 18 April 1865, Christian Churches of Madison, Indiana, to Andrew Johnson, 19 April 1865, Charles P. Smith to Andrew Johnson, 15 April 1865, AJP; Resolutions of the Cleveland Congregational Conference, *PAJ*, 7:586; Rollin H. Neale, "Matthew, IX:15," in *Sermons Preached in Boston on the Death of Abraham Lincoln* (Boston: J. E. Tilton, 1865), 172; Amory Dwight Mayo, *The Nation's Sacrifice* (Cincinnati: Robert Clarke, 1865), 13; Joseph S. Hartley to Andrew Johnson, 30 April 1865, *PAJ*, 7:765.

9. Simpson, *Reconstruction Presidents*, 71 (quote); Bergeron, *Andrew Johnson's Civil War*, 71–72; Christian Churches of Madison, Indiana, to Andrew Johnson, 19 April 1865, AJP; William R. Gordon, *The Sin of Reviling, and Its Work* (New York: John A. Gray and Green, 1865), 17; Gordon Hall, *President Lincoln's Death: Its Voice to the People* (Northampton, Mass.: Trumbull and Gere, 1865), 13–16; Abram Dunn Gillette, *God Seen Above All National Calamities* (Washington, D.C.: McGill and Witherow, 1865), 10–12; Sean A. Scott, *A Visitation of God: Northern Civilians Interpret the Civil War* (New York: Oxford University Press, 2011), 253–54.

10. *National Intelligencer*, 22 April 1865, in *PAJ*, 7:575–77. Compare this with his meeting with a group of southern African American ministers. Government largesse would not be forthcoming "like manna from heaven," he lectured, since "freedom simply means

liberty to work and enjoy the product of your own hands." Furthermore, the ex-slaves must cease living "in open and notorious concubinage," behavior that made them worse than Mormons. Viewing the ex-slaves as lazy, promiscuous, and unfit for American citizenship, colonization thus remained necessary. Hopefully a day will come, Johnson concluded, "when you shall be gathered together, in a clime and country suited to you." Andrew Johnson, Reply to Delegation of Black Ministers, 11 May 1865, *PAJ*, 8:61–63; Simpson, *Reconstruction Presidents*, 76.

11. Andrew Johnson, Proclamation for Day of Humiliation and Mourning, 25 April 1865, *PAJ*, 7:641–42n1; Henry A. Boardman, *The Peace We Need, and How to Secure It* (Philadelphia: James S. Claxton, 1865), 32.

12. Andrew Johnson, A Proclamation, 29 April 1865, in *A Compilation of the Messages and Papers of the Presidents, 1789–1908*, 11 vols., ed. James D. Richardson (Washington, D.C.: Bureau of National Literature and Art, 1907–9), 6:307; E. Mills to Andrew Johnson, 29 April 1865, *PAJ*, 7:666; "Letter to President Johnson," *NB*, 15 June 1865, p. 2. Some Methodists were distressed by Episcopalian influence at the Naval Academy. See S. D. Davis to Matthew Simpson, 11 July 1865, C. C. Cornwell to Matthew Simpson, 10 May 1875, MSP. Though some Episcopalians voiced similar civic-religious language, they tended to be Democrats and remained suspect to true-blue evangelicals. See Diana Hochstedt Butler, *Standing against the Whirlwind: Evangelical Episcopalians in Nineteenth-Century America* (New York: Oxford University Press, 1995); E. Brooks Holifield, *Theology in America: Christian Thought from the Age of the Puritans to the Civil War* (New Haven, Conn.: Yale University Press, 2003), 234–55; Paul Kleppner, *The Cross of Culture: A Social Analysis of Midwestern Politics, 1850–1900* (New York: Free Press, 1970); Blum, *Reforging the White Republic*, 34; Scott, *Visitation of God*, 101–3. Clearly evangelicals' anti-Catholicism survived the war, and this incident foreshadowed future conflict. Note Hodge, "President Lincoln," 450.

13. Johnson uttered variations of his promise as Tennessee's governor. See Bergeron, *Andrew Johnson's Civil War*, 22–23, 67; Benedict, *Compromise of Principle*, 100–101; Trefousse, *Andrew Johnson*, 155, 164, 168, 192; Simpson, *Reconstruction Presidents*, 68–72; Andrew Johnson, Remarks on the Fall of Richmond, 3 April 1865, *PAJ*, 7:543–46; idem, Remarks to Illinois Delegation, 18 April 1865, *PAJ*, 7:582–85.

14. George B. Cheever to Elizabeth Washburn, 24 April 1865, CFP; E. A. Thomas to Andrew Johnson, 18 May 1865, *PAJ*, 8:90–91; William S. Studley, "Lamentations V: 15–19," in *Sermons Preached in Boston on the Death of Abraham Lincoln* (Boston: J. E. Tilton, 1865), 230. See also William C. Harris, *With Charity for All: Lincoln and the Restoration of the Union* (Lexington: University Press of Kentucky, 1997), 266–67; George W. Cothran to Andrew Johnson, 19 April 1865, *PAJ*, 7:586–87; W. C. Hollyday to Andrew Johnson, 28 April 1865, *PAJ*, 7:650; Samuel R. Snyder to Andrew Johnson, 5 June 1865, *PAJ*, 8:184–86; William M. Blackburn, *The Crime against the Presidency* (Trenton, N.J.: Murphy and Bechtel, 1865), 20; Crane, *Sermon on the Occasion of the Death of President Lincoln*, 23–25; Hall, *President Lincoln's Death*, 14–16; Lothrop, "2 Samuel XIX: 2," 262; Seth Reed, *A Discourse Delivered on the Occasion of the Funeral Obsequies of President Lincoln* (Boston: Geo. C. Rand and Avery, 1865), 21–22; "Washington Correspondent," *Independent*, 11 May 1865, 8; Edwin Bonaparte Webb, "Isaiah XXI: 11, 12," in *Sermons Preached*

in Boston on the Death of Abraham Lincoln (Boston: J. E. Tilton, 1865), 158–59; Thomas Laurie, *Three Discourses* (Dedham, Mass.: John Cox Jr., 1865), 26; Henry E. Parker, *Discourse the Day after the Reception of the Tidings of the Assassination of President Lincoln* (Concord, N.H.: McFarland and Jenks, 1865), 11. Perhaps some had in mind Johnson's "Moses" speech, wherein Johnson chastised southern planters for sexually exploiting female slaves, appeared supportive of some land reform, and promised to be a Moses leading Tennessee slaves "through the Red Sea of war and bondage, to a fairer future of liberty and peace." See Andrew Johnson, "Moses of the Colored Men," 24 October 1864, *PAJ*, 7:251–53; Bergeron, *Andrew Johnson's Civil War*, 44; David Warren Bowen, *Andrew Johnson and the Negro* (Knoxville: University of Tennessee Press, 1989), 80–121.

15. Note a reporter's summary of Ulysses S. Grant's opinion: "[Grant] would treat the masses of the South with kindness and humanity especially in view of the fact that they had been forced to obey their own desperate leaders" (*New York Tribune*, 3 May 1865, quoted in Brooks D. Simpson, *Let Us Have Peace: Ulysses S. Grant and the Politics of War and Reconstruction, 1861–1868* [Chapel Hill: University of North Carolina Press, 1991], 99). See also Caroline E. Janney, *Remembering the Civil War: Reunion and the Limits of Reconciliation* (Chapel Hill: University of North Carolina Press, 2013), 47–49.

16. Henry Martyn Dexter, *What Ought to Be Done with the Freedmen and the Rebels?* (Boston: Nichols and Noyes, 1865), 33, 35; George Dana Boardman, *Addresses Delivered in the Meeting-House of the First Baptist Church of Philadelphia, April 14th, 16th, and 19th, 1865* (Philadelphia: Sherman, 1965), 18–20; Hall, *President Lincoln's Death*, 10.

17. Bergeron, *Andrew Johnson's Civil War*, 75.

18. Andrew Johnson, Amnesty Proclamation, 29 May 1865, *PAJ*, 8:128–31; Bergeron, *Andrew Johnson's Civil War*, 74–75; McKitrick, *Andrew Johnson and Reconstruction*, 7, 48–49, 120–52; Perman, *Reunion without Compromise*, 121–31; Gaines M. Foster, *Ghosts of the Confederacy: Defeat, the Lost Cause, and the Emergence of the New South* (New York: Oxford University Press, 1987), 22–35; Simpson, *Reconstruction Presidents*, 73–75; Carter, *When the War Was Over*, 24–25; Foner, *Reconstruction*, 190–91; Daniel W. Stowell, *Rebuilding Zion: The Religious Reconstruction of the South, 1863–1877* (New York: Oxford University Press, 1998), 39–48 (quote on 41); Charles Reagan Wilson, *Baptized in Blood: The Religion of the Lost Cause, 1865–1920* (Athens: University of Georgia Press, 1980), 58; Jason Phillips, "Rebels in War and Peace: Their Ethos and Its Impact," in *The Great Task Remaining before Us: Reconstruction as America's Continuing Civil War*, ed. Paul A. Cimbala and Randall Miller (New York: Fordham University Press, 2010), 165.

19. Hodge, "President Lincoln," 453–56. Cf. Moorhead, *American Apocalypse*, 178–79.

20. Andrew Johnson, Proclamation Establishing Government for North Carolina, 29 May 1865, *PAJ*, 8:136–38. See Perman, *Reunion without Compromise*, 57–67; McKitrick, *Andrew Johnson and Reconstruction*, 7–9, 49–51, 165–67; Bergeron, *Andrew Johnson's Civil War*, 75–84; Simpson, *Reconstruction Presidents*, 75–76; Carter, *When the War Was Over*, 25–28; Foner, *Reconstruction*, 185–95.

21. McKitrick, *Andrew Johnson and Reconstruction*, 18; George H. Stuart to O. O. Howard, 15 May 1865, OOHP.

22. W. H. Merrick to O. O. Howard, 15 May 1865, OOHP; "The Providences of the War," *NB*, 29 June 1865, p. 1; H. Tappen to O. O. Howard, 31 May 1865, OOHP. See also

"Capture of Jefferson Davis," *Independent*, 18 May 1865, p. 4. Some have made much of Davis's capture as a potential symbol for the South's emasculation. See Foster, *Ghosts*, 26–28; Nina Silber, *The Romance of Reunion: Northerners and the South, 1865–1900* (Chapel Hill: University of North Carolina Press, 1993), 29–31; Blum, *Reforging the White Republic*, 28–30.

23. Timothy L. Smith, *Revivalism and Social Reform: American Protestantism on the Eve of the Civil War* (Nashville, Tenn.: Abingdon Press, 1957; repr., New York: Harper and Row, 1965), 214; Albert Barnes, *The State of the Country* (Philadelphia: C. Sherman and Son, 1861), 27–30. Barnes was centrally involved in the split between Old and New School Presbyterians. See Albert Barnes, *Life at Three-Score and Ten* (New York: American Tract Society, 1871); idem, *Inquiry into the Scriptural Views of Slavery* (Philadelphia: Perkins and Purves, 1846); idem, *The Church and Slavery* (Philadelphia: Parry and McMillan, 1857); John R. McKivigan, *The War against Proslavery Religion: Abolitionism and the Northern Churches, 1830–1865* (Ithaca, N.Y.: Cornell University Press, 1984), 169; C. C. Goen, *Broken Churches, Broken Nation: Denominational Schisms and the Coming of the American Civil War* (Macon, Ga.: Mercer University Press, 1985), 145–46; George M. Marsden, *The Evangelical Mind and the New School Presbyterian Experience: A Case Study of Thought and Theology in Nineteenth-Century America* (New Haven, Conn.: Yale University Press, 1970); Mark A. Noll, "The Bible and Slavery," in *Religion and the American Civil War*, ed. Randall M. Miller, Harry S. Stout, and Charles Reagan Wilson (New York: Oxford University Press, 1998), 44, 51; idem, *America's God: From Jonathan Edwards to Abraham Lincoln* (New York: Oxford University Press, 2002), 302–3, 390–98; Holifield, *Theology in America*, 494, 503.

24. Hodge, "President Lincoln," 449; Barnes, *State of the Country*, 30, 39. See Gary W. Gallagher, *The Confederate War: How Popular Will, Nationalism, and Military Strategy Could Not Stave Off Defeat* (Cambridge, Mass.: Harvard University Press, 1997), 158–63; Michael Golay, *A Ruined Land: The End of the Civil War* (New York: John Wiley and Sons, 1999); Carter, *When the War Was Over*, 6–23; W. Harrison Daniel, "The Effects of the Civil War on Southern Protestantism," *Maryland Historical Magazine* 69 (Spring 1974): 44–63.

25. Joseph Parrish Thompson, "The Advancement of Christ's Kingdom by War," *NE* 24 (April 1865): 310; Joseph P. Thompson to O. O. Howard, 25 May 1865, OOHP; Pliny Butts Day, *A Discourse on Victory and Its Dangers* (Concord, N.H.: McFarland and Jenks, 1865), 14–15. See also George M. Randall, *Sermon before the Ancient and Honorable Artillery Co., on Its CCXXVII Anniversary, June 5, 1865* (Boston: Wright and Potter, 1965), 39–40; Alexander G. Cummins, *The Christian Church's Duty to the Freedmen* (Philadelphia: Sherman, 1865), 24–25; Conway P. Wing, "Christianity and Civilization," *APTR* 3 (January 1865): 102–4; Increase Niles Tarbox, "Universal Suffrage," *NE* 24 (January 1865): 162–65; Albert Barnes, "The Relation of Christianity to the Present Stage of the World's Progress in Science, Civilization, and the Arts," *APTR* 3 (October 1865): 596–98; Joseph F. Tuttle, "The College and the New Country," *APTR* 3 (July 1865): 460–71; Samuel Harris, "The Christian Doctrine of Labor," *NE* 24 (April 1865): 243–76; John W. Adams, *National Thanksgiving Sermon* (Manchester, N.H.: Mirror Steam Job Printing Establishment, 1866); Frederic Randolph Abbe, *"Wisdom Better Than the Weapons of War"*

(Boston: T. R. Marvin and Son, 1865), 5–6, 12; Andrew Leete Stone, *Elements of National Life* (Providence, R.I.: H. H. Thomas, 1865), 14–34; Chester Forrester Dunham, *The Attitude of the Northern Clergy toward the South, 1860–1865* (Toledo, Ohio: Gray, 1942), 204–37. On free labor, see Eric Foner, *Free Soil, Free Labor, Free Men: The Ideology of the Republican Party before the Civil War* (New York: Oxford University Press, 1980); idem, *Reconstruction*, 124–75; Heather Cox Richardson, *The Death of Reconstruction: Race, Labor, and Politics in the Post-Civil War North, 1865–1901* (Cambridge, Mass.: Harvard University Press, 2001), 6–40. Evangelical faith in the utility of common schools was widespread and continuous with antebellum opinion. See Carl F. Kaestle, *Pillars of the Republic: Common Schools and American Society, 1780–1860* (New York: Hill and Wang, 1983), 30–61, 75–103, 136–81; Ward M. McAfee, *Religion, Race, and Reconstruction: The Public School in the Politics of the 1870s* (Albany: State University of New York Press. 1998), 9–25.

26. Gaines M. Foster, "The End of Slavery and the Origins of the Bible Belt," in *Vale of Tears: New Essays on Religion and Reconstruction*, ed. Edward J. Blum and W. Scott Poole (Macon, Ga.: Mercer University Press, 2005), 147; Stowell, *Rebuilding Zion*, 16, 27–32, 130–45; Fletcher M. Green, "Northern Missionary Activities in the South, 1846–1861," *JSH* 21 (May 1955): 147–72; Richard B. Drake, "Freedmen's Aid Societies and Sectional Compromise," *JSH* 29 (May 1963): 175–86; Joe M. Richardson, *Christian Reconstruction: The American Missionary Association and Southern Blacks, 1861–1890* (Athens: University of Georgia Press, 1986); E. Allen Richardson, "Architects of a Benevolent Empire: The Relationship between the American Missionary Association and the Freedmen's Bureau in Virginia, 1865–1872," in *The Freedmen's Bureau and Reconstruction: Reconsiderations*, ed. Paul A. Cimbala and Randall M. Miller (New York: Fordham University Press, 1999), 119–39; Blum, *Reforging the White Republic*, 51–86; Robert C. Morris, "Educational Reconstruction," in *The Facts of Reconstruction*, ed. Eric Anderson and Alfred A. Moss Jr. (Baton Rouge: Louisiana State University Press, 1991), 141–66; Paul Harvey, "That Was about Equalization after Freedom: Southern Evangelicalism and the Politics of Reconstruction and Redemption, 1861–1900," in *Vale of Tears: New Essays on Religion and Reconstruction*, ed. Edward J. Blum and W. Scott Poole (Macon, Ga.: Mercer University Press, 2005), 73–92; Leon Litwack, *Been in the Storm So Long: The Aftermath of Slavery* (New York: Alfred A. Knopf, 1979), 450–501 (quote on 453); Jay R. Case, "The African American Great Awakening and Modernity, 1866–1900," in *American Evangelicalism: George Marsden and the State of American Religious History*, ed. Darren Dochuk, Thomas S. Kidd, and Kurt W. Peterson (Notre Dame, Ind.: University of Notre Dame Press, 2014), 110–37; William S. McFeely, *Yankee Stepfather: General O. O. Howard and the Freedmen* (New Haven, Conn.: Yale University Press, 1968), 84–106.

27. Henry Ward Beecher to Edwin M. Stanton, 3 May 1865, OOHP; McFeely, *Yankee Stepfather*, 60–61, 86; Abbe, "*Wisdom Better Than the Weapons of War*," 18–19. The Christian Commission's J. B. Waterbury insisted to Howard that "evangelical religion" must be the "controlling element" in Reconstruction, and he anticipated Howard's assistance in "wean[ing] the negro from his peculiar dialect and elevat[ing] him to a higher standard." J. B. Waterbury to O. O. Howard, 19 May 1865, OOHP. See also George H. Stuart to O. O. Howard, 15 May 1865, C. Kingsbury [?] to O. O. Howard, 17 May 1865, Samuel F. Colt

to O. O. Howard, 17 May 1865, L. A. Chase to O. O. Howard, 17 May 1865, Silas Hawley to O. O. Howard, 17 May 1865. E. B. Webb to O. O. Howard, 20 May 1865, Mary Seth to O. O. Howard, 22 May 1865, Joseph Parrish Thompson to O. O. Howard, 25 May 1865, H. Tappen to O. O. Howard, 31 May 1865, OOHP; Tarbox, "Universal Suffrage," 165–67; Edward Taylor, *Manliness* (New York: Office of the United States Service Magazine, 1866); William Adams, "The War for Independence, the War for Secession," *APTR* 4 (January 1866): 91. Many debated what accompanied "manhood." Silber, *Romance of Reunion*, 21–26, connects manliness to free labor ideals of striving and self-sufficiency; Blum, *Reforging the White Republic*, 12–13, conflates free labor with "racial radicalism and egalitarianism," while conceding that the amalgam "may not have reflected the opinions of the majority of northern whites."

28. Barnes, *State of the Country*, 30–32. See also idem, *Lectures on the Evidences of Christianity in the Nineteenth Century* (New York: Harper and Brothers, 1867). Barnes, like many evangelicals, was at home in the Scottish Common-Sense intellectual tradition; its empiricist epistemology made much of "evidences." See chapter 6, note 5.

29. Barnes, *State of the Country*, 34–35, 38. Charles Hodge made a similar appeal in 1861 to forestall secession; Barnes was now attempting to forestall resistance to reunion. See Charles Hodge, "The State of the Country," *BRPR* 33 (January 1861): 2. Hodge described the Union as "cemented by a common lineage, a common language, a common religion, and a common history. We were born in the same family, rocked in the same cradle, struggled through the same difficulties. We were united in the council chamber and on the battle-field. The blood of Northern and Southern patriots flowed in a common stream, and their ashes lie mingled in the same graves. These are not sentimentalities which men of sense can afford to despise. They are bonds of Union." See also Hodge, "President Lincoln," 449: "The object of the war from the beginning, [Lincoln] declared to be the preservation of the Union and the authority of the constitution. . . . It was not, and it never became an antislavery war. The abolition of slavery was no more a legitimate object of civil war than the abolition of false religion." Emancipation was, then, an unintended, though divine, consequence.

30. Barnes, *State of the Country*, 44–45, 47–49, 51–52. See also Herman Walther to Andrew Johnson, 15 June 1865, *PAJ*, 8:245–46; Hodge, "President Lincoln," 440–42. Hodge insisted that "the war has not destroyed the sovereignty of the States," though he also proclaimed, "We are a nation, and not a confederacy of nations, from which any member or any number of members may withdraw at pleasure. The United States is an indissoluble whole, composed of many self-governing communities, whose rights and sovereignty are limited. . . . The great point decided is, that the allegiance of every American citizen is primarily due to the United States, and not to the particular State to which he may belong." Hodge found the increased scope of the federal government "astonishing."

31. Boardman, *Peace We Need*, 6–9, 14. Pendleton quoted in Wilson, *Baptized in Blood*, 62–63.

32. Boardman, *Peace We Need*, 9–10, 12–14, 18–19, 32. See also Byron Sunderland, *Who Is My Neighbor?* (Boston: John Wilson and Sons, 1866); Hodge, "President Lincoln," 450–51. Hodge compared southern slavery to perceived religious idolatry and thereby

served up Lincolnesque empathy and grace: "No man can doubt that had we been born in India or Africa, we too would have been idolaters. Popery, the worship of the Virgin Mary, the adoration of the Host, are justly regarded by Protestants as great offences against God and Christ. But had we been born in Italy or Spain, we too had been papists. . . . [H]ad we been born and educated under that system [of southern slavery], we doubtless would have acquiesced in it or defended it."

33. This brings to mind Gary Gallagher's contention in *Union War* that the war's nineteenth-century meaning differs from its present-day meaning and that what appears clear to us was not necessarily so to Civil War–era Americans (Gary W. Gallagher, *Union War* [Cambridge, Mass.: Harvard University Press, 2011]). Regarding the blindness that has always characterized human experience, see Mark A. Noll, *God and Race in American Politics* (Princeton, N.J.: Princeton University Press, 2008), 176–81; George M. Marsden, "Human Depravity: A Neglected Explanatory Category," in *Figures in the Carpet: Finding the Human Person in the American Past*, ed. Wilfred M. McClay (Grand Rapids, Mich.: Wm. B. Eerdmans, 2007), 15–32; Merold Westphal, "Christian Philosophers and the Copernican Revolution," in *Christian Perspectives on Religious Knowledge*, ed. C. Stephen Evans and Merold Westphal (Grand Rapids, Mich.: Wm. B. Eerdmans, 1993), 161–79.

34. In May, the American Anti-Slavery Society held its annual meeting at George Cheever's church, where William Lloyd Garrison proposed that the pending Thirteenth Amendment meant that the society could dissolve; though the ex-slaves needed assistance, the society's mission was complete. Wendell Phillips, Parker Pillsbury, Frederick Douglass, and Cheever helped defeat Garrison's measure, and he resigned the presidency. Cheever became a vice president and argued alongside Douglass that emancipation meant little without suffrage. See "The Anniversaries," *Independent*, 18 May 1865, p. 1; Frederick Douglass, "The Need for Continuing Anti-Slavery Work," speech at the Thirty-Second Annual Meeting of the American Anti-Slavery Society, May [10], 1865, in *LWFD*, 4:167; idem, "In What New Skin Will the Old Snake Come Forth?: An Address delivered in New York, New York, on 10 May 1865," in *FDP*, 4:79–85; James M. McPherson, *The Struggle for Equality: Abolitionists and the Negro in the Civil War and Reconstruction* (Princeton, N.J.: Princeton University Press, 1964), 287–307; Henry Mayer, *All on Fire: William Lloyd Garrison and the Abolition of Slavery* (New York: St. Martin's Griffin, 1998), 586–94.

35. George B. Cheever to Elizabeth Washburn, 14 June 1865, 3 October 1865, CFP. See also "Reconstruction," *Principia and National Era*, 29 June 1865, p. 4; "Reconstruction of the Union," *Principia and National Era*, 29 June 1865, p. 5; "Negro Suffrage—Reconstruction," *Principia and National Era*, 6 July 1865, p. 2; Elizabeth Washburn to George B. Cheever, 20 October 1865, CFP; George B. Cheever, "The Right of Suffrage from God, and the Guilt and Peril of Withholding It," *National Principia*, 24 May 1866, p. 1; Gilbert Haven, *National Sermons: Sermons, Speeches, and Letters on Slavery and Its War: From the Passage of the Fugitive Slave Bill to the Election of President Grant* (Boston: Lee and Shepard, 1869), 599; Howard, *Religion and the Radical Republican Movement*, 90–105.

36. Blum, *Reforging the White Republic*, 49; Boardman, *Peace We Need*, 25–26.

37. Andrew Johnson, Speech to First Regiment, USCT, 10 October 1865, *PAJ*, 9:219–23; Boardman, *Peace We Need*, 27; idem, Sermon, 3 December 1865, HBP.

38. Dexter, *What Ought to Be Done*, 17.

39. See Thomas F. Gossett, *Race: The History of an Idea in America* (Dallas: Southern Methodist University Press, 1963), 36–48; George M. Fredrickson, *The Black Image in the White Mind: The Debate on Afro-American Character and Destiny, 1817–1914* (New York: Harper and Row, 1971), 137–64.

40. Dexter, *What Ought to be Done*, 8. Regarding expectations that ex-slaves labor for their former masters, see Fredrickson, *Black Image in the White Mind*, 175–86; Foner, *Reconstruction*, 234–39; Richardson, *Death of Reconstruction*, 6–40; Litwack, *Been in the Storm So Long*, 221–335; Tera W. Hunter, *To Joy My Freedom: Southern Black Women's Lives and Labors after the Civil War* (Cambridge, Mass.: Harvard University Press, 1997), 1–43.

41. Andrew Johnson to David Wills, 3 July 1865, *PAJ*, 8:344.

42. Joel Foote Bingham, *Bright Republic* (Buffalo, 1865), 1–2.

43. Clark E. Ferrin, *"Grateful Results of the War against the Slaveholder's Rebellion"* (Burlington, Vt.: Free Press Steam Job Printing Office, 1866), 8, 13. See also Albert Barnes, "Peace and Honor," in *National Preacher* 40 (January 1866): 1–28; Aaron Merrick Colton, *God's Dealings with Our Nation* (Northampton, Mass.: Trumbull and Gere, 1866), 8.

44. Henry Ward Beecher to Andrew Johnson, 23 October 1865, *PAJ*, 9:269–70; Henry Ward Beecher, *Patriotic Addresses: America and England, from the 1850s to 1885, on Slavery, the Civil War, and the Development of Civil Liberty in the United States* (New York: Fords, Howard, and Hubert, 1887), 713–34. The sermon appeared in print as Henry Ward Beecher, "Sermon," *Independent*, 2 November 1865, p. 2. Cf. Moorhead, *American Apocalypse*, 178–83; Blum, *Reforging the White Republic*, 87–104.

45. James M. Hoppin, "Henry Ward Beecher," *NE* 29 (July 1870): 425; Stampp, *Era of Reconstruction*, 50–82; McKitrick, *Andrew Johnson and Reconstruction*, 170–72; Bergeron, *Andrew Johnson's Civil War*, 8–11.

46. Andrew Johnson, Interview with George L. Stearns, 3 October 1865, *PAJ*, 9:179–80. Stearns, a staunch advocate of black suffrage, knew Johnson while serving as a recruiting agent for black troops in Tennessee and held out hope for Johnson through 1865. See Simpson, *Reconstruction Presidents*, 84; McKitrick, *Andrew Johnson and Reconstruction*, 171, McPherson, *Struggle for Equality*, 336–39; Bergeron, *Andrew Johnson's Civil War*, 92. Johnson believed he was following Lincoln, who had privately suggested that Louisiana's military governor might extend suffrage to the "very intelligent" and Union veterans. Johnson recommended that Mississippi's provisional governor support limited black suffrage but admitted that he desired to foil radicals "who are wild upon negro suffrage"; had that become policy in the South, Republicans likely would have been satisfied. However, only five northern states permitted black suffrage, and Connecticut, Minnesota, and Wisconsin rejected suffrage in fall referenda. See Abraham Lincoln to Michael Hahn, 13 March 1864, *CW*, 7:243; Andrew Johnson to William L. Sharkey, 15 August 1865, *PAJ*, 8:599–600; McKitrick, *Andrew Johnson and Reconstruction*, 56–59, 142–49, 166; Bergeron, *Andrew Johnson's Civil War*, 91–93; Foner, *Reconstruction*, 178–84,

216–24; Michael Vorenberg, *Final Freedom: The Civil War, the Abolition of Slavery, and the Thirteenth Amendment* (Cambridge: Cambridge University Press, 2001), 226–27; Simpson, *Reconstruction Presidents*, 79; McPherson, *Struggle for Equality*, 294–307, 318–40; Leslie H. Fishel Jr., "Northern Prejudice and Negro Suffrage, 1865–1870," *JNH* 39 (January 1954): 8–26. Most Republicans "were not Radicals," in Foner's words, "but moderates and conservatives who resented the 'element that seem to have the negro on the brain all the time' and feared the issue of black rights would prove fatal to the party's electoral prospects" (*Reconstruction*, 222).

47. Beecher did not discuss Johnson's third plank, Confederate debt repudiation. Beecher, *Patriotic Addresses*, 715, 721, 722, 724, 726; Beecher to Johnson, *PAJ*, 9:269. See also Henry Ward Beecher, "Reconstruction," *Independent*, 6 July 1865, p. 8. Beecher believed northern meddling in complex race relations could result in various unintended consequences; regarding racial violence, he commented, "One thing is certain: if [the freedmen] come up to manhood, to independence, to a civil estate, they will do it through suffering. You must not expect that any law, any administration, any policy, or any . . . societies are going to prevent that. You must not be disappointed or startled because . . . of shocking barbarities committed upon these people."

48. Paul A. Carter, *The Spiritual Crisis of the Gilded Age* (DeKalb: Northern Illinois University Press, 1971), 111–32; George M. Marsden, *Fundamentalism and American Culture: The Shaping of Twentieth-Century Evangelicalism, 1870–1925*, 2nd ed. (New York: Oxford University Press, 2006), 21–26.

49. Beecher, *Patriotic Addresses*, 715, 719–20. Beecher was sensitive to Robert E. Lee's treatment and forgave him for his "hour of great weakness"; there was no need to further humiliate Lee, especially given his noble surrender and subsequent presidency of Washington College. Beecher raised money for the institution. "Education at the South," *Independent*, 12 March 1868, p. 4.

50. Samuel Giles Buckingham, *A Sermon* (Springfield, Mass.[?]: Samuel Bowles, 1866), 10. Note Wilson, *Baptized in Blood*, 18–36; Foster, *Ghosts of the Confederacy*; David W. Blight, *Race and Reunion: The Civil War in American Memory* (Cambridge, Mass.: Belknap Press of Harvard University Press, 2001), 77–92, 181–92; Janney, *Remembering the Civil War*, 133–59; Tony Horwitz, *Confederates in the Attic: Dispatches from the Unfinished Civil War* (New York: Pantheon Books, 1998); G. Kurt Piehler, *Remembering War the American Way* (Washington, D.C.: Smithsonian Institution Press, 1995), 48–91.

51. Andrew Johnson, Thanksgiving Proclamation, October 28, 1865, in Richardson, *Compilation of the Messages and Papers of the Presidents, 1789–1908*, ed. James D. Richardson, 11 vols. (Washington, D.C.: Bureau of National Literature and Art, 1907–9), 6:332; Henry Hopkins, *Peace in Our Borders* (Troy, N.Y.: A. W. Scribner, 1866), 23; Theophilus Parsons Sawin, *Our Duty upon the Restoration of Peace* (Nashua, N.H.: Dearborn and Berry, 1866), 5–6. See also Charles B. Boynton, *National Thanksgiving Services Held on Thursday, December 7, 1865, in the Hall of the House of Representatives of the United States of America* (Washington, D.C.: W. H. and O. H. Morrison, 1865), 3.

52. Granville Moody to Andrew Johnson, 17 November 1865, *PAJ*, 9:398; Granville Moody, *A Life's Retrospect: Autobiography of Rev. Granville Moody, D.D. (Brigadier General by Brevet)*, ed. Sylvester Weeks (Cincinnati: Cranston and Howe, 1890), 264–67,

361–62; George V. Moody to Andrew Johnson, 20 August 1865, *PAJ*, 8:623–25; David M. Fleming to Andrew Johnson, 20 February 1868, *PAJ*, 13:568–69.

53. Andrew Johnson, Message to Congress, 4 December 1865, *PAJ*, 9:466, 468, 472, 484–85. Ratification became official December 18. Vorenberg, *Final Freedom*, 227–33; McKitrick, *Andrew Johnson and Reconstruction*, 253–58; Bergeron, *Andrew Johnson's Civil War*, 92–93.

54. I am not suggesting that Johnson did not have radical opposition. See John Weiss, *The Political Exigencies of Political Submission* (Boston: Walker, Fuller, 1865); Boynton, *National Thanksgiving*; Howard, *Religion and the Radical Republican Movement*, 91–105.

55. Elias R. Beadle, *Thanksgiving-Day Sermon* (Philadelphia: Jas. B. Rodgers, 1865), 19, 6–7; D. Hayes Agnew, "Biographical Sketch of the Rev. Elias R. Beadle, D.D., LL.D," *Proceedings of the American Philosophical Society* 22 (October 1885): 227–40; Henry Martyn Scudder, *A Discourse Delivered in the Howard Presbyterian Church, San Francisco, Thanksgiving Day, December 7th, 1865* (San Francisco, Calif.: Towne and Bacon, 1865), 16, 20; F. G. Notehelfer, *American Samurai: L. L. Janes and Japan* (Princeton, N.J.: Princeton University Press, 2014), 292n32. See also Adams, "War for Independence," 89–90; Adams, *National Thanksgiving*, 7–9; Heman R. Timlow, *A Thanksgiving Discourse* (Poughkeepsie, N.Y.: Platt and Son, 1866), 18; Henry Fowler, *The Country Saved* (Auburn, N.Y.: Daily Advertiser and Weekly Journal, 1866), 15–16; Caspar R. Gregory, *A Thanksgiving Sermon* (Bridgeton, N.J.: G. F. Nixon, 1865), 12–13.

56. Charles Smith, *What We Have Secured by the War, and What Remains to Be Secured* (Andover, Mass.: Warren F. Draper, 1866), 20–22. See also Cummins, *Christian Church's Duty to the Freedmen*, 29–30; Fowler, *Country Saved*, 15; Sawin, *Our Duty upon the Restoration of Peace*, 14–20; Timlow, *Thanksgiving Discourse*, 26–28; A. S. Twombly, *Escape from Danger a Cause for Thanksgiving* (Albany, N.Y.: J. Munsell, 1865), 15–22; George Leon Walker, *A Look Back, and Before* (Portland, Maine: Brown Thurston, 1865), 15–20.

57. George Duffield Jr., *The Dark Night and the Glorious Morning: A Thanksgiving Sermon: December 7, 1865* (Galesburg, Ill., 1866), 25, 5, 3. See also John C. Bliss, *Obedience the Fruit of Gratitude* (Carlisle, Pa.: Book and Job Office of the "American Volunteer," 1865); Buckingham, *Sermon*; T. Sandford Doolittle, *A Sermon* (Schenectady, N.Y.: Young and Graham, 1866); Walker, *A Look Back, and Before*.

58. Note Gardiner Spring Plumley, *Piety Secures the Nation's Prosperity* (New York: F. Somers, 1866), 8. Disconcerted by the large republic's ethnocultural diversity and particularly by Roman Catholicism, he wondered whether or not the Union would "cohere under one constitution as a well cemented whole." Security would come only through the glue of pervasive evangelical piety.

59. Harvey Denison Kitchel, *A Thanksgiving Sermon* (Chicago: Republican Book and Job Printing Office, 1865),5, 9; Henry A. Hazen et al, *Andover Theological Seminary: Necrology, 1880–1881* (Boston: Beacon Press, 1881), 195; Scudder, *Discourse Delivered in the Howard Presbyterian Church, San Francisco*, 5–6; James McDougall Jr., *God's Blessing of Peace* (Brooklyn: Daily Times, 1866), 6. For similar sentiments from returning soldiers, see Gallagher, *Union War*, 125–28.

60. McDougall, *God's Blessing of Peace*, 7–13.

5. The Union Saved Again

1. Edward R. Ames to Ulysses S. Grant, 28 March 1868, USGP. Stanton had tasked Methodist Bishop Ames with securing southern Methodist loyalty during the war. See Ralph E. Morrow, *Northern Methodism and Reconstruction* (East Lansing: Michigan State University Press, 1956), 33–35, 207–9. On 2 March 1867, Congress passed the Tenure of Office Act, requiring the Senate's consent to remove any Senate-confirmed official. The act covered Stanton, but on 12 August, with Congress recessing, Johnson replaced him with Grant; on 13 January, 1868, the Senate reappointed Stanton; on 21 February, Johnson replaced Stanton with General Lorenzo Thomas; and three days later Johnson was impeached. The trial began on 30 March, and on 26 May the Senate failed by one vote to convict—Republican moderates little desired the radical Benjamin Wade becoming president (next in the line of presidential succession). See Victor B. Howard, *Religion and the Radical Republican Movement, 1860–1870* (Lexington: University Press of Kentucky, 1990), 159–64; "The Secular World," *ZH*, 23 January 1868, p. 45; "Gen. Grant vs. the President," *ZH*, 6 February 1868, p. 65; "Secular World," *ZH*, 20 February 1868, p. 96; "Obedience to the Law An American Trait," *ZH*, 2 April 1868, p. 161; Michael Les Benedict, *The Impeachment and Trial of Andrew Johnson* (New York: W. W. Norton, 1973), 95–125; Paul H. Bergeron, *Andrew Johnson's Civil War and Reconstruction* (Knoxville: University of Tennessee Press, 2011), 181–208; Brooks D. Simpson, *Let Us Have Peace: Ulysses S. Grant and the Politics of War and Reconstruction, 1861–1868* (Chapel Hill: University of North Carolina Press, 1991),, 190–92, 225–36; idem, *The Reconstruction Presidents* (Lawrence: University Press of Kansas, 1998), 119–29; Eric L. McKitrick, *Andrew Johnson and Reconstruction* (Chicago: University of Chicago Press, 1960), 486–509.

2. Samuel T. Spear, "The President and Congress," *APTR* 5 (January 1867): 29; George L. Prentiss, "The Political Crisis," *APTR* 4 (October 1866): 625–26. Prentiss's wife, Elizabeth Payson Prentiss, was a well-known poet, author, and hymn writer. See idem, ed., *The Life and Letters of Elizabeth Prentiss* (New York: A. D. F. Randolph, 1882).

3. Henry A. Boardman, *A Reformed and Revived Christianity: Our Country's Great Necessity* (Philadelphia: J. B. Lippincott, 1867), 15, 21. Grant's slogan came from his nomination acceptance letter. Ulysses S. Grant to Joseph R. Hawley, 29 May 1868, *PUSG*, 18:264. Note Mark Wahlgren Summers, "With a Sublime Faith in God, and in Republican Liberty," in *Vale of Tears: New Essays on Religion and Reconstruction*, ed. Edward J. Blum and W. Scott Poole (Macon, Ga.: Mercer University Press, 2005), 112–32. Summers argues that Democratic political discourse privileged classical history, whereas Republicans privileged providence and the Bible. Perhaps—but plenty of evangelical Republicans synthesized the two.

4. No ex-Confederate state endorsed the Thirteenth Amendment in 1865, and Texas did not ratify until 1870 and Mississippi until 1995; some states refused to nullify secession or repudiate Confederate debt; and Georgia reserved the right to receive compensation for emancipated slaves. Though disconcerted by the response, Johnson continued to insist that the country was restored and that southern representatives should be seated. George C. Rable, *But There Was No Peace: The Role of Violence in the Politics of Reconstruction*, 2nd ed. (Athens: University of Georgia Press, 2007), 15; McKitrick, *Andrew*

Johnson and Reconstruction, 253–74 (quotes on 274); Michael Vorenberg, *Final Freedom: The Civil War, the Abolition of Slavery, and the Thirteenth Amendment* (Cambridge: Cambridge University Press, 2001), 227–33; Simpson, *Reconstruction Presidents*, 81–82, 91–93; Eric Foner, *Reconstruction: America's Unfinished Revolution, 1863–1877* (New York: Harper and Row, 1988), 192–99.

5. Gilbert Haven, "Prayer for Congress," *Independent* 18 [misdated 14] January 1866, p. 1.

6. Andrew Johnson, "Freedmen's Bureau Veto Message," 19 February 1866, *PAJ*, 10:121–22; Bergeron, *Andrew Johnson's Civil War and Reconstruction*, 106–8; Hans L. Trefousse, "Andrew Johnson and the Freedmen's Bureau," in *The Freedmen's Bureau and Reconstruction: Reconsiderations*, ed. Paul A. Cimbala and Randall M. Miller (New York: Fordham University Press, 1999), 29–45; Simpson, *Reconstruction Presidents*, 94–96; Patrick W. Riddleberger, *1866: The Critical Year Revisited* (Carbondale: Southern Illinois University Press, 1979), 72–74; McKitrick, *Andrew Johnson and Reconstruction*, 287–90; Michael Les Benedict, *A Compromise of Principle: Congressional Republicans and Reconstruction* 1863–1869 (New York: W. W. Norton, 1974), 147–48; Foner, *Reconstruction*, 243–49.

7. George Peck, *The Past and Present* (New York: Carlton and Porter, 1866), 42; William Adams, "The War for Independence, the War for Secession," *APTR* 4 (January 1866): 90, 92. See also S. G. Arnold, "The Suffrage Qualification," *MQR* 47 (October 1865): 582–93; Daniel Denison Whedon, "The Spirit of the Southern Methodist Press," *MQR* 48 (January 1866): 124–30; idem, "The Two Methodisms, North and South," *MQR* 48 (April 1866): 278–79; Donald G, Jones, *The Sectional Crisis and Northern Methodism: A Study in Piety, Political Ethics, and Civil Religion* (Metuchen, N.J.: Scarecrow Press, 1979), 264; Howard, *Religion and the Radical Republican Movement*, 106–10, 122–26.

8. Oliver Johnson to George Cheever, 1 March 1866, CFP. See also Howard, *Religion and the Radical Republican Movement*, 112–14; James M. McPherson, *The Struggle for Equality: Abolitionists and the Negro in the Civil War and Reconstruction* (Princeton, N.J.: Princeton University Press, 1964), 347–48; the *Independent* throughout late 1865 and 1866.

9. D. X. Junkin to Andrew Johnson, 27 February 1866, AJP. Junkin's nephew was Stonewall Jackson, under whom Junkin's son served; Junkin, however, was a staunch Unionist and regarded them as misguided. See David X. Junkin, *The Reverend George Junkin: A Historical Biography* (Philadelphia: J. B. Lippincott, 1871). See also Bergeron, *Andrew Johnson's Civil War and Reconstruction*, 108; Jane P. Thurston to Andrew Johnson, 27 February 1866, B. F. Benson to Andrew Johnson, 28 February 1866, Elizabeth I. Heustis to Andrew Johnson, 28 February 1866, Mrs. Leander Stone to Andrew Johnson, 28 February 1866, John H. Anketell to Andrew Johnson, 2 March 1866, Anson W. Jones to Andrew Johnson, 2 March 1866, David Page to Andrew Johnson, 2 March 1866, N. G. Sales to Andrew Johnson, 3 March 1866, AJP.

10. Henry Ward Beecher, "Our National Affairs," *New York Times*, 21 February 1866, p. 5. Beecher acknowledged remaining southern bitterness—all the more reason for letting the South alone. See also idem, "Love to Enemies," *Independent*, 18 [misdated 14] January 1866, p. 2; "Henry Ward Beecher on the Situation," *New York Times*, 21 February 1866, p. 4.

11. Illinois Senator Lyman Trumbull, Johnson's conservative backer who authored both the Freedmen's Bureau and Civil Rights Bills, hoped they would obviate the need for

black suffrage and pave the way for southerners' return to Congress. Regarding the Civil Rights Bill, Trumbull hoped the temporary threat of federal judicial jurisdiction would leverage states into guaranteeing equal protection; in doing so he could preserve federalism. Johnson disagreed precisely because he saw federalism threatened. See Benedict, *Compromise of Principle*, 148–49; Harold M. Hyman, *A More Perfect Union: The Impact of the Civil War and Reconstruction on the Constitution* (New York: Alfred A. Knopf, 1973), 463–64; Foner, *Reconstruction*, 243–45, 250–51; James H. Kettner, *The Development of American Citizenship, 1608–1870* (Chapel Hill: University of North Carolina Press, 1978), 341–42.

12. George B. Cheever [?], "Andrew Johnson, the Stump Speaker," *New York Principia*, 6 March 1866, p. 4; Andrew Johnson, "Washington's Birthday Address," 22 February 1866, *PAJ*, 10:152–53; McKitrick, *Andrew Johnson and Reconstruction*, 292–93.

13. Jean W. Freund to Andrew Johnson, 27 February 1866, AJP; George L. Prentiss, "The Political Situation," *APTR* 4 (April 1866): 306; idem, "Political Crisis," 628; "The Political Situation," *NE* 25 (April 1866): 359; "Impeachment and Military Government," *NE* 27 (April 1868): 361; Theodore Dwight Woolsey, "The New Era," *NE* 25 (April 1866): 179–99; Bergeron, *Andrew Johnson's Civil War and Reconstruction*, 109; McKitrick, *Andrew Johnson and Reconstruction*, 295; McPherson, *Struggle for Equality*, 349; Kenneth M. Stampp, *The Era of Reconstruction, 1865–1877* (New York: Vintage Books, 1965), 151.

14. Prentiss, "Political Crisis," 628; idem, "Political Situation," 298–99, 304.

15. Indicted for treason, Jefferson Davis languished at Virginia's Fortress Monroe until his release in May 1867; only Andersonville Prison's commander, Henry Wirz, was executed. William J. Cooper Jr., *Jefferson Davis, American* (New York: Alfred A. Knopf, 2000), 584–610; Charles Brandon Boynton, *National Thanksgiving Services Held on Thursday, December 7, 1865, in the Hall of the House of Representatives of the United States of America* (Washington, D.C.: W. H. and O. H. Morrison, 1865), 11; Oliver Johnson to George B. Cheever, 1 March 1866, CFP; S. W. S. Dutton, "Ought Treason against the Government of the United States to Be Punished?" *NE* 24 (October 1865): 778–85; Caroline E. Janney, *Remembering the Civil War: Reunion and the Limits of Reconciliation* (Chapel Hill: University of North Carolina Press, 2013), 79–81.

16. Mississippi, South Carolina, and Alabama passed Black Codes during 1865, as did several others in 1866. Boynton, *National Thanksgiving*, 9–10; William M. Grosvenor, "The Rights of the Nation, and the Duty of Congress," *NE* 24 (October 1865): 756–59; George B. Cheever, Edward Gilbert, and Parker Pillsbury, *Petition and Memorial of the Citizens of the United States to the Senate and the House of Representatives in Congress Assembled* (New York: Francis and Loutrel, 1865), 8–9; Stampp, *Era of Reconstruction*, 80–81; Leon Litwack, *Been in the Storm So Long: The Aftermath of Slavery* (New York: Alfred A. Knopf, 1979), 274–77, 366–71; Foner, *Reconstruction*, 119–20, 199–201; Simpson, *Reconstruction Presidents*, 82–83; McPherson, *Struggle for Equality*, 332–35.

17. Prentiss, "Political Situation," 303; Spear, "President and Congress," 46.

18. Moody praised the wisdom of Johnson's amnesty policy following the president's pardon of Moody's ex-Confederate brother. Granville Moody to Andrew Johnson, 26 January 1866, *PAJ*, 9:643–44. See also Granville Moody to Andrew Johnson, 17 November 1865, *PAJ*, 9:398–99; David M. Fleming to Andrew Johnson, 4 April 1866, *PAJ*, 10:354–55;

George V. Moody to Andrew Johnson, 13 April 1866, *PAJ*, 10:410–11; Clifford [?] N. Fyffe to Andrew Johnson, 25 July 1866, *PAJ*, 10:735–37; David M. Fleming to Andrew Johnson, 14 October 1866, *PAJ*, 11:349–50; David M. Fleming to Andrew Johnson, 4 February 1867, *PAJ*, 12:7–8; Bergeron, *Andrew Johnson's Civil War and Reconstruction*, 122–25; Michael Perman, *Reunion without Compromise: The South and Reconstruction, 1865–187* (Cambridge: Cambridge University Press, 1973), 198–201; Foner, *Reconstruction*, 260–62.

19. *NE*, "Political Situation," 360, 363–64; Spear, "President and Congress," 30; Prentiss, "Political Situation," 303, 307; "President Johnson's Tour, and His Policy," *NE* 25 (October 1866): 714. See also John Mooney to Andrew Johnson, 28 March 1866, Sam Godwin to Andrew Johnson, 29 March 1866, W. W. Duffield to Andrew Johnson, 31 March 1866, AJP; Benedict, *Impeachment and Trial of Andrew Johnson*, 49; Edward L. Gambill, *Conservative Ordeal: Northern Democrats and Reconstruction, 1865–1868* (Ames: Iowa State University Press, 1981), 20–33; Bergeron, *Andrew Johnson's Civil War and Reconstruction*, 125–28; Simpson, *Reconstruction Presidents*, 101–110; William Gillette, *Retreat from Reconstruction, 1869–1879* (Baton Rouge: Louisiana State University Press, 1979), 1–24.

20. Granville Moody to Andrew Johnson, 12 July 1866, PAJ, 10:679–83.

21. Johnson quoted in Bergeron, *Andrew Johnson's Civil War and Reconstruction*, 128; "The President's Pilgrimage," *Independent*, 6 September 1866, p. 4; Spear, "President and Congress," 41.

22. "Political Situation," *NE*, 361; Oliver Johnson to George B. Cheever, 1 March 1866, CFP; Samuel T. Spear, *The Citizen's Duty in the Present Crisis* (New York: N. Tibbals, 1866); H. T. Blake, "Judge Farrar on the Constitution," *NE* 26 (October 1867): 737; David Herbert Donald, *Lincoln Reconsidered: Essays on the Civil War Era* (New York: Alfred A. Knopf, 1956), 187–208; Daniel Walker Howe, *The Political Culture of the American Whigs* (Chicago: University of Chicago Press, 1979), 76–91; Richard J. Carwardine, *Evangelicals and Politics in Antebellum America* (New Haven, Conn.: Yale University Press, 1993), 64–68; Michael F. Holt, *The Rise and Fall of the American Whig Party: Jacksonian Politics and the Coming of the Civil War* (New York: Oxford University Press, 1999), 17–18, 26–34, 46, 58–59, 113.

23. Moderates generally began to take this stance. See Peter Cooper to Andrew Johnson, 12 September 1866, *PAJ*, 11:208–12; Augustus Woodbury, *The President and Congress* (Providence, R.I.: George H. Whitney, 1866); Benedict, *Impeachment and Trial of Andrew Johnson*, 50.

24. Daniel Whedon, supplement to John H. Caldwell, "Relations of the Colored People to the Methodist Episcopal Church, South," *MQR* 48 (July 1866): 442; "Political Situation," *NE*, 362–63; Rable, *But There Was No Peace*, 33–58; Woolsey, "New Era," 194; George F. Comfort, "Liberalism in Europe," *MQR* 48 (April 1866): 261; Spear, *Citizen's Duty*, 32; Howard, *Religion and the Radical Republican Movement*, 130–34.

25. John L. Smith to Andrew Johnson, 13 August 1866, *PAJ*, 11:74–76.

26. Prentiss, "Political Situation," 311, 327.

27. Benedict, *Compromise of Principle*, 162–209; Hyman, *More Perfect Union*, 446–71; McKitrick, *Andrew Johnson and Reconstruction*, 326–63; Simpson, *Reconstruction Presidents*, 102–3; Stampp, *Era of Reconstruction*, 135–45; Foner, *Reconstruction*, 251–61.

28. Henry Ward Beecher, *Beecher's "Cleveland Letters": Two Letters on Reconstruction of the Southern States* (New York [?], 1884), 14–17; Clifford E. Clark Jr., *Henry Ward Beecher: Spokesman for a Middle-Class America* (Urbana: University of Illinois Press, 1978), 166–78.

29. Beecher wrote his second letter to an unnamed congregant; his brother Edward and his sister Harriet were dismayed; and Frederick Douglass found Beecher inexplicable. See Beecher, *"Cleveland Letters,"* 15–28; Edward J. Blum, *Reforging the White Republic: Race, Religion, and American Nationalism, 1865–1898* (Baton Rouge: Louisiana State University Press, 2005), 93–96; Howard, *Religion and the Radical Republican Movement*, 138–39; Frederick Douglass, "We Are Here and Want the Ballot-Box: An Address Delivered in Philadelphia, Pennsylvania, on 4 September 1866," in *FDP*, 4:133.

30. "President Johnson's Tour, and His Policy," *NE* 25 (October 1866): 716; "Mr. Beecher," *Independent*, 6 September 1866, p. 4; Prentiss, "Political Crisis," 634, 636.

31. Spear, "President and Congress," 29.

32. George B. Cheever to Elizabeth Washburn, 2 April 1866, CFP; George B. Cheever, *Protest against the Robbery of the Colored Race by the Proposed Amendment of the Constitution* (New York: Robert J. Johnston, 1866), 5; idem, *The Republic or the Oligarchy? Which? An Appeal against the Proposed Transfer of the Right to Vote from the People to the State* (New York: American News Company, 1866), 19. See also idem, "The Right of Suffrage from God, and the Guilt and Peril of Withholding It," *National Principia*, 24 May 1866, p. 1, 14 June 1866, p. 2; "Citizenship a Birthright—Suffrage an Element of Citizenship," *National Principia*, 24 May 1866, p. 2. Cf. Howard, *Religion and the Radical Republican Movement*, 140–45, which identifies all support as radical, while overlooking radical opposition.

33. Frederick Douglass, "Reconstruction," *Atlantic Monthly*, December 1866, in *LWFD*, 4:199; David W. Blight, *Frederick Douglass' Civil War: Keeping Faith in Jubilee* (Baton Rouge: Louisiana State University Press, 1989), 191–95; George B. Cheever to Elizabeth Washburn, 4 March 1867, CFP; George B. Cheever, *Impartial Suffrage a Right; And the Infamy of the Revolution against It in the Proposed Amendment to the Constitution* (New York: Robert J. Johnston, 1866), 4. He was particularly angered that New York excluded African Americans in revising its constitution. See David Quigley, *Second Founding: New York City, Reconstruction, and the Making of American Democracy* (New York: Hill and Wang, 2004).

34. Prentiss, "Political Crisis," 630, 645; Benedict, *Impeachment and Trial of Andrew Johnson*, 50. Most congressional Republicans accepted Johnson's provisional governments, which included many ex-rebels, and foresaw the amendment ending Reconstruction.

35. Spear, "President and Congress," 47–50; McKitrick, *Andrew Johnson and Reconstruction*, 448–85; Simpson, *Reconstruction Presidents*, 110–19; Benedict, *Impeachment and Trial of Andrew Johnson*, 16–21; James M. McPherson, *Ordeal by Fire: The Civil War and Reconstruction*, 3rd ed. (Boston: McGraw-Hill, 2001), 563–66.

36. "Impeachment," *Christian Recorder*, 19 January 1867, 9; Blake, "Judge Farrar on the Constitution," 737; George B. Cheever to Henry T. Cheever, 28 August 1867, CFP; "What Next?" *Independent*, 14 November 1867, p. 4; Granville Moody, *A Life's Retrospect:*

Autobiography of Rev. Granville Moody, D.D. (Brigadier General by Brevet), ed. Sylvester Weeks (Cincinnati: Cranston and Howe, 1890), 383; George B. Cheever to Elizabeth Washburn, 6 February 1868, CFP. See also Prentiss, "Political Crisis," 637; George B. Cheever to Elizabeth Washburn, 1 October, 3 November 1867, CFP; "The Criminal in the White House," *Independent*, 5 March 1868, p. 4; "The 'Irrepressible Conflict' in Washington: Washington's Birth-Day—Johnson's Death-Day," *Independent*, 27 February 1868, p. 4; Benedict, *Impeachment and Trial of Andrew Johnson*, 15–25, 103; Gillette, *Retreat from Reconstruction*, 9–10; Howard, *Religion and the Radical Republican Movement*, 156–64; Stampp, *Era of Reconstruction*, 62; Simpson, *Reconstruction Presidents*, 125.

37. George B. Cheever, "Who Shall Set the Switches?" *Independent*, 16 April 1868, p. 1; "Work for President Wade," *Independent*, 7 May 1868, p. 8; "The Chicago Convention," *Independent*, 14 May 1868, p. 4.

38. Charles Dyer to Matthew Simpson, May 16, 1868, MSP; "The Country's Nomination," *ZH*, 28 May 1868, p. 263.

39. "National Republican Convention, 1868," in *A Political Manual for the Campaign of 1868* (Boston: A. Williams, 1868), 72; Ulysses S. Grant to Joseph R. Hawley, 29 May 1868, *PUSG*, 18:264.

40. "Correspondence—Words from Washington," *ZH*, 14 January 1869, p. 17; Samuel T. Spear, "The Duty of the Hour," *Independent*, 8 October 1868, p. 1.

41. Ulysses S. Grant to Joseph R. Hawley, 29 May 1868, *PUSG*, 18:264; Ulysses S. Grant to Matthew Simpson, 18 September 1868, *PUSG*, 19:284; Simpson, *Let Us Have Peace*, 246 (quote); idem, *Reconstruction Presidents*, 134; William S. McFeely, *Grant: A Biography* (New York: W. W. Norton, 1981), 244; Joan Waugh, *U. S. Grant: American Hero, American Myth* (Chapel Hill: University of North Carolina Press, 2009), 118–21.

42. Spear, "Duty of the Hour"; Moody, *Life's Retrospect*, 377; J. Russell Jones to Ulysses S. Grant, 11 October 1868, USGP. See also George C. Bates to Ulysses S. Grant, 21 May 1868, John McLean to Ulysses S. Grant, 5 November 1868, Methodist Bishops to Ulysses S. Grant, 19 November 1868, USGP; George Peck, *The Life and Times of Rev. George Peck, D.D., Written by Himself* (New York: Nelson and Phillips, 1874), 398; George B. Cheever to Elizabeth Washburn, 6 October 1868, CFP.

43. Daniel Curry, "The Africo-American," *MQR* 50 (April 1868): 252; Gilbert Haven, *National Sermons: Sermons, Speeches, and Letters on Slavery and Its War: From the Passage of the Fugitive Slave Bill to the Election of President Grant* (Boston: Lee and Shepard, 1869), 615.

44. *Christian Advocate*, 6 August 1868, p. 22, quoted in James H. Moorhead, *American Apocalypse: Yankee Protestants and the Civil War, 1860–1869* (New Haven, Conn.: Yale University Press, 1978), 212. Literature on the 1868 election generally overlooks evangelicals. See John Hope Franklin, "Election of 1868," in *History of American Presidential Elections, 1789–1868*, ed. Arthur M. Schlesinger Jr. (New York: Chelsea House, 1985), 3:1247–71; Foner, *Reconstruction*, 333–45; Simpson, *Let Us Have Peace*, 246–63; idem, *Reconstruction Presidents*, 128–39; Gillette, *Retreat from Reconstruction*, 12–17; McFeely, *Grant*, 274–84; Marie Ellen Kelsey, *Ulysses S. Grant: A Bibliography* (Westport, Conn.: Praeger, 2005), 191–200; William B. Hesseltine, *Ulysses S. Grant: Politician* (New York: Dodd, Mead, 1935), 112–44; Martin E. Mantell, *Johnson, Grant, and the Politics of Recon-*

struction (New York: Columbia University Press, 1973), 129–49; Charles H. Coleman, *The Election of 1868: The Democratic Effort to Regain Control* (New York: Columbia University Press, 1933).

45. Blake, "Judge Farrar on the Constitution," 737; J. B. Corey to Ulysses S. Grant, 1 June 1868, USGP; John Lothrop Motley, "Who Is General Grant?" *ZH*, 3 December 1868, 578–79.

46. "Representative Public Men," *Independent*, 6 February 1868, p. 1; Haven, *National Sermons*, 613. See also Aaron Merrick Colton, *God's Dealings with Our Nation* (Northampton, Mass.: Trumbull and Gere, 1866), 8; William M. Burleigh, "Grant: A Rhyme for the Campaign," *Independent*, 24 September 1868, p. 1; "A New Story of General Grant," *ZH*, 8 October 1868, p. 483; Charles Adams, "Our Three Generals," *ZH*, 18 February 1869, p. 75; Gilbert Haven [?], "A New President," *ZH*, 4 March 1869, p. 102; Prof. Hyde, "My Sight of Gen. Grant," *ZH*, 15 April 1869, p. 170; Waugh, *U. S. Grant*, 119.

47. Morrow, *Northern Methodism and Reconstruction*, 212–20; Joan Waugh, "'Pageantry of Woe': The Funeral of Ulysses S. Grant." *CWH* 51 (June 2005): 159–60; idem, *U.S. Grant*, 230–33; Robert H. Keller Jr., *American Protestantism and United States Indian Policy, 1869–82* (Lincoln: University of Nebraska Press, 1983), 24–25; McFeely, *Grant*, 503; John S. Bonnell, *Presidential Profiles: Religion in the Life of American Presidents* (Philadelphia: Westminster, 1971), 122–27; Vernon B. Hampton, *Religious Backgrounds of the White House* (Boston: Christopher, 1932), 241–45; Bliss Isely, *The Presidents: Men of Faith* (Boston: Wilde, 1953), 138–45; Franklin Steiner, *The Religious Beliefs of Our Presidents from Washington to F.D.R.* (Amherst, N.Y.: Prometheus Books, 1995), 71–76; Kelsey, *Ulysses S. Grant*, 318–20. For examples of Grant's interaction with evangelicals, see Matthew Simpson to Ulysses S. Grant, 18 February 1869, *PUSG*, 18:346; Mary E. Calhoun to Ulysses S. Grant, 25 March 1869, *PUSG*, 18:407; Matthew Simpson to Ulysses S. Grant, 13 April 1869, *PUSG*, 18:438; D. H. Mueller to Ulysses S. Grant, 3 May 1869, *PUSG*, 20:262; Cummings Hale to Ulysses S. Grant, 16 July 1869, *PUSG*, 19:520; Ulysses S. Grant to Methodist-Episcopal Church Benefit, 30 October 1869, *PUSG*, 18:267; Ulysses S. Grant to John P. Newman, 24 December 1869, *PUSG*, 20:73; Jacob C. Patrick to Ulysses S. Grant, 10 January 1870, *PUSG*, 20:360; Ulysses S. Grant to Matthew Simpson, 10 January 1871, *PUSG*, 21:134; Orville E. Babcock to Jacob B. Graw, 18 January, 13 April 1871, *PUSG*, 21:412; Matthew Simpson to Ulysses S. Grant, 1 March 1871, *PUSG*, 21:445. Regarding Simpson's influence, see William King to Matthew Simpson, 10 February 1869, Edward J. Allen to Matthew Simpson, 26 April 1872, J. Jaquese and J. E. Parker to Matthew Simpson, 6 November 1872, T. B. Poisal to Matthew Simpson, 10 January 1873, Henry J. Fox to Matthew Simpson, 13 October 1873, George Crawford to Matthew Simpson, 16 March 1875, John Titus to Matthew Simpson, 16 October 1875, R. F. Gaggin to Matthew Simpson, 21 December 1875, A. H. Carnahan to Matthew Simpson, 29 January 1876, W. L. S. Bayley to Matthew Simpson, 10 May 1876, MSP.

48. "A Woman's Letter from Washington," *Independent*, 13 February 1868, p. 1; W. E. Dodge to O. O. Howard, 2 June 1868, OOHP; McFeely, *Grant*, 282–83; Keller, *American Protestantism and United States Indian Policy*, 254n22. Perhaps there will never be a final word on Grant's drinking, though the nation knew something about it. See Frederick Law Olmsted, "The Genesis of a Rumor," *Nation* 6 (23 April 1868): 329–30.

49. E. F. Shepard to Ulysses S. Grant, 2 June 1868, John McLean to Ulysses S. Grant, 5 November 1868, Methodist Bishops to Ulysses S. Grant, 19 November 1868, USGP; Morrow, *Northern Methodism and Reconstruction*, 211–14.

50. Seymour's campaign biography tied him to Connecticut Puritan Thomas Hooker, but aside from occasional references to providential American history, the only other religious reference emphasized Seymour's criticism of perceived antebellum evangelical fanaticism. See James Dabney McCabe, *The Life and Public Services of Horatio Seymour together with a Complete and Authentic Life of Francis P. Blair, Jr.* (New York: United States Publishing Co., 1868), vi–vii, 17–19.

51. George B. Cheever to Elizabeth Washburn, 1 August 1868, 6 October 1868, CFP. Cheever never disdained Grant like he had Lincoln, and by spring 1868 most radicals had warmed to Grant. See "Gen. Grant's Resignation," *Independent*, 11 June 1868, p. 4; "The Outlook," *Independent*, 24 September 1868, p. 4; "It's Part of My Religion," *ZH*, 22 October 1868, p. 511; "Duty of Campaign Speakers," *ZH*, 29 October 1868, p. 522; Frederick Douglass, "The Work Before Us," *Independent*, 27 August 1868, p. 1; idem, "Horatio Seymour's Letter of Acceptance," *Independent*, 20 August 1868, p. 1; Howard, *Religion and the Radical Republican Movement*, 199–204.

52. Bernard H. Nadal to Ulysses S. Grant, 27 October 1868, *PUSG*, 19:306; *The Grant Campaign Songster* (New York: Robert M. De Witt, [1868]); Gillette, *Retreat from Reconstruction*, 8–10; Blight, *Race and Reunion*, 51–52; Janney, *Remembering the Civil War*, 127.

53. "The New Civil War" and "Danger and Safety of the Republican Party," *Independent*, 16 July 1868, p. 4. See also "The Lost Cause Regained," *Independent*, 6 August 1868, p. 4.

54. John Delany to Ulysses S. Grant, 22 September 1868, USGP. Regarding an American "paranoid style," see Richard Hofstadter, *The Paranoid Style in American Politics* (New York: Alfred A. Knopf, 1965); Gordon S. Wood, "Conspiracy and the Paranoid Style: Causality and Deceit in the Eighteenth Century," *WMQ* 39 (July 1982): 401–41; J. Eric Oliver and Thomas J. Wood, "Conspiracy Theories and the Paranoid Style(s) of Mass Opinion," *American Journal of Political Science* 58 (October 2014): 652–66.

55. Moody, *Life's Retrospect*, 381–82.

56. Gilbert Haven [?], "President Grant," *ZH*, 12 November 1868, p. 547; idem [?], "General Grant Elected President," *ZH*, 22 October 1868, p. 505; idem, *National Sermons*, 608, 618–20, 626. Congress submitted the Fifteenth Amendment for ratification on February 26, 1869, just prior to Grant's inaugural. Regarding Haven's extreme stand against caste, see D. Steele, "Politics and the Pulpit," 52 *MQR* 52 (April 1870): 194–200; George M. Fredrickson, *The Black Image in the White Mind: The Debate on Afro-American Character and Destiny, 1817–1914* (New York: Harper and Row, 1971), 122.

57. Jeremiah Eames Rankin, "A Philippic on Grant," *Independent*, 5 November 1868, p. 1; McPherson, *Struggle for Equality*, 417–22; "The New Order of Things," *Independent*, 5 November 1868, p. 4; "Washington Letter," *Independent*, 19 November 1868, p. 1.

58. Boardman, *Reformed and Revived Christianity*, 16–21; idem, *The General Assembly of 1866* (Philadelphia: J. B. Lippincott, 1867), 99–104; Curry, "Africo-American," 247, 251.

59. Gilbert Haven [?], "President Grant," *ZH*, 12 November 1868, p. 547; Charles Wadsworth, *A Call to Praise* (San Francisco: John H. Carmany, 1868), 8, 10; Brooks D. Simpson, "Consider the Alternatives: Reassessing Republican Reconstruction," in *A*

Political Nation: New Directions in Mid-Nineteenth-Century American Political History, ed. Gary W. Gallagher and Rachel A. Shelden (Charlottesville: University of Virginia Press, 2012), 218; Gary W. Gallagher, *Union War* (Cambridge, Mass.: Harvard University Press, 2011), 152.

60. Jesse T. Peck, *The History of the Great Republic, from a Christian Stand-Point* (New York: Broughton and Wyman, 1868), 668–69.

6. *Pax Grantis*: The Great Protestant Republic

1. Jesse T. Peck to George Peck, 1 June 1867, GPP; Jesse T. Peck, *The History of the Great Republic, from a Christian Stand-Point* (New York: Broughton and Wyman, 1868), viii. Though Peck expressed a typical covenantal understanding, he believed that Methodism was best suited to ensure a virtuous, republic-sustaining people because of its emphasis on free will and religious liberty. See also Thomas Mears Eddy, "The Centenary of Methodism," *MQR* 48 (April 1866): 165–87; S. D. Hillman, "The United States and Methodism," *MQR* 49 (January 1867): 29–49; "Methodism against the Papacy," *ZH*, 18 June 1868, pp. 294–95; Jesse T. Peck, "Methodism: Its Method and Mission," *MQR* 51 (April 1869): 252, 263, 267–68; John Atkinson, "Methodism in the Cities of the United States," *MQR* 59 (July 1877): 481–505.

2. Likely, Peck was aware of George Bancroft, *A History of the United States*, 10 vols. (Boston: Little, Brown, 1834–75); Benson J. Lossing, *Pictorial History of the Civil War in the United States of America*, 3 vols. (Philadelphia: G. W. Childs, 1866–68); John William Draper, *History of the American Civil War*, 3 vols. (New York: Harper and Brothers, 1867–70). Bancroft was Unitarian, and Draper, later famous for his scientific work, was secular. See Thomas J. Pressley, *Americans Interpret Their Civil War* (Princeton, N.J.: Princeton University Press, 1954), 60; Jonathan Townley Crane, "New American Histories—Peck and Draper," *MQR* 51 (January 1869): 5–30. See also Samuel L. Caldwell, "Is There a Science of History," *BQ* 1 (January 1867): 102–17; D. Steele, "Politics and the Pulpit," *MQR* 52 (January 1870): 190; George Nye Boardman, "Christianity Capable of Self-Defense," *APR*, n.s., 2 (April 1870): 288–90; E. A. Lawrence, "Plan in History," *BRPR* 43 (October 1871): 555–64; L. H. Shuck, "Christianity and Civilization," *BQ* 8 (January 1874): 50–57.

3. The epigraph is from Ulysses S. Grant, Inaugural Address, 4 March 1869, *PUSG*, 19:141. Note that Grant originally requested "the prayers of the Christian in behalf of this consumation [*sic*]." See Ulysses S. Grant, Draft Inaugural Address, 4 March 1869, *PUSG*, 19:139. Grant likely changed the text because of his infamous 1862 "Jew" order prohibiting Jews from his command in response to speculators. See USG to Isaac N. Morris, 14 September 1868, *PUSG*, 19:37; Tyler Anbinder, "Ulysses S. Grant, Nativist," *CWH* 43 (June 1997): 123–27; Brooks D. Simpson, *Let Us Have Peace: Ulysses S. Grant and the Politics of War and Reconstruction, 1861–1868* (Chapel Hill: University of North Carolina Press, 1991), 49; William S. McFeely, *Grant: A Biography* (New York: W. W. Norton, 1981), 123–24.

4. Note Rogan Kersh, *Dreams of a More Perfect Union* (Ithaca, N.Y.: Cornell University Press, 2001), 198–241; Francis Lieber, "The National Polity Is the Normal Type

of Modern Government," *APTR* 22 (April 1868): 304–5; "Nationalism," *Independent*, 23 April 1868, p. 1. Republicans were caught amid several aims: restoring the Union, providing some form of racial justice, and maintaining the party's well-being. They also had to respect the Constitution, federalism, and republican liberty. See Brooks D. Simpson, "Consider the Alternatives: Reassessing Republican Reconstruction," in *A Political Nation: New Directions in Mid-Nineteenth-Century American Political History*, ed. Gary W. Gallagher and Rachel A. Shelden (Charlottesville: University of Virginia Press, 2012), 214–30; Michael Green, "Reconstructing the Nation, Reconstructing the Party: Postwar Republicans and the Evolution of a Party," in *The Great Task Remaining before Us: Reconstruction as America's Continuing Civil War*, ed. Paul A. Cimbala and Randall M. Miller (New York: Fordham University Press, 2010), 183–203.

5. J. T. Peck, *History of the Great Republic*, 664–65, 689–90. Cf. Ulysses S. Grant to Henry C. Bowen, 21 April 1870, *PUSG*, 20:143. Peck's approach complemented evangelicals' stance toward nature. As with William Paley's watch analogy, the marks of design in American history seemingly compelled one to infer a providential designer. See Charles Hodge, *Systematic Theology* (New York: Charles Scribner, 1871), 1:53–54, 440–41, 587–88; John P. Newman, *Sermons of J. P. Newman, D.D.* (Washington, D.C. [?]: Reeves, Pagenhoff, 1877), 1:139–53; idem, *The Beneficence of Science* (Ann Arbor, Mich.: Board of Regents, 1881); Daniel Denison Whedon, "Position and Prospects of the American Union," *MQR* 56 (January 1874): 56–57. Secondary literature is voluminous: See E. Brooks Holifield, *Theology in America: Christian Thought from the Age of the Puritans to the Civil War* (New Haven, Conn.: Yale University Press, 2003), 159–394; Theodore Dwight Bozeman, *Protestants in an Age of Science: The Baconian Ideal and Antebellum American Religious Thought* (Chapel Hill: University of North Carolina Press, 1977), 139–43; George M. Marsden, "The Collapse of Evangelical Academia," in *Reckoning with the Past: Historical Essays on American Evangelicalism from the Institute for the Study of American Evangelicals*, ed. D. G. Hart (Grand Rapids, Mich.: Baker, 1995), 221–66; idem, *Understanding Fundamentalism and Evangelicalism* (Grand Rapids, Mich.: Wm. B. Eerdmans, 1991), 122–52; Herbert Hovenkamp, *Science and Religion in America, 1800–1860* (Philadelphia: University of Pennsylvania Press, 1978); Bruce Kuklick, *A History of Philosophy in America, 1720–2000* (New York: Oxford University Press, 2001), 97–110; idem, *Churchmen and Philosophers: From Jonathan Edwards to John Dewey* (New Haven, Conn.: Yale University Press, 1985), 117–45; Mark A. Noll, *The Scandal of the Evangelical Mind* (Grand Rapids, Mich.: Wm. B. Eerdmans, 1994), 83–107; idem, "Common Sense Traditions and American Evangelical Thought," *AQ* 37 (Summer 1985): 216–38; idem, *America's God: From Jonathan Edwards to Abraham Lincoln* (New York: Oxford University Press, 2002), 233–38.

6. "Christ in American History," *ZH*, 7 May 1868, p. 223; Cephas B. Crane, *Sermon on the Occasion of the Death of President Lincoln* (Hartford, Conn.: Lockwood, 1865), 5, 8, 29. Cf. "The Methodist Quarterly," *ZH*, 28 January 1869, p. 43, which criticized Peck and Crane for underemphasizing abolitionism.

7. Erastus Otis Haven, "The Approaching Centennial of American Independence," *MQR* 56 (October 1874): 541–42; Dexter A. Hawkins, "The Anglo-Saxon Race," *MQR* 58 (January 1876): 109; "The Coming Anniversary," *ZH*, 2 July 1868, p. 313. This was continuous with antebellum efforts to Christianize America. See Timothy L. Smith, *Revivalism*

and Social Reform: American Protestantism on the Eve of the Civil War (Nashville, Tenn.: Abingdon Press, 1957; repr., New York: Harper and Row, 1965); Richard J. Carwardine, *Evangelicals and Politics in Antebellum America* (New Haven, Conn.: Yale University Press, 1993), 18–22; Henry F. May, *Protestant Churches and Industrial America* (New York: Harper and Row, 1949), 3–63.

8. "Protestantism, its Dangers and Duties," *ZH*, 30 April 1868, p. 210; Augusta Moore, "Are We a Christian Nation?" *ZH*, 7 May 1868, p. 219; J. T. Peck, *History of the Great Republic*, 689–90; Mark Wahlgren Summers, *The Era of Good Stealings* (New York: Oxford University Press, 1993).

9. "The Nation's Bane," *ZH*, 19 March 1868, p. 139; "The Overflowing Scourge," *ZH*, 25 February 1869, p. 85.

10. John P. Newman, *Religious Liberty: A Free Church in a Free Country* (Washington, D.C.: Office of the "National Republican," 1875), 10; Sandford H. Cobb, "Farrar on the Constitution," *APR*, n.s., 2 (July 1870): 459; George Duffield Jr., *Rahab; or, "Dare to Do Right,"* (Lansing, Mich., 1877), 12–13; Benjamin Franklin Hamilton, *God in Government* (Boston: Albert J. Wright, 1877), 10–11. Note Gaines M. Foster, *Moral Reconstruction: Christian Lobbyists and the Federal Legislation of Morality, 1865–1920* (Chapel Hill: University of North Carolina Press, 2002), which ties this traditional stance to postwar intersectional reform movements, interest-group politics, lobbying efforts, and the growth of the modern state. See also Edward J. Blum, *Reforging the White Republic: Race, Religion, and American Nationalism, 1865–1898* (Baton Rouge: Louisiana State University Press, 2005), 173–210, which focuses on the Women's Christian Temperance Union and North–South reunion during the 1880s–1890s. Cf. Caroline E. Janney, *Remembering the Civil War: Reunion and the Limits of Reconciliation* (Chapel Hill: University of North Carolina Press, 2013), 241.

11. Samuel T. Spear, "Reformatory Legislation and Politics," *Independent*, 20 February 1868, p. 1. See also idem, "Religion and Politics," *Independent*, 13 February 1868, p. 1. Such sentiments persisted until at least 1884. See Mark Wahlgren Summers, *Rum, Romanism, and Rebellion: The Making of a President* (Chapel Hill: University of North Carolina Press, 2000).

12. Daniel Denison Whedon, "Position and Prospects of the American Union," *MQR* 56 (January 1874), 53; James Madison, *Federalist* 10; Gordon S. Wood, *The Creation of the American Republic, 1776–1787* (Chapel Hill: University of North Carolina Press, 1969), 356, 576; Jack N. Rakove, *Original Meanings: Politics and Ideas in the Making of the Constitution* (New York: Random House, 1996), 184–91; "The Democratic Party on Its Good Behavior," *NYE*, 13 January 1870, p. 4; "The Limits to Party Allegiance," *NYE*, 25 July 1872, p. 4; Elias R. Beadle, *"Gladness in the Works of God"* (Philadelphia: J. B. Chandler, 1873), 16–17.

13. Ulysses S. Grant, Inaugural Address, *PUSG*, 19:141; Joseph Parrish Thompson, *The Theocratic Principle; or, Religion the Bond of the Republic* (New York: American Home Missionary Society, 1868), 25; "Correspondence—Words from Washington," *ZH*, 14 January 1869, p. 17; Mark W. Summers, *Railroads, Reconstruction, and the Gospel of Prosperity, 1865–1877* (Princeton, N.J.: Princeton University Press, 1984); Matthew Simpson, "Correspondence—The Great Southwest," *ZH*, 18 February 1869, p. 77. Simpson

remained optimistic that southern recalcitrance would evaporate, while others were also enamored of the expanding nation's material prospects and beauty. See Calvin [?] Kingsley, "The Pacific Coast—How it Looks," *ZH*, 11 November 1869, pp. 530–31; Myron Munson, *God's Doing and Man's Doing* (Chicago: Lakeside Publishing and Printing, 1871); idem, *Iron More Golden than Gold* (Cambridge, Mass.: Riverside Press, 1873); idem, *Water as a Mirror of the Wisdom and Goodness of God* (Boston: Charles W. Kimball, 1877).

14. Nathaniel Clark Burt, "Nations vs. Countries," *NYE*, 4 May 1871, p. 1.

15. "The Jews," *ZH*, 10 December 1868, p. 589. See also "Pantheism on a New Field," *ZH*, 17 December 1868, p. 601, which criticized the government of Portland, Maine, for permitting equal usage of City Hall for religious services.

16. "The Mormon Question," *NYE*, 20 January 1870, p. 2; "The Mormon Question—II," *NYE*, 27 January 1870, p. 2; Ulysses S. Grant to John P. Newman, 6 November 1871, *PUSG*, 22:205–07; Ulysses S. Grant to Ulysses S. Grant Jr., 24 November 1870, *PUSG*, 21:28; Orson Pratt et al., *Does the Bible Sanction Polygamy? A Discussion between Professor Orson Pratt and Rev. Doctor J. P. Newman in the New Tabernacle, Salt Lake City, August 12, 13, and 14, 1870* (Salt Lake City: Deseret News, 1876); Ulysses S. Grant, Draft Annual Message, 4 December 1871, *PUSG*, 22:252; John W. Mears, "Our Protestant Nationality," *NYE*, 5 May 1870, p. 1.

17. Dexter A. Hawkins, "The Anglo-Saxon Race," *MQR* 58 (January 1876): 92; George B. Cheever to Elizabeth Washburn, 6 October 1868, 30 October 1870, 8 September 1871, 2 October 1871, 21 November 1872, CFP. Cheever regularly vacationed at Saratoga Springs and eventually retired to rural New Jersey. While tending his garden, pietism increased and anger subsided: "A farmer's experience," he wrote, "ought to teach him his dependence upon God, and make him feel it, as the streets and shapes of the city never can." Opposing slavery was unambiguous and easy compared to Gilded Age greed, corruption, and urban life. George B. Cheever to Elizabeth Washburn, 24 November 1871, 25 June (quote), 2 March 1872, 3 August 1874, CFP.

18. Thompson, *Theocratic Principle*, 20, 30–31.

19. E. P. Ree, "Defence of West Point," *NYE*, 16 February 1871, p. 1; Sandford H. Cobb, "Farrar on the Constitution," *APR*, n.s., 2 (July 1870): 466–67, 461–62. See also H. T. Blake, "Judge Farrar on the Constitution," *NE* 26 (October 1867): 725–40; Andrew P. Peabody, "Judge Farrar's Manual of the Constitution of the United States," *NE* 34 (July 1875): 498–518. All three were reviews of Timothy Farrar, *Manual of the Constitution of the United States of America* (Boston: Little, Brown, 1867). Farrar, a judge and Daniel Webster's former law partner, made strong Unionist arguments during the war. See Timothy Farrar, "Congress and the Territories," *NE* 21 (April 1862): 194–206; idem, "State Rights," *NE* 21 (October 1862): 695–725; "Are We a Nation?" *NYE*, 24 November 1870, p. 1.

20. Thompson, *Theocratic Principle*, 30–31. C. C. Goen, *Broken Churches, Broken Nation: Denominational Schisms and the Coming of the American Civil War* (Macon, Ga.: Mercer University Press, 1985), 120, contends similarly regarding antebellum evangelicals. Alexander Schmemann, *For the Life of the World: Sacraments and Orthodoxy*, rev. ed. (Crestwood, N.Y.: St. Vladimir's Press, 1973), 25, defines liturgy as "an action by which a group of people become something corporately which they had not been as a

mere collection of individuals." William T. Cavanaugh, *Migrations of the Holy: God, State, and the Political Meaning of the Church* (Grand Rapids, Mich.: Wm. B. Eerdmans, 2011), 116, says further, "In a basic sense, liturgy enacts and maintains community by the ritual remembering or re-presentation of foundational narratives, thereby helping to construct the perceived reality in which each member of the community lives." Regarding ex-Confederates' somewhat analogous Lost-Cause liturgical efforts, see Charles Reagan Wilson, *Baptized in Blood: The Religion of the Lost Cause, 1865–1920* (Athens: University of Georgia Press, 1980); Lloyd Hunter, "The Immortal Confederacy: Another Look at Lost Cause Religion," in *The Myth of the Lost Cause and Civil War History*, ed. Gary W. Gallagher and Alan T. Nolan (Bloomington: Indiana University Press, 2000), 185–218.

21. Gaines M. Foster, *Ghosts of the Confederacy: Defeat, the Lost Cause, and the Emergence of the New South* (New York: Oxford University Press, 1987), 36–46; David W. Blight, *Race and Reunion: The Civil War in American Memory* (Cambridge, Mass.: Belknap Press of Harvard University Press, 2001), 64–79; Janney, *Remembering the Civil War*, 87–102.

22. Thompson, *Theocratic Principle*, 30. Barbara Gannon, *The Won Cause: Black and White Comradeship in the Grand Army of the Republic* (Chapel Hill: University of North Carolina Press, 2011), portrays interracial, Americanizing camaraderie among Union veterans later in the century; Carolyn Marvin and David W. Ingle, *Blood Sacrifice and the Nation: Totem Rituals and the American Flag* (Cambridge: Cambridge University Press, 1999), argues that American national coherence and identity rest on shared blood sacrifice and commemorative ritual practices; Richard J. Ellis, *To the Flag: The Unlikely History of the Pledge of Allegiance* (Lawrence: University Press of Kansas, 2005), explores the pledge's Americanizing function beginning in 1892.

23. Even Haven's civic nationalism had its limits, as evidenced by his patronizing travel diary from a trip to Catholic Mexico. See Gilbert Haven, *Our Next-Door Neighbor: A Winter in Mexico* (New York: Harper and Brothers, 1875). Suggestive of continuity during the entire Civil War era, note John C. Pinheiro, *Missionaries of Republicanism: A Religious History of the Mexican-American War* (New York: Oxford University Press, 2014).

24. Thompson, *Theocratic Principle*, 27–29. See also idem, *Church and State in the United States, With an Appendix on the German Population* (Boston: James R. Osgood, 1873), which further discusses the distinctive American "race" emerging from an Anglo-Saxon core. Regarding beliefs in Anglo-Saxon superiority, Caroline Janney comments, "most white Unionists had believed in 1861, as they did in 1865 and into the postwar years, that they were socially, culturally, physically, and mentally superior to African Americans" (*Remembering the Civil War*, 200). See also Thomas F. Gossett, *Race: The History of an Idea in America* (Dallas, Tex.: Southern Methodist University Press, 1963), 84–122, 138, 244; George M. Fredrickson, *The Black Image in the White Mind: The Debate on Afro-American Character and Destiny, 1917–1914* (New York: Harper and Row, 1971), 98–102; John Higham, *Strangers in the Land: Patterns of American Nativism, 1860–1925* (Brunswick, N.J.: Rutgers University Press, 1963), 32–33. Note Samuel P. Huntington, *Who Are We? The Challenges to America's National Identity* (New York: Simon and Schuster, 2004), which argues for a "core" Anglo-Protestantism as the key to the republic's survival.

25. Thompson, *Theocratic Principle*, 29–30. Note Edward W. Blyden, "The Negro in Ancient History," *MQR* 51 (January 1869): 71–93; idem, "The Republic of Liberia," *MQR* 54 (July 1872): 466–90. Blyden, a white Congregationalist professor of Liberia College and avowed Burkean, was pessimistic that American law could effectually guarantee social equality because of centuries-long white racism; moreover, colonization remained blacks' best choice because they would cease to exist as a distinct group in America due to white immigration and natural increase.

26. Thompson, *Theocratic Principle*, 23–26; "Methodist Quarterly," *ZH*, 29 April 1869, p. 198; Ward M. McAfee, *Religion, Race, and Reconstruction: The Public School in the Politics of the 1870s* (Albany: State University of New York Press, 1998), 53–54.

27. Crane, *Sermon on the Occasion of the Death of President Lincoln*, 27; J. T. Peck, *History of the Great Republic*, 671. Knowingly or not, Peck was participating in a contest with southerners to define the war's meaning. See Edward Pollard, *The Lost Cause: A New Southern History of the War of the Confederates* (New York: E. B. Treat, 1866); Alexander H. Stephens, *A Constitutional View of the Late War between the States; Its Causes, Character, Conduct, and Results*, 2 vols. (Philadelphia: National Publishing, 1868–70); Jefferson Davis, *The Rise and Fall of the Confederate Government*, 2 vols. (New York: D. Appleton, 1881); Janney, *Remembering the Civil War*, 103–59; Blight, *Race and Reunion*, 258–66.

28. Joseph P. Thompson, "How to Build a Nation," *NE* 28 (January 1869): 29; Brooks D. Simpson, *The Reconstruction Presidents* (Lawrence: University Press of Kansas, 1998), 135, 145; idem, "Ulysses S. Grant and the Failure of Reconciliation," *IHJ* 81 (Winter 1988): 269–82; Ulysses S. Grant to Congress, 30 March 1870, *PUSG*, 20:130; "The National Thanksgiving," *NYE*, 17 November 1870, p. 4. Thompson also argued that Republicans should not do with blacks what many believed Democrats did with the Irish, namely, treat them as a separate voting bloc for partisan gain. Democrats had made "the crudest immigrant an active member of the body politic," while not bothering to enculturate them to the American way of life.

29. N. E. Cobleigh, "Southern Reconstruction," *MQR* 52 (July 1870): 380–84; Durwood Dunn, *The Civil War in Southern Appalachian Methodism* (Knoxville: University of Tennessee Press, 2013), 132–33; Daniel W. Stowell, *Rebuilding Zion: The Religious Reconstruction of the South, 1863–1877* (New York: Oxford University Press, 1998), 131; Matthew Simpson, ed. *Cyclopedia of Methodism*, 4th ed. (Philadelphia: Louis H. Everts, 1881), s.v. "Cobleigh, Nelson Ebenezer, D.D., LL.D."

30. S. G. Arnold, "The Ku Klux Conspiracy," *MQR* 55 (January 1873): 89–93. See also "The Bloody Klan," *ZH*, 24 September 1868, pp. 463–64. Regarding enforcement, see Ulysses S. Grant, Proclamation, 12 October 1871, *PUSG*, 22:161–62; Hezekiah Hunter to Ulysses S. Grant, 13 October 1871, *PUSG*, 22:168; Ira Mason to Ulysses S. Grant, 3 July 1871, *PUSG*, 22:182; Allen W. Trelease, *White Terror: The Ku Klux Klan Conspiracy and Southern Reconstruction* (New York: Harper and Row, 1971); William Gillette, *Retreat from Reconstruction, 1869–1879* (Baton Rouge: Louisiana State University Press, 1979), 25–37; Simpson, *Reconstruction Presidents*, 150–52; Blight, *Race and Reunion*, 108–22; Wilson, *Baptized in Blood*, 110–118; George C. Rable, *But There Was No Peace: The Role of Violence in the Politics of Reconstruction*, 2nd 3d. (Athens: University of Georgia Press,

2007), 106–8; Eric Foner, *Reconstruction: America's Unfinished Revolution, 1863–1877* (New York: Harper and Row, 1988), 454–59.

31. "Do We Want St. Domingo?" *NYE*, 6 April 1871, p. 4. The comments came in the context of Grant's proposal to acquire Santo Domingo. The author disagreed because he believed that America contained enough ethnocultural tension. Grant desired to shunt some African Americans to the island, spoke of Christianizing it, and saw its annexation as militarily and economically beneficial, but he exacerbated the controversy by permitting his personal secretary, who owned property on Santo Domingo, to negotiate the treaty. See Paul Harvey, "That Was about Equalization after Freedom: Southern Evangelicalism and the Politics of Reconstruction and Redemption, 1861–1900," in *Vale of Tears: New Essays on Religion and Reconstruction*, ed. Edward J. Blum and W. Scott Poole (Macon, Ga.: Mercer University Press, 2005), 89; Ulysses S. Grant to Congress, 5 April 1871, *PUSG*, 21:282; Francis Vinton to Ulysses S. Grant, 17 May 1871, *PUSG*, 21:367–68; Merline Pitre, "Frederick Douglass and the Annexation of Santo Domingo," *JNH* 62 (October 1977): 390–400; Simpson, *Reconstruction Presidents*, 145–46; Foner, *Reconstruction*, 494–97; Andrew L. Slap, *The Doom of Reconstruction: The Liberal Republicans in the Civil War Era* (New York: Fordham University Press, 2006), 117–20. Cf. Gilbert Haven, "The Government," *ZH*, 20 January 1870, p. 25; idem, "The Shot of Sumner," *ZH* 6 April 1871, p. 162.

32. "The Colfax Tragedy," *NYE*, 1 May 1873, p. 4; Ted Tunnell, *Crucible of Reconstruction: War, Radicalism, and Race in Louisiana, 1862–1877* (Baton Rouge: Louisiana State University Press, 1984), 189–93; idem, *Edge of the Sword: The Ordeal of Carpetbagger Marshall H. Twitchell in the Civil War and Reconstruction* (Baton Rouge: Louisiana State University Press, 2001), 173–74; Rable, *But There Was No Peace*, 126–29; Gillette, *Retreat from Reconstruction*, 115–16.

33. Cobleigh, "Southern Reconstruction," 386–87; Michael Perman, "Counter Reconstruction: The Role of Violence in Southern Redemption," in *The Facts of Reconstruction: Essays in Honor of John Hope Franklin*, ed. Eric Anderson and Alfred A. Moss Jr. (Baton Rouge: Louisiana State University Press, 1991), 121–40; Rable, *But There Was No Peace*, ix–xi; Harvey, "That Was about Equalization after Freedom," 89–92; Edward L. Ayers, *What Caused the Civil War: Reflections on the South and Southern History* (New York: W. W. Norton, 2005), 153.

34. Arnold, "Ku Klux Conspiracy," 111; Cobleigh, "Southern Reconstruction," 387–93; Henry J. Fox, "The Negro," *MQR* 57 (January 1875): 79–97.

35. Cobleigh, "Southern Reconstruction," 394–97; Stowell, *Rebuilding Zion*, 130–45.

36. Daniel Denison Whedon, "Position and Prospects of the American Union," *MQR* 56 (January 1874): 47, 52–54; Newman, *Religious Liberty*.

37. George B. Cheever to Elizabeth Washburn, 8 September 1871, 21 November 1872, Elizabeth Washburn to George B. Cheever, 10 December 1872, CFP.

38. The appellation comes from John G. Sproat, *"The Best Men": Liberal Reformers in the Gilded Age* (New York: Oxford University Press, 1968), and has since been enshrined. See Foner, *Reconstruction*, 488–511; Blight, *Race and Reunion*, 122–30. Historians characterize those "best men" opposed to Grant as well-bred elitists, primarily in terms of a classical liberalism that combined laissez-faire economic ideology with an aloof concern for the common good; they opposed an activist central government that threatened

free trade, hard money, and federalism; and by 1872 they sought civil service reform and Reconstruction's end. They often denigrated the ex-slaves and argued for a natural aristocracy. Cf. Slap, *Doom of Reconstruction*, xiv–xvi, 108–25, 215–21, which challenges the applicability of the phrase and adds republican ideology to the mix. Slap contends that many antebellum founders of the "liberal republican movement," a smaller group that contributed to the larger Liberal Republican Party's formation, were animated by a classical republican vision that rested on the importance of public virtue, fear of corruption, and vigilant attention to governmental power. Opposition to Grant, then, was not elitist, and many stuck by him. In any event, evangelicals were aware of so-called "best men" and reactively supported Grant in the face of Liberal Republicans' reform efforts and caustic criticism of him as incompetent and tyrannical.

39. On the election see James M. McPherson, "Grant or Greeley? The Abolitionist Dilemma in the Election of 1872," *AHR* 71 (October 1965): 43–61; Richard Allan Gerber, "The Liberal Republicans in Historiographical Perspective," *JAH* 62 (June 1975): 40–73; Slap, *Doom of Reconstruction*, 126–221; Sproat, *"Best Men,"* 64–66; Summers, *Era of Good Stealings*, 215–31; William Gillette, "Election of 1872," in *History of American Presidential Elections, 1789–1968*, ed. Arthur M. Schlesinger Jr. (New York: Chelsea House, 1985), 4:1303–37; idem, *Retreat from Reconstruction*, 56–75; Foner, *Reconstruction*, 499–511; McFeely, *Grant*, 380–86; Heather Cox Richardson, *The Death of Reconstruction: Race, Labor, and Politics in the Post–Civil War North, 1865–1901* (Cambridge, Mass.: Harvard University Press, 2001), 98–105; Blum, *Reforging the White Republic*, 111–118; Simpson, *Reconstruction Presidents*, 157–62.

40. George B. Cheever to Elizabeth Washburn, 7 April 1869, 30 October 1870, 30 October 1871, 2 March 1872, 26 August 1872, 25 September 1872, 30 September 1873, 9, 26 November 1873, 3 August 1874, John E. Lee to George B. Cheever, 30 January 1873, CFP; Gilbert Haven, "Policy and Principle," *ZH*, 10 November 1870; "The National Decree," *ZH*, 7 April 1870, p. 163; *ZH*, 26 January; Gilbert Haven, "The Shot of Sumner," *ZH*, 6 April 1871, p. 162; *ZH*, 23 March 1871; William Gravely, *Gilbert Haven, Methodist Abolitionist: A Study in Race, Religion, and Reform, 1850–1880* (Nashville, Tenn.: Abingdon, 1973), 172–77, 200–201, 224–26; McPherson, "Grant or Greeley," 47; David W. Blight, *Frederick Douglass' Civil War: Keeping Faith in Jubilee* (Baton Rouge: Louisiana State University Press, 1989), 210–16; idem, *Race and Reunion*, 127–28; Simpson, *Reconstruction Presidents*, 160; McFeely, *Grant*, 383.

41. Democrats circulated rumors that Matthew Simpson supported Greeley, though likely that was untrue. Nelson Long to Matthew Simpson, 3 September 1872, William A. Gleason to Matthew Simpson, 11 September 1872, J. Jaquese and J. E. Parker to Matthew Simpson, 6 November 1872, J. McKown to Matthew Simpson, 21 November 1872, W. Little to Matthew Simpson, 4 December 1872, J. Chester to Matthew Simpson, 1 December 1872, James Wright to Matthew Simpson, 9 December 1872, Robert Allyn to Matthew Simpson, 14 December 1872, E. Dew to Matthew Simpson, 15 December 1872, MSP. See also Summers, *Era of Good Stealings*, 217.

42. George B. Cheever to Elizabeth Washburn, 2 October 1871, 26 August 1872, 30 October 1871, 25 September 1872, CFP. Sumner also feuded with Grant regarding arbitration of financial claims associated with the British-built Confederate raider *Alabama*

and the Santo Domingo annexation. Simpson, *Reconstruction Presidents*, 146–48; McFeely, *Grant*, 332–55; Gravely, *Gilbert Haven, Methodist Abolitionist*, 176–77; McPherson, "Grant or Greeley," 55–56; idem, *Ordeal by Fire: The Civil War and Reconstruction*, 3rd ed. (Boston: McGraw-Hill, 2001), 590–96.

43. George B. Cheever to Elizabeth Washburn, 21 November 1872, CFP; Gilbert Haven [?], "A New Era in Politics," *ZH*, 8 August 1872, p. 378.

44. George B. Cheever to Elizabeth Washburn, 19 August 1870, 9 November 1873, 23 November 1875 (quote), Alfred Roe to George B. Cheever, 6 November 1869, S. H. Fairchild to George B. Cheever, 11 July 1872, John Lee to George B. Cheever, 30 January 1873, CFP.

45. Agreement between Second Presbyterian Church and George B. Cheever, 16 June 1873, Letter to George B. Cheever, 27 June 1873, George B. Cheever to Henry T. Cheever, 9 July 1873, George B. Cheever to Elizabeth Washburn, 30 September 1873, 9 November 1873, CFP; Jacob Todd, "A Common Basis of Knowledge for Science and Religion," *MQR* 57 (January 1875): 27–49; A. Winchell, "God in the World," *MQR* 58 (July 1876): 511–29; Beadle, *"Gladness in the Works of God,"* 9–10, 13–16; Henry A. Boardman, *Christian Fidelity and Its Reward* (Philadelphia: Collins, 1876). Note particularly George B. Cheever to Elizabeth Washburn, 12 November 1874, CFP. Cheever increasingly stressed the importance of religious experience, which, in the evangelical version of the Scottish Common-Sense tradition, objectively complemented natural science: "In science men can become learned and great by the observation and authority of others; but in religion we owe every thing to experience and the most learned of men is nothing at all without it. God be praised that every man has to go himself to the fountain, and has the original fountain to go to, for his own facts." Cheever thus supported Dwight Moody's experiential revivalism. See Henry T. Cheever to George B. Cheever, 6 November 1875, George B. Cheever to Elizabeth Washburn, 23 November 1875, 26 February 1876, 3 April 1876, CFP. See also Timothy E. W. Gloege, "A Gilded Age Modernist: R. A. Torrey and the Roots of Contemporary Conservative Evangelicalism," in *American Evangelicalism: George Marsden and the State of American Religious History*, ed. Darren Dochuk, Thomas S. Kidd, and Kurt W. Peterson (Notre Dame, Ind.: University of Notre Dame Press, 2014), 204–5.

46. Summers, *Era of Good Stealings*, 224–27; Slap, *Doom of Reconstruction*, 183; "Mr. Greeley's Nomination," *NYE*, 9 May 1872, p. 4.

47. William M. Martin to Matthew Simpson, 28 July 1868, MSP; William Eaton Knox, *Our Sabbath and our Morals* (Elmira, N.Y.: Horace A. Brooks, 1873); Letter to Ulysses S. Grant, 6 November 1872, Alfred A. Green to Ulysses S. Grant, 31 July 1874, USGP. See James Turner, *Language, Religion, Knowledge: Past and Present* (Notre Dame, Ind.: University of Notre Dame Press, 2003), 31–32. Turner ascribes "public intellectual" to Charles Hodge, "[who] behaved like Zeus pronouncing his high judgments and hurling his thunderbolts accordingly on the inferior mortals below." While Hodge's erudition distinguished him from many evangelicals, his Olympian disposition did not.

48. "Civil Service Reform," *NYE*, 25 January 1872, p. 4; "Dr. McCosh on Civil Service Reform," *NYE*, 25 January 1872, p. 2; Ulysses S. Grant to James McCosh, 23 June 1870, *PUSG*, 20:437; James McCosh to Ulysses S. Grant, 16 May 1871, *PUSG*, 21:208; Ulysses S. Grant, Draft Annual Message, 4 December 1871, *PUSG*, 22:255n5; James McCosh to Ulys-

ses S. Grant, 4 May 1876, USGP. McCosh also praised Grant for settling the *Alabama* dispute between the United States and Great Britain—those "bulwarks of Protestantism and the Bible." Quoted in the *New York Herald*, 28 June 1871, *PUSG*, 22:41. See also J. David Hoeveler Jr., *James McCosh and the Scottish Intellectual Tradition* (Princeton, N.J.: Princeton University Press, 1981), 284.

49. "The Limits to Party Allegiance," "Recent College Graduates," *NYE*, 25 July 1872, p. 4; "President Woolsey on Demagoguism," *NYE*, 26 September 1872, p. 4; George M. Marsden, *The Soul of the American University: From Protestant Establishment to Established Unbelief* (New York: Oxford University Press, 1994), 123–33, 181–218.

50. George E. Martin to Ulysses S. Grant, 5 November 1872, Kittie Dovel to Ulysses S. Grant, Jennie Richey to Ulysses S. Grant, John A. Bidwell to Ulysses S. Grant, 6 November 1872, USGP; Blight, *Race and Reunion*, 127.

51. "The Election," *NYE*, 14 November 1872, p. 4; "Our National Thanksgiving," "A Noble Beginning: Civil Service Reform in Earnest," *NYE*, 28 November 1872, p. 4; Elizabeth D. Scott to Ulysses S. Grant, 7 November 1872, J. Bruce to Ulysses S. Grant, 6 November 1872, Letter to Ulysses S. Grant, 9 November 1872, USGP. See also Polly Shorter to Ulysses S. Grant, 6 November 1872, Letter to Ulysses S. Grant, 8 November 1872, Mr. Kelly [?] to Ulysses S. Grant, Samuel T. Spear to Ulysses S. Grant, 9 November 1872, Mr. Hodgson to Ulysses S. Grant, 10 November 1872, H. H. Moore to Mrs. Ulysses S. Grant, 2 January 1873, USGP.

52. I. C. Wynn, "The Political Responsibility of the Christian Citizen," *BQ* 7 (October 1873): 463–65, 471–74. Theodore L. Cuyler, "A Thought or Two about Money," *NYE*, 13 February 1873, p. 4, insisted that the republic needed a revived Christianity that would elect new Daniel Websters and Henry Clays. Though sensing that republican and free-labor ideals were becoming anachronistic in the face of large-scale industrialization, some still looked to idealized antebellum labor-capital relationships infused with evangelicalism. See Leonard Bacon, "Constitution-Making," *NE* 33 (January 1874): 17; Lyman Atwater, "General Assembly," *BRPR* (July 1870): 430; idem, "The Labor Question in its Economic and Christian Aspects," *PQPR* 1 (July 1872): 468–95; idem, "The Eight-Hour Movement," *NYE*, 13 June 1872, p. 1; Foner, *Reconstruction*, 512–25; May, *Protestant Churches and Industrial America*, 39–63.

53. Wynn, "Political Responsibility of the Christian Citizen," 474, 477. There were willing applicants, though the motives were perhaps dubious. See Edmund Gardy to Matthew Simpson, 20 February 1869, MSP; G. H. Hall to Ulysses S. Grant, 21 April 1870, D. H. Mueller, 3 May 1870, *PUSG*, 20:262. See also "The Scandals in Congress," *NYE*, 6 February 1873, p. 4; "The National Shame," *NYE*, 27 February 1873, p. 4. The paper responded to the Credit Mobilier scandal by fusing the covenantal with the republican: It stressed the necessity of a citizenry possessing a well-educated conscience, hoped that such "national humiliations may bring down our pride and make us willing to be guided by the hand of God," and longed for a higher "standard of virtue in our public men," as in "the good old times when no profit or personal advantage was counted worthy to be weighed for an instant in the scales against a man's integrity and honor."

54. John E. Walker to Ulysses S. Grant, 12 November 1872, Letter to Ulysses S. Grant, 6 November 1872, USGP.

55. Ulysses S. Grant, Inaugural Address, 4 March 1869, *PUSG*, 19:142; Robert Ellis Thompson, ed., *The Life of George H. Stuart, Written by Himself* (Philadelphia: J. M. Stoddart, 1890), 239; McFeely, *Grant*, 305. Note Ulysses S. Grant to George H. Stuart, 26 October 1872, *PUSG*, 23:270: "I do not believe our Creator ever placed different races of men on this earth with the view of having the stronger exert all of his energies in exterminating the weaker."

56. Ulysses S. Grant, Annual Message, 6 December 1869, *PUSG*, 20:38–39; idem, To Congress, 30 January 1871, *PUSG*, 21:152–53; Robert H. Keller Jr., *American Protestantism and United States Indian Policy, 1869–82* (Lincoln: University of Nebraska Press, 1983), 1–71; McFeely, *Grant*, 305–18; Henry E. Fritz, "The Making of Grant's Peace Policy," *Chronicles of Oklahoma* 37 (Winter 1959–60): 411–32; Richard R. Levine, "Indian Fighters and Indian Reformers: Grant's Peace Policy and the Conservative Consensus," *CWH* 31 (December 1985): 329–52; David Sim, "The Peace Policy of Ulysses S. Grant," *American Nineteenth Century History* 9 (September 2008): 241–68; R. Pierce Beaver, "The Churches and President Grant's Peace Policy," *Journal of Church and State* 4 (November 1962): 174–90; J. C. Imoda and Francis J. Weber, "Grant's Peace Policy: A Catholic Dissenter," *Montana: The Magazine of Western History* 19 (Winter 1969): 56–61.

57. Gilbert Haven [?], "Editorial Paragraphs—President Grant," *ZH*, 29 April 1869, p. 193; W. G. Kephart to Ulysses S. Grant, 17 August 1869, *PUSG*, 19:532–33. See also "Notes," *ZH*, 18 March 1869; "Correspondence—The Administration: Its High Water Marks," *ZH*, 6 May 1869, p. 209; "Editorial Paragraphs—General Sheridan," *ZH*, 24 March 1870, p. 133. McFeely, *Grant*, 308–9, helpfully summarizes Grant's aims: First, he determined to cease dealing with tribes as sovereign nations; second, he desired to treat Indians as individuals rather than tribal members; third, though in tension with the second aim, he sought to confine Indians to reservations; and finally, he looked to education as the means of enculturation. Significantly, Grant believed the Indians had legitimate claim to the land and were capable of cultural transformation.

58. J. T. Tukesbury to Ulysses S. Grant, June 1869, *PUSG*, 19:508; Joel Benton, "Two Methods with the Indians," *ZH*, 14 April 1870, p. 170; "Treat Indians as Men and Brethren," *ZH*, 16 June 1870, p. 283; Ulysses S. Grant, Endorsement, 22 September 1870, *PUSG*, 20:271; San Francisco Baptist Association of California to Ulysses S. Grant, November 1870, *PUSG*, 21:392; "What the President Says," *ZH*, 15 December 1870, p. 595; Frederic Dan Huntington, *Two Ways of Treating the Indian Problem* (New York: Indian Commission of the Protestant Episcopal Church, 1875); S. G. Arnold, "President Grant's Indian Policy," *MQR* 59 (July 1877): 409–30; *Proceedings of the Sixth Annual Meeting of the Lake Mohonk of Friends of the Indian* (Boston: Frank Wood, 1888), 7, 16, 27, 112; Lawrie Tutum, *Our Red Brothers and the Peace Policy of President Ulysses S. Grant* (Philadelphia: John C. Winston, 1899).

59. Charles Little and James B. Chase to Ulysses S. Grant, 15 June 1869, *PUSG*, 19:497. Note Grant's comments quoted in the *New York Herald*, 8 June 1871, *PUSG*, 22:78; H. L. Wayland, "Our Indian Troubles," *Independent*, 1 October 1868, p. 1; "The Indians," *Independent*, 22 October 1868, p. 4; Keller, *American Protestantism and United States Indian Policy*, 1–16; Michael C. Coleman, "Not Race, but Grace: Presbyterian Missionaries and American Indians, 1837–1893," *JAH* 67 (June 1980): 41–60; Douglas Firth Anderson,

"'More Conscience than Force': U.S. Indian Inspector William Vandever, Grant's Peace Policy, and Protestant Whiteness," *Journal of the Gilded Age and Progressive Era* 9 (April 2010): 167–96.

60. Gilbert Haven [?],"Our Indian Policy," *ZH*, 12 May 1870, pp. 222–23.

61. "The General Assembly," *Princeton Review* 42 (July 1870): 432–34. The report implied that the Civil War could have been avoided had people approached slavery with similar caution.

62. "The New Indian Policy," *NYE*, 21 March 1872, p. 1; "Alaska as a Mission Field," *NYE*, 27 January 1870, p. 2; "Success of Our Indian Policy," *NYE*, 21 November 1872, p. 4; "Another Witness to Our Indian Policy," *NYE*, 5 December 1872; "The Indian Massacre," *NYE*, 17 April 1873, p. 4.

63. Francis. F. Ellinwood, "A Plea for the Indians," *NYE*, 26 June 1873, p. 1; "The Indian Question," *NYE*, 24 April 1873, p. 4.

64. Arnold, "President Grant's Indian Policy," 410, 413, 427–29.

65. Hiram Mattison, "Romanism in the United States," *MQR* 50 (October 1868): 508–9; idem, "The Decline of Romanism," *MQR* 50 (July 1868): 425–50; idem, *The Impending Crisis of 1860* (New York: Mason Brothers, 1858); idem, *Louisa Picquet, the Octoroon; or, Inside Views of Southern Domestic Life* (New York, 1861); idem, *Popular Amusements: An Appeal to Methodists, In Regard to the Evils of Card-Playing, Billiards, Dancing, Theatre-Going, etc.* (New York: Carlton and Porter, 1867); "The Outlook," *NYE*, 24 March 1870, p. 4; "The Mob Element and the Laws," *NYE*, 11 August 1870, p. 4.

66. Edwin Harwood, "Romanism," *NE* 28 (July 1869): 519–20; Leonard W. Bacon, "Forgery in Polemics: The Secret Instructions of the Jesuits," *NE* 28 (July 1869): 533–61; idem, "Moral Results of Romanism," *NE* 28 (July 1869): 561–75; Ray Palmer, "The Reformation Not Yet Finished," *Independent*, 18 June 1868, p. 1; Jeremiah E. Rankin, "Bible Labors among the Papists," *Independent*, 1 October 1868, p. 1; "The Triumph of Protestantism," *ZH*, 10 June 1869, pp. 270–71; E. H. Gillett, "Papal Infallibility and the 19th Century," *APTR* n.s. 2 (January 1870): 636–58; Henry B. Smith, "Roman Letters on the Vatican Council," *APTR* n.s. 2 (January 1870): 667–79; J. M. Macdonald, "The Temporal Power of the Pope," *BRPR* 43 (January 1871): 127–43; J. Colver Wightman, "Papal Infallibility," *BQ* 8 (January 1874): 37–49; Heman Lincoln, "The Vatican Council and Civil Allegiance," *BQ* 9 (April 1875): 200–215; Alvah Hovey, "Progress of a Century," *BQ* 10 (October 1876): 473. John McGreevy's *Catholicism and American Freedom* (New York: W. W. Norton, 2003) locates the conflict within a broader struggle between Ultramontane Roman Catholicism and Western liberalism. Regarding the struggle throughout Anglo-American history, see Peter Toon, ed., *Puritans, the Millennium and the Future of Israel: Puritan Eschatology 1600 to 1660* (Cambridge: James Clarke, 1970); Linda Colley, *Britons: Forging the Nation, 1707–1837* (New Haven, Conn.: Yale University Press, 1992), 11–54; Jenny Franchot, *Roads to Rome: The Antebellum Protestant Encounter with Catholicism* (Berkeley: University of California Press, 1994); Carwardine, *Evangelicals and Politics*, 80–89; William E. Gienapp, "Nativism and the Creation of a Republican Majority in the North before the Civil War," *JAH* 72 (December 1985): 529–59; Tyler G. Anbinder, *Nativism and Slavery: The Northern Know Nothings and the Politics of the 1850s* (New York: Oxford University Press, 1992); Higham, *Strangers in the Land*, 3–11.

67. George B. Cheever to Elizabeth Washburn, 19 August 1870, CFP; "Rome Reprobate," *ZH*, 18 August 1870, pp. 391–92.

68. "Protestantism, Its Dangers and Its Duties: Romish Tyranny Our First National Danger," *ZH*, 7 May 1868, p. 222; Granville Moody, *Popery and Its Aims: A Tract for the Times* (Cincinnati: Hitchcock and Walden, 1871), 11, 20. See also "Church and State," *Independent*, 7 May 1868, p. 4; "Papal Audacity," *ZH*, 21 May 1868, p. 241; "Rome's Plan to Subjugate America," *ZH*, 28 May 1868, p. 259; R. M. Hatfield, "Romanism in the United States," *Independent*, 10 September 1868, p. 1; "Shall the Bible or the Pope Be School-Master?," *ZH*, 16 December 1869, p. 590; "The Council at Rome," *NYE*, 6 January 1870, p. 4; Thomas H. Skinner, *The Progress of the Human Race* (Cincinnati: Gazette Company Print, 1875).

69. Beadle, *"Gladness in the Works of God,"* 17; Mrs. S. B. Perry to George B. Cheever, 7 April 1876, George B. Cheever to Elizabeth Washburn, 7 January 1876, CFP. Cf. McAfee, *Religion, Race, and Reconstruction*; R. Laurence Moore, "Bible Reading and Nonsectarian Schooling: The Failure of Religious Instruction in Nineteenth-Century Public Education," *JAH* 86 (March 2000): 1581–99; idem, "What Children Did Not Learn in School: The Intellectual Quickening of Young Americans in the Nineteenth Century," *CH* 68 (March 1999): 42–61.

70. "Recent Publications on the School Question," *BRPR* 42 (April 1870): 317, 320. The "Cincinnati Bible War" began in November 1869 when the school board attempted to end Bible reading; in 1873 Ohio's Supreme Court upheld the practice. Robert Michaelsen, "Common School, Common Religion? A Case Study in Church-State Relations, Cincinnati, 1869–70," *CH* 38 (June 1969): 201–17; McAfee, *Religion, Race, and Reconstruction*, 27–56. Henry Ward Beecher and Samuel Spear argued that ending the practice would not threaten a homogenizing common-school system; however, they did not assent to a division of school funds, while agreeing that Catholics did threaten Christian America. See Samuel T. Spear, *The Bible in Public Schools* (New York: Wm. C. Martin, 1870); idem, *Religion and the State; or, The Bible and the Public Schools* (New York: Dodd, Mead, 1876); Henry Ward Beecher, *Patriotic Addresses: America and England, from the 1850s to 1885, on Slavery, the Civil War, and the Development of Civil Liberty in the United States* (New York: Fords, Howard, and Hubert, 1887), 750–71; George R. Rudd, *The Bible in Our Public Schools* (Lyons, N.Y.: Office of the Republican, 1870); Gilbert Haven [?], "The Cincinnati Board of Education," *ZH*, 11 November 1869, p. 529; idem [?], "Down with the Common Schools," *ZH*, 2 June 1870, pp. 258–59.

71. William Aikman, "The Romanists' Attempt against the Public School Money Undemocratic," *NYE*, 6 January 1870, p. 1; "Recent Publications on the School Question," 318. See also McAfee, *Religion, Race, and Reconstruction*, 31–34; J. B. Bittinger, "Responsibility of Society for the Causes of Crime," *BRPR* 43 (January 1871): 18–36; Walter H. Lowrie, "The Philosophy of Civil Government," *BRPR* 43 (January 1871): 61–82; Charles Hodge, "Preaching the Gospel to the Poor," *BRPR* 43 (January 1871): 83–95; N. S. Burton, "The Higher Education and the State," *BQ* 8 (October 1874): 482.

72. "Recent Publications on the School Question," 322; George B. Cheever to Elizabeth Washburn, 21 December 1875, CFP; William C. Conant, "The Bible and the State," *BQ* 5 (July 1871): 288.

73. William H. Boole, *Our Bible, Our Schools, and Our Flag: One and Inseparable*, 3rd ed. (Brooklyn: L. Darbee and Son, 1870) 10, 12, 23; idem, *"Shall Our Common School System Be Maintained as It Is?"* (New York: N. Tibbals, 1870); Gilbert Haven, "America Protestant," *ZH*, 11 May 1871, p. 222.

74. Mears, "Our Protestant Nationality." Grant's nomination of Philadelphia Presbyterian William Strong to the Supreme Court heartened Mears; Strong was involved in the National Reform Association, which sought a reference to Jesus Christ in the Constitution. See John W. Mears, "New Supreme Court Judge," *NYE*, 10 March 1870, p. 1; McAfee, *Religion, Race, and Reconstruction*, 51–52. See chapter 1, note 59.

75. Newman was Grant's closest clerical friend, according to his aide Adam Badeau. Grant communicated frequently with Newman, apparently assisted him in attaining the Senate's chaplaincy, and appointed him as Inspector of United States Consulates and to the Board of Visitors to the Naval Academy. Additionally, the Grants attended Newman's church; the two families spent time together; and Grant gave money to Methodist causes. Ralph E. Morrow, *Northern Methodism and Reconstruction* (East Lansing: Michigan State University Press, 1956) 216–17; Keller, *American Protestantism and United States Indian Policy*, 37; McFeely, *Grant*, 503; J. P. Newman to George M. Robeson, 11 February 1871, *PUSG*, 21:445–46.

76. Newman, *Religious Liberty*, 7–8, 13, 24, 28–29. Newman also hoped that three great Protestant heads of state—England's Gladstone, Germany's Bismarck, and America's Grant—would turn back the global Catholic threat. See McGreevy, *Catholicism and American Freedom*, 98–103. Regarding Catholics, the war, and America, see Randall M. Miller, "Catholic Religion, Irish Ethnicity, and the Civil War," in *Religion and the American Civil War*, ed. Randall M. Miller, Harry S. Stout, and Charles Reagan Wilson (New York: Oxford University Press, 1998), 261–96; Christian G. Samito, "Thomas F. Meagher, Patrick R. Guiney, and the Meaning of the Civil War for Irish America," in *So Conceived and So Dedicated: Intellectual Life in the Civil War–Era North*, ed. Lorien Foote and Kanisorn Wongsrichanalai (New York: Fordham University Press, 2015), 193–216; William Kurtz, "'This Most Unholy and Destructive War': Catholic Intellectuals and the Limits of Catholic Patriotism," in *So Conceived and So Dedicated: Intellectual Life in the Civil War–Era North*, ed. Lorien Foote and Kanisorn Wongsrichanalai (New York: Fordham University Press, 2015), 216–35.

77. Hawley quoted in Gillette, *Retreat from Reconstruction*, 287. Simpson, *Reconstruction Presidents*, 188, contends that Grant "was casting about for new issues" to unite Republicans divided over Reconstruction. Anbinder, "Ulysses S. Grant, Nativist," contends that Grant perceived Catholicism as a threat from the 1840s until his death in 1885. Cf. Keller, *American Protestantism and United States Indian Policy*, 24–25.

78. Ulysses S. Grant, Speech, 29 September 1875, *PUSG*, 26:342–44. Some believed Newman was the author and that Grant, contemplating a third term, was pandering to evangelicals. Morrow, *Northern Methodism and Reconstruction*, 219; McAfee, *Religion, Race, and Reconstruction*, 192–202; McGreevy, *Catholicism and American Freedom*, 91–93.

79. Letter to Ulysses S. Grant, October 1875, Letter to Ulysses S. Grant, 30 September 1875, Edward W. Whitaker to Ulysses S. Grant, 30 September 1875, James A. Briggs to

Ulysses S. Grant, 1 October 1875, USGP. See also Samuel Goddard to Ulysses S. Grant, 14 October 1875, Theodore Bourne to Ulysses S. Grant, 30 October 1875, H. O. Wagoner Sr., to Ulysses S. Grant, 16 November 1875, USGP.

80. Ulysses S. Grant, Annual Message, 7 December 1875, *PUSG*, 26:387–88; "*Vivat Respublica*" to Ulysses S. Grant, 9 December 1875, USGP.

81. Ulysses S. Grant, Annual Message, 7 December 1875, *PUSG*, 26:386; Gravely, *Gilbert Haven, Methodist Abolitionist*, 224–28; Simpson, *Reconstruction Presidents*, 184–96; McFeely, *Grant*, 440; Frederick Douglass to Orville Babcock, 31 May 1875, USGP; Dee Brown, *The Year of the Century: 1876* (New York: Charles Scribner's Sons, 1966), 14–16, 125–26; Foner, *Reconstruction*, 564–65; Gillette, *Retreat from Reconstruction*, 300–301.

82. Granville Moody, *A Life's Retrospect: Autobiography of Rev. Granville Moody, D.D. (Brigadier General by Brevet)*, ed. Sylvester Weeks (Cincinnati: Cranston and Howe, 1890), 273–80. See also idem, *Memorial Days: A Centennial Sermon* (Cincinnati: Hitchcock and Walden, 1875), a similar covenantal sermon from September 1875; Frederick Merrick, *Religion and the State: A Centennial Sermon* (Cincinnati: Hitchcock and Walden, 1875), which exemplifies covenantal thinking from another Methodist; George Dana Boardman, *Conservative Progress* (Philadelphia: James B. Chandler, 1876), which recounts the divine narrative from a Baptist viewpoint.

83. Ulysses S. Grant, Proclamation, 26 June 1876, *PUSG*, 27:156; George B. Cheever to Elizabeth Washburn, 4 July 1876, CFP. See also A. B. Williamson to Ulysses S. Grant, 1 July 1876, USGP.

84. Brown, *Year of the Century*, 168.

85. Ulysses S. Grant to D. H. Chamberlain, 26 July 1876, in *Major Problems in the Civil War and Reconstruction*, 2nd ed., ed. Michael Perman (Boston: Houghton Mifflin, 1998), 408; Simpson, *Reconstruction Presidents*, 190; Rable, *But There Was No Peace*, 166–69; Foner, *Reconstruction*, 570–72; Gillette, *Retreat from Reconstruction*, 306–9.

86. Lindsay quoted in Daniel W. Stowell, "Why 'Redemption'? Religion and the End of Reconstruction, 1869–1877," in *Vale of Tears: New Essays on Religion and Reconstruction*, ed. Edward J. Blum and W. Scott Poole (Macon, Ga.: Mercer University Press, 2005), 145; Harvey, "That Was about Equalization after Freedom," 89–92; Foner, *Reconstruction*, 587–601; Michael Perman, *The Road to Redemption: Southern Politics, 1869–1879* (Chapel Hill: University of North Carolina Press, 1984); Michael Lemann, *Redemption: The Last Battle of the Civil War* (New York: Farrar, Straus and Giroux, 2006).

87. J. F. Chaffee to Ulysses S. Grant, 2 June 1876, USGP. See also George A. Peltz to Ulysses S. Grant, 19 April 1876, J. Henderson to Ulysses S. Grant, 10 May 1876, Mr. Gore to Ulysses S. Grant, 20 May 1876, USGP.

88. Simpson, *Reconstruction Presidents*, 193, 196; Gillette, *Retreat from Reconstruction*, 331–32; Roy Morris, *Fraud of the Century: Rutherford B. Hayes, Samuel Tilden, and the Stolen Election of 1876* (New York: Simon and Schuster, 2003).

89. Citizens of Baltimore to Ulysses S. Grant, 8 December 1876; McFeely, *Grant*, 441–42. See also Charles Milne to Ulysses S. Grant, 20 November 1876, John L. Pennington to Ulysses S. Grant, 20 November 1876, John L. Hooker to Ulysses S. Grant, 27 November 1876, J. Cory to J. D. Cameron, 27 November 1876, Julie R. Seavey to Ulysses S. Grant, 30 November 1876, Calvin Phelps to Ulysses S. Grant, 30 November 1876, P. N.

Davis to Ulysses S. Grant, 7 December 1876, John R. [?] to Ulysses S. Grant, 9 December 1876, L. Griggs to Ulysses S. Grant, 11 December 1876, M. Force to Ulysses S. Grant, 10 February 1877, John D. Lang to Ulysses S. Grant, 27 February 1877, E. Orr to Ulysses S. Grant, 3 March 1877, John W. Paine Jr. to Ulysses S. Grant, 4 March 1877, C. C. Parker to Ulysses S. Grant, 5 March 1877, USGP.

90. "The Two Presidents," *Christian Recorder*, 8 March 1877, 4. Note the recent celebratory remarks in "The Racial Views of Ulysses S. Grant," *Journal of Blacks in Higher Education* 66 (Winter 2009/2010): 26–27.

Conclusion: "The Nation Still in Danger"

1. Michael E. Strieby, "The Nation Still in Danger," in *The Nation Still in Danger; or, Ten Years after the War, A Plea by the American Missionary Association, with Confirmatory Articles* (New York: American Missionary Association, 1875), 3.

2. *Proceedings of Republican National Convention, 1876*, quoted in William Gillette, *Retreat from Reconstruction, 1869–1879* (Baton Rouge: Louisiana State University Press, 1979), 304.

3. Paul Harvey, *Freedom's Coming: Religious Culture and the Shaping of the South from the Civil War through the Civil Rights Era* (Chapel Hill: University of North Carolina Press, 2005), chap. 1; Edward L. Ayers, *The Promise of the New South: Life after Reconstruction* (New York: Oxford University Press, 1992), chap. 7; Kimberly R. Kellison, "Parameters of Promiscuity: Sexuality, Violence, and Religion in Upcountry South Carolina," in *Vale of Tears: New Essays on Religion and Reconstruction*, ed. Edward J. Blum and W. Scott Poole (Macon, Ga.: Mercer University Press, 2005), 15–35; W. Scott Poole, "Confederate Apocalypse: Theology and Violence in the Reconstruction South," in *Vale of Tears: New Essays on Religion and Reconstruction*, ed. Edward J. Blum and W. Scott Poole (Macon, Ga.: Mercer University Press, 2005), 36–52; Darren E. Grem, "Sam Jones, Sam Hose, and the Theology of Racial Violence," *GHQ* 90 (Spring 2006): 35–61; Mark A. Noll, *God and Race in American Politics: A Short History* (Princeton, N.J.: Princeton University Press, 2008), 87–89.

4. See C. Vann Woodward, *Reunion and Reaction: The Compromise of 1877 and the End of Reconstruction* (Boston: Little, Brown, 1951); Eric Foner, *Reconstruction: America's Unfinished Revolution, 1863–1877* (New York: Harper and Row, 1988), 575–87; Gillette, *Retreat from Reconstruction*, 318–34.

5. Martin S. Howard, *Address in Connection with Funeral Services in Honor of President James A. Garfield* (Springfield, Mass.: Weaver, Shipman, 1881), 3, 10. On Garfield see Allan Peskin, *Garfield: A Biography* (Kent, Ohio: Kent State University Press, 1978); Justus D. Doenecke, *The Presidencies of James A. Garfield and Chester A. Arthur* (Lawrence: Regents Press of Kansas, 1981); Kenneth D. Ackerman, *Dark Horse: The Surprise Election and Political Murder of President James A. Garfield* (New York: Carroll and Graf, 2003).

6. Henry Christopher McCook, *Garfield Memorial Sermons, Preached in the Tabernacle Presbyterian Church, Philadelphia, on the Occasions of the Assault, Death, and Burial of James Abram Garfield, Twentieth President of the United States* (Philadelphia: Lippincott's Press for the Congregation, 1881), 24. Regarding Garfield as exemplary, see

Caleb Davis Bradlee, *A Sermon* (Boston: Nathan Sawyer and Son, 1881), 11–13; Julius Orrin Converse, *Garfield: The Ideal Man* (Cleveland: William W. Williams, 1882), 10–13; Cyrus Huntington, *"A Great Man Fallen in Israel"* (Dover, Del.: James Kirk and Sons, 1881), 6–7; James McLeod, *A Sermon on the Death of Garfield* (Buffalo: Matthews, Northrup, 1881), 9–11; C. P. Osborne, *General James A. Garfield* (New Haven, Conn.: Hoggson and Robinson, 1881), 3–4, 9.

7. McCook, *Garfield Memorial Sermons*, 16–17.

8. Charles H. Parkhurst, *Sermon Preached by Rev. Charles H. Parkhurst, D. D., on Sabbath Morning following the Death of President James A. Garfield (September 25, 1881) at the Madison Square Presbyterian Church, New York City* (New York: Sharps, 1881), 12.

9. Elias Nason, *A Discourse on the Death of James Abram Garfield* (Boston: Moses H. Sargent and Sons, 1881), 4. See also Edwin B. Palmer, *A Sermon Suggested by the Death of President Garfield* (Boston: Lyman Rhodes, 1881), 14; Azel Washburn Wild, *On the Death of James Abram Garfield, President of the United States* (St. Johnsbury, Vt.: C. M. Stone, 1881); George Dana Boardman, *An Address in Commemoration of James Abram Garfield* (Philadelphia: Chandler Printing House, 1881), 19; Philip A. Strobel, "Sermon by Rev. P. A. Strobel," in George K. Ward et al., *Memorial Sermons* (Dansville, N.Y.: A. O. Bunnell, 1881), 23–26; George B. Spalding, *Discourse on the Occasion of the Death of President Garfield* (Dover, N.H.: Morning Star Job Printing Office, 1881), 22–24; George Leon Walker, *A Sermon on the Death of President Garfield* (Hartford, Conn.: Case, Lockwood and Brainard, 1881), 12–14.

10. The modernist/liberal challenge to evangelical orthodoxy involved a number of interrelated factors, including Darwinian evolutionary biology, geological findings regarding the earth's age, Comtean positivism, historicism, Romanticism, the experiential emphasis of Friedrich Schleiermacher, Kantian idealism, and higher criticism. See George M. Marsden, *Fundamentalism and American Culture: The Shaping of Twentieth-Century Evangelicalism, 1870–1925*, 2nd ed. (New York: Oxford University Press, 2006); idem, *The Soul of the American University: From Protestant Establishment to Established Nonbelief* (New York: Oxford University Press, 1994), 113–218; James Turner, *Without God, without Creed: The Origins of Unbelief in America* (Baltimore: Johns Hopkins University Press, 1985), 171–269; Bruce Kuklick, *Churchmen and Philosophers: From Jonathan Edwards to John Dewey* (New Haven, Conn.: Yale University Press, 1985), 128–261; Mark A. Noll, *The Scandal of the Evangelical Mind* (Grand Rapids, Mich.: Wm. B. Eerdmans, 1994), 109–45; William R. Hutchison, *The Modernist Impulse in American Protestantism* (Cambridge, Mass.: Harvard University Press, 1976), 1–110; Charles D. Cashdollar, *The Transformation of Theology, 1830–1890: Positivism and Protestant Thought in Britain and America* (Princeton, N.J.: Princeton University Press, 1989); Paul Jerome Croce, *Science and Religion in the Era of William James: Eclipse of Certainty, 1820–1880* (Chapel Hill: University of North Carolina Press, 1995); Peter Novick, *That Noble Dream: The "Objectivity Question" and the American Historical Profession* (Cambridge: Cambridge University Press, 1988), 1–46; Edward J. Larson, *Summer for the Gods: The Scopes Trial and America's Continuing Debate over Science and Religion* (Cambridge, Mass.: Harvard University Press, 1997).

11. McCook, *Garfield Memorial Sermons*, 37, 41. Note idem, *Some Characteristics of*

Abraham Lincoln (Philadelphia: I. Price, 1901). McCook, known for his research into ants and spiders, later became Vice President of the American Entomological Society and the American Academy of Natural Sciences. See idem, *The Gospel in Nature: A Series of Popular Discourses on Scripture Truths derived from Facts of Nature* (Philadelphia: Allen, Lane and Scott, 1887); idem, *Nature's Craftsmen: Popular Studies of Ants and Other Insects* (New York: Harper and Brothers, 1907).

12. Strobel, "Sermon by Rev. P. A. Strobel," 22.

13. Parkhurst, *Sermon*, 10–11.

14. Huntington, *"Great Man Fallen in Israel,"* 11.

15. Byron Sunderland, *"Our Republic in the Family of Nations"* (Washington, D.C.: R. O. Polkinhorn, 1885), 8.

16. Gaines M. Foster, *Moral Reconstruction: Christian Lobbyists and the Federal Legislation of Morality, 1865–1920* (Chapel Hill: University of North Carolina Press, 2002); idem, "The End of Slavery and the Origins of the Bible Belt," in *Vale of Tears: New Essays on Religion and Reconstruction*, ed. Edward J. Blum and W. Scott Poole (Macon, Ga.: Mercer University Press, 2005), 147–63; Edward J. Blum, *Reforging the White Republic: Race, Religion, and American Nationalism, 1865–1898* (Baton Rouge: Louisiana State University Press, 2005), 120–45; Michael S. Hamilton, "The Interdenominational Evangelicalism of D. L. Moody and the Problem of Fundamentalism," in *American Evangelicalism: George Marsden and the State of American Religious History*, ed. Darren Dochuk, Thomas S. Kidd, and Kurt W. Peterson (Notre Dame, Ind.: University of Notre Dame Press, 2014), 235; Michael Kazin, *A Godly Hero: The Life of William Jennings Bryan* (New York: Alfred A. Knopf, 2006), 45–108; George M. Marsden, *Religion and American Culture*, 2nd ed. (Orlando, Fla.: Harcourt, 2001), 123–30; Noll, *God and Race*, 77–86.

17. Joan Waugh, *U. S. Grant: American Hero, American Myth* (Chapel Hill: University of North Carolina Press, 2009), 216–17; idem, "'Pageantry of Woe': The Funeral of Ulysses S. Grant," *CWH* 51 (June 2005): 151–74.

18. See Paul R. Meyer, "The Fear of Cultural Decline: Josiah Strong's Thought about Reform and Expansion," *CH* 42 (September 1973): 396–405.

19. Robert T. Handy, "The Protestant Quest for a Christian America, 1830–1930," *CH* 22 (March 1953): 8–20; idem, *A Christian America: Protestant Hopes and Historical Realities*, 2nd ed. (New York: Oxford University Press, 1984), 57–100; Marsden, *Fundamentalism and American Culture*, 4, 206–11; idem, *Religion and American Culture*, passim; R. Laurence Moore, *Religious Outsiders and the Making of Americans* (New York: Oxford University Press, 1986), 150–72; Douglas W. Frank, *Less Than Conquerors: How Evangelicals Entered the Twentieth Century* (Grand Rapids, Mich.: Wm. B. Eerdmans, 1986). Some southern evangelicals became fundamentalists—notably symbolized by the Scopes trial—but southern evangelicals generally would not become fully "Christian Americans" again until after the civil rights movement and the turmoil of the 1960s. Marsden, *Religion and American Culture*, 179, 191–97; idem, *Fundamentalism and American Culture*, 184–89, 236–37; Noll, *God and Race*, 156–64; Foster, "End of Slavery and the Origins of the Bible Belt"; Darren Dochuk, "Evangelicalism Becomes Southern, Politics Becomes Evangelical," in *Religion and American Politics: From the Colonial Period to the Present*, 2nd ed., ed. Mark A. Noll and Luke E. Harlow (New York: Oxford University

Press, 2007), 297–326; idem, *From Bible Belt to Sunbelt: Plain-Folk Religion, Grassroots Politics, and the Rise of Evangelical Conservatism* (New York: W. W. Norton, 2011); Rick Ostrander, "The Southernization of the Evangelical Mind," in *American Evangelicalism: George Marsden and the State of American Religious History*, ed. Darren Dochuk, Thomas S. Kidd, and Kurt W. Peterson (Notre Dame, Ind.: University of Notre Dame Press, 2014), 357–78.

20. Joel A. Carpenter, *Revive Us Again: The Reawakening of American Fundamentalism* (New York: Oxford University Press, 1997), 5–6, 116.

21. Regarding neo-evangelicalism and the 1950s, see George M. Marsden, *Reforming Fundamentalism: Fuller Seminary and the New Evangelicalism* (Grand Rapids, Mich.: Wm. B. Eerdmans, 1987), 60–63; Garth M. Rosell, *The Surprising Work of God: Harold John Ockenga, Billy Graham, and the Rebirth of Evangelicalism* (Grand Rapids, Mich.: Baker, 2008); Grant Wacker, *America's Pastor: Billy Graham and the Shaping of a Nation* (Cambridge, Mass.: Belknap Press of Harvard University Press, 2014); Michael G. Long, *Billy Graham and the Beloved Community: America's Evangelist and the Dream of Martin Luther King, Jr.* (New York: Palgrave Macmillan, 2006); John G. Turner, *Bill Bright and Campus Crusade for Christ: The Renewal of Evangelicalism in Postwar America* (Chapel Hill: University of North Carolina Press, 2008); Stephen J. Whitfield, *The Culture of the Cold War*, 2nd ed. (Baltimore: Johns Hopkins University Press, 1996), 77–100; Kevin M. Cruse, *One Nation under God: How Corporate America Invented Christian America* (New York: Basic Books, 2015).

22. See John W. Jeffries, "The 'Quest for National Purpose' of 1960," *AQ* 30 (Autumn 1978): 451–70; Mark Silk, "Notes on the Judeo-Christian Tradition in America," *AQ* 36 (Spring 1984): 65–85; K. Healan Gaston, "The Cold War Romance of Religious Authenticity: Will Herberg, William F. Buckley Jr., and the Rise of the New Right," *JAH* 99 (March 2013): 1133–58; George M. Marsden, *The Twilight of the American Enlightenment: The 1950s and the Crisis of Liberal Belief* (New York: Basic Books, 2014).

23. The literature on the Religious Right is voluminous; see Noll, *Race and God*, 136–37, 197n2; William Martin, *With God on Our Side: The Rise of the Religious Right in America* (New York: Broadway, 1996); Ruth Murray Brown, *For a "Christian America": A History of the Religious Right* (New York: Prometheus Books, 2002); Marsden, *Fundamentalism and American Culture*, 231–57; idem, "Return to Christian America: A New Political Agenda?" in *The Search for Christian America*, ed. Mark A. Noll, Nathan O. Hatch, and George M. Marsden (Westchester, Ill.: Crossway, 1983), 125–44; David Hollinger, "The Secularization Question and the United States in the Twentieth Century," *CH* 70 (March 2001): 123–32; Gabriel Fackre, ed. *Judgment Day at the White House: A Critical Declaration Exploring Moral Issues and the Political Use and Abuse of Religion* (Grand Rapids, Mich.: Wm. B. Eerdmans, 1999); Gary Scott Smith, *Faith and the Presidency: From George Washington to George W. Bush* (New York: Oxford University Press, 2006), 325–413. Cf. David R. Swartz, *Moral Minority: The Evangelical Left in an Age of Conservatism* (Philadelphia: University of Pennsylvania Press, 2012).

24. Peter Marshall and David Manuel, *The Light and the Glory: Did God Have a Plan for America?* (Old Tappan, N.J.: Fleming H. Revell, 1977); Mark A. Noll, "The Search for Christian America: Introduction," in *The Search for Christian America*, ed. Mark A. Noll,

Nathan O. Hatch, and George M. Marsden (Westchester, Ill.: Crossway, 1983), 13–27; Isaac Kramnick and R. Laurence Moore, *The Godless Constitution: The Case against Religious Correctness* (New York: W. W. Norton, 1996); Christian Smith, *Christian America? What Evangelicals Really Want* (Berkeley: University of California Press, 2000); Stephen H. Webb, *American Providence: Nation with a Mission* (New York: Continuum, 2004).

25. Marsden, *Fundamentalism and American Culture*, 247; Rod Dreher, *The Benedict Option: A Strategy for Christians in a Post-Christian Nation* (New York: Sentinel, 2017).

26. Eric Foner, *Who Owns History? Rethinking the Past in a Changing World* (New York: Hill and Wang, 2002), 149–66.

27. Martin E. Marty, *The One and the Many: America's Struggle for the Common Good* (Cambridge, Mass.: Harvard University Press, 1997); David Hollinger, *Postethnic America: Beyond Multiculturalism*, rev. ed. (New York: Basic Books, 2000); Michael O. Emerson and Christian Smith, *Divided by Faith: Evangelical Religion and the Problem of Race in America* (New York: Oxford University Press, 2000); Mark A. Noll, *American Evangelical Christianity: An Introduction* (Oxford: Blackwell, 2001), 183–206; idem, *God and Race*, 176–81; James Brewer Stewart, "Reconsidering the Abolitionists in an Age of Fundamentalist Politics," *JER* 26 (Spring 2006): 1–23; John West, *The Politics of Revelation and Reason: Religion and Civic Life in the New Nation* (Lawrence: University Press of Kansas, 1996); John M. Murrin, "Fundamental Values, the Founding Fathers, and the Constitution," in *To Form a More Perfect Union: The Critical Ideas of the Constitution*, ed. Herman Belz, Ronald Hoffman, and Peter J. Albert (Charlottesville: University Press of Virginia, 1992), 1–37; Isaac Kramnick, "'Great National Discussion': The Discourse of Politics in 1787," *WMQ*, 3rd ser. 45 (January 1988): 3–32; James T. Kloppenberg, "The Virtues of Liberalism: Christianity, Republicanism, and Ethics in Early American Discourse," *JAH* 74 (June 1987): 9–37; Jon Meacham, *American Gospel: God, the Founding Fathers, and the Making of a Nation* (New York: Random House, 2006); Frank Lambert, *The Founding Fathers and the Place of Religion in America* (Princeton, N.J.: Princeton University Press, 2003); Edwin S. Gaustad, *Faith of Our Fathers: Religion and the New Nation* (San Francisco: Harper and Row, 1987).

Index

The North's Civil War
Andrew L. Slap, series editor

Anita Palladino, ed., *Diary of a Yankee Engineer: The Civil War Story of John H. Westervelt, Engineer, 1st New York Volunteer Engineer Corps.*

Herman Belz, *Abraham Lincoln, Constitutionalism, and Equal Rights in the Civil War Era.*

Earl J. Hess, *Liberty, Virtue, and Progress: Northerners and Their War for the Union.* Second revised edition, with a new introduction by the author.

William L. Burton, *Melting Pot Soldiers: The Union's Ethnic Regiments.*

Hans L. Trefousse, *Carl Schurz: A Biography.*

Stephen W. Sears, ed., *Mr. Dunn Browne's Experiences in the Army: The Civil War Letters of Samuel W. Fiske.*

Jean H. Baker, *Affairs of Party: The Political Culture of Northern Democrats in the Mid-Nineteenth Century.*

Frank L. Klement, *The Limits of Dissent: Clement L. Vallandigham and the Civil War.* With a new introduction by Steven K. Rogstad.

Lawrence N. Powell, *New Masters: Northern Planters during the Civil War and Reconstruction.*

John A. Carpenter, *Sword and Olive Branch: Oliver Otis Howard.*

Thomas F. Schwartz, ed., *"For a Vast Future Also": Essays from the* Journal of the Abraham Lincoln Association.

Mark De Wolfe Howe, ed., *Touched with Fire: Civil War Letters and Diary of Oliver Wendell Holmes, Jr.* With a new introduction by David Burton.

Harold Adams Small, ed., *The Road to Richmond: The Civil War Letters of Major Abner R. Small of the 16th Maine Volunteers*. With a new introduction by Earl J. Hess.

Eric A. Campbell, ed., *"A Grand Terrible Dramma": From Gettysburg to Petersburg: The Civil War Letters of Charles Wellington Reed*. Illustrated by Reed's Civil War sketches.

Herbert Mitgang, ed., *Abraham Lincoln: A Press Portrait*.

Harold Holzer, ed., *Prang's Civil War Pictures: The Complete Battle Chromos of Louis Prang*.

Harold Holzer, ed., *State of the Union: New York and the Civil War*.

Paul A. Cimbala and Randall M. Miller, eds., *Union Soldiers and the Northern Home Front: Wartime Experiences, Postwar Adjustments*.

Mark A. Snell, *From First to Last: The Life of Major General William B. Franklin*.

Paul A. Cimbala and Randall M. Miller, eds., *An Uncommon Time: The Civil War and the Northern Home Front*.

John Y. Simon and Harold Holzer, eds., *The Lincoln Forum: Rediscovering Abraham Lincoln*.

Thomas F. Curran, *Soldiers of Peace: Civil War Pacifism and the Postwar Radical Peace Movement*.

Kyle S. Sinisi, *Sacred Debts: State Civil War Claims and American Federalism, 1861–1880*.

Russell L. Johnson, *Warriors into Workers: The Civil War and the Formation of Urban-Industrial Society in a Northern City*.

Peter J. Parish, *The North and the Nation in the Era of the Civil War*. Edited by Adam L. P. Smith and Susan-Mary Grant.

Patricia Richard, *Busy Hands: Images of the Family in the Northern Civil War Effort*.

Michael S. Green, *Freedom, Union, and Power: The Mind of the Republican Party During the Civil War.*

Christian G. Samito, ed., *Fear Was Not In Him: The Civil War Letters of Major General Francis S. Barlow, U.S.A.*

John S. Collier and Bonnie B. Collier, eds., *Yours for the Union: The Civil War Letters of John W. Chase, First Massachusetts Light Artillery.*

Grace Palladino, *Another Civil War: Labor, Capital, and the State in the Anthracite Regions of Pennsylvania, 1840–1868.*

Christian B. Keller, *Chancellorsville and the Germans: Nativism, Ethnicity, and Civil War Memory.*

Sidney George Fisher, *A Philadelphia Perspective: The Civil War Diary of Sidney George Fisher.* Edited and with a new Introduction by Jonathan W. White.

Robert M. Sandow, *Deserter Country: Civil War Opposition in the Pennsylvania Appalachians.*

Craig L. Symonds, ed., *Union Combined Operations in the Civil War.*

Harold Holzer, Craig L. Symonds, and Frank L. Williams, eds., *The Lincoln Assassination: Crime and Punishment, Myth and Memory.* A Lincoln Forum Book.

Earl F. Mulderink III, *New Bedford's Civil War.*

David G. Smith, *On the Edge of Freedom: The Fugitive Slave Issue in South Central Pennsylvania, 1820–1870.*

George Washington Williams, *A History of the Negro Troops in the War of the Rebellion, 1861–1865.* Introduction by John David Smith.

Randall M. Miller, ed., *Lincoln and Leadership: Military, Political, and Religious Decision Making.*

Andrew L. Slap and Michael Thomas Smith, eds., *This Distracted and Anarchical People: New Answers for Old Questions about the Civil War–Era North.*

Paul D. Moreno and Johnathan O'Neill, eds., *Constitutionalism in the Approach and Aftermath of the Civil War.*

Steve Longenecker, *Gettysburg Religion: Refinement, Diversity, and Race in the Antebellum and Civil War Border North.*

Harold Holzer, Craig L. Symonds, and Frank L. Williams, eds., *Exploring Lincoln: Great Historians Reappraise Our Greatest President.* A Lincoln Forum Book.

Lorien Foote and Kanisorn Wongsrichanalai, eds., *So Conceived and So Dedicated: Intellectual Life in the Civil War–Era North.*

William B. Kurtz, *Excommunicated from the Union: How the Civil War Created a Separate Catholic America.*

Kanisorn Wongsrichanalai, *Northern Character: College-Educated New Englanders, Honor, Nationalism, and Leadership in the Civil War Era.*

Ryan W. Keating, *Shades of Green: Irish Regiments, American Soldiers, and Local Communities in the Civil War Era.*

Robert M. Sandow, ed., *Contested Loyalty: Debates over Patriotism in the Civil War North.*

Grant R. Brodrecht, *Our Country: Northern Evangelicals and the Union during the Civil War Era.*